Going for Gold

PERSPECTIVES ON SOUTHERN AFRICA

1. *The Autobiography of an Unknown South African,* by Naboth Mokgatle (1971)
2. *Modernizing Racial Domination: South Africa's Political Dynamics,* by Heribert Adam (1971)
3. *The Rise of African Nationalism in South Africa: The African National Congress, 1912–1952,* by Peter Walshe (1971)
4. *Tales from Southern Africa,* translated and retold by A. C. Jordan (1973)
5. *Lesotho 1970: An African Coup under the Microscope,* by B. M. Khaketla (1972)
6. *Towards an African Literature: The Emergence of Literary Form in Xhosa,* by A. C. Jordan (1973)
7. *Law, Order, and Liberty in South Africa,* by A. S. Mathews (1972)
8. *Swaziland: The Dynamics of Political Modernization,* by Christian P. Potholm (1972)
9. *The South West Africa/Namibia Dispute: Documents and Scholarly Writings on the Controversy between South Africa and the United Nations,* by John Dugard (1973)
10. *Confrontation and Accommodation in Southern Africa: The Limits of Independence,* by Kenneth W. Grundy (1973)
11. *The Rise of Afrikanerdom: Power, Apartheid, and the Afrikaner Civil Religion,* by T. Dunbar Moodie (1975)
12. *Justice in South Africa,* by Albie Sachs (1973)
13. *Afrikaner Politics in South Africa, 1934–1948,* by Newell M. Stultz (1974)
14. *Crown and Charter: The Early Years of the British South Africa Company,* by John S. Galbraith (1974)
15. *Politics of Zambia,* edited by William Tordoff (1974)
16. *Corporate Power in an African State: The Political Impact of Multinational Mining Companies in Zambia,* by Richard Sklar (1975)
17. *Change in Contemporary South Africa,* edited by Leonard Thompson and Jeffrey Butler (1975)
18. *The Tradition of Resistance in Mozambique: The Zambesi Valley, 1850–1921,* by Allen F. Isaacman (1976)
19. *Black Power in South Africa: The Evolution of an Ideology,* by Gail M. Gerhart (1978)
20. *Black Heart: Gore-Brown and the Politics of Multiracial Zambia,* by Robert I. Rotberg (1977)
21. *The Black Homelands of South Africa: The Political and Economic Development of Bophuthatswana and KwaZulu,* by Jeffrey Butler, Robert I. Rotberg, and John Adams (1977)
22. *Afrikaner Political Thought: Analysis and Documents,* Volume I: *1780–1850,* by André du Toit and Hermann Giliomee (1983)
23. *Angola under the Portuguese: The Myth and the Reality,* by Gerald J. Bender (1978)
24. *Land and Racial Domination in Rhodesia,* by Robin Palmer (1977)
25. *The Roots of Rural Poverty in Central and Southern Africa,* edited by Robin Palmer and Neil Parsons (1977)
26. *The Soul of Mbira; Music and Traditions of the Shona People of Zimbabwe,* by Paul F. Berliner (1978)

27. *The Darker Reaches of Government: Access to Information about Public Administration in the United States, Britain, and South Africa,* by Anthony S. Mathews (1979)
28. *The Rise and Fall of the South African Peasantry,* by Colin Bundy (1979)
29. *South Africa: Time Running Out. The Report of the Study Commission on U.S. Policy Toward Southern Africa* (1981; reprinted with a new preface, 1986)
30. *The Revolt of the Hereros,* by Jon M. Bridgman (1981)
31. *The White Tribe of Africa: South Africa in Perspective,* by David Harrison (1982)
32. *The House of Phalo: A History of the Xhosa People in the Days of Their Independence,* by J. B. Peires (1982)
33. *Soldiers without Politics: Blacks in the South African Armed Forces,* by Kenneth W. Grundy (1983)
34. *Education, Race, and Social Change in South Africa,* by John A. Marcum (1982)
35. *The Land Belongs to Us: The Pedi Polity, the Boers and the British in the Nineteenth-Century Transvaal,* by Peter Delius (1984)
36. *Sol Plaatje, South African Nationalist, 1876–1932,* by Brian Willan (1984)
37. *Peasant Consciousness and Guerrilla War in Zimbabwe: A Comparative Study,* by Terence Ranger (1985)
38. *Guns and Rain: Guerrillas and Spirit Mediums in Zimbabwe,* by David Lan (1985)
39. *South Africa without Apartheid: Dismantling Racial Domination,* by Heribert Adam and Kogila Moodley (1986)
40. *Hidden Struggles in Rural South Africa: Politics and Popular Movements in the Transkei and Eastern Cape, 1890–1930,* by William Beinart and Colin Bundy (1986)
41. *Legitimating the Illegitimate: State, Markets, and Resistance in South Africa,* by Stanley B. Greenberg (1987)
42. *Freedom, State Security, and the Rule of Law: Dilemmas of the Apartheid Society,* by Anthony S. Mathews (1987)
43. *The Creation of Tribalism in Southern Africa,* edited by Leroy Vail (1989)
44. *The Rand at War, 1899–1902: The Witwatersrand and Anglo-Boer War,* by Diana Cammack (1990)
45. *State Politics in Zimbabwe,* by Jeffrey Herbst (1990)
46. *A Democratic South Africa? Constitutional Engineering in a Divided Society,* by Donald L. Horowitz (1991)
47. *A Complicated War: The Harrowing of Mozambique,* by William Finnegan (1992)
48. *J. M. Coetzee: South Africa and the Politics of Writing,* by David Attwell (1993)
49. *A Life's Mosaic: The Autobiography of Phyllis Ntantala,* by Phyllis Ntantala (1992)
50. *The Opening of the Apartheid Mind: Options for the New South Africa,* by Heribert Adam and Kogila Moodley (1993)
51. *Going for Gold: Men, Mines, and Migration,* by T. Dunbar Moodie with Vivienne Ndatshe (1994)

Going for Gold

Men, Mines, and Migration

T. DUNBAR MOODIE
WITH VIVIENNE NDATSHE

University of California Press
BERKELEY LOS ANGELES LONDON

University of California Press
Berkeley and Los Angeles, California

University of California Press, Ltd.
London, England

Library of Congress Cataloging-in-Publication Data

Moodie, T. Dunbar.
Going for gold : men, mines, and migration / T. Dunbar Moodie with Vivienne Ndatshe.
p. cm. — (Perspectives on Southern Africa ; 51)
Includes bibliographical references and index.
ISBN 0-520-08130-7 (alk. paper). — ISBN 0-520-08644-9 (pbk. : alk. paper)
1. Gold miners—South Africa—Social conditions. 2. Blacks—South Africa—Social conditions. I. Ndatshe, Vivienne. II. Title. III. Series.
HD8039.M732S655 1994
305.9'622—dc20 93-38187
CIP

Printed in the United States of America
9 8 7 6 5 4 3 2 1

The paper used in this publication meets the minimum requirements of American National Standard for Information Sciences—Permanence of Paper for Printed Library Materials, ANSI Z39.48-1984.

For Meredith

Contents

Illustrations

Figures

Plates

Maps

Preface and Acknowledgments

In 1975, when Sam van Coller and Bobby Godsell of the Anglo-American Industrial Relations Division asked me to direct a study of the lives of black gold miners, I was intrigued because they wanted a study that would get behind local management's perceptions. With some hesitation, I agreed to conduct the mine ethnography on Welkom Mine on condition that the methodology be my own and that I be free to use the findings in scholarly articles. We hired four recent black university graduates, Aaron Matabela, Sibysiso Mbatha, Henry Mothibe, and Morris Tsebe, and, after an intensive seminar in what I considered relevant theoretical concepts, sent them to live at and work on the mine. They made no effort to conceal their research agendas. Each week I traveled with a team from the Industrial Relations Division to interview them and guide their progress. At the same time, Dale White of the Agency for Industrial Mission (AIM) approached me to direct a winter vacation internship in which groups of theological students from Lesotho would work on the Free State mines or interview people in the country districts or at recruitment centers. After an introductory seminar they set off with a commission to keep daily journals. The resulting material was published in an anthology titled *Another Blanket* (AIM 1976).

On the basis of both these projects, before leaving for the United States in 1976, I wrote up a report that was eventually published in two articles (Moodie 1980, 1983). I found the students' materials enlightening and intriguing but also unsatisfying, because the mines were clearly in a state of transition and the ethnographic research had snatched its conclusions from a system in fundamental transformation. After three years as department chair at Hobart and William Smith Colleges, when mine research was definitely on the back burner, I was invited to spend 1979–1980 in the

Southern African Research Program at Yale University, where I was once again able to focus on miners' lives.

Initially, I couched my project in terms of proletarianization and the difficulties of organizing migrant labor. My personal commitment to an interpretive methodology, I thought, would give me a unique perspective on the understanding of such systemic problems. I began to search the archives for voices of black miners. At Yale, I read widely in the secondary literature on black South African history and worked through early published evidence given to government commissions, paying special attention to the words of those directly involved in the control of the lives of black migrants. At once I realized that a simple structural approach was insufficient, and my focus deepened to include issues of domination and resistance at the mines. In 1981–1982, a summer grant from the National Endowment for the Humanities, an American Social Science Research Council Africa Fellowship, a University Fellowship at the Rhodes University Institute for Social and Economic Research, and a Hewlett-Mellon Faculty Development Grant from Hobart and William Smith Colleges enabled me to live and work in Johannesburg and Grahamstown. I returned to the United States with mountains of photocopies from various archives. At the same time, the Anglo-American Chairman's Fund made possible a study of "town women" in Thabong Township, near the Welkom mines, and I directed another mine internship for AIM, this time for Transkeian theological students.

While in Grahamstown, Meredith Aldrich, my wife, conducted the interviews for her doctorate in developmental psychology at the University of the Witwatersrand (Aldrich 1989). Vivienne Ndatshe, who is from Pondoland and whose father had been a mine worker, came from Durban, where she is a domestic servant, to conduct interviews and collect life histories in Grahamstown for Meredith. Before returning to Durban, she went home to Pondoland for a month, and, since I still had Hewlett-Mellon faculty development funds and Ms. Ndatshe was interested, I suggested she collect life histories from ex-miners in the countryside. I gave her several pages of interview protocols, mostly about strikes and other events from the 1930s and 1940s. She sent me forty extraordinary life histories that transformed my understanding of life on the mines and started us on a collaborative research effort that continues to this day. Thanks to summer grants from the Hobart and William Smith Faculty Research fund and two Humanities grants from the Rockefeller Foundation, I have been back several times with her to the Mpondo countryside, where she has acted as interpreter for interviews in which I initiated the questions and confirmed her findings. Others, most notably Palama Lelosa and Puseletso

Salae, performed similar functions for me in Lesotho, but it is the insistent originality of those early life histories she collected in 1982 (and a similar series of interviews in 1990 with women in the townships of the Western Transvaal funded by the Canadian International Development Research Council [IDRC]) that has earned Vivienne Ndatshe her place on the title page of this book. In a profound sense, for all that I have interpreted and contextualized her data, this is her book as well as mine. Despite what may seem like excessive theoretical baggage, I hope it remains true to the memory of her father, whom I never met, but of whom one old man told us, years ago in the hills of Pondoland, "he was a lion of the mines." (Copies of Ms. Ndatshe's original interview transcripts and later interview tapes are at the African Studies Institute, University of the Witwatersrand. Transcripts from the IDRC project are at Queens University in Kingston, Ontario.)

As the foregoing will have made clear, this book has been supported over the years by a multitude of funding agencies whose generosity I must formally acknowledge. During the years when I was writing and researching it, I was supported by three terms of sabbatical leave, numerous faculty summer grants and a Hewlett-Mellon faculty development grant from Hobart and William Smith Colleges, two Rockefeller Humanities Fellowships (one independent and one in which I was hospitably housed at the Center for the Humanities at Wesleyan University), a National Endowment of the Humanities summer stipend, a Social Science Research Council Africa grant, a University Fellowship at the Rhodes University Institute for Social and Economic Research, a fellowship in the Yale/Wesleyan Southern Africa Research Program (with support from the NEH and the Ford Foundation), support from the Anglo-American Chairman's Fund, and from the Canadian International Development Research Council. I am most grateful for the faith all these organizations have shown in my work and for their material assistance.

For more personal practical assistance, at the risk of leaving someone out, I must mention Jennifer and Alex Anderson, Charles van Onselen, Belinda Bozzoli, Eddie Webster, Luli Callinicos, Ian and Gusta Macdonald, Glenn Babb, John and Pam Parr, John Gay, Andre van Niekerk, John Moodie and Lyn Blore Moodie, the late Stella Blore, Stanley and Barbara Trapido, Aileen Dunbar Moodie, and my parents. Colleagues at the University of the Witwatersrand and then, for many years, at Hobart and William Smith Colleges have genially tolerated my preoccupation with this work. Besides my departmental colleagues, I must mention particularly the support of Ruth Freeman, Claudette Columbus, and Harmon Dunathan during a difficult time for me at Hobart and William Smith.

A work that has taken so long to produce and been through so many metamorphoses necessarily acquires streams of intellectual indebtedness in its wake. Risking invidiousness once again, let me mention Dan O'Meara, Stanley Greenberg, John Saul, Malusi Mpumlwana, Halton Cheadle, Sean Redding, Jeffrey Butler, Rick Elphick, Rick Johnstone, Leonard Thompson, Lee Quinby, David Ost, Patrick Harries, Shula Marks, John Comaroff, Jean Comaroff, Hoyt Alverson, Phil Bonner, Colin Bundy, Terence Ranger, Michael Burawoy, Eddie Webster, Luli Callinicos, Charles van Onselen, Belinda Bozzoli, David Yudelman, Jonathan Crush, Alan Jeeves, Gene Klaaren, Colin Murray, Patrick Pearson, Bob Shanafelt, Wilmot James, Martin Murray, Tim Couzens, Sean Moroney, Jeff Guy, Keith Breckenridge, Michael Kimmel, Nigel Unwin, Motlatsi Thabane, Dale White, Marcel Golding, Jean Leger, Richard Holway, Mark Ntshangase, Joh Seoka, Navan Adonis, Jeanne Penvenne, Geoffrey and Nomhle Moselane, and Leroy Vail, all of whom, in one way or another have offered insight, criticism, and encouragement for this work at various stages in its development.

I have benefited from feedback on various chapters of this work presented as papers at several Southern African Research Program seminars over many years, at Wits History Workshops, at the Center for the Humanities at Wesleyan University, at a research seminar of the Canadian Research Consortium on Southern Africa, at seminars and workshops in African Studies programs at Harvard, Northwestern, Emory, Chicago, Cape Town, Rhodes, Oxford, and Manchester universities, and at conferences of the African Studies Association in the United States and the Canadian Association of African Studies. William Beinart, Fred Cooper, and an anonymous reviewer from the University of California Press read the manuscript in its penultimate form and offered thoughtful and searching comments that sent me scurrying back to the text to clarify and revise.

My indebtedness to William Beinart goes back much farther than his useful comments on the manuscript. He has been reading my work for some years now, commenting on it, urging journal publication, and nudging me to write it up as a book. More than any other single individual, William's interest and encouragement have sustained me, bringing me to the point of writing this book. Bobby Godsell was an undergraduate student in sociology at the University of Natal when I first taught there in the early 1970s. I failed to persuade him to continue with graduate work, but he has remained an intellectual companion and an invaluable resource person within the mining industry. I have already mentioned Vivienne

Ndatshe's contribution to this work, as well as that of Puseletso Salae, Palama Lelosa, Aaron Matabela, Sibysiso Mbatha, Henry Mothibe, Morris Tsebe, and the AIM theological students. Others who have helped with interviewing and translating include Mark Ntshangase, Ntombeko Mlamlele, Dorothy Ramotsadi, and British Sibuyi, whom I have never met, but whose interview with Philemon, passed on to me by Patrick Harries, broadened my Mpondo-based understanding of male sexuality. Daniel Bregman's generous sharing with me of the minutes of his 1987 commission, with permission from Nigel Unwin at Anglo and Marcel Golding at the National Union of Mineworkers gave me access to unequaled insights into contemporary events on one compound of a large gold mine. That material complemented and contrasted in illuminating ways the ethnography conducted a decade before.

This book could not have been written without the willing assistance of the mine workers and ex-miners who spoke with Vivienne Ndatshe and myself in the countryside in Pondoland and Lesotho, the women who shared their life stories with Vivienne in Kanana, and the men Mark Ntshangase and I interviewed at Vaal Reefs. When I have quoted them, unless their remarks were on delicate matters, I have tried to mention their names. I was touched by how eager they were to tell their stories and hope this book conveys my respect for the courage of their achievements. I learned from them not only about the mines but also about living.

One of the wonderful things about growing older has been that my children have become colleagues. Conversations with Mary Jane, James, and Benjamin Aldrich-Moodie have forced me to clarify concepts and rethink assumptions. Mary Jane has been especially helpful in obliging me to confront gender issues and guiding me in reading on women, and Benjamin, who was three years old when this project started, gave the conclusion several close and searching readings.

Finally, Meredith Aldrich, my wife, has sustained me with her faith and integrity through months and years in which the demands of this work have taken me away from her and the children, sometimes on important family occasions, and have eaten away at family funds that might have been invested in other enterprises. As a companion, both intellectual and personal, she has never failed to keep me mindful that there is life beyond work and to help me live it fully. An inadequate tribute, this book is for her.

Earlier versions of some of the chapters in this book have been published elsewhere in journals and anthologies, and they are used here with permission. Details of original publication are as follows:

"The Formal and Informal Structure of a South African Gold Mine." *Human Relations* 33, 8, 1980.

"Mine Culture and Miners' Identity on the South African Gold Mines." In *Town and Countryside in the Transvaal,* edited by Belinda Bozzoli. Ravan Press, 1983.

"The Moral Economy of the Black Miners' Strike of 1946." *Journal of Southern African Studies* 13, 1, 1986.

"Migrancy and Male Sexuality on the South African Gold Mines" (with Vivienne Ndatshe and British Sibuyi). *Journal of Southern African Studies* 14, 2, 1988. Republished in abridged form in *Hidden from History,* edited by Martin Duberman, Martha Vicinus, and George Chauncey. NAL, 1989.

"Social Existence and the Practice of Personal Integrity: Narratives of Resistance on the South African Gold Mines." In *Tradition and Transition in Southern Africa: Festschrift for Philip and Iona Mayer,* edited by A. D. Spiegel and P. A. McAllister. Witwatersrand University Press, 1991. Also *African Studies* 50, 1 and 2, 1991.

"Alcohol and Resistance on the South African Gold Mines." In *Liquour and Labour in Southern Africa,* edited by Jonathan Crush and Charles Ambler. Ohio University Press, 1992.

"Ethnic Violence on the South African Gold Mines." *Journal of Southern African Studies* 18, September 1992.

"Town Women and Country Wives: Migrant Labor, Family Politics, and Housing Preferences at Vaal Reefs Mine" (with Vivienne Ndatshe). *Labour, Capital and Society,* October 1992.

Abbreviations

AAC/VR	Transcript of Evidence to the Bregman Commission, 1986–1987, microfilm at Yale University Library
Afr.	Afrikaans
AIM	Agency for Industrial Mission, a church organization set up to study the impact of industrial life on black South Africans
AMWU	African Mine Workers' Union
ANC	African National Congress
ARB	Files of the Department of Labour, Central Archives, Pretoria
AWB	Afrikaner Resistance Movement (Afrikaner Weerstandbeweging)
AZAPO	Azanian People's Organization (black power equivalent of UDF)
BBNA	Blue Book on Native Affairs
Beaumont	Published evidence of the Natives Land Commission
CM	Chamber of Mines archives, Johannesburg
COSAS	Congress of South African Students
COSATU	Congress of South African Trade Unions
CTH	Archives of Cheadle, Thompson, and Haysom, microfilm at Yale University Library
CUSA	Council of Unions of South Africa
DNL	Director of native labor, a Department of Native Affairs official in charge of Witwatersrand and other proclaimed labor districts; also (after 1923) native commissioner, Johannesburg
ERPM	East Rand Proprietary Mines

EWC	Evidence to the Economic and Wages Commission, Central Archives, Pretoria
GWU	Papers of the Garment Workers' Union, Cullen Library, University of the Witwatersrand, Johannesburg
ILC	Evidence to the Industrial Legislation Commission (also called Botha Commission), Central Archives, Pretoria
JCI	Johannesburg Consolidated Investments (a mining house)
JHB	Johannesburg
JSAS	*Journal of Southern African Studies*
JUS	Files of the Department of Justice, Central Archives, Pretoria
LGMC	Evidence to the Low Grade Mines Commission, Central Archives, Pretoria
LGOC	Evidence to the Low Grade Ore Commission, Central Archives, Pretoria
MIB	Evidence to the Mining Industry Board (obtained from F. A. Johnstone; now also at Yale University Library)
MNW	Files of the Department of Mines and Industries, Central Archives, Pretoria
MRC	Evidence to the Mining Regulations Commission, Central Archives, Pretoria
NA	Files of the Department of Native Affairs (early years), Central Archives, Pretoria
NEC	Evidence to the Native Economic Commission, Central Archives, Pretoria
NGI	Evidence to the Native Grievances Inquiry (also called the Buckle Commission), Central Archives, Pretoria (fragmentary)
NLB	Files of the Government Native Labour Bureau, Central Archives, Pretoria
NLC	Published evidence of the Natives Land Commission (also called Beaumont Commission)
NRC	Native Recruiting Corporation
NTS	Files of the Department of Native Affairs, Central Archives, Pretoria
NUM	National Union of Mineworkers
RDM	*Rand Daily Mail*
SAIRR	Files of the South African Institute of Race Relations, Cullen Library, University of the Witwatersrand, Johannesburg
SAP	Files of the South African police, Central Archives, Pretoria (includes confidential files, marked "conf.")
SNA	Files of the Transvaal Secretary for Native Affairs (pre-union), Central Archives, Pretoria

SNC	Sub-Native Commissioner
TEBA	The Employment Bureau of Africa
TMGC	Evidence to the Trading on Mining Grounds Commission, Central Archives, Pretoria
TUCSA	Papers of the Trade Union Congress of South Africa, Cullen Library, University of the Witwatersrand, Johannesburg
UDF	United Democratic Front (alliance of local organizations set up in the 1980s to confront apartheid)
WMNWC	Evidence (fragments) to the Witwatersrand Mine Natives' Wages Commission (also called Lansdown Commission), Corey Library, Rhodes University, Grahamstown
WNLA	Witwatersrand Native Labour Association (organization set up to recruit labor outside South Africa in Mozambique and tropical Africa—the NRC recruited within South Africa; rolled over into TEBA in the 1970s)
Xuma	Papers of Dr. Xuma, housed in the Cullen Library, University of the Witwatersrand, Johannesburg

After the Second World War, as proletarianization proceeded apace in South African secondary industries, mine owners—with the approval of the state—spread their recruiting networks deep into the heart of tropical Africa (Crush, Jeeves, and Yudelman 1991) in an effort to find cheap, nonproletarianized labor.

At this third and most general level, the argument of the book focuses on rural homesteaders' resistance to proletarianization and on the impact of uneven rates of proletarianization on relationships among workers once dependence on wage labor became more widespread on the mines during the 1970s.

In the years before the 1970s, the migrant labor and compound systems necessarily excluded proletarianized workers because the pay was so low. Between 1910 and 1970, despite substantial wage increases in manufacturing, real wages on the mines remained consistently low. Black South Africans without a subsistence base in the country, or at least the possibility of establishing one, might work on the mines for a contract or two but they would soon leave for better-paid industrial and other urban jobs. Thus, although there were some changes in work processes and in the management structure of the compounds, the mine workforce, whose "tribal" makeup was always changing, was never fully proletarianized, and indeed resisted proletarianization because of its links to rural homestead agricultural production.

After the rise in the price of gold in 1973, a radical change occurred in the makeup of the mine labor force.[1] A rapid rise in mine wages along with substantial restructuring of the South African economy led to a sharp shift on the mines from a largely illiterate peasant workforce (with its own migrant cultures) to one that included numerous better-educated, proletarian (if often still migrant) workers. This transformation, which took

[1]For workers from Lesotho, this change had occurred a decade earlier, when the South African state refused to permit Basotho workers in South African industry *except* on the mines. One of the mines, ERPM, had also earlier tried hiring proletarianized workers from Harare township, an experiment that was unsuccessful. Generally, problems associated with these earlier shifts were seen as resulting from the higher educational attainments of the new workers, and indeed, proletarianized workers in South Africa *are* generally more schooled. This is an additional variable to be taken into account, but our evidence suggests that education is less decisive than dependence on wage labor in explaining recent changes in mine-worker conduct and organization.

Workers from Mozambique, driven to work on the mines by forced labor in their homeland and early forced into peasant production, present a rather different experience and one that has been slighted in this volume for want of sufficient information and access. Studies dealing directly with workers from Mozambique include the doctoral theses of Jean Penvenne (1982) and Patrick Harries (1983) and First (1983).

place in less than a decade, was part of a conscious effort by certain mining houses to decrease and "stabilize" their black workforce in order to introduce more mechanized production techniques on deeper-level mines at the same time that they avoided dependence on labor from the increasingly hostile postcolonial frontline African states to the north.

Such systemic changes in the mine labor force in the 1970s have begun to break up traditional resistance to proletarianization and not only to redefine mine work but also to transform the structures of social order and control on the mines and alter the discourses of both miners and management. Notions of resistance and solidarity, management styles, types of collective action, conceptions of manhood, and styles of sexuality have all changed dramatically. Thus such terms as alcoholism, homosexuality, aggression, masculinity and femininity, work and family, and democracy may be deconstructed and relativized by their different meanings on the mines before and after the 1970s.

Increasingly miners' perceptions of themselves are proletarian, that is, they see themselves essentially as wage workers rather than as farmers striving to fund their rural homesteads. In more technical Marxist terms, these "new miners" have finally been "freed" from proprietorship on the land and from agricultural means of production. The coming of the National Union of Mineworkers has given a voice to the new workers' demands for the abolition of migrant labor.

Before the shift to a more proletarianized workforce (and the changes have been uneven, differing from mine to mine and on the same mines over time), the Chamber of Mines deliberately recruited migrants who continued to have substantial investments in rural livelihoods and to share a goal of rural self-sufficiency. Indeed, low mine wages made this the only viable recruitment policy for the chamber. The rise in mine wages since 1973, along with the restructuring of South African commercial agricultural production and the collapse of even marginal Bantustan rural subsistence, has attracted a substantial proportion of the contemporary mine labor force from rural proletarians (and on some mines even from urban youths) rather than from aspirant subsistence proprietors as in the past. My account of mine-worker experience of migrant labor thus seeks always to specify the historical period, the sorts of men who made up the mine workforce at the time, the nature of mine work, and, perhaps most important of all, the level of underdevelopment[2] in the migrant sending areas. All these variables have changed over time.

[2]I use the term *underdevelopment* in the sense in which it has come to be used in contemporary social science. It refers to a peripheral political economy that has

Notions such as "colonial despotism" fail to capture the historical complexity of the strategic exercise of power even in contexts of "ultraexploitation." Quite as important as political and economic exploitation for understanding men's lives on the South African gold mines are the changing ways in which power was actually exercised in the process of production and in compound life, the moral unity of subdominant cultures of resistance that made possible the maintenance of personal integrity and appeals to justice, and the strategies for social mobilization that linked practical interests and moral outrage in contexts of apparently total control.

I begin with a general discussion of the practices by which integrity was traditionally maintained on the South African gold mines before proceeding to accounts first of underground work and then of mine compounds as sites of struggle as well as centers of control. Next, I describe shifts in the meanings and practices among black miners of sexuality, drinking, and fighting as the processes of proletarianization brought different, sometimes incommensurable contexts for integrity and new forms of worker organization. This topic leads naturally to discussion of obstacles and achievements in black union organization on the mines in the 1940s and 1980s. After a brief theoretical discursive, I conclude with a detailed case study of two related faction fights at one compound on a Transvaal gold mine in 1986.

---

become economically dependent upon a more powerful central economy whose ongoing prosperity depends upon the systematic exploitation of the major resources of the dependent system. Instead of economic development, such dependency leads to systematic "underdevelopment," defined as the destruction of the potential for autonomous economic development of the dependent system. The fruits of productive activity by workers from the periphery are thus exported to sustain economic growth in the metropolitan center, leaving the dependent economy bereft of resources for investment. In the case of the rural areas in South Africa, it is literally the labor of its migrant inhabitants that is exported. As the rural areas become more underdeveloped, more and more of the wages remitted are invested not in sustainable agricultural production but rather in the simple day-to-day maintenance of family members who remain at home.

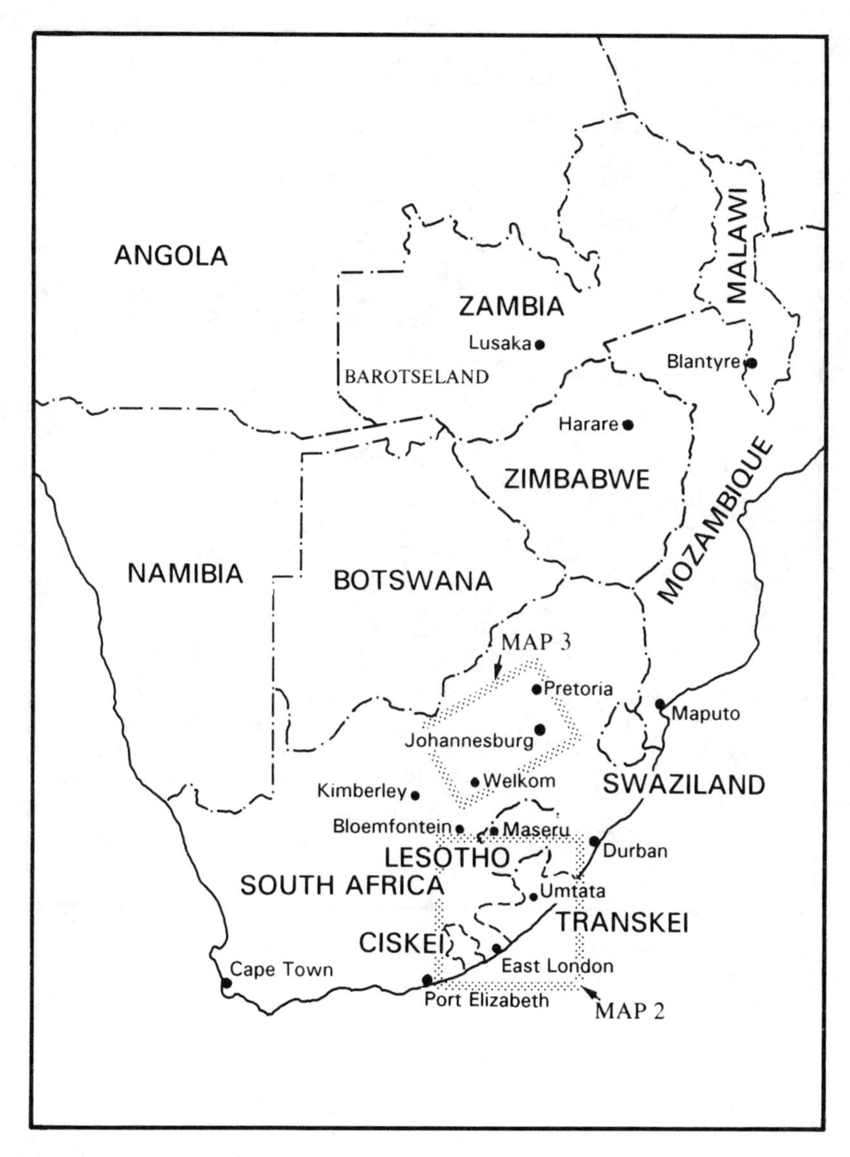

Map 1. Southern Africa, key map for maps 2 and 3, showing major labor supply areas for the mines.

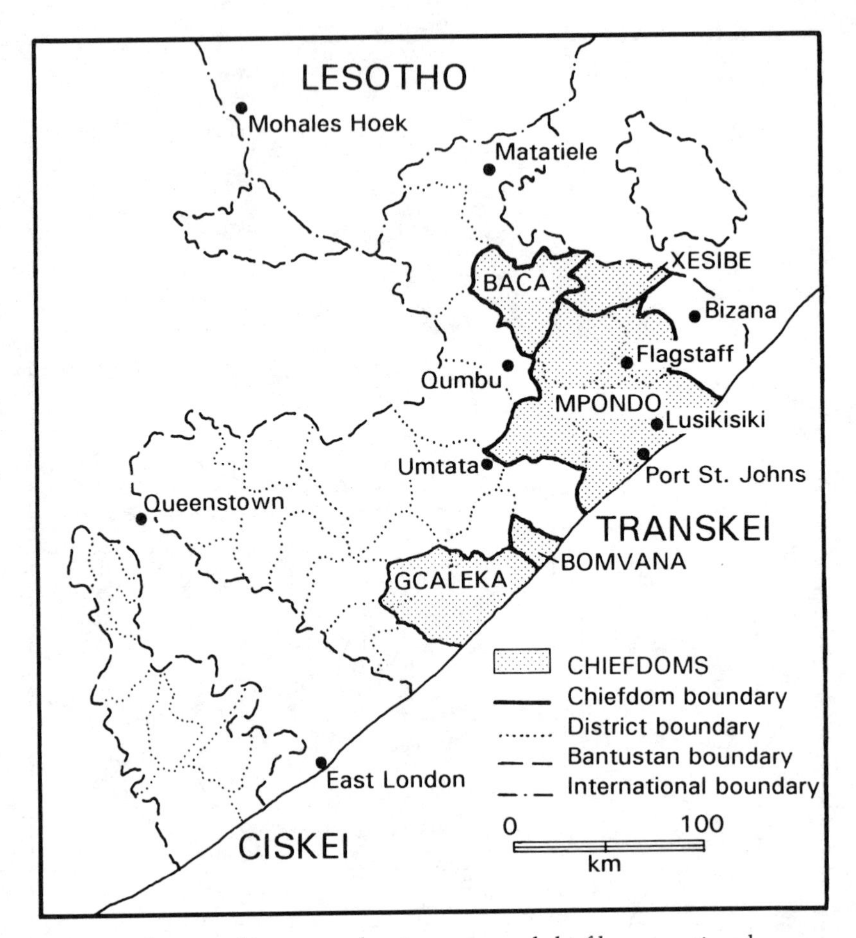

Map 2. Xhosa-speaking areas, showing towns and chiefdoms mentioned in the text.

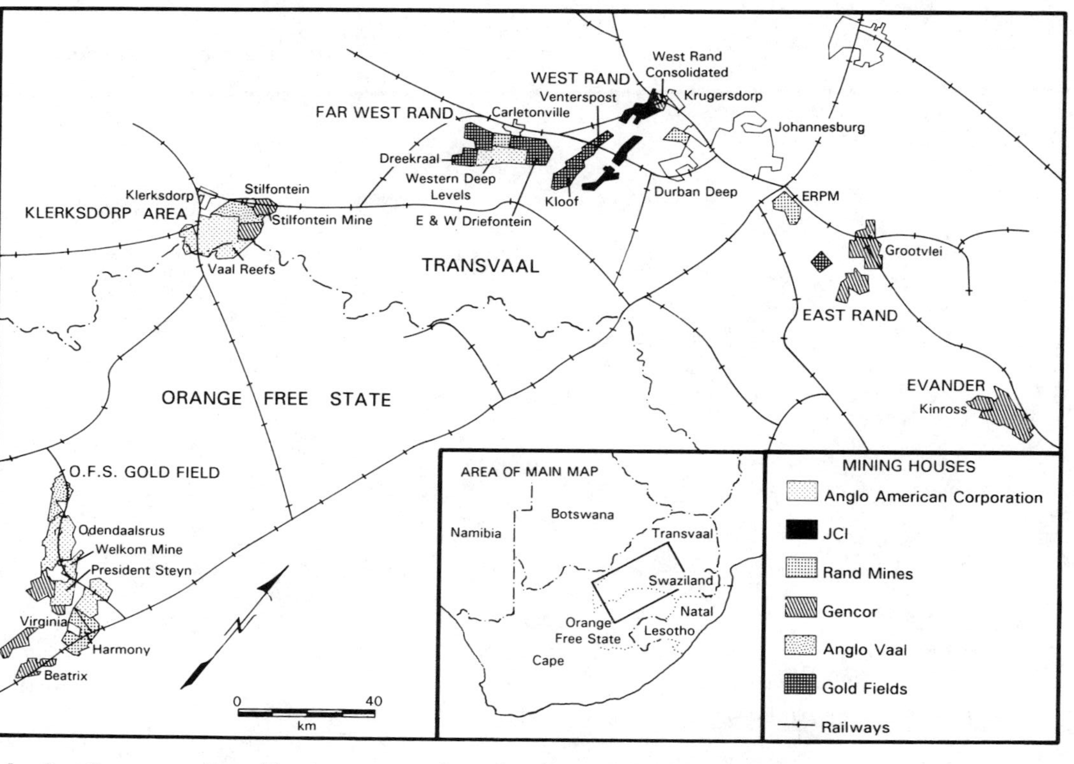

Map 3. Contemporary gold-mining areas of South Africa, indicating mines mentioned in the text. (Based on J. Crush, A. Jeeves and D. Yudelman, *South Africa's Labor Empire: A History of Black Migrancy to the Gold Mines* [Boulder: Westview Press, 1991], p. 1.)

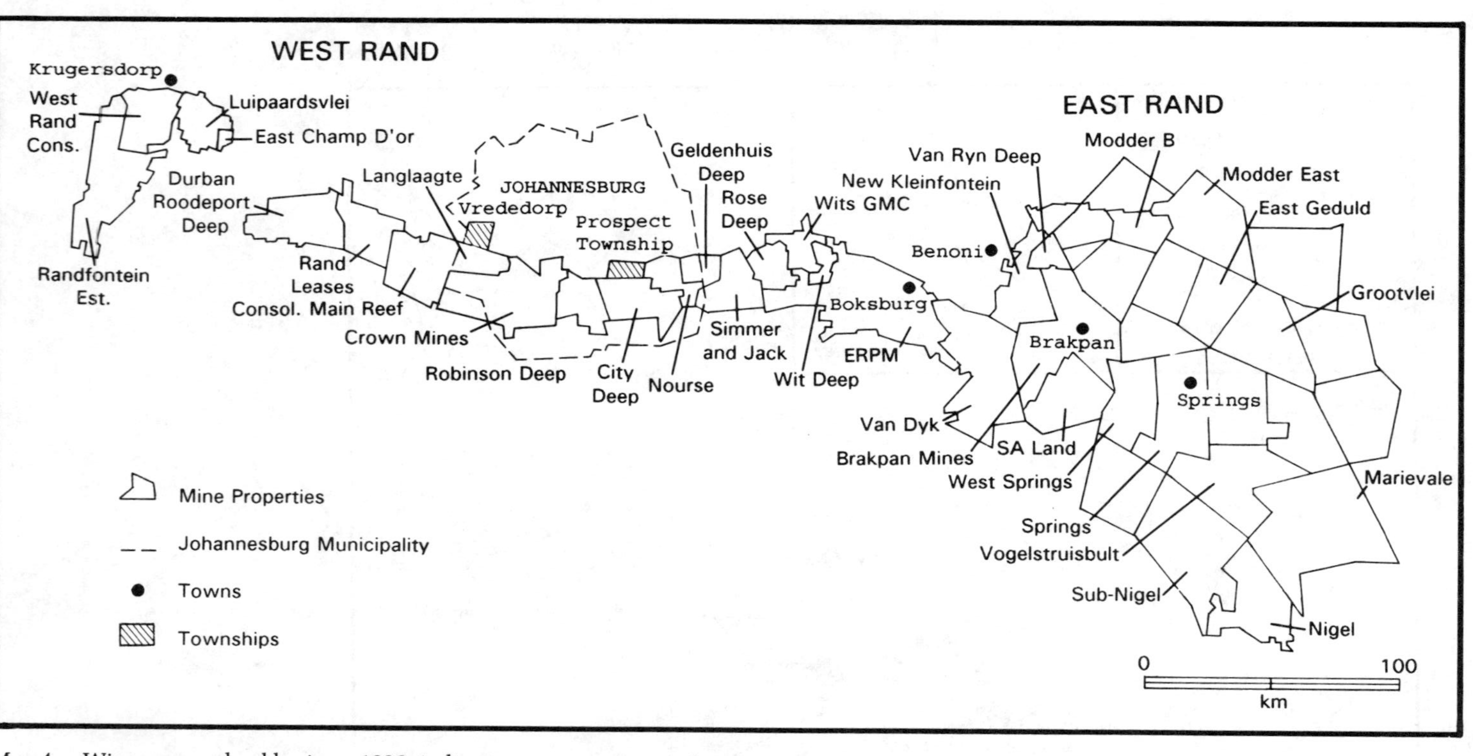

Map 4. Witwatersrand gold mines, 1938, indicating mines mentioned in the text.

1 Worker Identities

Migrant Cultures, Social Networks, and the Practice of Personal Integrity

Few environments are more totally regimented than those of black migrant workers on the South African gold mines. These men sign up at recruiting stations in their home territories and are then conducted great distances, usually hundreds of miles, to work on the mines. Their contracts have typically ranged from four months to two years at work away from homes and families for wages that were, until quite recently, pitifully low. They lived in compounds, fifteen to fifty to a room, under the close surveillance of management-appointed police. They worked in dangerous conditions at great depths underground, in work teams supervised by white miners and black "boss boys." Until very recently, when their contracts were completed, they were returned to their home territories, and no further management responsibility was assumed for them.

This system has been in operation for close to one hundred years; in some areas of Lesotho, Transkei-Ciskei, and, especially, Mozambique, miners look back on several generations of mine work. Whole areas of the Southern African countryside have been able to survive only because they are reservoirs of potential laborers for the mines—and now face disaster because of changing recruitment patterns or mine labor retrenchment. In this chapter I give an account of the various effects of the changing migrant system on workers' lives—not only upon their social organization but also upon their personal identities, their senses of themselves as men.

It has long been argued by sociologists that the compound system is one of the most effective forms of labor control ever invented (Rex 1973). It is the mainstay of what Michael Burawoy (1985:226–29) has called "colonial despotism." According to such scholars, black miners are locked into a total system in which they are little more than puppets of management. Every possibility for effective resistance has been systematically removed, leaving workers exposed to the self-formative effects of a veritable panopticon, a total institution controlling not only their productive but also their personal existences while at the mine.[1] Many scholars have considered migrants "men of two worlds." According to this interpretation, in migrating to work men cast off their rural home selves and take on mine selves. Migrant miners then bear on their very "souls" (in Foucault's sense [1979:29–30]) the scars of the articulation of two modes of production whose economic bases are mutually incompatible. Migrant labor implies a bifurcated identity.

In 1976, I directed an ethnography on Welkom Mine that was informed by precisely such assumptions.[2] Some of the evidence gathered in that study could be read to support the "two-self" theory of migrant identity. While archival research and interviews with old men in the countryside in both Lesotho and Pondoland have convinced me that the argument for dual identities is historically incorrect (and inadequate even for the contemporary period), I shall initially present the ethnographic evidence that seems most strongly to support the dual identities hypothesis before refocusing it into a more complex argument. The chapter proceeds on two levels: a theoretical debate between Erving Goffman, Alfred Schutz, and George Herbert Mead, and an overview of black miners' lives.

Recruitment and Mine Socialization

According to Sotho men recruited for the mines in 1976, management quickly asserted its control.[3] Having signed on at Maseru, Sotho migrants were taken into an eighty-room dormitory and told to strip naked for a medical examination. Such compulsory nakedness of young and old together was a source of great embarrassment to the Sotho, since it violated their conceptions of seniority: "Custom doesn't allow 'men'—the circumcised men—to strip before the 'boys'—uncircumcised men. As a young

[1]Burawoy (1985:230) does mention instances of worker resistance on the Zambian copper belt, but they have no place in his wider account of "colonial despotism."
[2]Material for the 1976 mine ethnography was collected from three sources: (1) the reports and journals of the Agency for Industrial Mission (AIM) theological students from Lesotho, referred to in the text as "informants"; (2) reports from black South African participant observers (referred to in the text as "participants") who lived and worked on Welkom Mine, wrote reports, and were interviewed weekly by a team from Anglo American Corporation's Industrial Relations Division under my supervision; (3) group interviews, mostly by Mark Ntshangase, with different types of black miners and officials, and my own interviews with white officials.
[3]This section is drawn from debriefing notes and the journals of Sotho theological students who worked on the mines during a fieldwork project organized by AIM with permission of Anglo American Corporation. For an anthology drawn from the 1976 journals, see AIM 1976.

man it was the first time that I saw a circumcised man." The medical examination was perfunctory. "The process seems to be unnecessary" said Tebanyane Ramahapu, one Sotho informant, "except as a way of initiating the miners into a subculture which is deprived of any values about human dignity. The doctor examines only the heartbeat and nothing more. The examination could be done with only the shirt off."[4]

So began a potent process of socialization. "These people are altogether not regarded as human beings," said another Sotho informant. "They are treated no better than animals because they are being insulted. . . . They are being kicked about like dogs." After a crowded train journey to Welkom in South Africa, the men arrived at the recruiting test center, where they again had "to strip naked and run in droves." They were "kicked and pushed to the doctor" after being doused in bitterly cold water. After the examination they were x-rayed and then fingerprinted. Having been assigned a number, they performed aptitude tests—and only then were they fed for the first time, on a thin gruel. Finally, a "police boy" escorted them to the mine. To further their acclimatization to strenuous work underground at high temperatures, once they arrived at the mine they were subjected every day for a week to four hours of monotonous exercise in a steam chamber to the metronomic beat of drums, supervised by unfeeling black overseers. In addition, they learned *fanakalo*, a pidgin language without nuance or subtlety, which is used by supervisors to order blacks about and which ensures that relationships between bosses and workers on the mine are as limited and impersonal as possible.

This management-imposed induction was accompanied, however, by a much more subtle anticipatory socialization among the workers themselves. According to Sotho informants in 1976, the migrants' presentations of self began to change on the trains in response to new patterns of interaction as they came closer to the mines. "Surely to be a miner is to change one's character," said one, ". . . because at home one has to behave one way and at work another way. For instance, all those people whom I know from my home are different people here on the mine." Once in the dormitories of the recruiting corporation, reported another Sotho informant, the attitudes of the men already began to alter: "The wildness and uneasiness of the migrants begins just here." They became both exultant and fearful. Their language became rough and boisterous. They shouted lewd invitations to women walking along the railway line. Older miners joked with young ones that they would take them for their lovers. They regaled

[4]Tebanyane V. Ramahapu developed his understanding of his mine experiences in his bachelor of arts thesis in history at the National University of Lesotho (1977).

one another with horrific accounts of the cruelty of the white man and work underground.

For the Sotho, these stories often took the form of *lifela* song cycles.[5] In 1976 they sang of underground conditions, loaders, winches, the occasional decent white miners, the money they would earn. They sang that in Lesotho they were like monkeys, that is, free; as they crossed from their mountainous kingdom to the flat land of the whites, they became mere men; underground they were like rats, going in a cage underground, trapped and harried. Their song told how they had left behind their children starving in miserable conditions. They sang of the mountains receding behind them:

> Lesotho, now I leave you with your mountains
> where I used to run.
> I am going to the white man's place—the tableland.
> Keep our children so that they may grow up on your sides
> as we did ourselves.
> I am leaving you in Lesotho
> I will never see your men with their beautiful mountains.
> I am going to the white mans' place—with electricity.
> I am leaving all the dark places here
> but I still prefer the mountains of Lesotho.

Then they recited the names of the mountains, "giving beautiful expressions to them," so attached were they to the land. They also sang of their nation with pride—how Sotho are strong and good, not needing training because they are naturally skilled.[6] They boasted of how "working in the mine strengthens one and one becomes a real man with all sorts of experiences and gifts for the family." Mining was thus at once attached to male maturation, household responsibilities, and ethnic solidarity.

Sotho on Welkom mines are fortunate in that from time to time they can return home for weekends. One Sotho participant observer in 1976 took the eight-hour bus trip several times. Before leaving for home, a man notified home friends on his mine and neighboring mines. He often carried letters, clothes, and even money, as well as personal messages by word of mouth. Upon his arrival, he would go from house to house delivering goods and messages. On the bus there was talk of wives and families, with a note of apprehension that the wife might not be alone. The men spoke softly of their regret at having had to leave home, while recognizing the necessity for it. They talked about cattle and property, and especially about

[5]For a useful discussion of *lifela* songs, see Coplan 1987.
[6]For Sotho pride in their skill as miners, see also Guy and Thabane 1988.

their children, for whom they bought gifts on the way. They dwelt on the freedom of Lesotho as opposed to the Republic, contrasting the unrestricted life at home with that of the compound. "They seem happier on the way home," said the participant. "They speak of love, not fear."

Thus did the passages to and from the mine ease the transition between wage work and country ways. Anticipatory socialization begins on the way to the mine, and recovery of the old life occurs on the way home for visits. Some miners never return home, however. For a while after their arrival, they send money home—but then "forget." There have always been individuals who absconded. The people at home call them "those lost to the mines" (in the Nguni languages, *amatshipa*; in Sesotho, *lekholoa*). Life at the mines could become so all-absorbing that some men would forget their purpose for coming there, abandoning rural commitments "left at home unfinished" and instead spending all their money on town women or pretty boys and heavy drinking.

It is on the basis of such evidence that many scholars have considered migrants "men of two worlds." The experience recounted so far seems poignantly to support a conception of the self in society that Erving Goffman derives from everyday interactions and from personal adjustments to "total institutions."[7] In Goffman's theory the self is no more than a transitory product of immediate social interaction. According to Goffman, personal identity is formed through a process of negotiation between *demeanor*, the presentation persons make of themselves, and *deference* (or lack of it), the response of others to that presentation. Selves become what they are within an interaction ritual in which individuals risk or impose their definitions of themselves on their immediate fellows. Thus Goffman's cast of characters moves from the con man who attempts to manipulate interaction to his benefit to the asylum inmate, re-formed within and conforming to a total institution. At either extreme, Goffman's characters work out their sense of self-esteem within a context of interaction over which ultimately they have very limited control.[8]

The self becomes what it is and is sustained within a field of personal performances that more or less conform to the expectations of others. These expectations are neither random nor idiosyncratic. They are organized in patterns that depend partly on the esteem accorded the individual,

[7]This exposition of Erving Goffman's work relies upon his early writings (1959, 1961, 1967), especially the essay on deference and demeanor in *Interaction Ritual* (Goffman 1967).

[8]Goffman's notion of role distance, while it seems to imply greater personal autonomy, fails to provide grounds for a Goffmanian theory of the self as agent. Role distance is itself "in role" for Goffman.

but largely on a structure of shared normative assumptions that reinforce power relationships. Subtle patterns of deference and demeanor, like more crude structures of domination, imply a common language of interaction, a cultural context in which, however delicate or demanding the process, we negotiate our self-esteem, indeed our very sense of self. Thus Goffman firmly anchors self-identity in social interaction. Presentation of self, he says, takes place within patterned social constraints, however these may be manipulated or arrogated.

Of course, Goffman's refusal to locate the self outside of social expectations does not necessarily imply a totally splintered self. To the extent that our interactions are consistent, our selves will be also. This consistency accounts for the power of total institutions or of totalistic bodies of knowledge like psychoanalysis in self-formation. Thus it might be argued, as I have argued in the past (Moodie 1983), that black miners are in fact men of two worlds, of bifurcated selves, with each self appropriate to a different mode of production. Let us turn to mining as an occupational culture, and more specifically mine culture in South Africa, as a further test of the Goffmanian concept of the self.

Mine Work and Migrant Cultures

The literature on occupational cultures contains strong evidence that mine work has important implications for a certain masculine self-formation. In fact, in all Western patriarchal societies, general identity-forming themes emerge as aspects of mine cultures. This holds as well for South African gold mining, in spite of its historical particularities.[9]

Mining is hard labor under conditions of extreme discomfort—deafening noise, intense heat and humidity, and cramped space—exacerbated by tension stemming from the need to watch constantly for signs of potential hazard. Every miner can recount several experiences of accidents or near-accidents. News of accidents spreads rapidly on a mining settlement. In the words of an old Sotho miner:

> Working in the mines is an agonizing painful experience. . . . Your work is in an extremely dangerous place. Anything can happen to you at any place. Whenever you go down the shaft, you are not sure that you will come out alive. You don't want to think about it. But it keeps coming. Whenever an accident occurs and someone is either killed or badly injured you think of yourself in the posi-

[9]This account of mine work is paralleled by a range of other mine studies on three continents: Leger 1992; van Onselen 1980; First 1983; Alverson 1978; Gordon 1977; Dennis, Henriques, and Slaughter 1956; Gouldner 1954; Trist et al. 1963; Gluckman 1961; Burawoy 1972; Nash 1979; and Bulmer 1975.

> tion, you think of your family and you become very unstable and lonely. You feel you want to see them for the last time, because the inevitable will come to you sometime. . . . Death is so real you keep on praying and thanking God each time you come out alive.

South African mines have a paraplegic unit on site whose men in wheelchairs serve as a constant reminder of the perils underground. Some mines are more dangerous than others, but danger lurks in them all. As Jose Kumbe told Alpheus Manghezi in Mozambique in 1979 (First 1983:96): "in a good mine you don't see the stretcher very often: you do see it, but only from time to time."[10]

There is an awesome quality about descent into the earth itself. The Bible speaks of those "strangers" who "cut galleries in the rocks" to reach "seams which lie in darkness," of those who "set their hands to the granite rock, laying bare the roots of the mountains" as "they drive forward far from men" (Job 28:1–11). Miners cope with the tensions of their elemental job in various ways. One is through supernatural lore, accompanied by a certain fatalism.[11] According to theological student informants in 1976, all the black miners "believe[d] in God . . . [but many] believe[d] that God does not pragmatically help them—He helps the whites only." Therefore they turn to *muti* (magical medicine) and their ancestors for help. One man "emphasized that in the work situation you need maximum protection. . . . The use of *muti* complements whatever help God might give you."

Jean Leger (1992) has recently described what he calls the "pit sense" of South African miners, the range of tacit skills developed to detect imminent collapses from the behavior of the rock. Miners share their "pit sense," cooperating closely with each other and exercising constant care while on the job. According to Sibysiso Mbatha, a participant observer who worked underground on Welkom Mine, black miners "are keen that every one of them should do a perfect job . . . else they all face the risk of danger from falling rocks. They try hard to prevent or minimize accidents at work places by giving advice and helping one another." Despite potential ethnic tensions among black workers in the compound in 1976, when they were underground they saw themselves "as members of their work team first and foremost and [did] not appear to have any interest in its ethnic composition." A warm team spirit and an atmosphere of rough male camaraderie typically exist among underground workers in most parts of the

[10]One important reason for the rapid success of the National Union of Mineworkers since 1982 is its stress on improving safety conditions underground. See, for instance, Leger 1985.

[11]See, for example, Alverson 1978:234; Gordon 1977:211–13; and Nash 1979.

world (Gordon 1977:163). Despite racial tensions with white miners, such solidarity among blacks also serves to ameliorate the isolation of underground work in the mines.

As in British shop-floor culture (Willis 1979), part of mine-worker camaraderie is to speak of women in crude and exploitative sexual terms. Sexual expletives and crude accounts of sexual activity pervade the underground conversation of miners everywhere.[12] To an extent this chatter is typical also of miners in South Africa. While waiting at the workplace, said Sibysiso Mbatha, men would discuss their sexual exploits in town, giving each other advice about how to meet women and entice them into having sex.

Physical strength is another basis of solidarity. Mining is for strong men, said one Sotho from Qacha's Nek (Sebilo 1976:23): "The work underground can be endured only by those with firm and tough knees; men suckled properly by their mothers. . . . Cowards and weaklings are revealed, the white man does not tolerate such 'Bed-Wetters.' " Fierce masculine pride in holding down such a tough job helps keep at bay incapacitating fears. "We are the bulls of the mines," sing the Sotho, exultant at the end of their contracts.

Even white surface officials in South Africa respect underground workers for their toughness and intransigence. On mines elsewhere in the world, a high rate of absenteeism is expected and tolerated as necessary for the miners' personal stability; by international standards the absenteeism rate of 1 or 2 percent on Welkom Mine in 1976 was thus incredibly low. In response, compound management there would overlook occasional refusals to go down by workers who claimed to be "tired."

Mining in general, then, is an occupational life-world characterized by both fear and pride, leading to warm but rough male camaraderie on and off the job, and personal tension resulting in high absenteeism and frequent work stoppages.[13] In addition, the need for solidarity in the face of mortal hazards typically softens lines of authority underground.

Historically, black South African mine culture has been different from the Western norm in two fundamental respects. First, the degree of hier-

[12]For a vivid account of the impact of the introduction of women into underground work on American coal mines, see Arble 1976:115, 131, 140–42, 174, 212–13, 235. Willis (1977:145–52 and 1979) provides a more analytical approach to British shop-floor life-worlds.

[13]Mining communities are noted for their solidarity and militancy. See, for example, Moore 1978:233–57; Epstein 1958:86–156; Nash 1979:87–120; and Kerr and Siegel 1954. My use of the notion of "life-worlds" is indebted to Habermas's (1989) rereading of Schutz. Its application to an occupational context is a deliberate, if immanent, critique of Habermas's tendency to restrict the notion to certain specific institutional spheres.

archical control on the South African mines would have been untenable if the labor force were "free." Until recently, most black miners contracted to sell their labor to the mines not on a daily or weekly basis but for six- or nine-month periods. Breaking such a contract was a criminal offense. The abrogation of the Masters and Servants Act in the 1970 and the coming of the black National Union of Mineworkers in the early 1980s began to erode the old system of control. Until these challenges, however, the coercive impact of white control of black labor in South African society was concentrated underground in the relationship between the white miner and his black team, supervised by a black boss boy[14] (nowadays called a team leader). White gangers (foremen) and their boss boys sometimes drove workers beyond their endurance, thus endangering general safety. Several different sources confirm the statements of Palesa Sebilo's (1976:25) informants that next to "fear of death or injury from a collapsing mine" the "constant fear of undefended hittings from their bosses . . . [made] their working conditions a constant strain and intolerable." Thus team spirit and camaraderie in South African mining tend to be poisoned by violent supervision and racial conflict.

Second, South African underground life-worlds differ from the Western norm in that they are located within a wider system of migrant labor that necessitates long-term separation from home and family in an alien living environment. In the South African case, work conflicts and solidarities are not dissipated at the end of the day by the miners' return from work to private or company-owned homes but are intensified by their crowding into male-only compounds subject to tight management control. To what extent does compound life, and the migrant cultures that arise in it, support the argument for black miners' two worlds?

Formally, everyday power on the compound was exercised by the compound manager and his white assistants together with the *indunas*—management-appointed black supervisors—and their police boys, clerks, and black personnel assistants. All of the latter exercised a considerable degree of discretionary power in a series of overlapping, sometimes con-

[14]At least until the 1970s, all black men who worked for whites in South Africa were called "boys." Ironically, black migrant men thus worked as "boys" of the whites in order to attain or retain manhood at home. Usually, I have retranslated such usages, so that "home boy" becomes "home fellow," "machine boy" becomes "machine operator," and "police boy" becomes "mine policeman." In the case of "boss boy" I have retained the original term precisely because it is ironical on two levels: both in the sense above that men became the "boys" of the whites and also because "boss boys" were *senior* supervisory black underground workers—they were "*boss* boys." The contemporary sanitized term, "team leader," fails to acknowledge the contradictions in the role.

flicting, sometimes complementary, black fiefdoms. Until very recently, management imposed very little formal limit to their power. The induna, for instance, was expected to maintain order in the compound and to prevent drinking in the rooms, *dagga* (marijuana) smoking, gambling, and homosexual liaisons. In carrying out that responsibility, however, he in fact permitted much that was formally forbidden so long as it did not threaten order.[15]

Thus, informally, power was not exercised according to management's blueprint. For all his pretensions to control, the white compound manager's power was expressed more in ignorance, or turning a blind eye, than in knowledge. Within the space created by this indulgence and delegation of power, black "authorities" and their refractory migrant worker subordinates worked out a modus vivendi, defined by what they called *imiteto* (rules, both formal and informal). For example, there were management imiteto (sing. *umteto*), legislated to reinforce and guide the indunas and mine police in the exercise of their authority but which left them wide discretion to administer their own rules agreed to by workers (sometimes these directly contravened management regulations, or at least ignored them). Such worker imiteto constituted the unwritten, constantly renegotiated, tacitly agreed-upon norms or codes of conduct that governed compound dwellers' daily interactions. I apply the notion of "implicit contract" (Moore 1978:203), among workers themselves and between workers and management, as specified by the imiteto, to define the moral economy of the mine.

Rob Gordon (1977:101–8) discovered a worker "brotherhood" on the small mine he studied in Namibia. On the larger, South African gold mine compounds there were myriad brotherhoods, formed around, for example, entrepreneurial services (hair cutting, bicycle repair, tailoring, or herbal medicine), religious concerns, burial societies, musical tastes, rural politics (as well as other informal activities based on home friend solidarities), homosexual dalliances, or other shared interests. Rackets abounded in this environment—including trafficking in illegal alcohol and drugs and gambling. Attempts by white management to control any of these activities or interests were met with fierce resistance.

Thus the mine compound left room for alternative cultural adaptations. Although the mine sought to control workers' leisure time, compound dwellers obliged management to leave space for their own activities. These

[15]Foucault (1979:82–89) provides a fascinating account of "tolerated illegality" in the social structure of preindustrial Europe. However, he fails to sustain his insight in treating modern total institutions, slipping instead into discourse about "soul-forming" power.

activities made up migrant cultures. They were worked out with fellow migrants in various social networks, not as individual adaptations. The networks often reached back into the rural areas from which the migrants had come and to which almost all of them would return.[16] Workers who came to the mines to realize some rural project, whether to earn cattle for their fathers, or obtain wives, or sustain rural production in building up a homestead, found like-minded fellows with whom to associate. In fact, they often went to the mines with home friends. They could smoke and drink and converse and relax and play together on the compounds and might eventually even explore the temptations of the red lights of town, insulated by each other's company. Thus was the home world integrated into the world of work.

I wish to suggest and in this book as a whole to demonstrate, against the conventional wisdom, that the material conditions of mine migration, at least before the 1970s, gave rise to variant strands of migrant culture whose common motif was commitment to the independence and satisfactions of patriarchal proprietorship over a rural homestead (Mayer 1980:39–44). Systemically, this attachment implied resistance to proletarianization, which, however, does not necessarily imply conflict with mine management or rejection of the compound system as such—nor does it deny such contestation. Resistance in the sense in which the term is used here is resistance to wider systemic pressures rather than to actual social institutions as such. In fact, I shall argue that the formal organization of the mine compound as a social institution was appropriated by migrant cultures for their own ends in a whole congeries of social practices and networks by those miners able to retain a social and economic subsistence base in the countryside (Mayer 1980:58–59; Sitas 1985).

Cultures must be understood and analyzed as overlapping aggregations of beliefs and practices inscribed with implicit and explicit understandings about the exercise of power and situated within and dependent upon social networks and economic bases. Notice the importance of access to land and patriarchal control for South African migrant cultures: "The elaborate de-

[16]It is the Comaroffs' (1987) failure to recognize the extent to which migrant cultures bridge the contrast between *tiro* and *mmereko*—indeed, carry aspects of *tiro* into the heart of *mmereko* (and vice versa, of course)—that is the major weakness of their paper. Not only Zionist "madmen" but also workers in their everyday routines live out this alternative hegemony, adjusting to but not conforming fully to the formal expectations of management. Such accommodations may be peculiar to mine work—although Sitas (1985) found them also among migrant metal workers on the East Rand. My own earlier work (Moodie 1983) certainly underestimated the extent to which rurally based mine cultures bridged work and home—partly, perhaps, because such patterns were already disintegrating by 1976.

fences developed by [migrant cultures] have lost their effectiveness once the possibility of obtaining arable land has fallen away, or when fathers and lineage elders no longer have a say in matters of land allocation" (Mayer 1980:50). Peasant proprietors resisted proletarianization as long as they had access to land and the means to work it, however dependent they were on the proceeds of wage labor.[17] Once workable land became scarce or migrant remittances were so fully used for basic subsistence that the land lay fallow, then proletarianization was complete, even if people continued to migrate and families remained in the rural areas.

Tenacious attachment to the land and to agrarian production along with the necessity for infusions of capital into rural agriculture (Murray 1981:65–85) thus gave rise to cultural patterns in which migrant men (and the women, children, and elders they left at home) forged continuities between wage work and subsistence agriculture. The ingenuity and integrity with which such migrants resisted proletarianization was indeed implicit in the very way they defined themselves as men and their wives as women. For both Mpondo and traditional Xhosa (McAllister 1980:208–13), for instance, "manhood" (*ubudoda*) was achieved essentially in presiding justly, wisely, and generously over an *umzi,* or rural homestead. At least since the 1930s, the achievement of such manhood has been predicated upon migrant labor. For the Sotho also, "the paradigm of the successful migrant career for a man is to establish his own household and to build up a capital base through the acquisition of land, livestock and equipment, to enable him to retire from migrant labour and to maintain an independent livelihood at home" (Murray 1981:41). That such independence is rare and household heads in contemporary Lesotho (if in fact they are men and not women) depend on remittances from younger migrants does not alter the ideal. Some access to land and the means to work it, however, are crucial.[18]

[17]In the *Grundrisse* (1973:471–72, 489), Marx shows a profound understanding of the tenacity with which rural proprietors cling to their traditional mode of subsistence:

> [In modes of production in which the worker is related to the soil as his or her natural workshop] the individuals relate not as workers but as proprietors—and members of a community, who at the same time work. The aim of this work is not the creation of [exchange] value—although they may do surplus labour in order to obtain alien, i.e., surplus, products in exchange—rather its aim is sustenance of the individual proprietor and of his family, as well as of the total community. . . . It is not the *unity* of living and active humanity with the natural, inorganic conditions of their metabolic exchange with nature, and hence their appropriation of nature, which requires explanation or is the result of a historic process, but rather the *separation* between these inorganic conditions of human existence and this active existence, a separation which is completely posited only in the relation of wage labour and capital.

[18]For an enlightening discussion of structural differences between different types of rural areas and their impact upon family politics, see Sharp and Spiegel 1991.

Rural Conceptions and Migrant Values

Migrant labor at an early stage (certainly by 1906) imposed a particular organization for the appropriation of surplus value upon the South African gold-mining industry (a form that became increasingly profitable and for which there were no real alternatives) not only because of cost constraints but also because most workers chose to migrate. Migrant miners were certainly exploited and disciplined, and knew they were. For some of them, the self-formative pressures of compound life were irresistible, and they became "creatures of the mine." Others left the mines and settled in urban townships nearby. Most, however, clung tenaciously to their country roots, finding support from fellow workers for their stubborn commitment to returning home, not only because of the cruel oppression of mine life but also because home was where fulfillment of true manhood lay. Informal networks of support among these workers gave them a degree of leverage against management, providing some protection against the worst depredations of work supervisors and compound overseers. The demand for labor was such that desertion or dismissal did not necessarily spell the end of mine work.

Unlike the diamond mines, compounds on the gold mines were open. Migrants were not confined to them outside of working hours, and on weekends mine workers traveled all over the Witwatersrand on foot and by train, visiting, eating, and sleeping with friends from home at other compounds. Migrants were thus able to sustain home networks across mines as well as within them.

As late as the middle 1970s, Hoyt Alverson (1978) found that instead of being psychologically impaired by their experiences on the mines, Tswana migrants who returned to homestead production reinterpreted their mine experiences in terms of their own wider rural life-plans and goals. They recomposed their experiences into narratives that organized their life histories, thereby retaining their sense of personal integrity and destiny despite their subjection to management control and exploitation.

I have argued that Hoyt Alverson's understanding of migrant reality is excessively individualistic, conferring too much autonomy on individual actors (Moodie 1983). The miners' reinterpretations did not take place in a social vacuum. They told stories not only to themselves or to admiring audiences back home but also to their peers on the mine. There is ample evidence that miners' accounts to each other of mine and home life, whether in the compound after work or underground while waiting at the workplace, served to reinforce their sense of themselves not only as individuals but also as members of a community.

Hoyt Alverson, in personal correspondence, disputes my reading of his work: "My emphasis was on the miners not as autonomous individuals but as individual agents of culture and community. Each is a bricoleur working within and in terms of a pre-existent material (cultural) world." My point is that as "agents of culture" the miners produced their bricolage not merely as individuals but also as part of a shared network of their fellows. Nor were rural cultures unchanged in the process. Social interactions mediate between "cultures" and "individuals," and cannot be ignored, because "individuals" themselves are social creations. On the mines, workers formed social networks supporting migrant cultures whose common sense was firmly rooted in commitment to rural practice. It is in such networks of sharing that cultures of solidarity and personal identities are maintained and recreated.

Hoyt Alverson asked all his Tswana respondents (both town and country dwellers) where they would prefer to live. Seventy-two of the seventy-four typically answered:

> Why do you ask me such a simple question? Of course I would like to be able to settle at home. Town has no life at all. In fact, there is no choice; if there were, no Tswana would live in town. I would definitely settle at my home. We don't like towns in Botswana. They are things of the Europeans. Even the Boers who live in town are screaming about the pains of town life. They want to go back to the farms. So, of course, the Tswana do. (Alverson 1978:238)

Indeed, in Setswana there are two words for work. *Mmereko* stems from the Afrikaans *werk* and refers to wage labor. *Tiro* refers to doing that which is "at once the means and end of wanting-to-do," that is, building a family and home for oneself in the countryside (in Xhosa, "building an umzi") according to proper custom (in Xhosa, umteto) in community with like-minded others (Alverson 1978:117–44).

The Xhosa too make a distinction between *ukwakha,* which refers to the material, social, moral, and religious senses of "building" the umzi (McAllister 1980:208), and *pangela,* meaning "working for the Whites" (Mayer 1980:58). Interestingly enough, according to Xhosa linguists, pangela originally meant to "seize" or "grab." This provides linguistic support for the argument (Beinart 1979, Harries 1982) that migrant labor was seen by migrants in the early years as in their interests, as a seizing of booty to maintain their desired ideal existence. Belinda Bozzoli (1991:97) makes a similar argument for the coming of women to the city as domestic workers in the 1920s, "raiding it for the resources they needed for their own dreams to be fulfilled."[19]

No linguistic distinction is made in Sesotho between different types of work. However, one Sotho informant did distinguish between work at home, which is fulfilling in itself, and mine work, which is a means to an end: "Work as an expression of oneself, as creative activity, is what is left unfinished at home. In the mine what comes first is the reward attached to work."[20]

It is important to stress that fulfillment in African rural life lies in communal struggle rather than in individual success. A profound expression of the distinction between tiro and mmereko in the lives of women is found in the words of the Tswana peasant proprietor Rre Segatlhe to Marianne Alverson (1987:43–44):

> Tiro is what you do here with your sisters. You work while you sing and talk. You are knowing each other when you are doing these things together. You are helping each other. And what you pick, you eat and you share with all in the lolwapa [homestead]. It is tiro, it is good for you and good for all.
>
> And if you and Maria and Seipate go to find a melon in the field, but there is no melon, you will come back with nothing. It is tiro; you tried to find the melon, and it is good. We will be sad that there is no melon in the field, but we are together, and we will share the head of a fly.[21]
>
> Mmereko is how they work in town. A woman will not go to find the melon with her sisters. Maybe she must buy it, maybe she must cook it for somebody else, but she does not eat it. She works

[19]The implication of the original meaning of *pangela* was captured by the early Marx in a discussion of exchange relationships:

> Thus the social relation I bear to you, the labour I perform to satisfy your need, is likewise merely an appearance and our mutual supplementing of each other is merely an appearance, based on our mutual plundering of each other. The intention to plunder, to deceive, inevitably lurks in the background. (1975:275)

[20]In personal correspondence, Colin Murray wrote to me:

> In Lesotho people do use different forms of the root *sebetsa* in different ways, although not altogether consistently: *motsebetsi* for a job or a piece of work or a specific task, or in the plural form *mesebetsi*, to cover the availability or otherwise of employment; *tsebetso* for a project or an undertaking with an implicitly longer timespan and an implicitly greater element of personal responsibility or investment effort and resources, to the extent of being synonymous with "occupation."

Bob Shanafelt made similar observations about Sesotho usage in correspondence with me about words for work in Lesotho.

[21]Geoffrey and Nomhle Moselane have pointed out to me that the phrase that Marianne Alverson translates as "the head of a fly" is actually an idiomatic expression referring to locusts, which people do in fact eat. Thus the expression is not merely metaphorical but also refers to the smallest available edible morsel.

> alone. If she is lucky there is a radio, and she sings with it. But, still, she does not like the work. She looks at the clock and thinks to finish it quickly. She does not know the people near her. Mmereko is only for the pocket . . . and if she has no mmereko, nothing for her pocket, she cannot buy food for her child. And in town, no one will share even the head of a fly.

For women at least, then, the communality of work in the homestead makes it tiro. Hoyt Alverson, who interviewed mostly men, stresses another component, the struggle for personal fulfillment, which he believes was even more important for Tswana men than community. Central to the notion of tiro through which one "builds family and home," he says, is the autonomy implied in the idea of "doing-for-oneself (*go itirela*)" (Alverson 1978:133).

Hoyt Alverson's interpretation is influenced by phenomenology, and his formulation of Tswana self-identity owes much to the theories of Merleau-Ponty and Alfred Schutz.[22] Schutz's phenomenological analysis of the self starts from self-conscious individuals actively molding a social world within which they seek to realize meaningful goals, or, in more technical language, from the experience of intentionality within the intersubjective world of everyday life. Self-esteem, Schutz implies, depends less upon the expectations of others and more upon the individual's realization of goals pursued within the world. The successful outcome of conduct undertaken by an autonomous individual (what he calls "working") seems to be at the heart of Schutz's notion of the self: "The wide-awake self integrates in its working and by its working its present, past and future into a specific dimension of time; it realizes itself as a totality in its working acts; it communicates with others through working acts; it organizes the different spatial perspectives of the world of daily life through working acts" (1962:212).

For Schutz, then, the self is founded upon purposeful conduct within a cultural-material life-world that draws on pre-existing horizons of meaning but is finally defined (and redefined) by individuals' intentions. Self-identity for Schutz is thus autonomous and consistent over time, interpreting and reinterpreting experience in accordance with its ongoing projects. While we may experience different realities (for instance, the realities of fantasy, dream, and play), says Schutz, all these realities are finally subject to the paramount reality of the world in which we work,

[22]The Comaroffs (1987) provide an alternative treatment in a different theoretical mode much closer to my own. Alverson's chapter on the "ecology of values" (1978:44–79) suggests a variation on my argument about proletarianization, however, and his book as a whole is enormously stimulating.

realizing our purposes in action. While such a conception of the self seems consonant with the Tswana notion of tiro as set forth by Hoyt Alverson, and captures the tenacious integrity with which rural migrants for so many years resisted proletarianization, it misses the alienative aspect of work captured by the notion of mmereko, coined in the experience of migrant wage labor. While an autonomous self-identity, "working" in the paramount reality, may to some extent be possible for members of the ruling class in capitalist society (or, for that matter, most men in at least some contexts in patriarchal society), Schutz seems to have little conception of the alienation experienced by subordinate groups in their "working." To what extent can migrant mine work be "working" as Schutz conceives of it—that is, purposive organization of life-worlds? Hoyt Alverson (1978:192–214) introduces the notion of the individual subject's reinterpretation of experience and "the trickster as hero" to avoid the dilemma. Such an understanding seems too individualist for my evidence, since reinterpretation of individual experience springs forth from and ultimately feeds back upon the myriad interactions of everyday social networks.

To be true to the life-worlds of migrants to the South African mines, Schutz's notion of "working" must be supplemented by an alternative and more communal notion of the self, however much this redefinition may threaten the "autonomy" so sacred to Schutz. If we stress the more communal aspect of tiro as set forth by Rre Segatlhe to Marianne Alverson, then, at least for black migrant mine workers who are actual or potential rural proprietors, the sharpness of the distinction between tiro and mmereko begins to break down. We can begin to understand why men might choose mine migrancy, because the choice of mmereko on the mines might sustain tiro at home later in life's course. What does this imply about notions of migrant identity?

Alfred Schutz's notion of "working" presupposes an individual self already formed, working meaningfully and creatively upon the world. While South African mine migrants are certainly more than passive products of socialization, Schutz fails to account adequately for the social origins of the self. Goffman's socially constructed and structurally situated notion of the self, however, fails to explain that socially sustained personal integrity which strives to build tiro in the midst of mmereko and enables resistance, not only systemically but also socially. Goffman overlooks the fact that the self formed in social interaction has a personal history rooted in strategic and moral practices over time. We need to conceive of socially constructed selves that also achieve some measure of self-determination. George Herbert Mead developed a theory in which freedom is exercised responsibly and responsively by actors whose conduct is limited by social structures and whose very capacity for self-conscious conduct is itself socially derived.

Mead's theory of self-consciousness is fundamentally social (1934:135). His theory also presupposes a philosophy of action, a pragmatics that implies reflective working upon the world. Such reflective action, which he roots in gesture and language, is self-modifying as well as world transforming. We are ourselves changed as we act upon or interact in the world. Self-reflection and meaningful action are possible, according to Mead, because human beings initially come to know themselves in a social context, by taking on the attitudes of significant others. Thus self-consciousness is irrevocably mutual.

Mead's metaphorical distinction between the "I" and the "me," two parts of the self, helps to clarify the relationship between social determinism and personal responsibility. The "I" may be said to represent immediate consciousness, consciousness in the specious present. Such consciousness, Mead believes, is biologically rooted, neurologically based. What is peculiar about human beings, Mead argues, is that their social existence and the development of language have enabled them to become self-conscious and so to reflect upon and control the action of the "I," to however limited an extent. A simple stimulus-response model (or for that matter, a socialization model like that of Goffman or Emile Durkheim) does not apply to human beings because the reflective self enables persons to some degree both to select their stimuli and to arrest and choose their responses. In the course of action and interaction, the human "I" constantly lays down a "me," a historical, cumulative self that is a product of that action and interaction. It is a dialectical product, placing limits and pressures on future action for the "I," rooting it historically and socially, and simultaneously extending its potential for creative and responsible action. Hence, according to Mead, we are all more or less responsible for ourselves as well as for one another, not only in the moral sense that we ought to care for each other, but also in the practical sense that as we form ourselves as persons in action and interaction with others we also form the selves of others and are ourselves formed by them. Mead's theory of the self combines the active ingredient of Schutz, the historical and practical continuity of Marx, and the social element of Goffman. Mead enables us to make theoretical sense of the way in which migrants build tiro in the midst of mmereko.

Mead's "self" is constituted in and derived from both practical action and social interaction. As Goffman so eloquently argues, any notion of pure autonomy is meaningless. However, Goffman plays down the fact that each self is not only social and cultural but also unique and potentially characterful, formed through time as meanings are appropriated over one's life.[23] Central to any notion of integrity is our ability to make sense of our personal formation within the social conditions which shape and limit us and to rework our past as we project our actions into the future.

The self formed in social interaction is thus not passive. It struggles to realize its intentions by "doing-in-the-world," as Hoyt Alverson's Tswana (and Alfred Schutz) would say. Those struggles are necessarily limited (but also enabled and empowered) by the prior history of the self, by its social origins, and by its social, cultural, and material milieu. Such struggles are seldom the work of individuals alone. Instead, they take place in the company of others who share our goals, support our commitments, and recollect our responsibilities—hence the importance of migrant cultures and home-based networks in maintaining the practical integrity of migrant miners. Rituals of social interaction do not merely limit action but also enable one to innovate strategically and more or less responsibly. Individual plans and projects are never wholly original because they are derived from culturally bounded social networks, but one can pursue them more or less skillfully and creatively, with greater or lesser integrity and responsibility. Strategic innovations, while they are rooted in and constrained by personal history and develop in a social and cultural context, if accepted may lead to collective action that itself forms alternative models of character and integrity. In this sense one may speak sociologically of agency and character without denying structural constraints. This theoretical insight was worked out practically by migrant South African mine workers as they migrated to and from the mines.

How did South African mine migrants maintain personal and social integrity while moving between the worlds of peasant proprietorship and industrial exploitation, of tiro and mmereko? Through migrant cultures that both modified home realities and created mine lives appropriate for maintaining rural identities. One key to understanding such cultures lies in the miners' stories and songs, rituals and relationships. These narratives and practices, rooted in the social networks of various and shifting migrant cultures, both created and sustained meanings. Such meanings transcended and interwove the disparate strands of the cultures of wage labor and peasant proprietorship. Miners at work told each other stories about their homes and about their work, stories full of advice and nostalgia. They told

[23]An essay in Goffman's *Asylums*, "The Moral Career of the Mental Patient," does seem to depart somewhat from his typical mode, although in the end his stress is not on the practice of integrity but rather on the "practise before all groups [of] the amoral arts of shamelessness" (1961:169). For Goffman, there seems to be no serious potential for sustained resistance in the total institutions he describes.

stories en route to the mines and on the way home again, stories of danger and pride, of family love and country ways. Indeed, migrant cultures came alive in such narratives as quests, epics of resistance to proletarianization built into the very self-formation of black mine workers.

Their stories were embodied in ritual as well. Traditional Xhosa had rituals of departure for the mines (McAllister 1980:213–19). One father described the speech he would give shortly before his son left for his first contract:

> I will tell him one thing only. I will tell him that whatever he does in town, he must do in order to build this homestead [umzi]. I have never borrowed oxen and he must be the same. I have worked hard and he must support me now that I am old and have worked to bring him up. I will tell him that he must . . . go to work and come back. I will say to him: "When the gate post of the cattle byre . . . is left with you, you must preserve . . . it. Don't lose the stock that are inside." He is going to be responsible for my children. He is just like myself and will one day take over my homestead.

At dawn the youthful migrant washed his body in the cattle byre with a special "medicine of the home" (*ubulawu*), invoked his father and the ancestral shades, took up special "food for the journey" prepared by his wife or mother, and left without entering the hut.

Sotho migrants prepared themselves for mine life by singing as they crossed the Mohokare (Caledon) River (the boundary with South Africa):

> Mohokare, now I assume another blanket,
> now that I have crossed you.
> Wash me from the profanations I have had
> with women at home.
> Here I cross to the other side
> and I do not know what dangers may face me.
> Perhaps this is the last time I cross you here.
> And if ever I have the chance of crossing you again
> wash me clean, Mohokare, and make me a pure man.
> Make me a man who is fit to go to heaven.
> Cleanse me from my sins because I am going
> to the dangerous place where I may lose my life . . .
>
> In crossing the river I become a new man,
> different from the one I was at home.
> At home I was secure
> but now that I am on this side
> I am in a place of danger,

where I may lose my life at any time.
So prepare me for death.

Now that [we] are this side
[we] assume a different attitude
from the one where [we] are soft with other men.
This side [we] have to be tough and assume manhood
not be soft like the women at home.

(AIM 1976:12)

Here "manhood" means strength and steadfastness. The song describes pilgrims' mutual progress into the valley of desolation. It is part of a shared epic narrative that prepared migrant selves for new ordeals. This narrative was a product of migrant culture, bridging rural identity and mine work. It actively prepared the singers for fears and hardships—even as other songs and rites of return later readied them for another, more important, aspect of manhood as heads of homesteads (McAllister 1980:219–34).

The rewards of migrant integrity were recounted by one old Mpondo homestead head who spoke to Vivienne Ndatshe in 1982:

> [As a result of my mine work] I bought cattle and mealies for the family. I have an umzi and children, and my wife was in charge when I was away. I trusted my wife and nothing went wrong in my absence. Now we stay together and I no longer go to the mines. . . . I own my umzi and plough my lands with oxen bought while I was on the mines.[24]

Although things did all too often "go wrong," such narratives and recollections—stories, songs, and ritual—mediated between the two worlds of migrant mine workers and sustained and unified their senses of themselves. These migrant narratives of stubborn resistance to proletarianization, reveal a practical integrity that not only is inconceivable outside of social existence but also lived out courageously within it. Over several generations, the integrity of migrant miners maintained tiro within the exploitation and barrenness of mmereko.

[24]In 1982, Vivienne Ndatshe conducted a series of interviews in Pondoland. Her interview notes are in my possession; copies have been housed in the African Studies Institute at the University of the Witwatersrand. In 1984, 1988, and 1989, Ms. Ndatshe and I conducted further interviews with miners and ex-miners in the area around Mantlaneni in the hills twenty miles from Lusikisiki. I conducted similar interviews in Lesotho with the assistance of Palama Lelosa in 1984 and 1988 and Puseletso Salae in 1988. In 1990, Ms. Ndatshe interviewed women living in shacks near the Western Transvaal mines. Her notes of those interviews are at Queens University in Kingston, Ontario. I have written in the acknowledgments of the initiative that Ms. Ndatshe showed in conducting those interviews and of my deep indebtedness to her.

It is important to note that this account deals explicitly with the self-formative narratives of men. Women told different if complementary stories, more rooted in the cycles of nature, I believe, and centered upon holding the umzi together rather than venturing forth on its behalf. Men certainly ruled these societies, but men and women worked to build the umzi together. It was known as their joint achievement.[25]

The notion of the umzi itself has changed over time. William Beinart has pointed out to me that a dehistoricized use of the term "homestead" (umzi) is too static. The umzi that migrants strove so mightily to build was itself changing during generations of migration, both materially (becoming smaller and more nuclear) and perhaps in imagery as well (Beinart 1980). Nonetheless, families clung tenaciously to different variants of what the Tswana called tiro. The commitment to building an umzi was dependent on a wider social and economic system, rooted in the potential for "doing-for-oneself" productively as a family (however constituted) on an agricultural small-holding. This way of life disappeared reluctantly as systemic processes of underdevelopment and resettlement destroyed its material base.

Young Men's Organizations and Women with Manhood: Mpondo Migrant Cultures

Migrant cultures have left their mark both on the organization of mine work and on rural production throughout Southern and Central Africa since the turn of the century. Migrancy as a social formation early marked both Southern African mining technology and the structures of country life in the labor-supplying reserves. The underdevelopment of African agriculture was a major theme of Southern African scholarship during the 1970s (Palmer and Parsons 1977).[26] Without denying the importance of underdevelopment as a systemic process in Southern Africa, one must note the tenacity with which rural proprietors resisted proletarianization and sustained rural production. Revivals of rural production (Ranger 1978,

[25]The best accounts of "women left at home" both deal with Lesotho. They are Murray 1981 and Gay 1980. Belinda Bozzoli (1991) describes the consciousness and life strategies of Tswana-speaking women who migrated from the western Transvaal to the Witwatersrand in the 1920s and 1930s and settled in town but who returned home on "retirement." Her account, with its stress on how these women established themselves "as active participants in and creators of households that embodied some of the values drawn from their youthful upbringing" (237), strikingly parallels that of Mpondo mine-working men and their women who stayed at home.

[26]Exceptions to this generalization are the work of William Beinart and Philip Mayer and his associates (especially Andrew Spiegel and Pat McAllister), whom I shall cite frequently throughout this study.

Beinart 1982) went hand in hand with pressures toward underdevelopment in an awkward dialectic whose final outcome was reached only in the 1960s (Simkins 1981) through massive intervention by the South African state in resettlement and rural development schemes.

Even now, there are pockets of resistance to proletarianization scattered throughout the Southern African countryside. Underdevelopment, most simply understood as the collapse of homestead agricultural production, has proceeded at different rates in different parts of rural Southern Africa.

Pondoland is one of the most agriculturally self-sufficient parts of the South African rural reserves and thus one of the last to be obliged to abandon homestead agriculture. Mine work has typically been popular among workers from such less underdeveloped areas because recruitment centers were convenient and because mine compounds insulated workers from full exposure to urban life. Furthermore, the system of full keep and deferred pay enabled workers to bring home a lump sum that could be invested in cattle and in homestead production.

Although cultures other than rural-based migrant ones existed, even on mine compounds,[27] compounds were particularly well suited for men with aspirations to rural patriarchal proprietorship like the Mpondo. Beinart (1980:145) found that in the 1940s "about 45 per cent of [Mpondo] mine workers from Lusikisiki were deferring their pay in full and that perhaps 60 to 70 percent of the total earned was repatriated." To this day, miners from other groups talk of the proverbial stinginess of the Mpondo. The Mpondo maintained, however, that they were "on business on the mine." According to ex-miner Zalele Sithelo:

> Most of the people who sent home money were either married or owned land. [It was safe to send money through the recruiting organization] but home friends trusted each other so that if one was going home he would deliver letters and money to others' families. Miners saved their money at the mine offices [keeping only a small amount of pocket money] to buy beer for friends on the weekends. We would visit each other and talk about girlfriends or [the married ones] their families, wives and children. . . . Those who were married always talked about their families and longed to see their new-born babies.
>
> Miners of those days didn't care about women. We camped for nine months [as did herd boys with their cattle in the countryside]

[27]For instance, considerable movement seems to have occurred between urban gangs, prisons, and the mine compounds. See, for example, van Onselen 1982, Breckenridge 1990, Guy and Thabane 1987, and Bonner 1988. One participant observer found such a multiethnic prison-based gang on Welkom Mine in 1976. It was running a *dagga*-dealing ring.

> and then left for our lovers and wives at home. We were afraid of the town women, believing that they were dangerous and would make us forget our families. Some of us had seen men with women in town who had left their wives and their lands and later came home penniless. They said town women loved these men only because of the money. If the man had no more money, he was kicked out.

Amongst the Mpondo before the 1970s there were actually two separate concatenations of migrant cultures bridging the gap between umzi building at home and mine work. The differences between them were expressed in the country areas as well as on the mines by two parallel types of youth organization.[28] The *igubura* were organizations of the traditional *amaqaba* ("red-blanket," sometimes called *nombola*) youth, and the *indlavini* (pl. *iindlavini*) youth organizations (Beinart 1988, O'Connell 1980, Mayer and Mayer 1972) represented the semischooled and churched segment of the rural community. Every older ex-miner we interviewed in Pondoland classified himself as either indlavini or amaqaba. The number of years of schooling (and to some extent churchgoing) was the major reason given for the differentiation. In our interviews Ms. Ndatshe and I found indlavini members with education through standard six (equivalent to the eighth grade in the United States), whereas amaqaba seldom had any education beyond the first couple of grades. Persons with education beyond standard six were likely to be called *amanene* ("respectables"). They seldom migrated to the mines unless they were hired as clerks, in which case they tended to bring their families and live in the mine village (*skomplas*), an area set aside as married quarters for senior black mine staff. In the Mpondo countryside as young men they were the butt of verbal and physical bullying from iindlavini, who despised them for being "soft." Although iindlavini were regarded as rougher and less under adult control than amaqaba, both groups disciplined their members and members of both groups migrated to the mines and moved on to become umzi heads. Amanene were generally perceived as having abandoned rural traditions—they had become "school" people in Philip Mayer's (1961) terms. Such accusations were not made about iindlavini, however much their roughness was deplored.[29]

The existence of indlavini migrant cultures in Pondoland points to the importance of education in separating young men and women from tra-

[28]For the importance of youth organizations amongst Xhosa-speaking Nguni, see Mayer and Mayer 1970 and 1972; Beinart 1987, O'Connell 1980; for Sotho, see Guy and Thabane 1987; for Pedi, see Delius 1989.

[29]For further discussion of *iindlavini* and comparisons with Sotho youth cultures, see the evidence to the Bregman Commission (AAC/VR:1704–52 and 2215–26).

ditional Xhosa culture (Mayer 1961, 1980). However, indlavini commitment to the rural economy also suggests that schooling (or even church attendance) as such was insufficient as an explanation for the abandonment of the homestead mode of production. The productivity of agricultural lands must be included in any account of social change in rural South Africa.

A counterfactual case exists in Lesotho, which has also been a traditional sending area to the mines. Before 1963, uneducated rural Sotho homestead heads from deep in the mountains chose mine work despite the scorn of their better educated and more wage-dependent fellows from the lowlands. The latter might use mine recruitment to get to the urban areas but would leave after one or two contracts to engage in better-remunerated jobs in the urban sector. In 1963, however, the South African state legislated against employment of citizens of Lesotho in all sectors except mining and agriculture. As a result, educated Sotho were obliged to seek mine work. Those with high school–leaving certificates (the equivalent of the amanene in Pondoland) were able to obtain clerical and surface supervisory positions, but others with only a middle school education and no land (often the most wage dependent of all but with an educational level equivalent to the Mpondo iindlavini) were obliged to work underground for miserable wages.

By 1975, when Palesa Sebilo (1976), who believed that education was the major variable in attitudes toward mine work, interviewed three groups of Sotho mine workers (high school graduates, those with standard six, and those from the mountains with little or no education), she found that members of the intermediate group were by far the most alienated because they aspired to white-collar jobs but had insufficient education to get them. Unlike the iindlavini, they had no migrant culture to insulate them from the stresses of mine labor and no workable land to return to, and their low wages (before 1973) brought them only scorn from people at home. Without a rural homestead like the iindlavini, they lacked the grounding that enabled both cultural encapsulation and a resistance base.

William Beinart is writing a history of the Mpondo that includes fascinating material on the indlavini movement.[30] He too has found that the decision to continue in school was a crucial factor in separating iindlavini from amaqaba—although the decision to run away from school to the mines or cane fields in later adolescence may have been just as important. The decision to stay in school beyond the first or second grade was apparently made by the potential indlavini's family; the decision to abscond

[30]For a statement of his current conclusions, see his paper in the Mayer *festschrift* (Beinart 1991).

before one became amanene while not necessarily actively encouraged by the parents was certainly condoned by them and was consciously planned with one's peers as an important step in the life course. All iindlavini, of course, expected to earn money for bridewealth in order to set up an umzi. Indeed, Beinart has found that obtaining access to young women was an important function of the indlavini organization.

Most important from the point of view of this study is that indlavini organizations incorporated variations of migrant cultures that bridged the worlds of mine and countryside for young men with access to land and who also had church affiliations and a measure of education. Beyond their longer schooling, their church adherence, their flashy dress and somewhat more swaggering behavior, and their different patterns of youth organization and courtship, which ensured somewhat greater independence from control by elders (but no less organizational self-discipline), in their material life the iindlavini were indistinguishable from the amaqaba. Certainly in regard to umzi building, they shared common aspirations to rural proprietorship. In 1987, an Mpondo consultant to the Bregman Commission (AAC/VR:2217) defined the place of iindlavini in the rural areas of Pondoland as follows:

> It is not that they are looked down upon by the community. No, they are a certain clique in the community. They are respected in their own circle. . . . But the people outside their circle look down upon them and fear them at the same time. . . . The red-blanketed do not go to school. The Ndlavinis come up to Standard Five, Standard Six . . . if you belong to that circle you start from boyhood, then early manhood and then there is a stage you are a Ndlavini, it is part of your growing. . . . After that you become an elder in the location. . . . At a certain stage you want to go, at thirty-five you are an old Ndlavini. Now at forty you forget about being Ndlavini, now you are an old man in the location. You have become a responsible. . . .
>
> You see in an enlightened area you can get the educated type and then there are few Ndlavini, a few sections of Ndlavinis but no Nombolas. In the less [enlightened areas] you get Nombolas and Ndlavinis and some few educated ones. . . . The situation of Ndlavinis and Nombolas is no longer as prevalent as ten years ago.

Beinart believes that indlavini groups superimposed urban youth styles upon traditional rural associations, grafting fragments of urban practices and discourse onto fundamentally rural structures of feeling. On the mines, indlavini groups provided important associational networks for their members, ensuring their somewhat better educated and churched workers a form of encapsulation similar to that provided by igubura youth associations for tradition amaqaba. Singing and dancing was the major activity of indlavini and igubura groups both on the mines and in the countryside (although the presence of women in the countryside, and fights over them, made mine gatherings but pale images of their country counterparts).

I have deliberately used the notion of "mine cultures" in the plural, because even the same "culture" differs from place to place and changes over time. To an extent, of course, migrants themselves struggled to reify elusive rural traditions even as the country base slowly eroded around them. Persons who came to town or mine to earn money for country pursuits did not return to the country unmarked by the wage work experience, however, despite their resistance to full proletarianization. Social structures in the countryside were modified by the impact of returning migrants (Beinart 1982, 1988). The archives are full of complaints by older men that youngsters were getting out of hand (see Harries 1982, Beinart 1979).[31] The powers of women in these patriarchal societies also gradually changed as they took on more responsibility in the absence of their men (Murray 1981). Families became more nuclear as the pressure on men to migrate increased with time.

Mpondo conceptions of masculinity and femininity themselves changed over time. Ms. Ndatshe and I originally asked questions about "manhood" in Pondoland in the Lusikisiki area in 1988 because I was interested in faction fights. I expected to uncover a "warrior syndrome," with fighting ability as at least part of the definition of manhood. So, with the twenty-odd men we spoke to that time, young and old alike, we raised the issue of fighting, for which the Mpondo are famed on the mines, to lead into questions about manhood.[32] Imagine my surprise when every older man we interviewed, whether indlavini or amaqaba, denied categorically that strength in combat had anything to do with manhood (*ubudoda*).

What then did constitute manhood? we asked. In a typical conversation with two ex-iindlavini, Ntelezi and Msana, at Gcuda, Ntelezi said: "Ubu-

[31]The evidence of Chief Jico to the Native Economic Commission (NEC:3043) on 10 December 1930 mentions young men who have run away from home: "[They are] rascals who have stayed for a long time on the mines. Then, when they go wrong, the mining people send them back to us and they are useless to us and they cause a lot of trouble and quarrels." The word *indlavini* is often translated "rascal." Could this be an early reference to the indlavini groups?

[32]For Xhosa from the Ciskei and Western Transkei and for Sotho, manhood is not as profound a talking point as it is for Mpondo, since the Mpondo do not circumcise. Questions to Sotho about "manhood" simply elicited answers about circumcision. The Mpondo were obliged to be more complex.

doda is to do things, to put things right, to help a person in need." Msana added:

> Ubudoda is to help people. If somebody's children don't have books or school fees or so, then you are going to help those children while the father cannot manage. Or if there is somebody who died, you go there and talk to people there. Or, if someone is poor—has no oxen—then you can take your own oxen and plow his fields. That is ubudoda, one who helps other people.

I was still not willing to drop my search for the warrior syndrome, however, and asked whether there was not also a sort of manhood displayed by strength in fighting. Msana replied at once: "No, that is not manhood. Such a person is called a killer." Ntelezi agreed: "That is not manhood."

Whether iindlavini or amaqaba, without exception the old men to whom we spoke in Pondoland agreed that ubudoda, the essence of manhood, had to do with competent and benevolent management of the umzi, aiding in homestead decision-making, settling disputes, and generous sharing of homestead resources with guests and visitors.[33] A second, subsidiary, conception of manhood, which became fundamental on the mines, referred to consistency, staying power, strength in remaining true to one's purposes and in solidarity with one's friends and neighbors. To Mpondo elders, however, this was merely an extension of the original meaning, since mine life was seen as a means to building and maintaining a homestead. The mines were a testing ground for true manhood, manifested in presiding justly over a rural homestead.

We asked Ntelezi and Msana about "womanhood" (*ubufazi*). Msana said at once: "If a woman looks after people in the kraal [homestead], does things for them, helps them, that woman has got ubufazi." For Ntelezi, who had been an indlavini chief, the essence of womanhood too resided in her relation to the umzi, especially in a context of migrant labor with frequent male absence. Asked if a woman could have ubudoda, Ntelezi and Msana agreed that she could. In fact, with only one exception, a very old nombola, all the older Mpondo men stated categorically that a women could have ubudoda. Since they defined manhood morally rather than biologically, this assertion was not illogical. Sometimes they explained that a women would have such attributes when the man was absent from the homestead. All but Msana denied, however, that a man could have womanhood, except in a metaphorical sense that implied cowardice.

[33]It is no accident that Kuckertz (1990) centers his entire ethnographic description of Mpondo social life around the umzi.

Ntelezi actually said that ubufazi refers to "a woman who, when the man is away in the mines, looks after his things at home, she does everything." He thus implied that the two terms "woman" and "man" had the same meaning in the context of indlavini migrant culture. Msana, in correcting him, alone of all the men worked through to the patriarchal power that lies behind the moralistic understanding of the umzi and the migrant conception of manhood, although he linked it to patrilocality. He was also the only man to say that men could have ubufazi:

> These words mean the same. If you are a man you can have ubufazi. If you are a woman you can have ubudoda. The difference is that if you are *indoda* [a man], if you have ubudoda, you have power—more power than ubufazi, because this ubufazi comes from home where if ubudoda is being practiced she must always listen—so this ubufazi is powerless whereas ubudoda is powerful.

In speaking of female "manhood," then, Mpondo men were not denying male power in the last instance. That, it seems, was firmly located for them in patrilocality. However, migrant cultures clearly brought to the fore the conception of male-female partnership, which is embedded in the notion of "building the umzi." This aspect became more pronounced as the homestead became more nuclear (which may explain the very old amaqaba man who denied ubudoda to women).

During the years of intensive Mpondo mine migration, women, in fact if not formally, were left in charge when married men left for the mines.[34] The secondary sense of ubudoda, as "strength," the ability to see things through, obviously also applied to women left behind to build the umzi. If notions of "maleness" necessarily imply "femaleness" (however repressed or negated), in Mpondo migrant cultures awareness of the terms' complementarity was close to the surface. After all, a major function of indlavini organizations was to control courtship patterns as the arrangements of the amaqaba broke down with schooling and male youth migration. The conception of manhood that formed the basis of migrant culture made no sense without a woman left at home building the umzi and presiding over it in the absence of the man.

There is another sense also in which women were important to African migrant cultures and reinforced patriarchal power. The system of bridewealth became a means whereby money earned through migration could

[34]Philip Mayer (1978:97–115) years ago made the point that migrancy strengthened the position of women at home. More recently this has become an important theme in the work of several feminist scholars. See, for example, articles by Deutsch 1987, Guendelman and Perez-Itriago 1987, and Schmidt 1990. I am indebted to Mary Jane Aldrich-Moodie for these references.

be transferred to older men back home. Kenelm Burridge (1969:114), points out the irreconcilable contradictions that migration to work for money created for Melanesian men:

> In the indigenous prestige systems of Melanesia, only mature men could have any influence. But when money appeared the young had the readiest access to it through their labour, and they could outbid their seniors. On the other hand, when a young man settled down and married he re-entered the traditional prestige system and could no longer earn money. . . . Either they could return to their villages and become men of stature in traditional terms without the aid of money, or they could remain in the European settled areas, with money, and be considered men of small account.

Migrant cultures overcame this dilemma in Southern Africa, but they did so only because, despite undoubted generational tensions, the exchange of women through the bridewealth system redistributed wealth upward across the generations. Furthermore, access to women was important in a practical sense as well as sexually and symbolically because without women the building of the homestead—and hence manhood itself—would have been impossible.

The Erosion of Migrant Cultures

At the same time that migrant cultures were forcing adjustments upon rural societies, there was a seepage of more impoverished individuals from the reserve areas to the white farms and towns, with a stint or two on the mines often providing a conduit to urban employment. State policies of massive resettlement into the rural areas during the 1960s, along with "betterment schemes," are finally, if unevenly, destroying the resilience of country lifestyles as individuals are resettled on land that is insufficient for rural proprietorship (Sharp and Spiegel 1985, 1991). The rise in mine wages in the 1970s has brought a much more proletarian, if still migrant, workforce to the gold mines, often from the burgeoning rural slums. For these men, the full alienation of wage labor is exacerbated by separation from families who are now completely dependent on their wages. As the men say: "Our families eat our money." In those cases, women in the country, who had been somewhat empowered by productive partnerships with their husbands, are no longer able to complement migrant men by cultivating the fields and presiding over the umzi in the absence of their husbands. Now they are totally dependent on the men's moral obligation to make remittances although these are no longer investments in their futures for the men. Often the remittances stop coming as men increasingly find women in the towns and farms around the mines. More and more women from the country areas themselves migrate to town, where they often find themselves in deeply dependent situations—whether they find their husbands or move in with other men (Ramphele 1989, Moodie and Ndatshe 1992). Younger men in Pondoland no longer associate "manhood" (ubudoda) with the ability to preside over an umzi competently, generously, and humanely—a quality that women could retain in the absence of their migrant husbands. Instead, "manhood" is now simply "maleness"—a biological fact.

Thus, for the present generation of Mpondo, maleness and femaleness have been dichotomized again. The suggestion that women might have ubudoda is categorically denied, if not ridiculed. On ubudoda and ubufazi, young men to whom we spoke disagreed with their elders fundamentally and universally.[35] There is no point in reproducing their conversations because their attitudes were so cut and dried. Ubudoda, the young men said, denoted biological maleness and ubufazi biological femaleness. They looked at me as though I were slightly dippy when I asked if a women could have ubudoda. Of course not, they said politely, implying that my question had been nonsensical. For some, ubudoda had a directly sexual reference. I learned that one may say to a man with his fly open: "Your ubudoda is showing."

Young Mpondo men in the Mandlaneni district of Lusikisiki in 1988 spoke to me of their work underground, of the union, of the recent strike that had locked out many of them from mine work. One quietly sang me a song of the "comrades": "Ask Oliver Tambo, to tell P. W. Botha, to release Nelson Mandela." Those who still had jobs, especially those with families, were determined to keep out of trouble. They were constructing fairly large and elaborate houses—square houses with tin roofs. Boys go to school now and play soccer in the afternoons. No longer are they out herding cattle and playing with sticks—indeed, cattle are sparse. Indlavini organizations are defunct, reflecting the small minority of adherents of the old migrant cultures left on the mines. It is thus hardly surprising that older conceptions of women with manhood, adjusted to long absences of men when women were left with the responsibility for the productive work of the umzi, are also things of the past. Women are now virtually com-

[35]Both my colleague H. Wesley Perkins and participants at an SSRC conference on "Towards a Gendered History of African Men" at the University of Minnesota in 1989 suggested that the differences between older and younger men might be a matter of position in the life course rather than a historical shift. I do not have a definitive answer to this objection except a contextual one. So much else is changing so fast in Pondoland that I cannot believe that the young men of today will say in their old age that women can have manhood. It seems unlikely that their conceptions will mature along lines of migrant culture.

pletely dependent on remittances from migrating men since the umzi is no longer much of a productive unit.

Young, unionized mine workers living a stone's throw from old miners firmly contradicted their testimony on the meaning of masculinity. The "women with manhood" who had been so important in maintaining the home end of migrant culture have disappeared in the younger circles at Mandlaneni. They have been replaced by women who can have only womanhood, presiding over fancier houses, but without "homesteads" to sustain and be sustained by.[36] Although the word "umzi" is still used to describe one's house and home, its moral meaning has been narrowed and constricted to physical housing and the nuclear family. While some rural traditions of hospitality remain, migrant cultures are disappearing with the demise of the rural political economy that maintained them. Modern black mine workers with rural homes may indeed be "men of two worlds." It makes better sense, however, to conceive of them as professional miners whose families continue to reside in the countryside. That is, they have become rural commuters.

Conclusion

Can any single notion of self-identity apply both to migrant cultures and to their demise? Probably not, for personal identities make sense only within wider sets of social practices and commitments. When life-worlds are breaking down and others have not yet been constituted to take their place, identity formations become fragmented and Goffman's sorts of selves may be found. The potential for deeply divisive social conflict increases. In practice, however, resourceful persons create lives of integrity together as they build new life-worlds out of fragments of the old. The rapid growth of the National Union of Mineworkers among both "traditional" and "new" workers shows that even across systemic divides between fundamentally different material bases, everyday social networks and alliances around common interests can build new organizational contexts for social action and new practical identities. There is always room for integrity, that personally practiced and socially supported virtue in which one lives a life true to culturally derived but personally constructed purposes. Bozzoli's study of Tswana women who came to settle in Johan-

[36]In the transition in Africa from agricultural self-sufficiency to wage labor, migrant cultures seem to have provided an intermediate state of greater autonomy for women. For the precapitalist African age-gender system of exploitation, see Jeff Guy 1990; for the great dependency that migrant labor and influx control imposed on women once the rural base was destroyed, see Mamphele Ramphele 1989.

nesburg in the 1920s and 1930s, for instance, discovered identities that were made up "historically, within the limits set by the material world," not arbitrarily:

> [E]ach fragment of identity—involving the women's perception of themselves as Christians, as Bafokeng, as Tswana, as women, as mothers, wives, "respectables" or whatever—has a history, and a link with a prevailing discourse. Each fragment is an inherent tradition which was once derived from a particular past situation, socially created, and yet brought into idiosyncratic and individual expression by its incarnation in the character, the "self" of each particular woman. (1991:241)

So too individual miners created their own identities in both traditional migrant cultures and the democratic practices of the National Union of Mineworkers. They engaged in characterful conduct that maintained integrity but situated it differently, forming alliances with different others for particular political purposes. Part of the importance of the National Union of Mineworkers is that it not only represents all workers in wage negotiations and disputes over unfair dismissals, but also that local union branches seek to create new moral orders with new integrities where the old imiteto are breaking down.

A more complete treatment of such developments, however, requires more extensive sociohistorical analysis of miners' lives at work and in the compounds on South African gold mines during the twentieth century. This book sets out to delineate changes in the social conditions by which black miners were made workers and men but also to show how mine workers made each other and themselves, as they struggled to practice integrity in an alienated world.

2 Production Politics

Workplace Control and Worker Resistance

The existence of massive deposits of gold ore brought thousands of men to work underground on the Witwatersrand, and later the western Orange Free State. Behind the pressures of mine work, the contestation of compound life, and the integrity of migrant cultures lay the reason for it all—vast networks of tunnels branching out from vertical shafts at different levels to intersect with the gold reef. Men and machinery and explosives were moved underground, and massive amounts of rock were brought to the surface to be treated to extract minute proportions of gold. The grade of South African gold ore is poor. What makes mine controllers and investors rich is the huge quantity of ore deep beneath the thin South African soil, so that colossal capital investment brings forth dividends as long as costs can be kept down.

Unlike any other commodity, gold has a guaranteed international market, but until the early 1970s the price was fixed. Price controls exacerbated the effects of already stringent cost constraints. The South African gold-mining industry dealt with the peculiarities of its cost structure in three ways. First economies of scale were achieved through large mining investment houses that managed and shared in the engineering and development costs of individual mines. Second, labor was divided racially between well-remunerated white supervisory workers and management and exceedingly low-paid, compounded, and indentured migrant black miners. Third, the Chamber of Mines provided a monopsonist arrangement among the various mining houses, partly for research and development, but primarily to control wages and organize the labor supply. These are the constraints under which South African gold production has traditionally operated, setting the parameters within which management control and worker resistance have typically been exercised.

Given the importance of cheap labor for the industry prior to the 1970s and given the integrity with which black migrants pursued their own specific goals, it is hardly surprising that complaints about shortages of labor and fluctuation of supply run like a refrain through the history of South African mine management. Uncertainty stemming from the ability of peasant proprietors to withhold their labor—at least for a few years—gave migrants a lever against management. Despite the many measures encouraging recruitment (advances up front) and controlling the labor force (taxes, pass laws, lengthy contracts, and the compound system), black migrant workers (especially those South African–born) *did* exercise strategic choices. They chose gold mines over coal, copper, salt, or asbestos mines and over plantation-type farm work, and, especially as the twentieth century wore on, some of them chose secondary industry, dock work, railway work, even domestic labor, over the mines. These were not free choices nor were all black workers as free as some to make them, but workers from within the political boundaries of South Africa certainly had strategic options—and they exercised them. Experienced black miners, even those from outside the country, were able to return to the mines they had worked on before. In fact, in certain periods all South African–born workers had such choices. As a result, over the years Mozambican labor (and from the 1950s, "tropical," largely Malawian, labor), with fewer options, has been especially useful to the mining industry. Unpopular gold mines always had high proportions of Mozambicans and "Tropicals," and Mozambicans supplied virtually all the labor for the high veld coal mines. Thus, among the many constraints facing mining managements—the low grade of the ore, the depth and unevenness of the reef, the hardness of the rock, the fixed price of gold, fluctuations in the cost of stores, and often militant white miners' unions—were uncertainties about the black labor supply, both overall and between individual mines.

There were limits to the options even of South African–born workers, of course, but the formal system also constrained mine managers' alternatives. Thus, workers could choose individual mines only as long as their preferences did not already have a full "complement" of labor, allotted to them by the chamber's committee of consulting engineers. Likewise, individual mine managements could use wages to compete for black workers but only within the parameters of a "maximum average wage" for their total black labor force decided by the chamber, and the committee of consulting engineers decided on the proper size of any mine's labor force. The monopsony of the recruiting arms of the Chamber of Mines controlled individual mining companies, like Hobbes's Leviathan, in their own interest.[1] The hegemony of individual mine managers, despotic though it may have seemed to their thousands of working minions, was tightly limited by group controls and recruiting organization concerns—not to mention the political and industrial clout of the white miners' unions and informal collective action by black workers.

Furthermore, by 1910, government inspectors from the Department of Mines as well as Native Affairs Department inspectors had Witwatersrand mining fairly firmly regulated. There were strategic exceptions, of course. A blind eye tended to be turned to contraventions of regulations by low-grade and almost-worked-out mines, and inspectors of mines could be controlled by personal ties with mine managements if not by outright bribery. Similar problems arose with the appointment of underground "native overseers" by the mines themselves. B. G. Lloyd, who was in charge of the Witwatersrand Native Labour Association (WNLA) staging compound on the Rand told Commissioner Buckle (NGI, 28 April 1914, 66):

> [Compound managers] hear grievances from underground and they want to make complaints but the costs are running too high and they do not get much sympathy. . . . In theory it would look a beautiful system to put an underground overseer on a mine and many mines have got them and I think on the whole they are doing a lot of good but a mine is a very big place underground and there are great difficulties. If that underground Inspector makes himself a nuisance to the powers that be underground they have various insidious ways of getting back at him so that his first job is to be able to run smoothly with the [white] underground staff.

Such informal power notwithstanding, mine managements on the Witwatersrand always had to operate with an eye to state regulations, however much they might contravene them in practice.

In most capitalist enterprises hegemony is derived from the technological organization of work, structures of supervisory surveillance (and the strategies of informal power associated with them), and incentives. What now seem to have been straightforward technological "improvements" in mining methods sometimes did not seem so to management at the time

[1]Until the 1970s, there were two recruiting bodies, the Native Recruiting Corporation (NRC) for South African labor and the Witwatersrand Native Labour Association (WNLA) for Mozambican and tropical labor. They have now been combined into one company under the acronym TEBA (The Employment Bureau of Africa). For the development of these bodies and their complex relationships with the South African government and neighboring labor supply states, see Jeeves 1985 and Crush, Jeeves, and Yudelman 1991.

because they affected workplace hegemony. New technologies and methods of work organization could become tactical weapons in the struggle to control the workplace. To illustrate this point, we shall examine examples of two of the most important innovations in South African gold mining: the introduction of machine drills in the first quarter of the twentieth century and the vicissitudes, over a seventy-year period, of schemes to give more responsibility to black underground supervisors.

Underground Work: Technological Methods and Developments

Deep-level gold mining involves sinking a shaft into the earth and then driving development tunnels out of the shaft to intersect the reef of ore. From these development drives, stopes lead off into the reef itself, cutting it out like the roast beef for a huge sandwich. The width of the gold-bearing reef, often thousands of feet below the surface, is measured in inches. Thus to get it out, waste rock must be blasted also and trammed along the haulage to the shaft, where it used to be raised to the surface with the ore, forming Johannesburg's distinctive mine dumps. Railed trucks, either locomotive drawn or continuous haulage, are used for tramming. Until the 1930s, pick-and-shovel men, called *layishas,* or "lashers," manually removed rock from the stopes and into the trucks in the haulage. Mechanical stope scrapers were introduced on most mines in the 1930s, although the ubiquitous human lasher is by no means outmoded.

Before the reef can be removed, it must be broken. This requires drilling holes up to four feet deep into the rock surrounding the packed ore and then blasting it. Until 1915 or thereabouts, the most common form of drilling was hand drilling:

> In 1908 or so 100,000 "holes," 3 feet to 3 ft. 6 ins. deep, were drilled in stopes daily by native "hammer boys" on the Witwatersrand in hand drilling. The pointed solid steel rod "borer," or "jumper" as it is called locally, is struck with an iron hammer, withdrawn a short distance to free it from the broken chips, and twisted so as to maintain the round shape of the hole. Water is used to assist in removing the chips and sludge formed; they are sucked up by withdrawing the jumper from time to time from the hole, and periodically clearing the hole completely with a wooden stick. A wetted ring or "swab" is placed round the drill at the mouth of the hold to minimise the quantity of dust escaping from the hole. (Jeppe 1946:148)

The jumpers, steel rods with flattened ends, usually came in sets of four, weighing from four to eleven pounds (Jeppe 1946:183).

In the late teens, relatively light, small compressed-air jackhammer drills were introduced on a large scale. The jumpers fitted into these drills were hollowed out so that water could pass through them to damp down the hole continuously since dust was found to cause miners' phthisis (*pneumosilicosis*). The African drill operator (*machine boy*) would be accompanied by an assistant (called a *spanner boy*) to help steady the drill and to change jumpers as the hole got deeper.

The important categories of black workers underground after 1920 until the 1970s, then, were machine drillers, who worked in pairs; lashers, who worked in teams under the supervision of black boss boys; teams of timberers, who constructed and installed waste packs to hold up the hanging; and pipelayers, who led water and compressed air to the drills. Teams of trammers worked on trucks and trains in the haulage. When mechanical stope scrapers were introduced in the 1930s, they were also operated by black workers, who were usually regarded as part of the lashing team. White miners, whether under contract or paid by the day, were essentially supervisors, although until the 1980s only they were legally permitted to blast and handle dynamite. White officials (shift bosses) supervised white miners in turn. Figure 1 provides a general summary of the formal hierarchy on the South African gold mines (underground and in the compounds) in the 1970s.

Although there have been recent technological improvements in shaft-sinking and development work (Guy and Thabane 1988), stoping has changed little since the introduction of the scraper winch in the 1930s. Before the rise in mine wages in the 1970s, labor-intensive stoping technologies were apparently regarded as adequate for the job (especially given tramming speeds). Now, however, greater mechanization is being planned at the larger mining houses although, given the unevenness and narrowness of the reef, new techniques may not necessarily be at hand. A recent article, by Horst Wagner (1986) of the Chamber Research Division, does mention improvements in firing shot-holes (presumably through electrification) during the early 1960s as a means of increasing productivity per worker. As I understand this improvement it includes two different aspects. First, all blasting is now centralized so that the mine may be completely cleared before daily blasting takes place. Second, improved explosives and drilling jumpers have eliminated the necessity for mining skills in the placing of holes. These are relatively minor improvements. Indeed, despite an intensive search for new techniques, South African gold-mining stoping technology has changed little in its fundamentals. Reorganization of the labor process, however, has brought an acknowledged need for a more skilled and stable black workforce. In the long run it is believed that

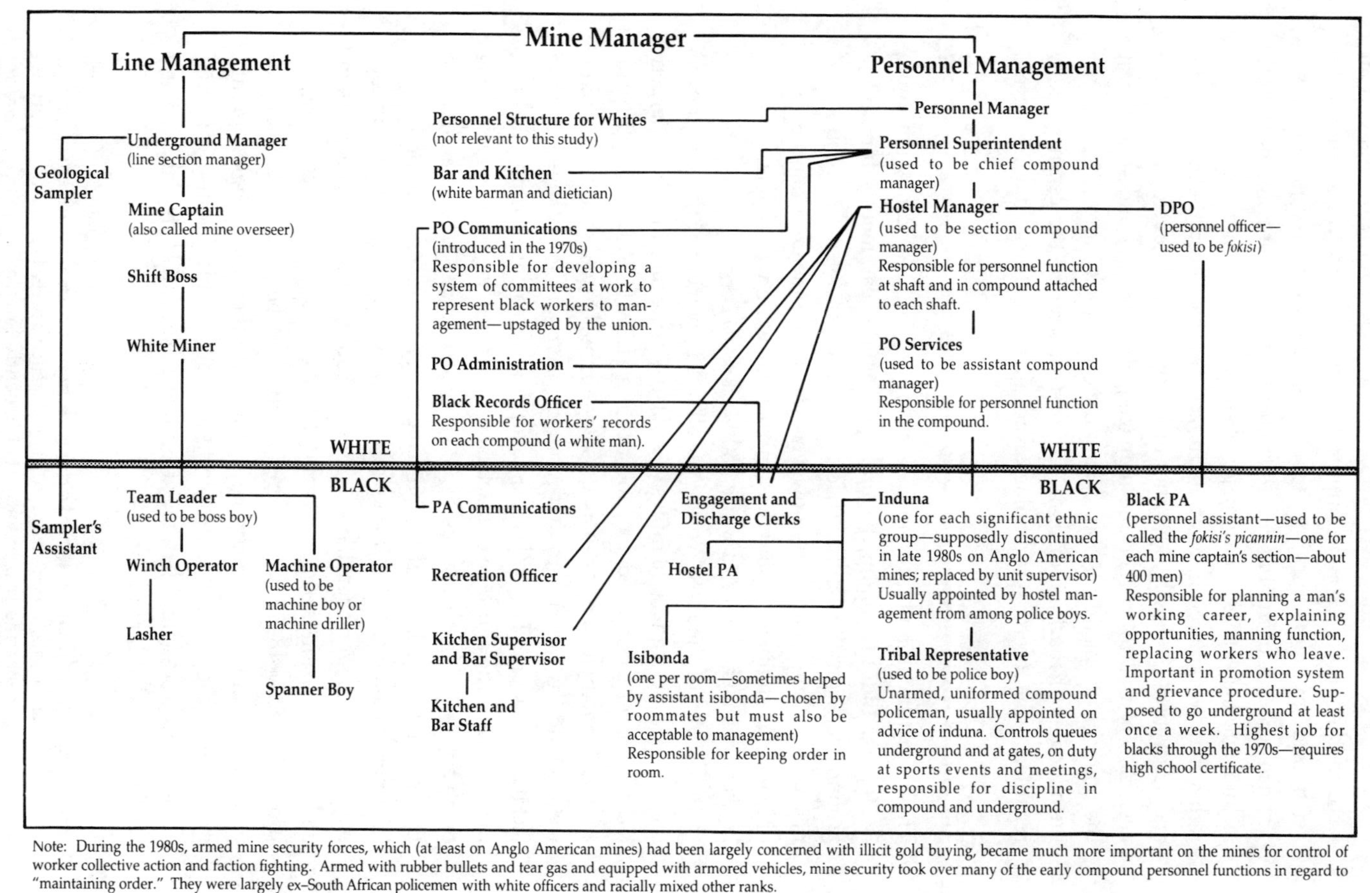

Note: During the 1980s, armed mine security forces, which (at least on Anglo American mines) had been largely concerned with illicit gold buying, became much more important on the mines for control of worker collective action and faction fighting. Armed with rubber bullets and tear gas and equipped with armored vehicles, mine security took over many of the early compound personnel functions in regard to "maintaining order." They were largely ex–South African policemen with white officers and racially mixed other ranks.

Figure 1. Formal organizational structure of a typical gold mine, c. 1975.

this will be best attained by phasing out migrant labor, although current labor market surpluses and computerization of worker registration have "stabilized" migrants, turning them into career miners (Crush 1987).

Such accounts of mining developments leave the impression of smooth technological advances whose major obstacles were engineering problems rather than workplace contestation. In fact, however, even the most simple and apparently obviously advantageous technological developments have been closely tied to worker and management strategies and struggles at the point of production. As an example we will look more closely at the introduction of machine drills in the first quarter of the century—now regarded as the foremost technological advance since the gold mines began.

The Introduction of Machine Drills

The most difficult and labor-intensive part of South African gold mining is stoping. Indeed, stoping technologies set the parameters for underground work on the South African gold mines.[2] Even the adoption of machine-drilling technology, however, was by no means a neutral result of scientific engineering but was introduced within a complex struggle between managements and white and black workers.

By the end of the First World War all but 15 percent of the rock moved on the Witwatersrand gold mines was blasted using machine drills (largely jackhammers) as opposed to hand drilling (LGMC, August 1919, para. 16203). Nonetheless, mine managers unanimously held that hand drilling was technically superior to and less expensive and less dangerous than jackhammer work. The widespread adoption of machine drilling was primarily due to the shortage of black labor (at prices the mines were willing or able to pay). In the words of G. H. Beatty, manager of Randfontein Estates: "I do not know that you have many managers who prefer jack hammers to hand stoping, if they can get natives. . . . If I can get hammer boys I utilize them rather than machines, because it is much easier working and the supervision is easier, and the capital cost is low, and so on" (MIB, July 1922:4852, 4840). Jackhammers came, not because of technical superiority in fathomage produced, nor because they made higher profits, nor because they deskilled the workforce, but simply because with machines more rock could be moved by fewer black workers; labor supply was thus the deciding factor.

[2]Coal mining is a different story. There, with more favorable work environments and wide, even seams, mechanization has proceeded apace. Not only the narrowness of the gold-bearing reef but also its frequently broken and uneven character makes technological improvements in stoping difficult.

Management testimony was unanimous on this point. In the best of all possible worlds, with an infinite, cheap labor supply, hammers were preferable to machines. When he was challenged in 1922 about whether there was actually a black labor shortage, William Gemmill of the Chamber of Mines expostulated that "a permanently adequate supply of natives" was "the ideal condition, when [the mines] would not be required to employ machines instead of hammer boys" (MIB, July 1922:3900).

The managers had technical reasons for preferring hand hammers: the vibration caused by machines was more likely to loosen the hanging (stope roof), leading not only to accidents but also to the need to remove more waste rock; the early machines used more explosives because they drilled wider holes, again leading to less precise blasting of ore; and machines required wider stopes in which to operate (NGI, 5 February 1914:5). All these factors produced greater amounts of waste that had to be hauled to the surface, sorted, and discarded.[3] The extra waste required larger lashing teams to clear the stopes. Faster rock breaking simply bottlenecked in the haulage.[4]

In fact, one of the strongest arguments for hand drilling was that hammer workers lashed their own stopes for up to two hours to clear the face prior to beginning work. The requirement that hammer drillers shovel before beginning work led to one of the major complaints of these workers, who were the most experienced and most militant black miners. Sometimes so much lashing would be required that drillers would not be able to complete their requisite thirty-six-inch hole and they would be marked as "loafers" and not paid for the shift. The objection was not that "hammer boys" had to lash—that had always been the case—but rather that in situations where excessive lashing was required the mine obtained free lashing and the white contractor obtained free drilling by blasting a short hole. Since hammer drillers were actually contracted to drill a hole of a particular depth (usually at least thirty-six inches) and not for shovel work, the requirement that they lash at all was technically against the law (NGI Report, paras. 65–91). Nonetheless, especially on mines, like those on the West Rand, with steep stopes (up to seventy degrees), where gravity could be used to good effect, "hammer boys' lashing" was a major money-saver

[3]Backfilling waste rock in worked-out stopes, which was introduced fairly early, also requires substantial labor, although it does cut down the demand for hoisting space, and on some mines such "waste packing" can help save on the use of artificial supports.

[4]To some extent this explains the lack of management sympathy for those occasional skilled white miners who managed to break prodigious amounts of rock and then complained to commission after commission that managements cut their rates.

for management. Few cost savings arose in the shift to machine drills as long as ample cheap labor was available—especially given the initial expense for machines and for piping of compressed air and maintenance costs.

Furthermore, machines required closer supervision than did hammer drillers. It could thus be contended that management objected to the introduction of machine stoping on strategic grounds, mainly because machines required more expensive white supervision. Representatives of the white unions, who were strongly in favor of the greater efficiency of machine drilling, certainly believed that management's aversion to machines stemmed from the cost of white supervision. In fact, wholesale management acceptance of machine drills had to wait until the white unions had been broken in the major strike that occurred in 1922. Evidence given by managers to the Mining Industry Board that was convened immediately after the strike stated clearly their determination to retain control of the workplace. In this they were successful, regaining control from militant white union shop stewards, despite the National/Labour party victory at the polls in 1924 (Yudelman 1983).

No one doubted that machines could break more ore more quickly, but management held that the extra rock simply backed up in the stope and haulage. Hence the development in the early 1930s of scraper winches to clear the stopes. The technological advantage of the underground jackhammer drill was not really substantial until the invention and deployment of mechanical means to clear the stopes. As late as October 1930, the manager of Randfontein Estates explained the problem to yet another commission:

> Q: But as your labour drops, why do you not put more boys onto machines?
>
> A: It is no use doing so if you cannot get the rock out of the stopes.
>
> Q: So it is really the tramming and lashing that is the important question here?
>
> A: Yes, and reclamation. . . . The advantage of the hammer boy is that he moves a lot of his broken rock himself but the machine boy does not. (LGOC, October 1930:863, 870)

Randfontein Estates, which was on the West Rand, still did about a quarter of its stoping by hand because of its very steep stopes. The nearly level stopes on the East Rand required massive numbers of lashers. There the major concern was to reorganize the work to ensure more efficient lashing, hence the early introduction of scrapers in the 1930s. However, in the 1930 struggle for labor, East Rand managers looked with some envy on West Rand colleagues who had managed to retain hand stopers, since mines that retained hand stoping could lay claim to a larger complement of labor from the recruitment agencies. Then, when a shortage of labor occurred, they could shift to machines and keep up production (LGOC, October 1930:1734).

This discussion points up the extent to which the introduction of new mining technology depended on the available supply of black labor and the outcome of the struggle with white miner organizations for control of the workplace. Wholesale management acceptance of the jackhammer drill, which looks to present-day engineers like an obvious and simple innovation, actually took several decades even *after* the development of lightweight drills. As we have seen, the delay was partly because of backlogs at other points of production in stope clearing and haulage, partly because mine managers had grown up with hand drilling and considered it safer, partly because white miners insisted on a higher ratio of black workers to whites in machine production, partly because of a struggle among mines for a larger share of the available complement of black labor from the recruiting organizations, and partly because black workers on machines refused to shovel their own stopes whereas it had become traditional for hand hammerers to do this.

If the adoption of what appears to be such a simple technological improvement as the jackhammer drill was so dependent on its strategic context, reorganization of the social relations of production was far more difficult to achieve. We shall examine management efforts since the First World War to provide independent training for boss boys as black supervisors underground, arguably the most important reorganization of work on the mines during this century, but which was not fully implemented until the 1980s.

Physical Coercion in Underground Work: Assaults on Black Workers

After the Anglo-Boer War of 1899–1902, the mining houses consciously opted to mine their low-grade ore with cheap "ultraexploited" migrant labor. The debit side of that policy was a fluctuating labor force with few industrial skills and little or no motivation to work hard once on shift. Indeed, given an indentured, contract labor force, working underground in small teams scattered along many work faces and in long tunnels, the puzzle is not why black miners were "lazy" but why any of them did any work at all.

In capitalist industrial enterprise, where surplus value is extracted from workers in exchange for wages, employees are obliged to put in their time on the job. The question Michael Burawoy (1979) rightly asks is, Why do they work hard? Managements are obliged to make profits for the owners of the firm by extracting surplus value from workers, whereas workers, to the extent that they are rational in the capitalist sense, seek to get by with as little work as possible short of dismissal.[5] That is the basis, at the level of agency, for class conflict in industry, and for on-the-job management controls and incentives for workers. It was also, in a much more direct way, the cause of workplace assaults underground on the South African mines.

Until the 1970s, assaults upon black workers were endemic on the South African gold mines. Commissioner Buckle's 1914 report stated:

> A complaint which is all but universal throughout the mines is that natives are frequently assaulted by Europeans, generally underground. A certain number of such cases seem inevitable when the conditions of work are considered. The mines consist of an enormous mileage of tunnels, in which a number of Europeans, many of them of no high standard of education or ethics, are each in practically unchecked control of several members of a subservient race. As a rule, neither the master nor the servant understands the other's language, yet the master has to give directions and the servant to obey them. Both parties are working under unhealthy and unnatural conditions. In these circumstances the temptation to and the opportunity for assaults on the servant by the master are constantly present; and these circumstances may be modified but cannot be altogether removed. (NGI, para. 33)

Theodora Williams, an Anglican missionary to the mines, who met with Buckle in October 1913, concurred with his conclusion on the matter of assaults (NGI, 15 October 1913:12). "It is the white miners themselves," she said. "Until you can change human nature you cannot do much good. It is the personality of the white miners and the language and blows and the sordidness of the whole thing underground."

Whether they argued from circumstances underground or human nature, such observers agreed that the basic problem lay with the white miner. It was he who could not resist the temptation to assault his workers. The law clearly forbade assaults—and from time to time a white miner

[5]One must also consider the issue of "independent ego energies" (White 1963), that is, whether human beings perhaps get inherent satisfaction from competence in meeting challenges, in Burawoy's language, from "making out." Some such notion is surely presupposed by Marx's account of alienation, which has no meaning without a prior assumption of free and fulfilling life-activity from which one is alienated. Even in the midst of alienation, *homo faber* (our "species-being") always threatens to break through. While such independent ego energies may be exploited by management, they are also an ongoing source of resistance on the job.

would appear in court and pay his fine if found guilty. Representatives of management would point proudly to such examples of evenhandedness, although they might also admit the "human nature" problem.

White workers themselves, however, provided much more structural reasons for underground brutality, pointing to the drive for production in explaining the regular nature of assaults.[6] D. D. Reich of the Mine Workers Union remembered (LGOC, October 1930:2301): "There was no question about the sincerity of the manager nor the compound manager, with regard to his instructions [to treat the workers well]. But as soon as your tonnage fell, then the mine captain and the shift boss wanted to know 'What the hell . . . what I had a pair of boots for!' " Especially in the early years, it was the immediate responsibility of the white miner and his black boss boy (at this time a personal retainer) to make black migrants work their contracts once management had delivered them underground. Black workers received little or no formal training in mining, and white miners and black boss boys received none in supervision. Supervisor and supervised, especially new recruits, seldom spoke the same language. Kicks and clouts replaced meaningful verbal communication. Although loud and foul language was certainly the order of the day,[7] it was the tone of voice and

[6]An analogous contemporary debate has arisen around issues of underground safety, with the National Union of Mineworkers setting forth similarly structural arguments (Leger 1985) in response to management's longstanding emphasis on "human factors" (cf., for example, Stobart 1960 and Lawrence 1974).

[7]See, for example, the evidence of Masole of the Johannesburg Joint Council to the Trading on Mining Grounds Commission in 1934 (965–66):

> I have heard language underground which I could not understand. In one case a good boy who was discharged from underground was hired by a very respectable European and when he worked in the kitchen he kept on swearing although he did not know what he was saying and he was discharged. . . . As to the ordinary [white] miner, you would be surprised if you heard the language they use to the boys.

Again, a 1945 article on "native labour control" reported as follows:

> Much concern was felt over the high accident and assault rate involving "tropicals" and the large number of complaints of "loafing" and general uselessness made by gangers and underground officials. In investigating these complaints and assaults, one point, that of misunderstanding, was found to be common to nearly all issues. As a result of this finding it was decided to inaugurate a "Fana-ka-lo" or "Mine Kaffir" class to be attended by all tropical natives each day during their period of surface acclimatization. The results have surpassed all expectations, due to the amazing enthusiasm shown by them in their desire to understand not only the Europeans but also natives of other tribes. Tropicals are now successfully filling the roles of boss boys, machine and spanner boys, and many of the other specialized underground tasks. (Rushton 1945:836)

These comments were written at a moment when "tropical" labor was just beginning to return to the South African mines. By 1967, "tropicals" (mostly Malawians) made up almost a third of the mine labor force and fanakalo classes were standard for all new recruits. Nonetheless, a study as late as the early 1980s (Leger

the accompanying slap that conveyed meanings to raw mine recruits. Violence was so common that the union representative on the Low Grade Mines Commission, B. Pohl, took for granted the need for "a lift with your foot or a gentle reminder with the flat of your hand" (LGMC, para. 1463) to "insist" that black workers get on with the job. Government mining officials and Chamber of Mines representatives were shocked at his openness, but Pohl kept coming back to the issue in cross-examining witnesses. "In your practical experience of natives," he asked one mine manager (para. 1855), "have you not found that when you have given a cantankerous boy a good hiding or thrashing that that boy is afterwards your best boy? Have you never heard of a man saying that a boy attempted to bully him and he gave the boy a hiding and since then that boy has been his best one?" When the manager demurred, saying that he would lose workers in the long run under such a regimen, Pohl persevered:

> If the law allowed a manager to order that a boy should receive cuts [a caning] or a good thrashing—I do not mean hit him across the head with an iron bar, I mean a respectable good thrashing—don't you think that if the natives know that they were going to get a hiding if they did not do their work, and they were paid a little better than they are, you would get more work out of them and you would be able to do with fewer boys? . . . Rhodes was a far seeing man, a deep seeing man, and he advocated the strap law for the native.[8]

Even H. Wellbeloved of the WNLA, renowned for his knowledge and experience of the "native," who advocated that respect of black workers be gained by just and fair treatment, admitted under cross-examination by Pohl (para. 5306) that "occasionally a man may lose his temper and box a boy's ears, but it certainly is wrong to knock a boy about brutally." A measure of assault in the push for production was taken for granted. "They are chasing you all the time," Gerhardus Stephanus Ackerman, a white miner at Rose Deep told the Mining Regulations Commission (MRC, November 1924:27), "for holes, for footage, fathomage and everything else." As a result, he said, "we have to chase the nigger." Pohl summed up the white miners' dilemma:

1985:89–90) found that the majority of "new workers could not speak [or understand] enough fanakalo when they started work underground." The problem of adequate training for recruits when communication is so poor remains so serious that some mines have finally decided to train new workers in their own vernaculars.

[8]For a brief history of corporal punishment in South Africa, see Sloth-Nielsen 1990.

> He is forced to get a job and he goes underground and he is told that [this and] that is required of him and of the natives. His boss—the mine captain or the shift boss or the underground manager, tells him at the same time "you must not hit the boys, you will get fired if you do." Well, if he does not he gets fired as well because the work is not done; if he does not get the work out of the boys, he stands a chance of being fired. What position do you put him in? (LGMC, 21 August 1919, para. 13488)

It is clear from testimony of black ex-miners that a certain measure of assault was taken for granted by workers as an aspect of the moral economy of underground work. Part of the acceptance of assaults by recent recruits stemmed from their experience of corporal punishment back home. Hoyt Alverson (1978:220), for instance, summarizes conversations with young men in Botswana on this issue: "He gets beaten at the mine, but he also gets beaten at home, and he doesn't get paid to be beaten at home. So, better to be beaten at the mine. The welts from home beatings meld with those of the compound boss." Jeff Guy's recent article (1990) on "precapitalist" African patriarchy provides a systemic analysis of the rule of older men in the countryside. On the social level, such rule was enforced by violent "discipline."

Nonetheless, moral outrage at grievous assault leading to serious injury might occasionally lead to collective action by black workers underground. Ncathama Mdelwa, in Pondoland in 1982 years later, remembered that in the 1940s and 1950s:

> The boss boys were cruel to us underground because they were scared of the white man, who simply sat on his box and charged up. What could we do? Because we didn't go to school, we thought everything was all right, because we didn't know anything. In one case the lashers fought back against the boss boy and had to be separated from him.

More often, however, individual workers had to stand up for themselves, perhaps with advice from their fellows. Masheane Matela remembered, when interviewed in 1984 at Butha Buthe in Lesotho, that "assaults were common in those days."

> In 1932 when I first got to the mine, the shift boss got my name wrong and when I didn't respond to his summons, he hit me hard on the nose so that it bled all day. In the evening when I went to complain to the native controller, I was told that I was lazy. This made me feel that the mine was not a good place to work, but as I went on I got used to it. Thereafter I fought for myself. If anyone tried to push me around I would say, "Hey!" Boss boys would hit

> their own people because they were trying to gain the confidence of the whites. Each time a man was hit he would become more "cheeky" and angry. After work we would sit around and there would be some talk of the assaults—we would teach each other how to resist (pick up stones, hit back, pick up a shovel), else a man would be beaten every day. You had to stand up for yourself—they would not help each other.

The Role of the Fokisi

Commissioner Buckle in 1914 had proposed the appointment of white "native overseers" underground to arbitrate disputes and handle black worker complaints, and by the end of the war most mines had such individuals in place. The underground overseer (called by management the native controller and by the workers, *fokisi*) did in fact quickly became a part of the underground system of control, less because of his personal advocacy for black workers than because his structural role as supervisor of labor allocation improved production. He assigned black workers to work teams, handling their promotions and shifting them around in the event of trouble. A retired compound manager explained to me in 1984:

> The fokisi dealt with complaints underground, and with loafers and so on. He ran the black situation underground, falling under both the compound manager and the underground manager. There were one or two to a shaft. All the native controllers fell under a chief supervisor to whom they would go for advice. Fokisi would have boss boys under them who would actually investigate cases where production was falling off in certain teams or sections. Promotions would be decided on the basis of efficiency on the job. The fokisi would make the promotions on recommendation from the white miner.

However, Ikaneng, a Tswana chief who had been on the mines, testified to the Witwatersrand Mine Natives' Wages Commission (WMNWC, 7 June 1943:18) that the fokisi might try to settle disputes between black workers "but if the complaint [was] against a European, it [was] either referred to the Compound Manager or the General Manager. . . . [T]he Controller [fokisi] [was] unable to settle the matter because the compound people [were] also Europeans."

There is ample testimony that the fokisi would himself assault workers who came to complain to him, calling them "loafers." For instance, senior mine clerks interviewed in 1984 on Vaal Reefs reported that in their youth:

> Boss boys were very very rough, and the fokisi was just like the other whites who were working underground. If you went to him

> to complain that someone had assaulted you underground, he would ask you: "If your ox does not pull well, what are you going to do? That is what they are doing underground." If you persisted, he would just close the door and *sjambok* [whip] you himself.

Enforcement, even by conscientious native controllers, of complaints against assault underground, was well-nigh impossible.[9] Philip Vundla, a black mine clerk giving evidence to the Witwatersrand Mine Natives' Wages Commission on 14 July 1943 (12) succinctly summed up the problem:

> If a labourer has a quarrel with a [white] ganger underground, the first person who comes up is the ganger, of course, who [always] gets up first. He has to report with that boy's ticket to the Controller [fokisi] that so and so has been cheeky or has done this and that. And then later the labourer comes up to lodge his complaint to the Supervisor. Where he states that he has been assaulted, then he will be asked by the supervisor if he has any witnesses. That is the first question. He will say yes, he has witnesses, only to be disappointed by the witnesses who dare not speak against the boss because the same treatment will be inflicted upon them. [Or alternatively the white man would produce his own witnesses who would deny that the assault took place.]

Vundla himself was intimidated by his white boss for agreeing to give evidence to the commission, his own witnesses let him down, and he was dismissed from the mine.

[9]The difficulty was illustrated also by black witnesses from the Cape to the Mine Industry Board (MIB) on 17 July 1922 (4789–95, 4817–19):

> When the natives are in the mines, they are always afraid, they do not trust. A man cannot speak openly against another man. If a man goes round to find out whether the natives have any complaints, the natives are afraid to say much. . . . You may go forward and try to rectify these cases, and then the man who may have brought his complaints to you may say "I have not said such a thing, I have never said it" because he is afraid to give away the man he is working under, and then you are left in the lurch. (4791, 4793)

In 1943, the African Mine Workers' Union statement to the Witwatersrand Mine Natives' Wages Commission made essentially the same point:

> Assaults occur daily on the Mines. . . . The Native Supervisor investigates cases of assault and decides if the European must pay the African for the days lost in hospital as a result of the assault. Where there are no witnesses and it is a matter of deciding between the word of the European and that of the African, the former's word is usually accepted. In practice these cases are usually dropped. The African has no legal knowledge and no legal advice is provided. It is very difficult for him to stand up against the word of a European. . . . The appointment of European Native Supervisors has not helped the Africans very much. Complaints are not taken to them, for fear of victimization.

Giving evidence to the same commission in 1943 (NTS 2224, 442/280), R. Woodley, the inspector of native labor in Springs, at that time the fastest-growing mining area, urged that

> native Controllers/Supervisors be accorded a sufficiently high status as to place them above underground officials lower in rank than a mine captain and have direct access to underground Managers. All complaints made to them by labourers should be recorded and brought to the notice of Compound Managers, under whose control they should be. Supervisors should not in any circumstances be utilized by underground officials for forcing boys to greater efforts at work. Once this is done confidence in the official, as one who labourers may look to to protect their interests, is destroyed.

Commissioner Buckle had given similar advice thirty years before. Whatever the personal inclinations of individual native controllers, however, they had become part of the formal underground structure of production. If they had sympathetic attitudes toward black workers, that might ameliorate the situation somewhat, and shrewd workers made strategic use of the fokisi's formal powers to obtain promotions or to arrange transfers from supervisors showing personal animus against them, but the fokisi's primary structural function had to do with the organization of work. This was clear in the opening to the chamber's statement on the role of the "native controller" to the Witwatersrand Mine Natives' Wages Commission (WMNWC, #12, 1):

> As the allocation of new Natives to gangs and the transfer of Natives from one gang to another are primarily duties of the Supervisor, it follows that he must keep, and provide to the Underground and Compound staffs, daily returns of the mine numbers of the Native labourers in all gangs, and arrange for the replacement of discharged Natives in the gangs. To assist him in the maintenance of these records he is provided with a staff of Native clerks.

Almost as an afterword to the onerous duties described above, the chamber added the following:

> [A]n important section of the duties of a supervisor on all mines is the investigation of complaints made by natives either in respect of their conditions of work, incorrect payment of wages or bonuses, their ability to perform the duties allotted to them, ill-treatment by their gangers or any other matter.

With those priorities it is little wonder that assaults continued.

Black supervisors also assaulted black underground workers. Indeed, the full flowering of the functions of the fokisi went in tandem with the reorganization of work after 1922 and the introduction of management-trained boss "boys."

Reorganizing Labor for Lashing and Tramming— Boss Boy Training

In the early years, skilled white miners argued that the need for their supervision was even greater when machines were used than with hand drilling. We have seen that this constraint was one of the factors that slowed down the wide-scale introduction of machines in stopes. What though of lashing and tramming teams? How was higher output, whether by white or black supervisors, attained? Rock drillers had productivity incentives: they were paid by the number of inches or holes they drilled. For shovelers matters were different. Any incentive scheme for lashing and tramming ran smack up against the maximum average system—a major means of keeping black mine wages low. Thus it was here that productivity was most often attained through the threat of coercion, that is, beatings. The moral economy of underground work tolerated a measure of physical coercion not only from white miners but also from black boss boys. Peter Tshezi told Vivienne Ndatshe at Port St. Johns in 1982: "I was a boss boy. If you were a boss boy, you should be cruel because there were people who didn't want to listen. Also, boss boys had to be rough because the shift boss wanted the job to be done. If the layisha boys didn't finish lashing in time, there would be trouble, and the white staff would be cross with the boss boy."

During the pre-1922 period, boss boys were personal retainers of their white overseers, following them about from mine to mine and coercing production from recent arrivals in exchange for a share of the contract or simply for the privilege of being the beater rather than the beaten. "In those days, the boss boy was not attached to the gang—he was attached to the man," said Munnik, an ex-mining inspector, to the Mining Regulations Commission in 1925 (MRC:1732), stressing how things had changed since the defeat of white labor in 1922. "The timberman had his boss boy to assist him and he was looked on in that way. . . . There was a specific man underground in charge of the timber gang and he had his own boss boy, and if that man left then the boss boy fell, but now your boss boy still continues, after the white man leaves."

The mines lost many skilled white men to the armed forces during the First World War. While this strengthened the white miners' unions (Johnstone 1976:96–118), it also led to the employment of many Afrikaans-speaking white underground supervisors, hastily trained and totally inexperienced. Thus, at the same time that white miners' unions successfully pushed for greater workplace privileges and controls, white mine workers were less and less skilled. Managements responded by selecting experienced black miners and setting up training and reward systems to make them into boss boys accountable to the mine rather than to individual white miners.[10]

Experiments on Simmer and Jack in mid-1917 produced great enthusiasm from experienced black workers for a "leading hand" scheme and some improvement in production. Three levels of "leading hands," with higher wage scales (released in small numbers from the maximum average wage system), were created. They were awarded badges and were set to work marshaling work teams and getting them to the workplaces, training "green natives," attending to minor first aid matters, and alerting white miners and mine officials to potential danger (NTS 215, 768/18/473, Taberer's Memorandum, 20/8/17, annexures E and F). Such schemes were immediately adopted, especially on the large East Rand Proprietary and Crown Mines complexes.

When the new scheme came into effect on City Deep, early in 1918, twenty-five old-style boss boys, who had been promoted by their own white miner bosses and then demoted by management, brought other workers out on strike and were fined ten pounds each. Arbitrary introduction of the new scheme had contravened the underground moral economy. F. A. D. Edmeston, the local Native Affairs Department inspector, was almost as outraged as the workers themselves. "I must say," he wrote to Cooke, the acting director of native labor:

> I consider the general attitude of the Management, in this matter, most arbitrary. Natives promoted to boss boy would not be able to understand whether the promotion was valid, or otherwise; and since each had been so employed, for some time, and paid at boss boy rates, each was naturally confirmed in his appointment. They must have imagined they were being treated unfairly, and even illegally. . . . The least management could have done, was to offer to discharge all those who would not agree to revert to hammer work; instead of which they were coerced, and those refusing, seriously punished. I deem it my duty to point to the altogether op-

[10]See, for example, Taberer, "Memorandum on Native Employment," August 1917 (NTS 215, 768/18/473). The immediate impetus for the policy of training boss boys was the reduction in white working hours called for by the white unions and introduced in January 1918. I have not the space to treat in detail the introduction of the "night examinations" that followed this new deal, except to say that night examinations also required trained boss boys.

> pressive sentence. They are sentenced to [a] ten pounds fine, which, at two shillings per shift, would take each 100 shifts to pay. (NLB 183, 938/14/154)

Cooke, who saw the case as a "purely judicial matter" refused to intervene.

A new kind of boss boy system was emerging out of the struggle between white unions and mine management. It is surprising that no further fallout from untrained boss boys is recorded in the archives. Presumably other mines used more tact in introducing the scheme.

By 1919, trained boss boys were being used to circumvent the mining regulation "that no member of a gang [may] enter a work place unless instructed to do so by a white ganger." Once again Pohl, sitting on the Low Grade Mines Commission in 1919, blew the cover of mine management, saying to C. D. Leslie, a Gold Fields consulting engineer, "You seem to have implied [that] the fact that the natives have to wait for the white man before they enter the stope holds back the work?" Leslie replied by asserting the law: "Yes, that is while the white man is making safe a working place in the morning. The natives are not allowed into the stope until the white man has seen that all is safe." Pohl, once again bringing a touch of refreshing realism to the deliberations of his commission, responded with skepticism: "Do you think that any of the mines on the Reef would be payable if they stuck to the Regulations laid down by the Government?"

In the years immediately after the First World War a great struggle ensued between white miners and management as the miners' unions rode a worldwide tide of labor militancy that also affected white South African workers (Yudelman 1983). The 1919 Low Grade Mines Commission heard testimony from worker and shop steward committees and were quite sympathetic to their cause. Mine managers refused to cooperate with the unions in the running of "their" mines, however, and confrontation was the order of the day. In South Africa, however, white miners fought not only to improve work conditions and gain control of the workplace but also to maintain the black-white ratio in underground work. They feared competition for skilled jobs with migrant "indentured workers." Productivity dropped. For a couple of years after the war, there was a premium on the world price of gold, and the white miners held their own with this help from the world system. In 1922, however, the premium was dropped, and management forced a massive strike on the racial issue. Civil war broke out on the Rand between striking militants and South African troops. Working-class areas of Johannesburg were shelled and bombed into submission. The army's triumph handed the Chamber of Mines a crucial victory. Mine managers regained absolute control of the organization of work on the mines. They proceeded to pull the teeth of the miners' unions by a combination of coercion and co-optation.[11]

One basic way in which management cut costs after 1922 was to "stretch" white miners by obliging them to supervise many more workers. Efforts were also made by some managers to introduce scientific management.[12] In addition, most mines followed the wartime example and began to train numbers of boss boys for underground supervisory responsibilities. Management also arranged for new recruits to receive instruction in mining from more senior boss boys. Within months of the strike, a majority of mines had tightened up their system for distribution and training of recent arrivals and set up primitive schools in which boss boys were taught the rudiments of mining under the rubric of "safety training."[13]

By November 1924, David Stephanus Jacobs, a white miner at the East Rand Proprietary Mines, testified before the Mining Regulations Commission that his boss boys (note that now there were more than one) went into workplaces first to make them safe. They also charged up. Each action was strictly against the law. He said, "We were allowed a boss boy to each three ends to assist us. It was never told us definitely that this boy would assist in charging up, but this boy was instructed and trained in the compound how to do it as well as in regard to first aid. He had been shown how to cap a fuse and other things, and these boys got badges, first grade, second grade or third grade" (MRC:336). The system started, Jacobs said, "after the strike. It was not known before the 1922 strike. . . . It is a customary thing on the mines at the present day. Whatever the European miner cannot do he has two or three boss boys to do it for him." Later, in cross-examining managerial witnesses, an ex-mining inspector concluded:

[11]Johnstone (1976), Davies (1979), and Yudelman (1983) provide the best accounts of these developments.

[12]One chapter of Leger's fascinating doctoral dissertation (1992) deals with scientific management. From 1916 to the present, mine managers' publications go into much detail on methods to standardize underground tasks in order to instruct unskilled workers and increase production. While waves of interest in scientific management in South Africa do seem to coincide with increases in productivity, it is difficult to know whether the former is a cause or a symptom of the latter. That increases in production coincided with management obsession with production hardly seems surprising and may require no other explanation. Experienced managers themselves seem to have had their doubts about the practical efficacy of scientific management (Hildick-Smith 1944).

[13]For detailed treatment of these changes, see the extensive 1922 discussion of the suggestions by S. A. M. Pritchard, director of native labour, for improving "native efficiency" on the mines (MIB 3816ff.) and individual mine responses in SAIRR B36.3 and NLB 340. See also the 1925 MRC (1509ff., 1715ff.) on boss boy training at Crown Mines.

> The whole policy today is that greater responsibility is placed on the shoulders of the boss boy, and on the men, and as the boss boys become more and more efficient they are able to take over more responsibility. . . . These boss boys are being trained now to stand out from the rank and file of the coloured workers and become more efficient in the duties of supervising the different working places at times when the white man cannot be in attendance. (MRC:1642, 1649)

By the time the chamber gave evidence to the Witwatersrand Mine Natives' Wages Commission in 1943, it was able to boast of the "promotion opportunities" (*Star*, 16/6/43) of "boss boys and supervising boys," comparing their promotion ratios to those of white supervisors on the mines, without mentioning, of course, the huge disparity in wages. Indeed, the outcome of the struggle between militant white workers and mine managements *had* led to greater use of black skilled mine supervisors, but, partly because of the maximum average system and partly because of the high turnover of migrant workers, it was difficult to provide adequate incentives for boss boys. For instance, comments made by A. H. Krynauw, a longtime manager of the East Rand Proprietary Mines, in 1945 suggest that the training of boss boys had not advanced much since 1925. He "looked forward to the day," he said, "when the boss boy is more generally regarded as a staff employee. . . . if the Industry generally adopted a high degree of selection and training of boss boys and could inculcate in them a keen sense of responsibility, a great step forward in efficiency and safety should result" (Heywood 1945:995). Krynauw also felt that the incentives for boss boys should be changed:

> [T]he boss boy's job should be made sufficiently attractive to make him jealous of it and demoting should be a real hardship compared with the present practice where degrading a boss boy to the ranks is but a small economic punishment. In this connexion a special schedule of rates might be established for boss boys and be excluded when arriving at maximum average rates permitted, which, at present, limit the scope of materially improving the boss boy's rates of pay.

The maximum average system precluded the development of sharp wage differentials in the black labor force. In fact, black machine drillers made more money than boss boys—and without the responsibility. That boss boys took their supervisory responsibilities seriously emerged particularly clearly in a conversation with Ryna Dushu, a former boss boy, in October 1984:

> If there was a disagreement between the boss boy and the white man about a workplace, the boss boy had to listen to the white man because he had more power; however, if there was an accident, he would remind the white miner of their disagreement. If he really feared an accident, the boss boy might go to the mine captain and explain everything, so that the mine captain could come and check. . . . If the teams worked well together, they were very happy, satisfied, and friendly with each other. They also should be friendly with their boss boy so that they could work together. If they were not friendly with their boss boy, the work did not go right. The boss boy did have the right to change some of the members of his team if they did not work well together or for him. Workers could also ask for transfers.

This picture of happy rationality, however, rooted in the experience of a successful boss boy, overlooks the fundamental problem—that the most important attribute of boss boys remained their ability to coerce work out of lashing and tramming teams. "If a man was a loafer," even Dushu said, "the boss boy could not beat him, but instead would report him to the fokisi, who would take him out. That is the ideal—there were people who hit loafers. If the boss boy was reluctant to beat a man, he could always call the white miner to do it for him." Obviously, in structural terms such a system differed little from the coercive and violent one that preceded it, except that boss boys now possessed formal authority from management rather than informal support from the individual white miner. Over the years, white miners became somewhat more likely to leave the assaults to their black supervisory subordinates.

What remained from the reorganizational flurry of the 1920s was the system of boss boy training, the awarding of badges and the granting of substantial supervisory powers to larger numbers of boss boys at just slightly higher wages. Behind the apparent rationality of the post-1922 reorganization lay the reality of production pressures—now placed more directly on the boss boys' shoulders. Unlike Dushu, most of them responded with the kind of brutality white miners had made traditional. The testimony is overwhelming. Clerks from Vaal Reefs interviewed in 1984 were clear and explicit about mining in the 1940s and 1950s:

> The boss boys [beat the men] because they wanted to keep their jobs. At that time the white supervisors wanted someone who could fight. They believed that if the boss boy could fight production would come up. At that time most of the boss boys were Mozambican and Sotho (mainly Mozambican), the drillers were mostly Mpondo. No one complained because there was no one to complain to. There were no promotions underground at that time.

> If you started as a lasher, you lashed until you finished your contract—unless you assaulted the boss boy and took all those first-aid badges and put them on yourself and said, "Hey, lash." Then you would become the boss boy. The white miner didn't mind if you beat up the boss boy as long as you pushed the people: "Keep up the dust!" If you wanted to be a boss boy, you took the job.

So much for the reality of "boss boy training" underground. This depiction was confirmed by Robert Mahlati, a boss boy on a completely different mine during the 1940s and 1950s:

> On those days underground there was a bit of roughness, although on the surface it was tame. People could become team leaders by means of roughness. You might well find a boss boy who had been in the school of mines pushing a *cocopan* [tramming trolley] because another lasher was brave enough to hit that boss boy and take all his badges off. The white man wouldn't care whether his boss boy had been [replaced]. . . . They were after production. . . . They would abuse their men in *fanakalo,* referring to them by their mothers' private parts. There was a fokisi but he was just as rough as anyone else.

Again, older workers at Vaal Reefs, interviewed separately from the clerks quoted earlier, had the same story:

> Boss boys were chosen based on how hard they worked and how belligerent they were (you looked like you could handle the other people very strictly). . . . If the boss boy beat you in those days, it was under orders from the white man—he could not do otherwise. If he did not handle the people as he was told (that is, beat them), he would be fired. There were no criteria for choosing boss boys in those days—except how well a man could fight. If he was afraid of his men, he was fired, and an aggressive man chosen in his place. There was no training center or ability training in those days. This was why people worked so badly. Nowadays men know their jobs and are not pushed around. No one has to be taught his job underground.

Underground Work Relations since the 1970s

All black worker comments about the failures of the boss boy system in the past imply that matters have since changed. As we have seen, since the First World War, mine managements have made sporadic efforts to improve boss boy training. The papers and printed discussions of meetings of the Association of Mine Managers for the 1950s and early 1960s are peppered with moral admonitions about the advantages of improved training for black supervisors. Such exhortations implied that for all the urgency of mine managers' expressed wishes and their actual efforts to reorganize work at the mines, the structural reality of social relations in production underground made their realization impossible.

Leger and Van Niekerk (1986:71) point to contemporary problems of supervision in terms strikingly similar to those mentioned by Commissioner Buckle seventy-two years before:

> To understand restraints on the productivity of gold mines one has to understand the physical nature of the work. Underground work is extremely difficult to supervise. A typical gold mine has 250 working rockfaces, each 40 metres long. If all these workplaces were strung end to end, they would form a line ten kilometres in length. For management, a production line this long in a well-lit factory would be difficult enough to supervise. But in a mine where the working faces are scattered over many square kilometres, direct supervision is almost impossible.

It is insufficient, however, to speak of the difficulties involved in physically supervising the mine labor force. While the layout of the mines themselves certainly made supervision harder, constraints built into the very organization of mine work itself impeded change. What occurred in the later 1960s to reverse previously existing limits to reform?

By 1976 on Welkom Mine, our researchers had few reports of assaults on black workers by whites. The white personnel officer (the modern equivalent of the fokisi) did not automatically take the word of a white against a black. Witnesses had to be produced and the basis of the grievance established. The old fokisi system was replaced in the early 1970s by a new underground personnel system under which, for the first time, underground assaults were properly investigated and prosecuted by mine management. Black high school graduates were hired as personnel assistants (whom the workers called *masizas*) to enforce the new system. The outcome of this rationalization, no doubt introduced largely in the interest of increased productivity, was evident in increased coordination and supervision at the stope face by team leaders. Thus, at least on Anglo American mines by 1976, even before the coming of the National Union of Mineworkers in 1984, there was some avenue of appeal against the absolute power of the white man underground and blacks availed themselves of it. As Jack Mpapea, a former mine worker, recalled:

> At work there's a little change because that oppression that was [there] previously is no longer there. Because in those days when a boss boy would report to the white man that you did this and this

> and this, he wouldn't even sit down with you to listen to your views. He would immediately take action on this, even hit you physically. . . . Now things have changed because now the mine has introduced what they call a complaint form, and if the boss boy [or white miner] or shift boss is not happy with you he will not kick you like in those days but he will now try to fill that complaint form and send it to the masiza of that section. . . . In 1962, they replaced the fokisi with the masiza.

Nonetheless, as late as 1976, the white miner's insistence upon the respect due his white skin and his demand that blacks jump unquestioning to his every command definitely increased the tension at the point of production. Mpapea added:

> It did happen that sometimes the white man was not interested in filling in that complaint form and jumped you and kicked you and even though the case might be taken straight to the masiza, who tried to bring the two parties together, still the white men had powers. They had powers to say you had no right to fight with the white man and you'd be dismissed for doing that.

A wide range of sources suggest that by 1976 for most of his time underground the typical white miner sat on his box in the haulage, his *picannin*[14] (personal retainer) on guard, relaxing in the company of fellow white miners or reading his newspaper. Periodically he would send out instructions and ask for reports about work progress. He appeared occasionally at the stope, shouting orders left and right and "pushing blacks around" and "criticizing them." Said one informant, "pushing around means driving them hard, making the men work as if they did not know their work and should rush around in slavish response to the white man's bidding." The whites gave orders without giving reasons, forgetting that blacks did the work most of the time without them. In other words, the interference was counterproductive, breaking the cooperative rhythm of the work team and arousing resentment.

On the whole, by 1976 the white miner had little control over a situation in which he claimed to be boss. Naturally, blacks had no respect for him: "They think that the white man is physically incapable of doing hard labour and that he cannot fight as well as they can." The white miner's

[14]Although the position was no longer part of the formal organizational structure of the mine, every white miner had a *picannin,* who served as his personal servant underground, and sometimes at his home, and who informed him of black opinion and kept an eye out for the mine overseer who might be coming to inspect. The job of *picannin* was considered desirable by many black miners, who appreciated the lack of hard labor involved. Contemporary union members despise the job.

discretion on the job, his technical authority, had largely passed to his subordinates. One would expect that such a situation of uncertainty would have given greater power to black workers. However, because of his position in the hierarchy of domination, and the political clout of his union, the white miner could still claim a certain arbitrary power (especially the power of dismissal), which was the more resented because of his diminished technical authority on the job. Since arbitrary personal power interfered with production, however, it seemed to be expressed relatively infrequently on Welkom Mine in 1976.

The farther white miners were removed from direct supervision, let alone skilled labor, the greater the responsibility placed on the shoulders of boss boys. The latter were now called "team leaders" and had been upgraded in status since the introduction of the Paterson scale on Anglo American mines in 1972 and 1973. The Paterson principle set out to reward responsibility, and as a result, for the first time in South African mining history, team leaders began to be paid more than machine drillers. They have also been given higher status on the compound and since the early 1980s have been housed and messed separately from ordinary workers—at least on Anglo American mines. Jack Mpapea, who was on Vaal Reefs, distinctly remembered the change when interviewed in Lesotho in 1988: "I can still remember quite well that the person previously called the boss boy was first called the team leader in 1972. And then the management started dividing them from other workers. The process started in early 1972, but it went on until 1977, when it was now visible that the team leaders stayed in beautiful rooms—twelve to a room—and the other workers stayed in the regular rooms."

The 1976 ethnography concluded that the team leaders' relationship to the white miner was an ambivalent one. Our participant observers were of the distinct opinion that productivity was essentially a function of the team leaders' supervisory and mining skills. Workers alleged that their team leaders drove them so hard that they sometimes overlooked safety in the interests of increased production. Nonetheless, it was the white miner, working on a contract, who profited from his team leader's ability, not the team leader himself. Since the team leader was paid a flat rate,[15] why should he be so strongly motivated to produce?

In most cases, he did not work out of respect for the white miner. Team leaders in 1976 shared the general black resentment of white miners. Thus

[15]On some mines, by the middle 1980s, work teams were paid a productivity bonus. However, the manner in which such bonuses were paid was so complex that Jean Leger (1985:54–62) was able to demonstrate convincingly that the majority of team leaders were quite ignorant of the terms under which such incentives were paid.

one of our informants said of team leaders that "they see the white miners as their enemies because they do no hard labour but earn more on payday. They are very conscious that they are the people who do more work for the mine than the white supervisors but they get less money. They are very envious of this salary disparity." In fact, a group of team leaders themselves specifically complained in a 1976 interview that white miners "interfere with our men; will not heed our advice; and when, because of their interference, work is held up or goes wrong, then we are still supposed to get the production, to get the men to work." When asked why they drove so hard for the white miners' benefit, team leaders replied that "if we drive for production it is because we wish to keep our jobs." They claimed that white miners could and did get team leaders transferred, demoted, or even fired for poor production.

Jean Leger's (1985) excellent 1984 study of safety underground,[16] which was commissioned by the National Union of Mineworkers, fully supports our findings in 1976 but achieves greater analytical insight. Although team leaders were no longer supposed to be assaulted, 67 percent of his sample of team leaders reported that their job security was threatened by the risk of being "charged," a judiciary procedure before a management disciplinary committee. While charging seems more often threatened than carried out, nonetheless, Leger argues that it had become an important negative sanction used by the white miner against team leaders, all the more effective because team leaders' new status and remuneration meant they had more to lose. In one instance, for example, a team leader reported:

> If we do not finish the work of the day, we report to the white miner. If we have not finished, then he instructs me to go to the shift boss's office. He says I am reluctant to do work—he promised to charge but ultimately he charged me by demoting me from team leader to stope team [member] for nine months. [This meant a drop in wages of about fifty percent.]

According to Leger (1985:51–54), team leaders disliked the threat of being charged mostly because it seemed to them that charges were brought so arbitrarily. Most work delays were the unavoidable result of unsafe conditions. As team leaders began to accept more informal responsibility for production, supervision, and coordination in the stope, they also were obliged to take on a quasi-legal responsibility for safety. White miners pushed for production, but as one team leader noted (Leger 1985:61): "If there is any accident and they find any mistakes I will be picked up for

[16]Much of what follows is based on Leger's splendid study—by far the best account of underground production relationships so far undertaken.

that and charged." Another said, "If people die I will be the one to be blamed."

While the stabilization of the mine labor force means few inexperienced workers are recruited on the mines these days and team leaders thus revert to assault infrequently, a change in blasting methods has actually increased production pressures on black supervisors. Jean Leger (1985:98–99) summarizes the changes as follows:

> The essential "skill" required of a miner engaged in conventional mining in the past . . . related to the marking off of drill holes so that the maximum amount of rock would be broken with every hole drilled. Only a limited number of holes . . . could be drilled, charged and blasted in a single shift. . . . If holes were well located, face advance would be rapid, but if poorly placed, explosives would detonate with little effect. Since the shape of the face changed with each blast the miner had to draw on his skill and experience in siting each individual hole to best advantage.
>
> The development of concentrated mining techniques, partly due to improvements in blasting ancillaries and in rock drill jumpers, has eliminated the skill required to locate each hole for maximum breaking. [Holes] are now marked according to a standard sawtooth pattern along the length of the face. The skill of the traditional miner having been rendered superfluous, management since the early sixties has set about re-organising the production process.

Because of these changes in blasting techniques, says Leger, mine managements have tolerated the noninvolvement of white miners in day-to-day production work underground. White mining skills are no longer needed for close supervision at the stope face. Increased remuneration and training for the boss boys have combined with technical advances to render the supervision and coordination functions of the white miner redundant in the system of production. Why then do the mines retain white miners at all?

Of course, management will insist that the power of the white workers' union has maintained their sinecures. That is part of the story, but it is a political rather than a systemic explanation. Leger's answer to this question is both intriguing and convincing. He locates his explanation in the way in which the production system actually operates. While white miners were no longer necessary for coordination and supervision or for their mining skills in placing holes, they nonetheless still were important in ensuring production. With new centralized blasting techniques, it is often impossible to make up time safely when conditions are bad. A face that is not fully drilled and charged up during any particular shift cannot be blasted until the end of the following day's shift.

All over the world, production incentives persuade miners to take risks underground, but in South Africa in the mid-1980s the sharp separation between productivity bonuses (earned by white miners) and supervision and coordination (undertaken by black team leaders) meant that the risks were undertaken by black workers on the white miners' behalf. White miners earned 80 percent over and above their basic pay in bonus payments if their teams maintained high levels of production. Leger (1985:105) concluded: "Bonus payments inevitably lead to workers taking risks, but in gold mining two aspects exacerbate this problem: bonus payments form a substantial portion of total earnings, and payments are related to the risks that other men are required to take." As a result, in the words of one team leader (Leger 1985:48), "The white miner is not interested in safety whatsoever, he is only interested in production. So he does not do a damn thing about [dangerous conditions]. He does not come at all, he says it is up to the team leader to do it, he wants to blast every day." The division of labor between production incentives on the one hand and concern for the safety of the team on the other leads to constant tension between white miner and black team leader, especially given the white man's ability to "charge" the black. It provides an additional, more systemic reason than simple racism or political power, a reason built into the production process itself, for the hostility between blacks and whites underground on Welkom Mine in 1976.

In the late 1980s, tension began to arise between team leaders and black miners. The increasingly hostile relation between these two black groups—whose members are often in the same union—also has a systemic as well as an attitudinal and social dimension. It is not just that the status of team leaders has been improved by management and that they have been housed and fed in separate and superior fashion on the compounds. Nor is it merely that team leaders tend to be older workers with migrant values and rural integrities. In the late 1980s and early 1990s, as racial barriers to skill and authority on the job underground gradually begin to dissipate, black supervisors began to take greater responsibility for production goals and to earn more substantial bonuses. Now it is their turn to push for production and perhaps to ignore danger signals in the interest of being ready for the blasting hour.

Relations between Workers and Team Leaders in the Early 1990s

At first the new black National Union of Mineworkers (NUM) recruited primarily among team leaders but soon started to concentrate on the lower work categories as well. Now team leaders are identified with management. Resentment against team leaders emerged clearly in an interview Ms.

Ndatshe and I conducted with an Mpondo team leader, Zithulele Mkhaza, in the Vaal Reefs mine village (*skomplas*) on 4 August 1990. Although he told us that he was still a dues-paying union member he had stopped going to meetings because he "would be called an *impimpi* [informer]." He cited a case in which he had quarreled with a shift boss and a white miner. The union shaft steward listened to his complaint but failed to help because Mkhaza was a team leader. Indeed, Mkhaza said, "All the team leaders are now called impimpi by the shaft stewards." If he should die, he said, his wife was to go straight to the Klerksdorp offices of the NUM rather than to the local compound office. Furthermore, if he were sacked, he would go directly to the Johannesburg head office of the union because "there I won't be called an impimpi."

Mkhaza's wife sells meat and beer, and since we were interviewing him on a Saturday morning, a group of Mpondo home fellows (home boys) began to gather. One of them was a militant member of the African National Congress and the "political" wing of the NUM. He insisted heatedly that team leaders were in fact impimpi because, at least on his shaft (No. 5), Sotho team leaders charged Xhosa-speaking workers who were "guiltless." The whites listened to the team leaders, he said. He was himself sacked because he had refused to work at a certain place for safety reasons and had been reported by the team leader. He went to the time office with his shaft steward and was reinstated. But, he said, "Team leaders act like managers now. They think they are superior. They get an incentive bonus to make workers work harder. On Number Five shaft, the team leaders don't work hard. They go down with the whites. And they get more leave."

The team leader, Mkhaza, responded by attempting to contextualize and particularize such an attack. It is because they are closer to the whites that team leaders are called impimpi, he said. He himself, to avoid the charge, always sought to work problems out with his team rather than run to the whites. He also disliked team leaders who did take complaints straight to the whites. They should have communicated with their teams in the waiting places. "The white men started the trouble by separating team leaders and ordinary workers," he said. "When team leaders are told by whites in training to push workers, not all of them take it so literally. I try to motivate my team by understanding and working with them."

Such a debate was possible because the disputants were from the same home village in Pondoland. No doubt it was stimulated by our questions. Normally, the topic would not have been raised among home fellows over their beer. Indeed, informal conversations between team leaders and ordinary workers have become increasingly rare on contemporary mines, where team leaders tend to keep to themselves or associate with senior black management. The reorganization of production during and after the First World War gave boss boys responsibilities without much additional remuneration and placed them in an invidious structural double bind. Prior to the 1980s they resolved their dilemma by identifying as workers; in the 1980s the new "team leaders" have been incorporated into lower management. For some team leaders, as we shall see, the result of their identification with management has been fatal.

Conclusion

This chapter was written to achieve two ends. One was to introduce readers to the complexities of South African gold-mining technology and changes in the organization of work underground. The second was to use the example of the introduction of machine drills to demonstrate the validity of Harley Shaiken's (1986:15) argument that "the design of technology is not only a question of machines and systems but of power and political choice." In addition, it examines the changing nature of black supervisory authority to indicate how the organization of work at the point of production depends upon strategic resources and relationships among management, white and black supervisors, and black workers. None of the class actors are completely powerless but their struggles are limited by and predicated upon the conditions under which they are obliged to get gold out of the ground. It is because management sets the parameters for this common priority that it is able to exercise hegemony, but it does not do so unchallenged, nor do its particular strategies always have predictable outcomes. Management control is in a precarious equilibrium at best, despite the ultimate sanction of dismissal or retrenchment. Management's provisional power becomes even more apparent when one turns to life in the residential compounds and the squatter camps, townships, and villages around the mines.

3 Confrontations and Collaborations

Compound Hegemony and Moral Economy

After the discovery of gold in 1886, the tens of thousands of black workers who poured into the Witwatersrand were initially housed in huts clustered around the mine shafts without any state or management effort at control. The coming of Chinese labor for a few years after 1904 briefly brought closed compounds to the Rand and established architectural standards for compound construction. Although African compounds on the Rand were never closed, once the importation of Chinese labor had provided a model, police and officials pressed for enclosed compounds, walled barracks of concrete bunks, with one or two guarded gates that could be closed in event of trouble.

The files of the Government Native Labour Bureau between 1901 and 1912 are full of the reports of Native Affairs inspectors attempting to enforce standards of compound construction, dealing with sanitation primarily but also with security. The state, not managements, took the initiative for reasons made quite clear in the 1914 Buckle Commission report (NGI, para. 474):

> There are normally 200,000 native mine labourers on the Reef. They are all male, practically all adults and the large majority in the prime of life. They are scattered over 50 miles of country in blocks from 1,000 to 5,000 in each compound. They can mobilize themselves in a few minutes, armed with such weapons as assegais, jumpers, axes, etc. A good many of them consider, whether rightly or wrongly, that they have grievances against the Europeans, and most of them are savages, whose only idea of reform is violence. All of them want more pay, and most of them are under the impression that the employment of force by European miners during the riots of last July resulted in the latter obtaining their demands.

Closable compounds may have been incidentally useful to management for the control of production, but they were considered essential by police and officials concerned with public order. Maintenance of order rather than pursuit of profit was the primary reason for compound construction.

The notion of the compound as a spatial means of maintaining order was expressed in precisely panoptical terms by J. S. G. Douglas, deputy commissioner of police in Johannesburg, in his evidence to the Buckle Commission:

> The compound must be suitably constructed to contain the natives and I know of no better attempt at this than the City Deep compound. . . . It is surrounded first of all by a high galvanised iron fence. It has barbed wire at the top which prevents anybody getting in or out. . . . The gates are so constructed that they have turnstiles by which each native can file in singly. The buildings are so constructed that from the compound manager's office he can see down any direction along the line of huts. The buildings are arranged like the spokes of a wheel with the office as a hub [and] by that means they are able to see exactly what goes on in the compound and practically almost in the rooms. (NGI, 6/3/14:3, 6)

City Deep compound in Johannesburg was unusual in 1914, however. More typical was Langlaagte B, whose compound manager reported to Buckle that it was "a very higgeldy piddledy [*sic*] sort of place" (NGI, 27/10/14:34). Although it had only two gates, they were not very substantial and, since the workers had "all got jumpers, it would be quite easy for them to break through."

"Improvements" were uneven, depending on the profitability of the mine, but by the early 1930s the majority of gold mines seem to have conformed fairly well to Buckle's requirement of "closable" space. Workers were literally packed into that space. For instance, on 1 June 1943, the compound manager at East Geduld Gold Mine wrote to the Witwatersrand Mine Natives' Wages Commission (WMNWC), rebutting the evidence of Blyth Koko of the African Mine Workers' Union regarding overcrowding but inadvertently giving an impression of how crowded compound rooms actually were:

> The Compound has 52 rooms of 60 bunks each, 2 rooms of 40 bunks each, 260 rooms of 20 bunks each (Total bunks 8,400). The 60 bunk rooms accommodate an average of 54 Natives per room. A strict check is kept on the number of Natives in each room and overcrowding is *not* permitted. (WMNWC Evidence, 1/6/43)

Or, for Simmer and Jack: "The allegation that 80 Natives are housed in a room 25 feet by 16 feet is incorrect; no more than 40 Natives are ever housed in a room this size. . . . Rooms to accommodate 80 natives measure 40 feet by 32 feet'' (Chamber of Mines 1943:127). These cramped ''accommodations'' were arranged in squares of barracks-like buildings surrounding dusty quadrangles in the center of which might be found the kitchens, mine offices, indunas' houses, and change houses (see figure 2 for a typical 1950 compound layout).

In 1976, when I directed an ethnography on Welkom Mine in the Orange Free State, there were sixteen persons to a room, but otherwise the physical structure had changed very little. However, new compounds then under construction at Anglo American mines were being built on a more open plan with eight to a room and a common sitting-dining room.[1]

Compound Social Structure

By the time of the Buckle Commission report in 1914, the compound manager-induna–police boy structure of compound administration was already set. In later years, as we have seen, some mines appointed ''native controllers'' (fokisi) to handle underground complaints and supervision. In the 1960s that office expanded to include black personal assistants, but it was not until the middle 1970s that any serious effort was made to reform the compound manager system. Meanwhile, compound managers, their white assistants, and their black indunas and police boys ran the compounds. Compound managers were licensed by the director of native labor and subject to the mines' general managers, of course, but as long as they produced a satisfactory flow of labor down the shaft every morning and committed no criminal or egregiously oppressive acts, they were seldom called to account (Jeeves 1985:49–50). Their formal power was well-nigh absolute. Frequently, compound managers used their power to run ''sidelines'' in their own interests. One ex–compound manager I interviewed had for a while owned a pig farm whose animals had been fed on leftovers from the compound kitchen. In 1944, there was the celebrated case of Gilchrist, the compound manager on Nourse Mines, who was alleged before the Witwatersrand Mine Natives' Wages Commission to have run a farm on mining ground, selling his produce to the workers (WMNWC Majoro, 16/7/43:1515–33).

[1]For an overview of different compound layouts and management conceptions of their functions in 1975, see J. K. McNamara and P. de Bruyn, *Hostel Organization and Management in the Gold Mining Industry,* Chamber of Mines of South Africa Research Organization, Human Resources Laboratory, September 1975. Crush (1992) provides a useful treatment of how surveillance methods on the mines have been transformed in recent years by the introduction of computerized methods of control.

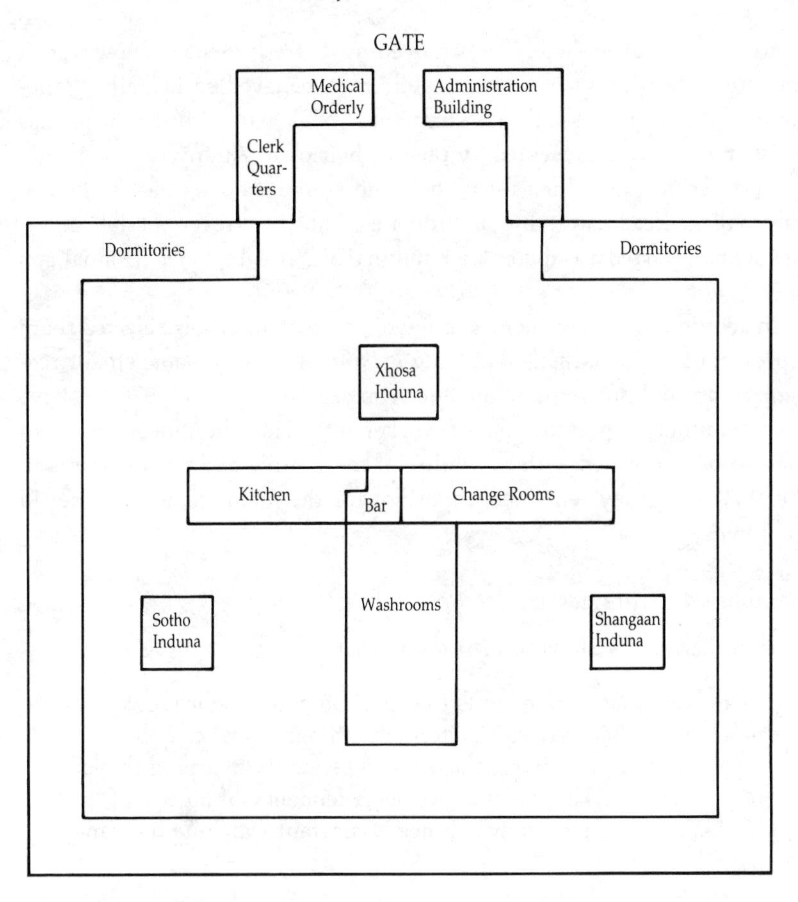

Figure 2. Schematic of a typical compound layout, c. 1950s.

To effect their power in the compounds, compound managers appointed black "police" who acted as their surrogates to "maintain order" on the compound. These men were (illegally) empowered by the compound manager to commit any black miner at any time to the mine lockup (called by workers the *stokkies* or *stokisi*). Cases that came before the Department of Native Affairs inspectors often mention two or three days incarceration without food or water. At the head of the black compound police was the induna, whom Buckle (NGI, para. 143) called "a person of very great consequence indeed in the compound." On large mines there would be an induna for each of the major ethnic groups, and he would appoint mine police (police boys) from his own group. From time to time in the files one comes across a demand from a new group of workers for their own "policeman." Such demands were invariably met. Unlike on the Rhodesian mines (van Onselen 1980), on South African gold mines the dreaded "Zulu police" collaborators had been removed by 1914. In a sense, however, it was precisely because black mine policemen behaved so brutally ("allegations of habitual assault are common" [NGI, para. 146]) that groups insisted on being represented by one of their own. At any rate, management expected the induna for each of the ethnic groups to act in lieu of tribal village headman to his subordinates. Thus, wherever possible, management preferred to appoint an induna of "royal" blood (Ramahapu 1977).

In addition to management-appointed police, workers also elected room representatives, called *izibonda* (sing. *isibonda*), whom management recognized but did not remunerate and who seem before the 1970s to have been genuinely representative of worker interests. The independence of these izibonda waned with the influx of more proletarianized workers in the 1970s, but they remained important for the maintenance of order in the rooms.

Compound Strategies: Police Power

In 1914, Buckle (NGI, para. 148) found that

> there were many complaints that the compound police took too much upon themselves, interfering with natives who wished to speak to the compound manager, and generally usurping the latter's functions. This must always be a tendency of a body of this kind; and it is an abuse which needs constant watching by compound managers.

In "a body of this kind," however, there was also an incentive for compound managers to turn a blind eye to excesses of zeal on the part of their appointed police. To explain this tendency, I turn to a brief discussion of power in complex organizations.

When the power to command is institutionalized, it becomes *authority*, which implies that rules promulgated by certain actors or groups of actors will be obeyed by themselves and others. Authority is exercised whether or not those who are dominated consent to the domination, as long as they, and those in authority who impose the rules, accept them and are thereafter subject to them. My use of the term differs from that of Max Weber, whose terminology proved unfruitful primarily because, for him, the notion of authority applies only to rules legitimated by followers. In dealing with authority on the South African mines, imposed rules are as important.

Rules may be formal or informal as long as infractions can be sanctioned in some way. Institutionalization of commands within rules is a means of extending the range of domination more widely, but those who dominate by authority pay the price of being subject to their own rules. If rule changes are to be authoritative, they must necessarily apply to all who are subject to them. Coercive or despotic power is inconsistent with authority, in that rules provide subjects with grounds and procedures for appeal against arbitrariness. Management, to the extent that it is dominant, can decide to ignore the rules, but if it does so it will be choosing to undercut its own authority. Crozier (1964:163) expresses the management dilemma well:

> To achieve his aims, the manager has two sets of conflicting weapons: rationalization and rule-making on the one side; and the power to make exceptions and to ignore the rules on the other. . . . Proliferation of the rules curtails his own power. Too many exceptions to the rules reduce his ability to check other people's power.

Arbitrary power, unlike authority or directly coercive power, is strategically exercised in situations of uncertainty (Crozier 1964, ch. 6) where the rules cannot be applied or are deliberately ignored by dominants or dominated. The one who has power in a situation of uncertainty is the one who has the ability to effect his or her decision in such a situation. The uncertainty may be inherent in the situation itself, for example, in the interpretation of a rule, or it may be created by persons who choose to ignore or transgress the rules in individual cases. The classic example of one who strategically transforms structural authority into arbitrary power is the foreman in Gouldner's study of an American gypsum mine. He chose to ignore the no smoking rules but then applied them arbitrarily when he wanted to victimize other individuals (Gouldner 1954:172–74).

On the South African mine compounds before 1973, the best example of strategic use of uncertainty to increase personal power was the behavior of the mine clerks. Better educated than mine workers, clerks interpreted for black workers to white management, who tended to speak at most one African language. White managers to whom I spoke insisted that clerks had no power on the compound at all. In fact, they had a gate-keeping role, controlling access to white management and interpreting black worker representations to serve their own ends or perceptions where they thought it necessary. As a result, they exercised considerable informal power. In such situations the *amanene* ("respectables"), bullied by rural youth for their continued commitment to schooling in their adolescence, could get their own back. Some took malicious pleasure in condescending to their "ignorant" fellows. There were also predictable structural tensions between clerks and indunas, who had usually risen from the ranks and had their own sources of authority.

According to the 1976 ethnography, on the gold mines, compound managers and indunas faced the dilemma of whether to use their power authoritatively, by enforcing or promulgating rules, or arbitrarily, by ignoring or getting around the rules. Of course, they did not work in a vacuum or on totally malleable materials. We have shown that beliefs and action patterns underground are primarily conditioned by a combination of pride and fear, with fear and tension predominant in the actual underground situation. One of our informants wrote: "One man told me that when he goes to work underground he leaves his intellect above, that when he is underground he is not a full person. Another said: 'When I am underground I do not think of anything else except coming out of the mine.' " Another informant spoke to a drill operator:

> Like all the other workers I talked to, he expressed to me the difficulties of work and stressed that one does not feel hunger underground because of the anxiety to come out once more to see the world again. When this man talked of anxiety to come out of the mine, he gave me an idea of why people are so happy and noisy when they come out.

Certainly, workers emerging from underground display a curious elation. One can feel the sense of released tension as they emerge from the shaft and make their way across to the compound. Their attitude is exalted and devil-may-care. An observer who worked in the change room on Welkom Mine in 1976 noticed: "they become aggressive when they come out from work and are not afraid of anything that faces them. This element of aggression may be observed in the changing-house. You must not delay them, else you invite insults." This release of nervous energy was not dispersed into individual homes, however. It was poured into a densely packed compound, impersonally structured and administered for white management by indunas and their police.

The induna was caught in a bind imposed by management, since he was expected both to control the hostel and to represent the inmates to management. If he had been an elected official, this feat might have been possible. But he was not. He was a management appointee, and compound policemen were his appointees in turn. "We don't elect him, he is appointed in the night," said the Mozambican workers in 1976. "His appointment by white management makes him irresponsible," said a group of boss boys. "He does not care about worker problems. He sides with management."

It is useful to distinguish heuristically between those who have a position in a bureaucratic hierarchy and whose authority therefore lies in their right to administer rules from above, and those who are responsive and responsible to those below them, whose ultimate source of authority is the "will of the people," although, in any event, authority is always a combination of the two. In the latter case those in authority are much more likely to respond to popular pressure. One of the problems for the induna was that he and his associates fell largely into the first category but management operated under the illusion that he ruled in terms of the second.

The authority imbued in the induna by compound management was diffuse, not specific. That is, the "rules" that he was expected to administer consisted of a general insistence on law and order in the compound (i.e., he should prevent disturbances and get the men out to work on time) rather then specific dictates. Such diffuse power left much discretion in its exercise to the officeholder. Such discretion, from the ordinary workers' point of view, implied uncertainty with an accompanying potential for the arbitrary exercise of power by the indunas. The induna could invoke management authority for a wide range of actions. "He will favor his friends in the choice of compound police; he will communicate to management only those grievances that he and his favorites deem worth communicating and overlook others," said a group of senior black mine officials in 1976. The opposite of favoritism, of course, is victimization. The diffuse power of the induna lent itself well to both.

The induna's power gave him a considerable amount of patronage to bestow. People played up to him. One of the indunas on Welkom Mine in 1976 was very "traditional." He liked workers to refer to him as *baba*—"father"—or *morena*—"my lord." He always carried a whisk, made from a cow's tail, to frighten away the spirits. On the compound he would behave like one of royal blood, distributing largess, always with a policeman on hand—"just like a chief at home would always have one of his councilors with him." Here the observer noted the role-playing: "This man was promoted to the position of induna after having been a boss-boy. He projects this image because he is just an ordinary man with very little education. People call him 'baba,' but actually they laugh at him and tease him." The teasing remained strictly in limits, of course. People would turn to their indunas when in trouble. A man needing leave, for instance, might first approach the induna with a great show of subservience, knowing that if the induna approved the leave he would get it.

Although they despised some (but not all) the indunas as people, black miners on Welkom Mine in 1976 did not ask for the abolition of the induna system when suggesting reforms. Rather, they asked that the induna be made genuinely representative of worker interests, with workers having a right to overrule him, rather than an instrument of management control. One can see why black miners later so readily accepted the National Union of Mineworkers, and why rivalry immediately erupted between union shaft stewards and indunas.

Even in the 1970s, however, the induna, although he had apparently absolute power, also operated at the heart of the normative structure of the compound. In addition to his management-ordained powers, the induna also had informal authority, derived from the *imiteto,* the informal rules of the compound community. This was even more true of the izibonda.

The word *umteto* (pl. *imiteto*) is Nguni for law, custom, regulation, or way or manner of doing anything; a habitual way of behavior; or a bent or an inclination.[2] It includes both the commands of authoritative individuals and communal agreements. On the mine there are at least three interlinked levels of imiteto involving the black worker: first, the formal rules and regulations established by management; second, the unwritten but well-established rules developed by workers and supervisors underground and in the hostel to define their relationship not only among themselves but also to management (the moral economy of the mine); and, third, those less well established, informal customs among workers, which made up migrant cultures.

On Welkom Mine in 1976, each compound had its imiteto as did each block and, indeed, every room. Imiteto include formal management regulations as well as the unwritten, tacitly agreed-upon rules by which men interacted every day. Mutual trust is based on imiteto, as is popular authority. A management umteto forbade homosexuality, but the indunas scrupulously administered informal imiteto concerning "homosexual" contracts (for example, the senior "husband" had regularly to pay his "wife" the sum agreed upon at the outset of the relationship or face the prospect of dismissal). Management forbade drinking in the men's rooms, dagga smoking, and gambling, yet all these took place with the knowledge of the indunas and compound policemen (in certain rooms and at certain times and without disturbing the proper order). Mine police searched for knives only at specified times, in accordance with the umteto, but there were imiteto for using knives and, of course, for fighting with sticks! Indunas, with their "councillors" the police boys (later dubbed "tribal representatives"), presided over their own courts, which adjudicated minor disputes among the workers packed into compounds, according to the imiteto proper to the various spheres of compound life.

[2]I owe this definition to Mark Ntshangase.

Of course, the norms, both written and unwritten, were broken by the indunas and their "councillors"—and quite often. Different types and levels of imiteto were often incommensurable. Bad indunas violated certain imiteto most of the time. Nonetheless, there was sufficient consistency to maintain social order so that it was umteto-ruled authority, in combination with the indunas' strategic use of their widely discretionary power, that made the compound run. Strategies, even for those with substantial arbitrary power, work best if mediated by authority. Of course, the most effective imiteto were based on common agreement. When black miners asked for "an induna appointed by the workers," they were requesting a representative who would be more fully subject to informal imiteto against arbitrary management power.

Strategies of Resistance: The Workings of the Moral Economy

In 1984, Ms. Ndatshe and I interviewed fourteen men who had been on the mines in the 1940s. Two of them, brothers, were resigned to their complete powerlessness. The most extreme of these was Ziphumele Nkawana:

> You can't say that the indunas are just—in fact they are unjust, favoring some people. But one can do nothing about it and must behave as though one respects them. We couldn't trust the induna but we were afraid to show him because we feared that he would take us to the compound manager and then we would get a reputation for trouble-making in the compound. We didn't want to lose our jobs. He was already unjust when we arrived and we simply accepted him—on all the mines I was on. We talked among ourselves but we didn't want anyone to know for fear that we would be reported and thus lose our jobs. Even the isibonda was afraid of losing his job. Thus although the isibonda is chosen by the people of the room, he doesn't have much power. Whether we were satisfied or not we had to abide by the will of the compound manager. We trusted him because he was a bigger person than us. We were afraid to get together to go to him because we would be told we were on strike. People who made trouble were always sacked, for instance, those who started fights. Right from the beginning when we were first told the imiteto of the mine we believed that if we went to the compound manager we would be breaking the imiteto of the mine. But no one tried. We had agreed to the imiteto when we first came. . . . I saw people in other rooms being picked up and taken to the induna by the police. Some people got bigger rations than others but I didn't know why.

His brother added that they "trusted" the induna because they had to. "The induna ruled not by any inherent right," he said, "but because he was the manager's nominee. His power came from the manager."

On the basis of the 1976 ethnography, I had expected such attitudes. In fact, however, they were quite unusual. Ten of the fourteen ex-miners I interviewed in Pondoland in 1984, as well as others in Lesotho and retired compound managers, insisted that workers strenuously resisted unjust indunas, getting rid of them if need be. Some of them exaggerated, perhaps, but all were clear on the methods of the moral economy for resisting excessive partiality by black officials.

In addition to the terms of the explicit and one-sided written contract binding black miners to the mines, then, were the imiteto for relations with management, constituting an implicit contract, again unequal, whose bounds were moral but whose sanctions were political and quite effective. Like the moral economy described by E. P. Thompson (1971) for eighteenth-century England, the moral economy of the mine implied certain obligations from mine officials (indunas and police boys as well as white compound and underground staff). Workers expected food of a certain minimal quality, as well as wages comparable to those at other mines, a limit on the amount of personal assault underground, fair adjudication of personal disputes, equal treatment for each "tribal" category of workers, and a considerable measure of latitude in allowing workers private lives of their own in regard to matters such as homosexuality, beer brewing, hospitality for visiting friends, dagga smoking, and other "forbidden" practices.

Indispensable concepts such as "moral economy," "plebeian culture," or "cultural hegemony" are tricky because they so easily slide over into notions of a "common value system" or "dominant ideology" so dear to many social scientists. Following E. P. Thompson, moral economy is perhaps better described as encompassing mutually acceptable rules for resistance within systems of domination and appropriation. On the mines, the moral economy sorted out those aspects of compound life that dominant and subordinate groups could take for granted as inevitable from those which would be contested by workers, often with fierce outrage, or forbidden by management outright.[3]

[3]While the notion of moral economy is borrowed from E. P. Thompson (1971), my reading of it is much indebted to the ideas of Barrington Moore's *Injustice* (1978), especially his notion of an "implicit contract" and his use of "moral outrage" as an analytical concept, and to Thompson's later development of his ideas (1974 and 1978). My use of moral economy as interactive and constantly contested should be distinguished from that of James Scott (1976), which is much closer to dominant ideology theory.

One old man interviewed in Pondoland in 1984 expressed very well the acceptance of inevitability: "We were quite happy. We knew we were being oppressed but it did us no harm." Better wages they could all have used. One reported: "We would talk of the injustice of the white miners' higher pay, but we could do nothing about it since we were under them—the whites had power." However, none of the men interviewed were able to think of any changes (other than in wages) they might have made. Although several of them said that their sons (current mine workers) would never have put up with the underground beatings they suffered, they themselves accepted them as inevitable, joking with each other about them in the trains en route to the mines. As several men said, their fathers had warned them of the hard work and cruelty underground but they had "wanted to taste the bitterness" themselves.

Like mining men elsewhere, the work they did was a source of male pride to them:

> The pay was bad, but we liked the work. Long ago it was an Mpondo pride to go and work in the mines. You could get work in town but people looked down on you then: "You are not strong, you are not a man. Why do you not go to the mines?" Mine-work was our pride, a source of self-respect. "A man must work in the mines, underground. The Mpondo like very much to be *machine boys*. If you work in town you are taken to be lazy because you do not do the hard jobs that men can do." When we met at dances, at home, those working on the mines would scorn those working in town or the cane-fields. Even mine surface workers were scorned.

When asked why he did not migrate to Cape Town, where wages were higher, one dignified old man answered simply: "There are no gold mines in Cape Town."

Such acceptance of the rigors of mine life by workers, which certainly constituted an important means for control by management, did not imply that control could be taken for granted, whether at work or on the compound. The pride and independence of Mpondo men in this period, the fact that most of them did not have to come to work out of immediate economic necessity, shaped them as the most active troublemakers on the mines.

In the ten years between 1939 and 1948, excluding faction fights, 101 gold and coal mine disturbances occurred that were important enough to be the subject of police or native affairs inspectors' reports filed in the Department of Native Affairs. For other periods the records are less complete but point to similar patterns. Such disturbances tended to focus on local issues at individual mines, but together they involved thousands of black miners. Statistics on such rapid wildcat strikes are almost certainly unreliable. Many times management must have dealt with collective strategic resistance without summoning the South African police or Native Affairs officials. Half the old men I interviewed in Lesotho and Pondoland could remember at least one such event during their working lives.

The hand of the moral economy on the mines ruled a particularly unequal and constantly contested set of relationships. Nonetheless, it existed. The mobilization of the moral outrage of the entire workforce was an infrequent and hazardous enterprise. But it did happen, and that it might happen placed definite limits on complete autocracy. Compound existence is subordinated to the overriding needs of production. That compound inmates were productive workers makes Goffman's (1961) "asylum" model less useful for mine compounds than for total institutions like prisons or mental hospitals. A compound manager or induna whose charges repeatedly rioted or struck work would not last long. The same applied to underground supervisors.

Compound managers and indunas from the period admitted to constant vigilance to ensure that the men in the compound were both "disciplined and happy." The compound manager paid careful attention to his two sources of information about black discontent on the mine: black appointees (indunas and compound police) and his informal "friends" in the compound. Such "trusties" enabled the compound manager to "keep his finger on the pulse" of compound life. Neither indunas and police boys nor compound managers were ever completely free to dominate. The moral economy of the mine confined and defined their hegemony, even though it never sought to abolish it.

Ten of the Mpondo I interviewed in spring 1984, as well as all the black officials (two indunas and seven clerks in all) and both retired compound managers, mentioned collective resistance of compound dwellers to injustices. The pattern described varies slightly in its details, but the outline is clear enough to be formulaic. Most of the ordinary workers interviewed had had at least one personal experience of such collective action, and those who had not nonetheless knew the procedure.

The process was quite simple. Persons with grievances would go through their isibonda to the induna. Usually that was enough. If the induna himself was unjust or unresponsive, however, the people in each room would discuss their complaints and would instruct the izibonda to get together (sometimes with other respected or older men in the compound) and arrange to summon everyone to a meeting at a given time outside the compound manager's office. There they would sit, often several thousand of them, until he noticed and sent someone to find out what they wanted. By most accounts the izibonda took the lead in these affairs:

> If the induna is unjust, the people of every room come together and they talk about it, and so they will either send a policeman or a clerk to the compound manager to come and meet with all of them from all the rooms. It was the izibonda who organized such meetings. Each isibonda would tell his people that on such and such a day we have to meet at such and such a place. Nobody would organize the izibonda; they organized themselves. Sometimes the workers would talk among themselves and agree to call the izibonda or other men whom they regarded as clever, who would come together with the izibonda. But the izibonda would organize this themselves, and then they would tell certain men from different rooms whom they regarded as wise, whom they trusted. They would choose men from all the different tribes to consult with them. These meetings would occur only when there was trouble. They would speak *fanakalo* to ensure mutual understanding.

Compound managers understandably dreaded such meetings and did their best to conciliate them when they occurred, usually promising an inquiry. Large numbers of workers who assembled to make demands from management sometimes resorted to violence, especially when management proved intransigent. Such violence was generally directed against compound property that represented the source of a grievance. If the original complaint was about food, for instance, the kitchen might be wrecked and food taken. If the complaint was about management injustices, compound offices might be destroyed and associated persons, especially black officials, attacked. Breaking windows in the compound, however, was a standard expression of displeasure with white management. Even relatively minor damage to property effectively emphasized the importance of a grievance. Typically, management would summon the South African police and often representatives of the recruiting organizations and the Department of Native Affairs as well, and compound dwellers would be given a hearing.

Because compound managers feared that "things might get out of hand" and become violent, nonviolent "protest demonstrations" were often successful. After all, the compound manager was hired by the mine to keep the workforce "disciplined and happy." Violent expression of grievances would bring him the unfavorable attention of the mine manager. Occasionally, he might fear for his own physical safety, although records of such cases are surprisingly rare. Violence against persons tended to be restricted to so-called faction fights (discussed in chapter 6). Deaths that occurred during demonstrations generally resulted from police action against the demonstrators. For example, it is unusual for the archives to contain police reports such as the one describing a Sotho disturbance at Nigel Mine on 8 February 1914:

> they were throwing stones at Mr Pithey's [compound manager's] house, he could not come out, he was sitting there with his revolver trying to protect his house in which were his wife and children. Mr Pithey could not get word to the Police Station as the Rioters were throwing stones at [him]. . . . We were only four European Policemen and Mr Pithey inside the Compound, while there were at least two hundred natives. We stood no chance at all when they rushed us. There were about eight shots fired. (JUS 195, 3/170/14, SAP Nigel, 9/2/14)

No doubt the event cast serious doubt in the general manager's mind on Pithey's competence as a compound manager.

In the "rationalized" hostels of the present day with their more proletarianized workforces, the disintegration of local management hegemony has meant both beefed-up internal security forces on the mines and increased violence. Nonetheless, McNamara's careful analysis of worker confrontation with mine managements in the 1970s and early 1980s demonstrates clearly the continuing success of such events, slightly more than 40 percent of which were violent (McNamara 1985:347–62).

A classic case of a protest meeting against management in which police intervention led to violence took place at Van Ryn Deep on 19 July 1928 (NLB 197, 987/13/68, police report, Benoni, 20/7/28 and 27/7/28, SNC's reports, Benoni, 23/7/28, 14/8/28, 4/9/28, Compound Manager's statement, 20/7/28, and letter to SNC, Benoni, 23/8/28). Three or four hundred workers (mostly Xhosa speaking) held a meeting in the compound and decided to bypass normal grievance channels (the indunas, the black mine police, and the compound manager) and to approach the general manager himself. So "with a great noise of shouting and whistling by mouth" they "came running out of the main gate . . . across the veld" to seat themselves "in the garden in front of the manager's house." He happened to be away at one of the outlying shafts, so they settled down to wait for him. However, because "[the manager's] wife was getting anxious," said the compound manager, he decided to address the crowd, who shouted "that they had a complaint to make to the manager and did not want to speak to me. I told them that complaints had to be made to me at the compound and that if they were not satisfied with my ruling they could see the manager at the compound" later. Refusing to return to the compound, they began yelling "Beta!" (meaning "attack" in Xhosa), so an assistant compound manager had the mine police arrest one who seemed particularly vociferous. When the crowd forced his release, the compound manager called the

South African police in Benoni and informed the crowd he had done so. "They became abusive and more noisy" and began to move off into an adjoining plantation. When the police arrived, they heard "branches of the trees being broken off to get weapons." The miners "shouted in Si-Xhosa they did not care [about] the police." Mounted constables were stoned when they attempted to drive the workers back into the compound, and one horse collapsed with his rider. The miners' attack with sticks and stones necessitated "very firm and definite action" by police with batons, who nonetheless took a full hour to get people back into their rooms.

Worker outrage in this case seems to have focused on the thinness of the *marewu* (a porridge-like beverage made from maize) served in the kitchen, although workers on a distant shaft also complained bitterly that they had not been served their evening meal because they had arrived back too late. The compound manager claimed to know nothing about either of these complaints and thought the whole affair had been engineered by a Xhosa induna he had sacked two months previously. The sub–native commissioner was told, however, that "the reason these natives go in a large body to complain is that members of a deputation would be marked and victimized by the Compound authorities." Certainly after the violence management tried to meet the demands. Yet, the "leader," who had been arrested and then released outside the manager's house, was sentenced to three months' hard labor, which could hardly have reassured workers about victimization.

This account is typical of collective action against mine authorities (see also NTS 7675, 102/332, reports dated 3/3/39, 12/3/39, 16/2/40, 25/2/40, 20/10/41, 16/3/43, 11/2/44). Such worker mobilization was often ethnically based. Interethnic organization could be risky because it involved sending messengers from one ethnically segregated section of the compound to the other. Occasionally during the 1930s and 1940s, violence occurred because the compound manager, getting wind of a potential mass meeting, would arrest "messengers" who were announcing the meeting (NTS 7675, 102/332, 20/6/42) or "agitators" who were setting it up. On 15 April 1940, for instance, a certain Dynbele was arrested at Consolidated Main Reef by the South African police for inciting his fellow workers to strike because of delays in the hoisting of day shifts, shortages of hot water, and insufficient food. The latter two complaints often accompanied the former because workers delayed in the hoisting would often return to the compound so late that the hot water was cold and the food finished. When Dynbele was taken to the police station in town, three hundred to five hundred workers congregated outside the compound. The compound manager went to the meeting and offered to listen to the workers, but they refused to speak to him unless Dynbele was released. Eventually, rioters wrecked all the administration buildings in the compound. Stones were gathered from a dump through the back gate in anticipation of the arrival of the police. It took the latter three hours and the use of tear gas to disperse the angry workers (NTS 7675, 102/332, police report, Krugersdorp, 17/4/40).

From time to time, more "spontaneous" violence against the brutality of "native police" would occur. This was often, but not always, exacerbated by ethnic differences (NLB 197, 1440/14/48, 30/8/14, Nourse Mines and Randfontein Estates, 8/4/17, Brakpan Mines; NTS 7675, 102/332, 17/2/42; NTS 7686, 256/332, 10/3/46). Very occasionally, workers would resort directly to organized violence against management without having voiced prior demands, most often when complaints about food were involved (NTS 7675, 102/332, 13/3/39). However, violence was surprisingly rare in the fifty-seven odd demonstration meetings and strikes mentioned in the state archives and press between 1938 and 1947.

In my evidence for the period before 1973, especially given the thousands of mine workers housed in crowded compounds over the years, gold miners were remarkably disciplined in expressing grievances and turned to violence against management only when representation by other means failed. McNamara reaches similar conclusions for 1973–1982. Nor was management liable to dismiss such collective action as "irrational violence." Characterizations of irrationality tended to be reserved for supposedly more primordial violence associated with "tribal faction fights" among black workers themselves.

Certain specific conclusions may be drawn from the stories of ex-miners and police reports about resistance strategies against management. The position of the induna and his compound police was by no means as secure or despotic as it might have seemed. The induna himself was caught up in the moral economy of the compound (as was the compound manager himself). Masheane Matela, interviewed in Lesotho in 1984, who was himself an induna for many years, remembered frequent dismissals of indunas when he was a young man on Springs Mine:

> If the people did not like the way the induna was acting against them, they would lodge a complaint by calling a big crowd and appointing a spokesman from among themselves to let the compound manager know that they wanted to see him. When the compound manager came, they would tell him their complaint. When he saw that the people were not going to work, he would decide that the best thing would be to dismiss the induna. . . . If it was too late when the induna was dismissed, he was taken to security to sleep

> and next morning transportation was waiting to take him to the station. When the people came up from underground, he was gone. In my experience the complaints varied; maybe the induna was not deciding cases impartially; maybe he had some bad rules and regulations which did not meet the approval of the compound manager; maybe the induna was taking bribes in exchange for promises of promotion, say to mine policemen, and could not deliver on them; maybe he did not report back to the hostel manager when food was not well prepared in the kitchen.

In cases in which the induna was completely the compound manager's creature, he was easily dismissed or demoted, thus giving indunas some incentive to please their mine-worker subjects. One particularly clear instance of the demotion of an induna because he had alienated his subjects is found in a 1948 report dealing with Vogelstruisbult No. 2 compound (NTS 7689, 320/332, 15/3/48, Labour Inspector, Springs). In this instance, the induna was criticized by the Mpondo for referring every complaint he received to the acting compound manager. This particular induna had previously been a clerk, which might explain some of the workers' hostility toward him and his ineptitude in exercising authority. Marsh, the acting compound manager, decided to fire him because of these complaints, but the labor inspector prevailed on him to give the man one more chance and informed a large gathering of the Mpondo of this. One month later, the men of No. 2 compound held a meeting "at which they demanded the removal of both Marsh and the induna, failing which, they said, trouble would follow." Next day the labor inspector met with six hundred of the workers. Their grievances were now both more specific and more wide ranging. There were too many discharges and discharged workers hanging around the mine ("the veld was covered with men and the fact that there were so many robbers around was the Compound Manager's doing") and too many arrests for petty offenses. Also the mine detective and his men had been allowed to search their rooms while they were underground, a clear contradiction of mine imiteto. In this case the major spokesmen were boss boys.

Marsh denied that the mine detective had been given permission to search any rooms. Apparently, the induna had been told to send compound policemen to the rooms to "tell the inmates that the Police were perturbed at the liquor brewing in the Compound and that the practice had to stop." Instead he had used the loudspeaker system to announce that if brewing did not cease the mine detective would conduct a search. Since such a practice was so clearly out of order according to the rules of the moral economy, the labor inspector decided to demote the induna to his previous job of compound clerk. He informed the assembled Mpondo of this, but told them that he had recommended that Marsh be retained. The gathering then dispersed peaceably.

Two important subsidiary points emerge from this particular case. First, the strategic mobilization of moral outrage around a single issue had a kind of halo effect, in that having crossed the threshold from accommodation to collective action, the workers brought up a substantial number of accumulated additional grievances. As a result, the outburst was both more potent and more diffuse than it would have been if minor issues had been dealt with as they arose. Second, many of the cases that reached the Native Affairs files have as a leading figure a compound manager who is either new or acting. As one retired compound manager said, getting "one's finger on the pulse" of compound life took many years of cultivating "friendships" with trusted informants. New managers often tried to introduce new rules or tighten up on old ones, thereby upsetting the delicate equilibrium of compound life. Beer brewing especially precipitated such upsets.

Beer brewing's weight in the contested equilibrium of the moral economy varied from mine to mine. The beer served on the compounds was virtually nonalcoholic. However, if sugar were added to it, after a few days it could build up quite a kick. On the one hand, everybody knew that such beer brewing was illegal. Also, especially for compounds close to urban areas, drunkenness in and around a compound often led to raids by the South African police. On the other hand, the compound manager and especially the induna ignored a certain amount of beer brewing as long as drunkenness was kept within bounds. Sometimes, in fact, both to control them and to show a profit, the induna would supervise the brewing and liquor sales himself (chapter 5 deals at greater length with the place of alcohol in compound life).

In the Vogelstruisbult case described above, the combination of an acting compound manager and an officious induna was clearly too much for the workers, and they ensured the removal of the induna. In situations where the induna was himself involved in brewing or the illegal liquor trade, the support of the workers might enable him to defy the compound manager. On Witwatersrand Deep Gold Mine in 1949, for instance, a new compound manager, C. H. Oliver, "found that illicit brewing of Kaffir Beer and Skokiaan [a potent home-brewed liquor] were rife in the compound and illicit liquor dealing was also taking place" (NTS 7675, 102/332, SAP Boksburg, 9/8/49). Furthermore, he discovered through the appointment of a clerk as an informer "that the induna was the prime mover in this evil." The induna decided that he "was going to remove the informer by hook or by crook." After unsuccessful efforts to frame him on charges of corruption and illicit gold-dealing, the induna staged an evening meeting outside the compound manager's office to demand the discharge of the informer. The crowd rioted, smashing windows in the office. At that point the general manager of the mine arrived and promised to discharge the informer. The crowd dispersed. The manager went back on his word, no doubt having talked over the matter with Oliver, and a compound meeting was called to announce the reinstatement of the dismissed clerk and informer, this time with four officers and thirty-five other ranks of the South African police on hand. The crowd was again hostile but scattered on the appearance of the police. No further police report was filed, so apparently a new equilibrium had been established on the mine—but there is no mention that the induna was fired. The power of the induna, then, resided to a considerable extent in his acceptance by the workers. Certainly, he was appointed by management, but the informal veto power of his subjects on his future success was quite substantial, and their support could grant him a measure of autonomy.

Compound managers who interfered with the established imiteto on their mines often had to face moral outrage. Not only did such interference upset the already unequal balance of the moral economy but it also almost always affected the recreational, sexual, or financial interests of some group of strategically powerful individuals on the mine—like the induna in the case above. At North Compound on Randfontein Estates in 1944, for instance, the compound manager prohibited the sale of *vet koekies* (doughnuts) by Sotho in the compound and then had to call out the South African police to put down resistance. Even instructions to clean up the rooms caused a riot at City Deep in 1940. But perhaps the most serious infringement of the moral economy of a mine occurred at New State Areas in June 1942, when a new compound manager "tightened up the organization and instructed that the natives must produce their tickets on Saturdays also, when drawing food" (NTS 7675, 102/332). To a man my Mpondo informants stated that their most common form of recreation was crisscrossing the Witwatersrand on weekends, by train or on foot, visiting friends and "home boys" on other mines. Invariably, they would sleep over on Saturday nights and eat with friends on their mines. Thus, although the compound manager's new ruling at New State Areas may have been technically legitimate, it ran directly counter to one of the most important, common practices of the various compound cultures. The workers responded immediately:

> At about 7 p.m. the Police Boys discovered that messengers were going round the rooms telling the natives to attend a meeting to

> complain about the food, the showing of tickets on Saturdays and to strike. Two of the messengers were detailed by the Police Boys and while they were interrogated the attack started. . . . About 80 Xosas and Basutos attacked the Compound Police Boys. They retired and later returned in greater numbers and started throwing stones at the kitchen and offices. (NTS 7675, 102/332, New State Areas, 20/6/42)

Three mine policemen were injured.

Compound managers who refused to negotiate with worker petitionary gatherings, or who failed to placate them, ran the risk of riots, either against compound property (especially their own offices and the kitchens) or between tribal groups. While the South African police could be and were readily called if violence occurred on a mine, frequent rioting was costly in terms of damages and work lost—especially the latter. A compound manager could not afford more than an occasional disturbance without having his competence called into question.

The Organization of Resistance

Moral economy is not suspended in a cultural vacuum. Rather it is rooted in an intricate pattern of informal interactions among workers that both informs it and provides the collective power to enforce it. The moral economy of the mine could be sustained only to the extent that people mobilized to support it. Such mobilization was not "spontaneous" but emerged from established social networks. Mpondo ex-miners remembered that in the 1940s and 1950s collective mobilization on the compound was usually organized by the izibonda. Were they the only source of resistance by black mineworkers? That question can best be answered by examining three nodal points for networks of social interaction on the mines in this period—"home boy" networks, compound room organization, and underground work teams.

For the Mpondo the most important group ties on the mines were with home friends (home boys), especially home friends who belonged to the same youth groups. Men would leave for the mines together and take note where their friends were sent. They would also choose mines on the advice of local gossip and so often ended up together. Sometimes letters from home would tell them who was where. On weekends they would travel, often crossing the Rand by train ("from Durban Deep to Benoni") to be together and often to dance in *igubura* or *indlavini* style together and with like-minded fellows. News from home thus traveled surprisingly rapidly around the mines. A neighbor or relative who had become "lost" or who had absconded would be sought and often found. Young men would go to older men from their home districts for advice on personal matters. The Mpondo on the whole avoided black townships, although home friends might go together to the municipal beer halls on the east Rand or to Syrian eating houses in Johannesburg. There too they would often meet home fellows from other mines. They would discuss home matters with such friends, keeping alive memories of rural gossip. They also discussed mine matters with their home fellows, for example, the type of workplace they found themselves in underground (hardness of rock, etc.), their treatment by white miners and boss boys, and so on. There can be no question about the importance of such home-based networks for all the traditional Mpondo miners.

While home friend networks may have lent reinforcement in certain cases, and were sometimes important in faction fights, I know of no instance in which they were identifiably the organizational foundation for collective resistance to management on the mines. As much as men relied on their home friends for personal sustenance, the networks were still dispersed and their foci tended to be individual and parochial. Mpondo who said they went to old men from home for personal advice would turn to the isibonda or induna if they encountered a mine problem. A man charged by the induna might be supported by his home friends (they would pay his fine, for instance), but he would be represented in the induna's court by the isibonda of his room. Of course, some overlap occurred. Izibonda, for instance, would gather to discuss serious matters with older men on the mine, and such older men tended to be elected as izibonda anyway. When the izibonda did consult elders, however, the role of the latter was essentially advisory, for the izibonda were the organizers.

As we have seen, izibonda were chosen by the men of their rooms. Usually they were perceived as quiet and reasonable men who would represent the room faithfully in compound matters. Often they were older men; almost always they had had more mine experience than most of the other room inhabitants. The isibonda's appointment invariably required the consent of all the men in the room. If even one man dissented, the room would look for another isibonda. He was a mediator within the room and a spokesman for the room to the outside; the Mpondo made it quite clear in interviews that the isibonda was more the voice of people in the room than he was their leader.

The position of izibonda seems to have had its origins in the workers' own need for solidarity and self-regulation rather than any management initiative. The isibonda was unpaid, for instance, and thus could not easily be threatened. Although management recognized him, it had not co-opted him. The induna was selected by management and presented to the workers; the isibonda was selected by the room and presented to the induna. Those who had been izibonda clearly regarded the position as one of great responsibility.

The precise role of the isibonda in "protest disturbances" is unclear. According to the Mpondo, he was decisive as a facilitator for collection action, but they are ambiguous, or they do not agree, on whether he and his fellow izibonda actually initiated worker resistance on the compound. The Native Affairs files are little help because reports never mention whether participants were izibonda or not. We do have one uniquely detailed deposition from a certain Ngonqela, presumably Xhosa, who was said to have been a ringleader in a huge food riot on Modderfontein East Gold Mine (also called Modder East) in March 1946 (NTS 7685, 254/332). Even though the deposition does not identify the izibonda, the importance of the room and room ties in initiating collective action is made abundantly clear. My surmise from the context is that Ngonqela was the isibonda in his room.

There was a general shortage of food, especially maize, in South Africa in 1946. On Modder East, workers coming up late from work were receiving no *marewu* (the same yeasty maize porridge beverage whose poor quality provoked the 1928 Van Ryn affair) "because the natives who came off shift first drew double and treble rations." Thus the compound manager introduced rationing. Ngonqela takes up the story at this point:

> On Thursday, 28/2/46, or Friday, 1/3/46, I heard from my room mates that as from the next day all natives who draw rations at 12.00 midday would be required to produce their tickets. . . . The following day . . . [w]hen I entered the room I was reminded by my room mates to take my ticket along. I went and drew my marewu where my ticket was taken and marked in pencil; from there I proceeded to draw my food, where my ticket was stamped. From there I proceeded to my room and sat down and started eating. Whilst eating, I remarked to the others, "so it is true that tickets are being marked for marewu. I thought it was only a joke that you passed." After making this remark I kept quiet.

Ngonqela himself did not initiate any grievance. However, "on Monday evening," he says, "when I entered my room back from work a Pondo (No. 954) addressed me personally and told me that a meeting would be held that same afternoon in our room."

Notice that no room meeting was proposed during the weekend. Presumably, people were away visiting, so the room could not be got together. In fact, since marewu was not being rationed on other mines in the district, home friend visiting might have stoked up the indignation of the Modder

East workers. At any rate, on Monday, Ngonqela and his Pondo roommate, along with three others, told the rest of the room: "All right we will hold this meeting and get rooms 29 and 30 to agree with us." They then sent a youngster to room 29 and 30 with a message to the occupants to attend a meeting on Tuesday afternoon. Since each room contained about fifty occupants, the initial meeting would have had about 150 people present. All would have been Xhosa speaking. Ngonqela continues:

> On Tuesday afternoon, before we went to the spot where the meeting was to be held, the occupants of rooms 29 and 30 came to room 28 and asked us why there was a delay in holding the meeting. We replied that we are just up from underground, and hungry and are now eating, but will come along just now. We then came out and joined them under the tree where they were sitting.

It would seem that Ngonqela and his room were among those workers who came up last from underground. They would thus have suffered most when the marewu ran out:

> A native named George from room 30 then got up and asked what this meeting was about. I then got up and replied that the reason why we are here at this meeting is that we are starving. We come up from underground late and the porridge we get is little, and the marewu is also little and we finish it while we are still standing where we have drawn it. Then the Pondo (No. 954) got up and said "The previous speaker was right: only he lies when he says we get a little porridge. As for myself, I do not get any porridge at all, only soup and that is also very little." The whole gathering then shouted "Yes, we do not get any porridge at all." Two natives, one from room 29 and one from room 30 then got up and asked if this meeting was going to be the end of their complaint. Then the Pondo (No. 954) got up and replied "No, we are only holding this meeting to get agreement. If agreement is obtained we will notify the rest of the compound." A man (whom I know) from room 29 then got up and said "Gentlemen let us not delay this thing, let us notify the whole compound right away and hold another meeting tomorrow afternoon on the same big spot." He then pointed to a youngster from room 29 and said "I will send this man from room 29 to go round the compound." No. 954 asked me who was a fast boy to send from our room. I then pointed out a youngster and said that he could do it quickly. Then George from room 30 also chose a youngster from his room. We had now selected three youngsters. The man from room 29 got up and said "Three youngsters are not enough, we want four," so I chose that youngster to make four. Then George, the man from

> 29, No. 954, and I agreed that we will separate the four youngsters and send two of them to start at room 75 and work their way East around the compound, and two to start at the middle rooms. . . . The meeting then dispersed and we went back to our rooms.

Again from the context, George was likely the isibonda of room 30 and the speaker from room 29 was possibly the isibonda there. The Mpondo referred to as "No. 954," who instigated the meeting, was probably a member of the African Mine Workers' Union, which was active on the mines during this period. He seems to have been quite new to the room, evidenced by his deferral to Ngonqela in the selection of runners. Thus, although the isibonda of the room was not the leader of the affair, once a room meeting had agreed upon a line of action, the izibonda were at the fore in organizing the compoundwide meeting.

"The next day," said Ngonqela, "after we arrived in the Compound, we were still busy eating when we saw that the natives started to congregate at the meeting place. After the hooter sounded, the crowd increased rapidly." The Mpondo (No. 954) arose and called for an interpreter from each of the Xhosa, Shangaan, Sotho, Mpondo, and Zulu groups. This appeal served, of course, to identify publicly all the different groups represented at the meeting. Next, "No. 954 got up again and said 'The reason that we are all here today is that we have a complaint, our complaint is that we are starving. We should ask for more food, and if we don't get more food, then we should ask for more money.' "

Since the Chamber of Mines insisted that one of the reasons for low wages on the mines was that workers were amply remunerated in kind, this line of argument was eminently a fair one. It was used in speeches by representatives of the African Mine Workers' Union all along the Rand during the food shortage. At the Modder East meeting, having stated the position, the Mpondo leader made sure that the Xhosa understood the complaint—"they all said that they understood."

> A Basuto (British)[4] from the crowd got up and said "I agree fully with what has been said, it is exactly what is in my own heart, and all the Basutos agree with me." A Zulu got up from the crowd and said that he agreed with the last speaker—everybody agreed to it. A Xosa got up from the crowd and came close to the centre and said "All that you people have said here today is correct, but there is a question, where are we going to lay this complaint first?" The crowd replied that we will lay the complaint before the boss. The

[4]Since Sotho-speakers live in both South Africa and Lesotho (which was the British colony of Basutoland at this time), "British Basuto" identifies a Sotho from Basutoland (Lesotho).

> same Xosa replied that it would not be in order to lay our complaint to the boss, but that we should first lay it before Tshawe, the Head Induna.

Ngonqela rose to support the last speaker, but he was shouted down by other Xhosa who said, "No, we don't even want to hear that name, Tshawe." Ngonqela gave up and sat down, and the whole crowd said, "Let us go to the Manager straight away." The indunas and compound police barred the main gate, so the crowd straggled through the north gate, gathered sticks from the plantation en route and congregated over two thousand strong on the general manager's lawn.

The compound manager appeared at the general manager's house and asked the workers to appoint a spokesman. They shouted him down. According to Ngonqela:

> The Manager and the Compound Manager came out to us and the Compound Manager asked us what we wanted. We all shouted "We are starving." He told us that we have broken the law [umteto?] by coming here, and that if we have a complaint we should send for him. . . . We all got up and proceeded to the Compound, where we found the big gate shut. . . . We ran back to the North gate. We found the gate open and went into the Compound. We went towards the kitchen and picked up lumps of coal at the boilerhouse. We started throwing them at the kitchen windows and the boilers.

By this time the South African police, under a certain Chief-Inspector Coetzee, who had a reputation for being hotly imperious, had arrived to find that most of the demonstrators had returned to the compound and taken it over, driving out all the white officials, indunas, and black mine police and apparently trying to wreck the place. Coetzee, concerned at the destruction of property, attempted to storm the compound with an inadequate force of men. Nine policemen sustained minor injuries. "In order to divert an immediate catastrophe to the members of the Force," said the police report, Coetzee "gave the order to open fire on the assailants, in consequence of which a few revolver shots were actually fired. This had the desired effect in that the assailants broke and fled."

Surprisingly little damage actually occurred to mine property (although the contents of the indunas' and police boys' rooms had been either stolen or burned). The kitchen and beer hall were relatively intact, and the intrepid Chief-Inspector Coetzee and his men had saved the recreation room piano from destruction. One Xhosa was killed "by a bullet through the chest," one Zulu died with a fractured neck, there were eighty-seven seriously wounded workers, and one police boy was hospitalized. The police had exacted their price for the minor injuries suffered by some of their number and for the damaged piano. The matter had clearly been mishandled. A similar affair at Simmer and Jack on 8 August 1945 had been dealt with without excessive violence (NTS 7685, 233/332). However, Ngonqela's story gives us an excellent account of how mine workers arranged such compound protest meetings.

Although the izibonda had a leading role in organizing strikes or compound meetings, apparently they did not do so without a strong sense of support from their rooms and indeed neighboring rooms—nor did they necessarily initiate the collective action. There is an interesting case of an isibonda on Union Collieries in Breyton who persuaded his roommates to go on strike without wider support. The whole affair fizzled out, and he was dismissed (NTS 7687, 290/332). Thus although roommates were seldom a closely knit group, the organization of resistance on the compound tended to be room based, with the izibonda assuming a substantial measure of responsibility—but also seeking to exert a moderating influence on the most militant of the rank and file.

What of work teams? The Mpondo provided ample testimony that friendships on the mine were not restricted to home friends or roommates. People established friendships with fellow workers or members of the same team, and although these were initially hampered by the language gap they would often grow into genuinely close relationships:

> Sometimes it happened that even though you are a Mosotho man, staying with Basotho only, it is possible that maybe you've got a friend who is Xhosa . . . and you can visit him and have him over to visit. That is typical of the life of the compound. We used to mix going to visit each other. . . . Sometimes to make a friend was simple. You could just meet him around the compound. But this friendship always used to start right at the workplace. You would find that when working together "You handle that side and I'll handle this side," and that [you] are doing the work together. Automatically, you become friends. (Jack Mpapea, Lesotho, 1988)

At first such friends would speak *fanakalo*, but it is a "language" with little subtlety and no nuance designed to drive people at work, so in time they would learn each other's languages. They delighted in exploring the differences in each other's customs and in sharing stories about their homes, families, and girlfriends. They also talked about work. Sandiso Madikizela in Pondoland captured well the spirit of those exchanges:

> I was friendly with people from other tribes who were work mates from the same team. So we became friendly with Sotho and other

> tribes. We used to visit each other on weekends. When I went to a Sotho room, I would be the guest of that Sotho acquaintance, who would go to the kitchen and fetch food and meat and beer for me. If I drank tea, that man would go to the concession store to get food for me. We would talk to each other about work and about our different customs. When we discussed work, we would talk about the cruelty of the boss boy or the white man. We would also talk about our work if we happened to be working in a very dangerous place and were scared.

Mixed friendships were not restricted to teammates. Boss boys would get together, for instance, and discuss the difficulties and complexities of supervision, comparing techniques by which they were able to get the most work out of their teams. They would brag to each other about their workers' production, thus confirming their self-formation as agents of management. Ryna Dushu described this best:

> When we discussed our work, if one was a boss boy he would say, "Well, my people are working like thus and so," and another would respond, "My people are working much harder than others." We would then talk about how each was handling his team. Most of the people from other tribes that I was speaking to were boss boys because I was myself a boss boy. We also talked about accidents, because the boss boys' work was to go in first and make [the work area] safe.

Mpondo workers readily discussed the good team spirit that developed underground under the stress of hard work and danger. As we have seen, a certain level of abuse—by both white miners and boss boys—was taken for granted. Workers would react against serious and continued cases of assault, however. Sometimes the team would go as a group to the mine captain to complain of ill treatment by boss boys or because they were being sent to work in a place perceived by them to be dangerous. Several remembered cases of individual resistance to the boss boy or white miner, which were usually resolved by the worker's transfer to another team by the fokisi. In the rough and tumble underground in those early days, being tough was what mattered.

Assaults underground by blacks upon blacks were thus worked out by the workers themselves according to a rough moral economy enforced by mutual threats and retaliation. As we shall see in chapter 6, such action could sometimes escalate into a "faction fight." A certain level of white assaults and abuse was accepted beyond which individual workers would retaliate or request a transfer.

Collective action against higher management underground, when it occurred, seems most often to have been associated with delays in hoisting, involuntary overtime, or tickets incorrectly stamped or directed against the compound manager and underground staff for ignoring worker complaints. So rare were cases of underground collective action that none of the Mpondo interviewed could personally recall any. Occasional accounts are scattered through the Native Affairs files. In September 1939, a delay in hoisting led to a protest demonstration outside the compound manager's office at Geldenhuis Deep (NTS 7675, 102/332, SAP Jeppe, 29/9/39). On New Kleinfontein Gold Mine in July 1941, about three hundred workers refused to return to the surface at the end of their shift until their grievances about hours had been attended to. The compound manager agreed to talk to them (NTS 7675, 102/332, SAP Boksburg, 9/7/41, and *Inkululeko,* August 1941). At Marievale in 1940 and at West Springs in 1944, there were compound gatherings to complain about overstamped tickets. At Marievale the workers "demanded that the gates be opened as they intended marching to Johannesburg to place their complaints before Mr. Taberer in person" at the head office of the Native Recruiting Corporation. In the end the police dispersed them with a baton charge (NTS 7683, 194/332, SAP Boksburg, 31/3/40; see also NTS 7675, 102/332, and *Guardian,* 21/1/43; SAP Krugersdorp, 8/9/43, and *RDM,* 9/9/43).

One case definitely was associated with production problems (NTS 7675, 102/332, Memos 9 and 11/1/43). The manager of Langlaagte Estate and Gold Mining Company, A. S. Ford, was an enthusiast for "scientific management" (Ford 1944).[5] On 6 January 1943, underground workers from Block "B" Compound at Langlaagte called a meeting to which Ford was summoned. "In a rather rowdy and insolent manner . . . the machine boys, especially Pondos . . . put their complaints" to him. Their complaints had to do with problems at the point of production underground: double, even treble shifts and insufficient remuneration for overtime; the requirement that they use a measuring string with their machine drills; the demand that they be able to recite underground working regulations by the numbers of the paragraphs and regular assaults when they were not word perfect; and the failure of the compound manager to attend to their complaints. Ford promised to stop the double and treble shifts immediately and to investigate complaints about overtime pay, but he insisted that "learning instructions and the string . . . had been used for the past five years and was in the interest of the African."

[5]I am grateful to Wilmot James for pointing the Ford article out to me. Jean Leger's doctoral dissertation (1992) deals fully with efforts to establish scientific management on the gold mines. A. S. Ford figures prominently in his argument.

The grievances thus had primarily to do with machine drilling. The ethnic character of the complainants can be explained by the fact that most machine drillers in the 1940s were from Pondoland. Because of the concurrent threat of a strike at Victoria Falls Power Station (Moodie 1988:28–30), the affair was taken more seriously than would otherwise have been the case. A large force of police stood by, and at three o'clock the next morning workers who appeared outside the compound were driven back and five hundred were arrested. Police claimed that they were picketing, but according to the workers themselves, they were heading for the Native Recruiting Corporation offices to turn in their tickets and make their complaints. Forty-eight "ringleaders" were tried, defended by an advocate retained by the recently established African Mine Workers' Union, and were given relatively light sentences. The mine actually reemployed all but eight of them.

A final case in the Department of Native Affairs files before the 1950s of underground collective action against management occurred in September 1943 at Rand Leases Gold Mine (NTS 7675, 102/332, SAP Krugersdorp, 6/9/43, and *RDM*, 9/9/43). Three hundred forty-eight workers (339 according to the press report) refused to come to the surface, and "mine officials who went down to hear their grievance and induce them to enter the skip were threatened with assault." The South African police arrived, and the mine manager descended with ten policemen to speak to the strikers, "who were armed with pieces of timber and iron bars." When they saw the police, the miners dropped their weapons. When "the manager spoke to them, informing them that the Police of the Government had arrived, . . . they agreed to come to the surface." They were all "detained by the police" and twenty-two were "charged with refusing to obey a legitimate order," which can hardly have encouraged their faith in the "government's" justice. Their mates in the compound rioted, smashing windows, stripping trees, and causing a general panic among the policemen and authorities in attendance, who feared an uprising of the compound's ten thousand inmates. Tear gas and a baton charge, however, dispersed them.

These fragmentary cases suggest that the informal organization of workers could occur underground according to a workplace moral economy. We have no reports on who was responsible for them, but the sit-down strikes underground were no doubt work team based and probably boss boy led. This theory fits well with what we know of work team friendship groups. Alternatively, as in the Langlaagte case, the strikes may have been led by the machine drillers who worked the stopes relatively independently of boss boy supervision and were in fact better paid than boss boys in this period. The machine drillers tended to be independent and individualistic (often they were Mpondo), they were respected by the others as "kings of the mine."

Extemporaneous underground strikes were unusual, however, and apparently occurred at the end of shifts. Mpondo ex-miners interviewed in the countryside asserted that underground disturbances were rare "because they came to the mine for money" and did not want to miss a single day's pay. In this period, workers' commitment to putting in their time seems to have been almost as absolute as management's commitment to production. The two are of course not necessarily complementary. It is quite possible to "put in one's time" in a most unproductive manner.

There is no evidence that work teams formed the bases for compound resistance, which was much more common than collective action underground. Although boss boys and machine drillers do seem to have led some underground resistance at the point of production, especially around issues of safety and hoisting delays, compound resistance under the old regime on the mines seems clearly to have been room based and was probably organized by izibonda as the Mpondo said.

Wage Raises, New Workers, Different Strategies: Challenges to Management Hegemony in the 1970s

For about sixty years, from the time of the successful establishment of the Native Recruiting Corporation and its alliance with the Witwatersrand Native Labour Association in the late teens of this century (Jeeves 1985; Crush, Jeeves, and Yudelman 1991), mine labor recruitment shifted from one area to another in a relentless search for cheap labor. Offering low wages also ensured the recruitment of a particularly desirable class of worker—rural peasant proprietors with a stake in the countryside, who worked on the mines to build up equity in a rural homestead. Unlike more fully proletarianized workers, for whom the mines was the job of last resort, rural proprietors chose mine work because food was provided, savings for rural investment were possible, and compound life enabled encapsulated solidarities with other rural migrants and protection from urban crime. In the words of an Mpondo ex-miner, who is now working in construction: "I prefer mines to town. In town we eat our money, whereas in Johannesburg there were rations. And there were no *tsotsis* [urban gangsters] around us there."

As long as the mines could maintain a labor force with such attitudes and such an economic base, fluctuations in labor supply areas did not affect basic continuities. Thus, social order on the South African gold mines before the 1970s was handled by a combination of local mine management paternalism, the informal authority of management-appointed and worker-accepted black officials, and the operation of a moral economy, with imiteto defining relationships among workers and between workers and management.

The new type of worker, who started coming to the mines from Lesotho in the late 1960s and from Zimbabwe and then the Ciskei and Transkei and the South African rural resettlement slums in the 1970s, was deeply alienated from compound life in general and the paternalistic authority of compound manager and induna in particular (McNamara 1980). He had little understanding of, indeed considerable scorn for, the operations of the moral economy that had served to maintain the equilibrium of resistance and control on the compounds for so many years.

By 1976 on Welkom Mine, our participant observers found that black perceptions of white management could be divided into two broad categories. On the one hand, to some workers, management seemed vaguely benevolent as a result of its very distance from them: "The indunas, boss boys, and others who are next to us are weak in that they favor their district neighbors, their friends, or those who bribe them with money. The compound manager is much better than the lower authorities but unfortunately he is not known by us because we are stupid or not told." The implication is clear. White management would help if they could be reached, but they were simply inaccessible. Let us call this the inaccessibility view.

On the other hand, another perception recorded by one of our observers was probably more typical—certainly of the newer workers: "The black miners see the power of white management as being adamant and arbitrary. They do not believe that, on the whole, justice is done to them by white management." Thus, the inaccessibility of the whites was seen as a result not of the machinations of black officials but of mine rules administered by black officials for management's own protection:

> [Management wants] to make a barrier around themselves, to cut themselves off from the miners in order to force them into submission, to make them into a sort of receptacle that swallows everything, not knowing whether it is good or bad. Some of the indunas and the police boys are trying their best, but the thing is that they cannot send their complaints because there is a barrier between them and those who are really in authority, that is, the management.

With regard to white management, these miners said that they "feel the kick of a horse, but they do not see the man [riding the horse] giving these kicks." Again the implication is clear. Black officials were simply the agents of management injustice. This we will call the total despotism view.

Of course there were variations among these two general views of white management, and in fact both were overstated, but their differences demonstrate the transition taking place on the mines in 1976. Under the old manager-induna regime, workers were not genuinely represented to management, as was argued in the inaccessibility view. However, black officials also failed to represent the views of ordinary miners because they were the agents of management, as represented in the despotism view. Black officials had more discretionary power than the despotism view credited them with but rather less arbitrary power than the inaccessibility view argued.

The "new workers," who were so scornful of their "uneducated" elders' acceptance of management controls, failed to see that the older black miners' experience of domination on the compound was a complex combination of management-ordained authority and discretionary power held by white compound managers and black indunas and compound policemen. Arbitrary power was held in check, or at least in stable if unequal equilibrium, by a moral economy that justified local collective resistance against particular injustices. The sense of injustice that undergirded resistance justified and sanctioned collective outbreaks of moral outrage. As we have seen, the organization of resistance appears to have been based on room solidarities centering on the izibonda.

It is interesting that on Welkom Mine by 1976, however, our participant observers found little evidence of strategic resistance from izibonda. My own perusal of minutes of the monthly meetings of izibonda presided over by a white compound official at that time suggests that downward communication predominated at those meetings. By 1976, then, on Anglo American mines, the potential for izibonda organization of resistance (or even protest) seemed moribund, although their importance in keeping order in the rooms was acknowledged by all. The Anglo American Industrial Relations Department investigated the position of the isibonda in May 1976. They concluded as follows:

> Most respondents could not conceive of peace and order without the Isibonda. They regarded him as a guarantee for their personal security and the safety of their belongings in the room. They felt that without him men would want only to quarrel and fight and steal. They saw him as the symbol of law and order, without, however, the odium that often attaches to the office of a police constable. In this role he is indispensable. (1976:6)

In an extremely interesting chapter of his honors dissertation, Patrick Pearson (1975) argued for the genuinely democratic and representative nature of the isibonda system on Stilfontein Mine in 1975. Since Stilfontein Mine does not fall under control of the Anglo American group, this difference points up the unevenness of changes in compound structures during the 1970s. In earlier years there can be little doubt that the isibonda system was an important basis for worker representation.

By 1976, policy differences between the various mining houses seem to have been reflected in their compound organization. The Anglo American report on the isibonda, for instance, confirmed our findings for their mines:

> Isibondas are accused of tale-bearing. Some respondents held that once a dispute between parties had been settled in the room, it was not necessary for the Isibonda to mention it to the Tribal Representatives [compound police under their new name] or the induna, but some do still report, either to curry favour with the induna or Tribal Representatives or to ensure that one of the parties in the dispute is penalised, or just to denigrate his character. [One black official,] in making the case for the indispensability of the office of Isibonda, stated that they could not, so to speak "secure convictions" against some people brought before the induna but for the invaluable evidence which they obtained from Isibondas.

Small wonder, then, that the National Union of Mineworkers, when it started to organize on Anglo American mines in 1982, found little support from the izibonda, whom union representatives scornfully dismissed as "management stooges."

Changes on the Compounds after 1970

The "new workers" who arrived on the mines in increasing numbers after wages started to go up in 1973 were quite intolerant of the old moral economy. In their opinion, traditional indunas and their "police"—and even izibonda—had no legitimacy, their authority being dependent on white control. "The rules are made by those with power only," one of the new workers said in 1976. They rejected the informal imiteto of compound life, failing to appreciate the integrity of the old-timers. They also challenged the (always questionable) legality of the mine police system with its "arrests" and "*stokkies*" and fines meted out by the induna's courts and clerks in the compound manager's office.

In response to such challenges (and perhaps because top management in the Gold Division had had Zambian experience and thus knew other ways of running things), Anglo American in particular began to reform the entire compound system. The indunas were increasingly relatively educated men, appointed from outside rather than from the ranks of the mine "police." Training in industrial relations became standard for local mine officials, black and white alike. Many Anglo American compounds (now called "hostels") no longer ethnically segregated its workers but rather housed them by work team. Indunas were renamed "unit supervisors" and by the middle 1980s were set to administrating ethnically integrated blocks in the hostels rather than ethnic groupings as such. Compound policemen were renamed "tribal representatives."

The position of the compound manager (now renamed "hostel manager") also changed. Paternalistic compound authority rapidly became bureaucratic, with less discretion and more rules. The hostel manager became subject to the authority of a wider "personnel structure" in which he was a mere cipher. The crumbling of the old moral economy under the challenges of the "new workers" of the 1970s was thus exacerbated on Anglo American mines by rationalization of management controls. Increased consciousness of alienation on the job was accompanied in the compounds by apparent anomie and disintegration of the order established by the imiteto. The resulting collapse of the compound "police" apparatus led to the transformation of mine security forces, which on Anglo American mines had traditionally been concerned largely with guarding bullion and preventing illicit gold buying, into a full-scale private police force with a complete panoply of riot-control equipment.

The coming of the National Union of Mineworkers in the early 1980s, with its job- and wage-related demands, thus filled a moral as well as a power vacuum as it confronted rationalizing authority in the compounds. However, old compound structures and practices were not eliminated overnight, and old-style worker and local-level management strategists fought a last-ditch battle against union organizers within the new structures. This period of transition, which still continues today, has been chaotic. We shall return frequently in the chapters that follow to continuities and contestation on supposedly "rationalized" compounds—especially on Vaal Reefs No. 1 compound, where testimony to the Bregman Commission (AAC/VR) in 1987 provides detailed evidence.

A Case Study: Vaal Reefs No. 1

Case studies inevitably risk generalizing the particular. This one will be no exception. The Bregman Commission was a private commission called into being by Anglo American Corporation because of excessive collective violence at Vaal Reefs. It took uniquely detailed evidence from black workers, who were cross-examined by representatives of the mine, the National

Union of Mineworkers, and the governments of the Transkei and Lesotho, as well as by Commissioner Bregman himself.

Before the 1987 strike, of all the Anglo American mines, the local management at Vaal Reefs seems to have been the most reluctant to recognize and deal with the union (Crush 1989). While the Vaal Reefs case may thus not be fully representative of Anglo American mines, the situation there was probably closer to that of other mining houses like Anglo Vaal or Gencor. From our point of view, Vaal Reefs is then probably as representative a mine as one could find.

What is most striking about the Vaal Reefs case is the extent to which, despite rationalization of authority and collapse of the moral economy, the hostel manager, his black officials, and many of the black workers still operated according to the old rules of compound authority. The hostel manager at Vaal Reefs No. 1, Hendrik Maritz (not his real name), emerges as a particularly pathetic figure. According to Mlamli Botha, who was a prominent figure in the union:

> [The workers] take him as a manager who does not have a very good hand. . . . They actually gave him a nickname, a colloquial term, saying he is a "tsotsi." That means he is of a vacillating character.[6] . . . In the first place he has got to see to it that he maintains law and order amongst the inmates. . . . but at the same time he has got to be close enough to them and not stand aloof in order to know their needs and wants. . . . The hostel manager is supposed to be a man who can handle faction fighting situations and be able to prevent them, but in March 1986 he never did it. . . . In March a report was made to him but he took no action. In November again I made a report to him concerning disturbances in the hostel, but as manager he never took any definite action, though he is an overseer in the hostel. Yes. He is shepherd of a flock that he really has no interest in, in that rivers of blood have flowed in this hostel but he has taken no action. (AAC/VR:2629)

Botha compared this compound manager unfavorably with his predecessor:

> The previous hostel manager . . . we used to call . . . Mashukumisa. . . . Mashukumisa is the person who normally shakes things up, or a person who is alert [lit., of "fast action"]. . . . [Mashukumisa] had the interests of the inmates at heart. He was so concerned with their lot that he used to go to them and find out what

[6]Botha was actually being kind in translating *tsotsi* so. Tsotsis are South African urban gangsters, noted (and hated) by rural and other respectable folk for their brutal assaults on innocent citizens. To call a man "tsotsi" implies, at least, "sneakiness" and "unreliability" as well as "vacillation."

their needs were even if there were no problems. He would even instruct them and inform them on various other items that were relevant to their resident situation. And he was very popular with the inmates in that he understood the needs of the Black mine worker. I think, if I am not making a mistake, [Mashukumisa] was the hostel manager until 1982. (AAC/VR:2631–32)

The date is significant. In 1982 the National Union of Mineworkers was founded. Mlamli Botha, despite his commitment to the union, clearly expected the hostel manager to continue his patrimonial role, not noting that this was much complicated by the coming of the union and management rationalization going on at Vaal Reefs at the time.

While the hostel manager in 1986 was clearly a rather weak and devious individual, the structural pressures he experienced should not be ignored. In his own evidence, Maritz kept referring to the blueprint of formal authority on the mine. Asked to explain the role of the hostel manager in the event of collective violence, for instance, he responded:

> Mr. Chairman in an event like this we report to, according to our disciplinary procedure, a report has got to be made to my superiors, in which case Mr. Goosen was my superior at the time. . . . I presume he summoned the Security Officer or he reported that to the Security Officer, any unrest like that. And then the security take over. . . . Under circumstances like that I have no control because it has been taken over by the security forces. (AAC/VR:224)

His testimony became smoother when describing the formal authority structures on the mine:

> Mr. Chairman, I am in charge of Number One Hostel, being appointed by Mr. Dicks, the Mine Manager. Under my control I have two white Personnel Officers, [two Assistant Personnel Officers,] . . . seven Unit Supervisors, twenty-two Unit Prefects and then ordinary labourers. I am accountable to my Personnel Superintendent, Mr. Simpson, Mr. Simpson to the Personnel Manager, at this point in time Mr. Goosen, and Mr. Goosen to the Mine Manager, Mr. Dicks. (AAC/VR:266–67)

He seemed on the defensive when cross-examined about the responsibilities of his job, essentially disclaiming any part in the maintenance of order in his compound (AAC/VR:336): "I cannot protect the people, I can only rely on security, but it is impractical to protect people inside the hostel because we have got . . . I have got about in the region of plus/minus five thousand people and I cannot protect them, impossible." A traditional compound manager would have squirmed to hear such talk. Long gone was the notion of the hostel manager's finger on the pulse of compound life. Now he seemed more concerned to slough off his responsibilities, eager to admit his impotence.

Asked about his relationship to the union at the hostel, "Tsotsi" Maritz responded (AAC/VR:255–56) that it was "very good" but admitted at once that he did not even know the names of the shaft stewards. Asked which workers the union represented, and in relation to what aspect of work or compound life, he was able to say only: "All I can say is that we have a very good relationship with the Union work-wise. All I can say here is that in all aspects when we want something done then we speak to the Union and the [so-called] Union shaft stewards, . . . [who] always said that they represent the workers."

In fact, Maritz had earlier complained (AAC/VR:183–84) that the union shaft stewards had met with him only twice and then stayed away. According to him, the National Union of Mineworkers should have played a role in his compound similar to that of the Hostel Consultative Committee, a body of "very respectable people" (AAC/VR:327) appointed by his unit supervisors (erstwhile indunas), with essentially top-down authority:

> [The committee is there] to advise management, or in this particular case, to advise me on matters arising in the hostel, anything that goes wrong, we get their opinion, we get their co-operation, participating [with] management. . . . Anything that does not or is not right or that should be put right, comes to that meeting. From management's side we put certain things over to them, requests, over to this Consultative, as well as to the Union, meetings [matters?] which management feel . . . should receive their attention, should be rectified. (AAC/VR:185)

Given the arrogance of such a conception of "consultation," it is hardly surprising that the union shaft stewards failed to show up after a couple of meetings with their hostel manager at Vaal Reefs No. 1. Apparently, he made no effort to pursue the matter. He had blocked out certain times on his calendar, and if they chose not to appear, so be it. Commissioner Bregman asked Mlamli Botha why no "representations were made by the hostel dwellers or their representatives to higher management . . . that they were dissatisfied with [the compound manager's] performance" (AAC/VR:2632). Botha's reply was revealing of how completely the old moral economy had been eroded on Vaal Reefs by 1986—and how the union had not yet replaced it. "The hostel inmates," he said,

> have no other way of actually voicing their complaints in this way except that they have to be called to a meeting where they could

> air their views, and since they had never made a report before to higher management they would still have to go through the hostel manager. . . . [Furthermore] they never resorted to us shaft stewards. Well, I could only assume that possibly they thought if they were to come with a complaint about a manager possibly no action would be taken against that manager.

Given higher management's attitudes to the union on this mine, the workers were probably correct that a complaint from the shaft stewards at No. 1 hostel about their hostel manager would have been ignored by higher management.

The thought that the union could organize collective action on *hostel* matters seems not to have crossed Botha's mind. The official position of the union on hostels, after all, was simply that they were illegitimate and should be abolished. In practice the hostels became the sites of struggle over work issues, like favoritism toward team leaders or wage strikes, or wider national political issues, like Bantustan elections or boycotts and stay-aways. But, officially at least, the union on Vaal Reefs Eastern Division claimed little part in compound politics except insofar as they effected workplace issues. Unofficially, however, as we shall see, elected shaft stewards were perceived as a major threat by indunas, whose traditional base was being eroded by ethnically mixed rooming and whose discretionary power from management was now delimited by detailed job descriptions for their new roles as "unit supervisors."

When the commission examined the Xhosa sub-induna, he was asked the induna's duties. His response was simple (AAC/VR:2982): "To report all the incidents taking place in the hostel." Small wonder that one of the Transkeian government advisers to the Bregman Commission was able to say:

> There has been bandying of the term "sell-outs," "informers," etc. Now this has also been said, but not explicitly, that indunas were actually being used by management in order to syphon out information of the happenings within the hostel and take it up to management, so that management should know what is actually going on on a day to day basis. (AAC/VR:3528)

This description of the induna's job was also true for the old compound regime, of course, although it overlooked the extent to which because they were the compound manager's major source of information about compound goings-on, the indunas also gained substantial informal strategic power. At Vaal Reefs No. 1, the hostel manager did continue to meet regularly with his indunas and their "police," but they had become increasingly irrelevant to a substantial number of more proletarianized workers in the compound and would have given him biased opinions, especially concerning these "new workers," who were much more adequately represented by the union.

As a National Union of Mineworkers' shaft steward, Mlamli Botha's position on the induna system was explicit and to the point. "From my point of view," he said, "there is nothing that they do. Maybe they can tell their roles, but I see nothing" (AAC/VR:1324). The previous Xhosa induna, Machain, was quite respected, Botha said, because "he was close to us, because Machain, he was always amongst us discussing things with us, advising us, counselling us about the ways and means of life in the hostel, generally" (AAC/VR:1330). Now, however, the induna's authority had become completely derivative (AAC/VR:1325). People "have to give due respect to a management appointee" because they are "still . . . under the hostel manager in the hostel." But, for himself, said Botha: "Since I came here in 1975, there is nothing that I can pin-point and say this was solved by an induna."

Despite Botha's disdain, he did admit that certain functions currently undertaken by shaft stewards had been carried out by indunas before the coming of the union. Before 1984, with "the inception of the shaft stewards in the hostel," he told the commission, indunas "handled cases of the dwellers before [they were] . . . referred to the hostel manager" (AAC/VR:1323). The mine policeman, who had often acted as induna, amplified (AAC/VR:3517–26): "[The induna] investigates a case before he could refer it further. . . . The complainant has got the choice to choose the court where the case should be dealt with." Should the complainant choose the induna's court, he would be tried there according to "the law [umteto?] of the mine." If the indunas could not finish the case, only then was it referred to the white compound staff. The accused was given the option of bringing a representative to such hearings, and once the National Union of Mineworkers entered the picture he invariably brought a shaft steward. In fact, according to Mlamli Botha (AAC/VR:1323), since the coming of the union to Vaal Reefs in 1984, very few cases had been tried in the indunas' courts, so that the induna's traditional function was increasingly redundant. Indeed, on Vaal Reefs, a new formal arrangement for supervisors to deal with complaints came into being, and it applied to indunas as "unit supervisors" as well. Thus, at least technically, the induna has been placed on a par with all other supervisors on the mine (AAC/VR:3531–39). His discretionary authority has been removed. Whether either local management or hostel inmates recognize that limitation is an important point to consider.

Management has set up "consultative committees" to hear worker grievances. Workers on Vaal Reefs No. 1 complain, however, that such committees are merely management tools, with appointed not elected representatives, and with no mechanism for feedback. Black officials, and even senior white management representatives, agree that the communication system has broken down completely (AAC/VR:3563–93). Members of the consultative committees put forward personal grievances rather than worker concerns. Workers, whether or not they are formally union members, turn with their problems to the shaft stewards rather than members of the nonrepresentative consultative committees, whose personnel apparently differ little from those of the old induna system supplemented by management trusties.

At least on Vaal Reefs No. 1 in 1987, however formally diminished the authority of indunas was, they continued to have informal representative functions in relation to management. The retirement of the Sotho who was chief induna is a case in point. With his departure in March 1986, the Sotho at Vaal Reefs No. 1 were without formal representation at the induna level (AAC/VR:3735–40). In theory, according to the new formal structure, tribal representation should no longer have been necessary because blocks of rooms occupied by work teams would be represented by well-qualified and trained unit supervisors whose ethnic identity should have been irrelevant. In practice, "Tsotsi" Maritz still thought in terms of tribal indunas and apparently continued to meet with the unit supervisors on that basis. The new rational, "detribalized" management structures had no hope of working if those with authority chose to ignore them and operate according to the old "tribal" system. Furthermore, at least during the time of transition, workers confronted with a changed formal system that still operates informally under the old rules are caught in a catch-22. For instance, when asked what he and his fellow Sotho were doing about the fact that the security forces had disarmed the Sotho but not the Xhosa after "tribal violence" in November 1986 and January 1987, Matsepi Mokheti, a Mosotho underground worker, replied: "There is nothing we are doing, because we have not got any indunas" (AAC/VR:3828–29). Asked why they had not complained to management, he responded that "we reckon that before we take anything to management it must first of all start from our indunas." Did that mean that the Sotho still felt the need for an induna? he was asked. "Oh yes," Mokheti replied, "as long as the Xhosa still have indunas, we need one too."

As long as local management plays by the old rules, and there are workers like Mokheti who remember them, it makes sense for the local union leaders to try to do so as well. Take the case of Thabang, a Sotho shaft steward who left the mine after a faction fight in March 1986. A charismatic character, Thabang mobilized Sotho support around himself and the union, thereby threatening the already declining powers of the Sotho chief induna. As a Transkeian government representative argued before the Bregman Commission:

> People from any ethnic group would, in a work situation, automatically follow people who improve their own work conditions and their salary scales. . . . And this is what actually happened with Thabang because he was a shaft steward and he was a strong one too, trying to improve the lot of the mine workers, not only Sothos but even other ethnic groups at Number One Shaft. So now you will not deny the fact [he asked Mokheti] that he had some following of the people, including Sothos at Number One? (AAC/VR:3939–42)

Of course, Mokheti responded, "People are going to follow any man that does a good thing for them." The popularity of Thabang the shaft steward was thus well earned. The traditional authorities on Vaal Reefs No. 1 had reason to resent Thabang.

The Transkeian representative pursued his point with vigor. "Will you deny," he said, "that there were those followers of [the Sotho induna], who because of this tug-of-war between him and Thabang [the Sotho shaft steward] . . . decided to have a meeting . . . with the Pondos on the question of shaft stewards being flushed out of Number One?" The Transkeian representative had heard rumors of an effort by the traditionalist Sotho on the mine to recruit traditionalist Mpondo militants to drive the union out. Mokheti's response was typically careful but revealing: "I only know . . . I was told that some of the Sothos and Pondos wanted to . . . yes, I heard that there were some Sothos and Pondos who wanted to come together to fight the shaft stewards."

I describe in detail in chapter 7 and the conclusion the faction fights that followed. In this chapter, which has drawn generalizations about compound authority, I have tried to point up the enormous potential for the strategic practice of arbitrary power when hegemonic structures are changing rapidly. In the chaos of the 1970s, different groups of workers fought each other and demonstrated against management as they jockeyed for power in the new environment. Nor could local compound management resist getting involved.

Head office, with the advice of industrial relations experts, scrambled to rationalize control of the compounds and humanize local management despotism. Local management resisted, with the assistance of what remained of the old moral economy and the entrenched induna system. The coming of the union with head office approval brought solidarity to the "new workers" and truly effective challenges to local management. As a new order struggled to emerge, local union leaders working for representative worker democracy had to count the cost of confrontation and devise disciplined strategies that were effective in local disputes. At the grassroots level, union solidarity on workplace issues papered over ongoing systemic divisions among union members, but it did not annul them. This issue will arise again and again in the chapters that follow.

First, however, we must examine more closely the workings of the traditional order among workers and black compound authorities under the old compound regime. We shall then be better able to appreciate the problems in the transition to the new unionized order.

1. *Underground work.* A crew that obtained the world deep-level-mining record in 1958 at East Rand Proprietary Mines. That record has since been surpassed, but the pride and integrity of this top-notch team at the bottom of the mine are captured clearly in the photograph. Note that as late as 1958 on the ERPM only white miners had battery-operated lamps. Black workers had to make do with candles. (Barlow-Rand Archives)

2. *Underground work.* Hand hammer stoping in Crown Deep Mine (later Crown Mines) in the 1900s. A typical stoping team consisted of a white miner and twelve to fifteen black "hammer boys." The average black worker would drill 36–42 inches a day. Notice the timber support for the hanging in the foreground. (Barlow-Rand Archives)

3. *Underground work.* Jackhammer stoping on East Rand Proprietary Mines in 1938. Notice the black machine operator (usually called a "machine boy") at the back with the "spanner boy" in front to guide the drill and replace the jumpers as longer ones were needed. (Barlow-Rand Archives)

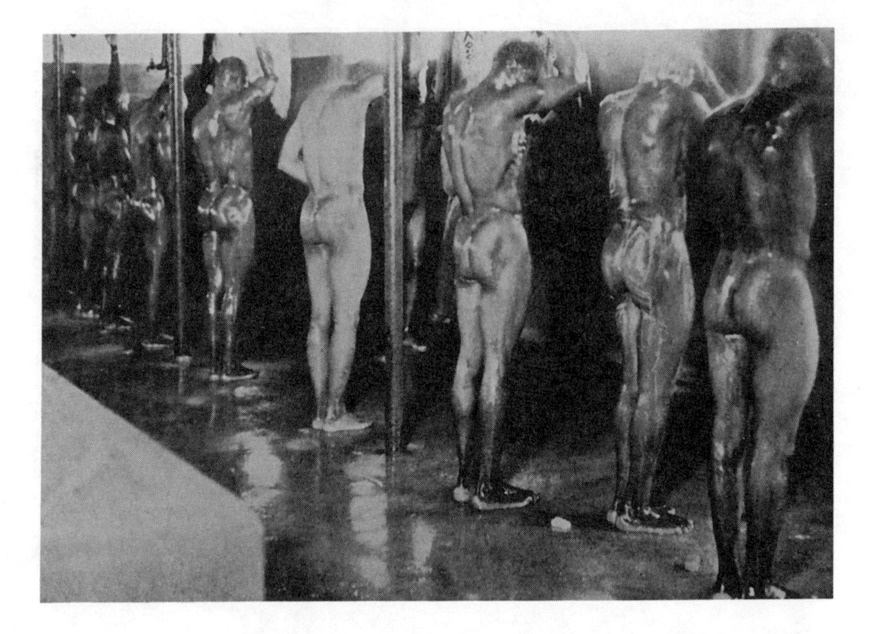

4. *Compound life.* A shower room at a Crown Mines compound in the 1930s. The toilets were set low to the ground about ten feet behind the standing men, making a vantage point from which more senior men seeking ''wives'' could survey their juniors. (Luli Callinicos, History Workshop Collection, University of the Witwatersrand)

5. *Compound life.* A Basotho compound room in the late 1940s or early 1950s. Notice the shoemaker on the left and, in an excellent example of how compound life obscured gender roles, the man knitting in the center. (Leon Levson, Mayibuye Centre, University of Western Cape)

6. *Compound life.* Miners mending clothes in a compound yard. A typical example of entrepreneurial activities after work. (Leon Levson, Mayibuye Centre, University of Western Cape)

7. *Compound life.* A typical scene on the East Rand during the 1930s or 1940s of workers walking alongside the mine dump and the ore-trolley tracks. Since the compound would have been near the hoisting mechanism in the far distance, the picture gives an idea of how free workers were to go to town or to visit friends on other mines. Notice how miners tended to move around the Rand in groups rather than singly. (Luli Callinicos, History Workshop Collection, University of the Witwatersrand)

8. *Life at home.* A rural homestead near Morija in Lesotho in the early 1950s. Notice the preponderance of women and the relatively scattered huts. This settlement was typical of recruitment areas for the mines before 1970. (Mayibuye Centre, University of Western Cape)

9. *(Opposite, above) Life at home.* A section of the Botshabelo resettlement area in 1981. This was a typical source of mine labor after the 1970s. The close settlement made agricultural activities impossible so that families became totally dependent on wages from migrant workers. Notice the vehicles used for transporting migrants to and from work. (Colin Murray)

10. *Unionization.* A National Union of Mineworkers rally in the 1980s. (*Weekly Mail*)

4 Sexualities

Variations on a Patriarchal Theme

Participant observers on Welkom Mine in 1976 reported that miners had three main preoccupations in the compound after work—drinking, the seduction of town women, and homosexual encounters. Each of these may be seen as a response to the two most important exigencies of migrant life—the pressures of work and separation from home. In 1976, participant observers and theological student informants alike saw miners' drunkenness, their womanizing, and their homosexuality as pathological examples of "release activity," outcomes of the horror of migrancy, although they also recognized the collective character of such conduct and the constraints of mine imiteto on its exercise (Moodie 1983:183–89).

To some extent perceptions of anomie by the participant observers were a product of their own ideological bent and the period of transition during the 1970s. In the next two chapters I hope to situate sexual practices and drinking activities both in the old integrities and in new exigencies. As the new miners of the 1970s forced changes in compound administration and brought different self-conceptions and new solidarities to mine life, so patterns and meanings of sexual activity and social drinking also changed. Their new life projects demanded new imiteto for sex and alcohol with new judgments of moral character brought to bear on old ways. The old integrities themselves also took on new meanings, even for some of the more traditional workers, especially after the coming of the National Union of Mineworkers in 1982.

The argument of this chapter is framed by Foucault's (1980) suggestion that the inclination to define the psychological character of individuals in terms of their sexual preferences is a recent phenomenon. I also follow Foucault in demonstrating the impossibility, at least in the case of black miners, of sensibly discussing sexuality outside the context of power relations, both power structures on the mines and the power of men in marriage.

I start with a descriptive analysis, a phenomenology, of male sexual experience on the mines. I deal first with miners' sexual relationships with "boys," known as "the wives of the mine," and then turn to relationships with women living on farms or in townships near the mines, known to the miners as "town women." The second part of the chapter picks up on the major systemic theme of the volume, arguing that for junior partners in the men-boy relationships (and to some extent even for senior men) homosexual relationships were used as resources in the long-standing resistance by migrant miners to proletarianization. Proletarianization, however, as it eventually came to the gold mines, has had sexual implications that have helped to reinforce the rejection of migrancy by contemporary black miners and their wives.

It is important to stress the tentative nature of the conclusions reached in this chapter. My discussion of "mine marriages" depends on material collected by Vivienne Ndatshe in a remarkable series of life histories from old men in Pondoland in 1982 (and several follow-up interviews of my own in 1988) in which they recounted events in the 1930s, 1940s, and 1950s, and an interview with a single Tsonga individual by British Sibuyi.[1] While rather scanty archival evidence confirms these accounts and thus enables us to generalize with some certainty, most such written material dates from an earlier period (1900–1920). A more recent article by Patrick Harries (1990), based on Shangaan material, supports and amplifies my conclusions. The material on town women dates from participant observational material collected by two female African research assistants in the Welkom area during the early 1980s and from life histories collected by Vivienne Ndatshe at Vaal Reefs Mine in 1990. Their work is supplemented by archival material and the recollections of old men in Pondoland and Lesotho.

Thus, while the account offered here conforms to the evidence available to me, it is presented as an initial foray into a complex and sensitive area. It might well be modified and amplified by further enquiry, especially by more intensive interviewing. Meanwhile, this chapter represents a tentative sociohistorical description of a delicate but often avoided aspect of the lives not only of black miners but also of all men and women everywhere, namely, the relationship of sexual desire and structural and personal power.

[1]I am grateful to Patrick Harries for making a transcript of the latter available to me.

Mine Marriages

In February 1987, in the Bushbuckridge area, British Sibuyi interviewed an old Tsonga-speaking Shangaan[2] man named Philemon, who had worked on the mines from the late 1940s to the early 1960s. This man discussed what he called *bakontshana,* or "boys" who were "wives on the mine":[3]

> On the mines there were compounds which consisted of houses, each of which had a *xibonda* [Tsonga for *isibonda*] inside. Each of these *xibonda* would propose a boy for himself, not only for the sake of washing his dishes, because in the evening the boy would have to go and join the *xibonda* on his bed. In that way he had become a wife. [The "husband"] would "double his join" [stay twelve months instead of the normal six] on the mines because of this boy. He would "make love" with him. The "husband" would penetrate his manhood between the boy's thighs. You would find a man buying a bicycle for his boy. He would buy him many pairs of trousers, shirts and many blankets.

In important particulars this story summarizes many other accounts mentioned in interviews with Mpondo mine workers and scattered through early archival records under the heading "unnatural vice." First, the sexual activity itself hardly ever involved anal penetration but took place externally through "the satisfaction of sexual passions by action between the thighs" (Taberer Report 1907, Chamber of Mines, 1899–1910, N series, N35[4]). Such sexual intercourse was typical of a form of sexual play, called *ukumetsha* among Xhosa-speakers, *hlobongo* by the Zulu, and *gangisa* in Southern Mozambique, common among traditional adolescent Nguni boys and girls. Second, these young men of the miners were not merely sexual partners but were also "wives" in other ways, providing domestic services for their "husbands" in exchange for remuneration.

Such homosexual activity on the mines seems to have taken place almost exclusively between senior men (men with power in the mine structure) and young boys. In fact an entire set of rules governed these relationships, whose parameters were well known and enforced by black compound authorities. Observers in 1976 reported that "those who are

[2]The shifting and crosscutting nature of ethnic categories is especially apparent in dealing with mine workers from Southern Mozambique. While many of them are Tsonga speaking, some are M'Chopi, and not all Tsonga speakers live in Mozambique, as the example of Philemon indicates. On the mines, the term "Shangaan" has tended to be used to describe Southern Mozambican and related South African peoples. I shall vary my usage depending on the context.

[3]Junod (1962:492) states that *inkontshane* is an Ngoni word meaning "girlfriend," that is, the junior partner in love affairs.

[4]I am indebted to Charles van Onselen for a copy of this document.

engaged in this business know each other, give advice to each other and help each other pay the . . . boys in due time and accordingly." It is the rule-bound nature of these relationships, their subjection to imiteto, and their integration into the nexus of homestead resistance to proletarianization that distinguishes "mine marriages" from similar arrangements in prisons worldwide.

"Men" and "Boys"

Among traditional Xhosa, *ukumetsha* is the most common form of erotic activity prior to marriage. According to the Mayer and Mayer (1970), it is fundamental to peer group socialization. Premarital sexual play is expected and indeed prescribed among young persons, but premarital pregnancy incurs disabilities in the adult world and "instant complete exclusion from the pleasures of the youth organisation." The expectation is that traditional young unmarried Nguni couples will practice that mode of external sexual activity that we find described by Philemon for mine marriages.

In 1907, H. M. Taberer, at that time in the Transvaal Native Affairs Department, investigated missionary charges of endemic "unnatural vice" in the compounds (in the wake of a furor about Chinese "catamites"). Significantly, these inquiries took place at the insistence of missionaries working on and around the compounds and not at the request of management, who turned a blind eye to such affairs. Taberer reported that *metsha* sexual practices were common among Mozambican mine workers, but that "actual sodomy [was] very rare and [was] generally looked upon with disgust," even by Mozambicans. In 1916 a compound manager told the Boksburg native inspector that he had recently seen heavily scented young Mozambicans at a dance "wearing imitation breasts" (NLB 229, 583/15/145, 16/2/16). He noticed that they had greased themselves heavily in the crotch and asserted "that a great deal of what goes on is *hlobongo* [Zulu for *ukumetsha*] and not the other." According to Patrick Harries (1990:329), his Tsonga informants emphasized the exaggerated masculinity of the senior partners in such relationships and the femininity of their "wives":

> Gender roles were often advertised at parties where men drank heavily, swore and engaged in bouts of horseplay, bravado and generosity while singing explicitly erotic songs celebrating their sexual dominance over boys and women. The young men displayed markers of femininity at these parties by wearing imitation breasts fashioned from wood and cloth, strong perfumes, skirts, and tight jackets. They further masked their masculinity by wear-

ing head-scarves and using creams that hid their need to shave. The female role of the *nkhontxana* was reinforced by their sexually suggestive dancing.

When in 1928 the Transkeian Territories General Council moved that a delegation of senior councillors be sent to the Witwatersrand compounds to lecture Xhosa mine workers on the evils of "immoral practices obtaining among labourers working on the mines" (NLB 374, 110/28/110, TTGC 1928 Session, 4/5/28), the delegation was informed by the director of native labour, H. S. Cooke, that the immorality that did occur involved taking an *inkotshane* (*nkhontxana*). He continued that "except that the subject was a male and not a female [the sexual practice] took the form of what is known amongst Transkeian Natives as *ukemetsha* which, when girls were concerned, was to some extent condoned by Native Custom" (NTS 2091, 213/280, 30/11/28).

Ukumetsha was consistently condemned by Christian missionaries, however, and among the urban African elite its extension to men was quite repugnant. For instance, when one of the commissioners on the Native Economic Commission asked A. W. G. Champion "whether this bad practice amounts to *hlobongo* between man and man," he was answered in the affirmative (NEC:8241). However, when the questioner implied that it was thus not sodomy in the European sense, Champion was indignant, saying, "I do not know what is used among Europeans; all I know is that this thing is very low among the natives—it is unspeakable."

One old Mpondo was nonetheless quite open with Vivienne Ndatshe about his affairs on the mines: "There were boss boys who liked boys. I did that once myself. There were boys who looked like women—fat and attractive. My 'girlfriend' was a Sotho young lad. I did not ill treat him as other boss boys did. I was very nice to him." He smiled while talking to Ms. Ndatshe about this matter and asked her not to tell others at his home. She promised not to and asked him why he got involved with the boy. He replied:

> First, miners were not allowed to go and visit women in the township.[5] Also I felt very lonely for all the long period without meeting a woman. Because of boredom I needed someone to be with

[5]Many workers mentioned this fact, although several of them later described relationships with town women in their interviews. Apparently, management discouraged forays into town but could not legally forbid them. As a result, novices tended to obey the instructions given them at initial orientation sessions as imiteto whereas more experienced men were liable to ignore them. Also, since prospective senior partners conducted the orientation sessions for new recruits, it was in their interest to play up the dangers of visits to women in town.

> me. I was not doing that in public—not in the room but in the old section underground where people no longer worked. I proposed love to him in the compound—called on him in our spare time. I did promise to give him some of my pay, but not all of it as others did. Then he agreed. I warned him that everything was our secret because I did not want my home friends to know that I was doing that as they might tell people at home or girlfriends in the country. I loved that boy very much.

Ms. Ndatshe asked about the feelings of the Sotho youngster when they slept together. The response was revealing about the expectations of "men": "He had quick feelings, but he had to control himself as he was my girlfriend."

Although these relationships for the Mpondo seldom extended beyond one contract and were never brought home ("it was only friendship on the mines"), and although Mpondo men preferred to conceal these liaisons from their home fellows, everyone knew that such affairs existed and joked with each other about them. Young men en route to the mines from Lesotho in 1976 were told jokingly that they would become "girlfriends of the Shangaans." According to Ms. Ndatshe, old men, long since retired from the mines, sit around at their "beer drinks" in Pondoland and talk of men who wanted to make love to them. They laugh because they know that "among us there were those who practiced it." One man, when asked whether such homosexual relationships hampered a man's prospects as a lover of women back home, smiled quietly and said, "No, it actually helps because you understand the woman's point of view. You learn to be more gentle."

According to Philemon, among Shangaans "mine marriages" were accepted, indeed taken for granted by women (including wives) and elders at home, and relationships might extend beyond a single contract ("when the time to go back arrived, one partner would inform the other through a letter so that they could [meet] at a stipulated place . . . on the mines"). As early as the turn of the century, Junod (1962) wrote of the Tsonga: "The immense majority of the Natives themselves do not consider this sin as of any importance at all. They speak of it with laughter."

At home in Pondoland, however, people did not openly admit to it, "because it was a disgrace." According to Philip Mayer (1978:116–26), the same ambivalence prevailed among the traditional Xhosa about extramarital affairs with married women at home. Everyone knew it went on but expected the parties to be discreet about it (Monica Hunter [1936:203–10] makes the same point for the Mpondo). Even among the Tsonga, said Philemon, "the elders would not talk about it because it was taboo. It's just like now, son. If you had a wife, surely you would not tell me what you do with your wife behind doors?"

Testimony is divided over how widely these affairs were public knowledge on the mines themselves. One reason that pinning down what was known is difficult is that young men were expected to serve their elders anyway and many did so without sexual exchanges. There were reports from time to time, however, of dance parties involving sexual inversion, especially, but not only, among the Mozambicans. Ethnic differences were apparently manifested in regard to public display, with mine marriages much more publicly acknowledged in Shangaan quarters. People chose not to interfere in such matters. In 1976, an induna explained:

> What is public knowledge is that it goes on. Otherwise, the culprits keep it scrupulously discreet. One does notice unnatural closeness and attentiveness, for example, one may walk into an otherwise empty room and discover a couple talking in undertones. I know this, myself. What I do is discreetly withdraw. It comes out into the open . . . when disaffection sets in. But we all know it takes place.

For all this induna's implication of wrongdoing, in fact the indunas' courts enforced the monetary aspects of such agreements. A code of behavior informally governed mine marriages, and, despite the varying intensity of management opposition to these relationships in different periods, the code and its enforcement seems to have changed little before the 1980s, although by then the practice was restricted to narrowing traditional circles.

In 1976, certain rooms specialized in these relationships. One of the Sotho-speaking participant observers found himself in such a room, where all but two of the inmates slept in pairs (one of the other two slept out), and they spoke of fellow miners as they would have of women. There was much talk of "marriage" in the room, and when they got drunk men kissed each other openly. They were quite discreet outside the room, however. Even within the room, Philemon reported, "People would not make love when others were still conversing in the evening—they would wait for everybody to 'sleep.' "

Mine marriage implied more than casual sex underground or in the rooms. These relationships were supposed to be exclusive, and hence "men" might sometimes fight over attractive young men. For instance, a certain Mpondo, when he was senior enough, wanted to have his own "boy." He made an arrangement at Luipaardsvlei, where he was a boss boy: "I had a young Xhosa boy from Ciskei. I was paying him, but not all my money, without knowing that he had another man. I was nearly stabbed by the man." Another Mpondo said that as a "boy" he was not able to get a woman in town "because [his] man was very jealous." Typically, when sexual infidelity by a "boy" took place, the older initiating partner would be blamed and often assaulted, not the "wife."

The older men paid their "wives" generously for their services, which often went well beyond the merely sexual, and included food preparation, fetching and carrying and other domestic chores, and companionship. According to Taberer's report (1907:2): "An *inkotshane*'s duty appears to be to fetch water, cook food and do any odd work or run messages for his master and at night time to be available as bedfellow. In return for these services the *nkhontxana* is well fed and paid, presents and luxuries are lavished upon him." According to Philemon, the Tsonga informant, young men were paid generously in kind; however, the Mpondo reported payments in cash.

Philemon explained how mine marriages were built into the everyday social lives of Shangaan compound dwellers. On the weekends, for instance,

> people from different houses would bring money together and then buy things like tea and bread (which were considered to be luxuries) and eat together. "Husbands" would bring along their wives. Also, when somebody was leaving the mines forever, farewell parties would be made where workers from different houses would come together. . . . The boys would make the tea when the "husbands" were seated around the tables.

As part of their normal duties, boys "would wash and iron their husbands' clothes and pack everything neatly. They did not wait to be told because it was their job." Philemon, who at the time of his interview still worked as a migrant but had a room in town, was mildly nostalgic for the advantages of mine marriage. On the one hand, he said, "It was just for the sake of 'satisfying' one because really, what pleasure? I mean . . . it was just as good as making love to oneself. But anyway, one would get the psychological relief because I mean . . . [being alone] was bad." On the other hand, his present arrangements left much to be desired:

> It's just [that] now a man can rather starve himself to death as long as his woman has all the things that she wants in the world. But I mean it was better [then] because the boy would look after your things, wash your clothes, and so on. It [was] unlike now, [because now] you spend all your money buying clothes and giving money to your wife with whom you are not even staying. That's somehow a loss of money. I mean, she does not even wash your vest, while with those it was better because evenings were for "legs."

Shangaan mine "wives" took on the attitudes and behaviors of women in their relations with their "spouses": "The boy [would] tell his 'hubby' if ever he was going away, say, home or to the shops, . . . and, if the 'hubby' had time, he would also come along." Furthermore, "he would not just stand up and say it. He had to say goodbye or any other thing . . . in a kneeling position." The boys would "gossip, just like women, . . . perhaps discussing things like 'my husband bought me this' or 'my husband is good for this and that.' And if a husband was stingy he would also come under discussion."

"Wives" were also expected to "look feminine," according to Philemon.

> They would get pieces of [cloth] and they would sew [them] together so that [they looked] like real breasts. They would then attach . . . strings that made it look almost like a bra so that at the evening dancing "she" would dance with the "husband." I mean it would appear very real. Don't forget that guys used to play guitars there. . . . [Another] thing that a *nkonkana* [nkhontxana] had to do was either cover his beard with [cloth] or cut it completely off. He was now so-and-so's wife. How would it [be] if a "couple" looked identical! There had to be differences and for a *nkonkana* to stay clean shaven was one of them. Once the *nkonkana* became a "grown-up" he could then keep his beard to indicate his maturity, which would be demonstrated by his acquiring a boy.

In their sexual relations, too, the young men were expected to behave with womanly decorum. You will recall the comment made by the Mpondo about his Sotho "wife" when asked about his partner's feelings: "He had to control himself because he was my girlfriend." The Tsonga informant expanded such hints, saying, "Don't forget, the boy would never make a mistake of 'breathing out' into the 'hubby.' It was taboo. Only the 'hubby' could 'breathe out' into the boy's legs."

The implication is inescapable. Proper "wifely" sexual behavior was essentially passive, at least receptive rather than intrusive. Boys might "wish they were so-and-so's wife . . . for the sake of security, for the acquisition of property, . . . and for the fun itself," but they were certainly subordinate, both socially and sexually. Although the relationships might end in "divorce" after a quarrel or upon returning home, there was also a "natural" point at which they could be terminated. As a boy became "old enough," he might "wish to start his own family" on the mine, becoming the senior partner. Nor could his partner refuse him that right, according to the Shangaan custom:

> When the boy thought he was old enough, he would tell the "husband" that he also wished to get himself a "wife" and that would

> be the end. Therefore the "husband" would have to get himself another boy. . . . As long as you [were] old enough there would be no problem. I mean that was the way of life. You would just have to explain that you [were] experiencing some biological problems at night. (It was not possible for the boy to penetrate the *sibonda*, only the *sibonda* could.) You would then have to wait for newcomers where you could choose. After choosing you would just show him which bed was yours.

There was thus a "biological" period (apparently occurring sometime in his middle twenties, but also based on the extent of his mine experience) when a "boy" would become a man, unable to endure any longer his nonejaculatory sexual role. That would be the end of it for the "marriage." Thus men who were sexually active with senior men in their youth themselves took "boys" when they became boss boys. If the dominant mores of white society decreed that all black men, even senior mine supervisors were "boys," black workers themselves graduated from being "boys" for their fellow workers to being "men" with their own "boys" as they gained mine experience. In fact, the entire system of mine marriages was thoroughly interwoven with the power structure of the mines.

The Rules of Mine Marriage (Umteto ka sokisi)

Giving evidence before the Native Economic Commission, H. S. Cooke stated that the "evil" at the root of migrant labor was "the natural tendency of the male animal to give expression to his desires" (NEC:229). The problem with that statement is not with the conclusion that men in certain types of patriarchal society will seek sexual release and sexual domination but with the assumption that this tendency is a universal, natural, and irresistible biological given rather than a social construction and that all biological males are "men." That "men" are considered "men" in all sexual encounters entirely overlooks the incidence and organization of sexual relationships between black miners. These relationships are much more a prerogative of those with power than universal gender-linked outcomes of "natural necessity." As we have seen, young men at the height of what we believe is their biological sexual development were the objects rather than the subjects of sexual activity.

Of course, our own understandings of sexual "biology" may themselves be social constructions. I make no effort here to address the issues of whether or not there are "real" differences across cultures in the biological stages of sexual development or the biology of sexual preference. If differences in sexual development do "exist," they function much like "temperament" in the thought of Margaret Mead (1935) in that they may be overridden by cultural forces or situational factors. How else can we explain the cultural variability discussed in this chapter?

The parallels with social formations at home are striking. Bantu-speaking communities are not only patriarchal but also gerontocratic, organized on principles of seniority. Without respect for elders the entire political and moral economy of traditional Bantu-speaking societies would unravel. In the words of Mayer and Mayer, "Respect for seniority is essentially the same as respect for law as against mere force" (1980:16).

Principles of seniority on the mines coincided to a considerable extent with age and status in the home societies, and they governed definitions of masculinity and sexual relations in both locales. Junod notes how such affairs were part of the compound authority structure:

> When a gang of new workers arrives in a Compound, the Native induna, who has the supervision of the Compound, and the Native policemen, who have their rooms at the entrance of the yard, come and *humutsha*, i.e., make proposals to the younger ones, not only to little boys (there are only a few of these) but also to boys up to the age of twenty or more. If these lads consent to become their *bakontshana*, they will be treated with greater kindness than the others. Their husbands will give them ten shillings to woo them (*buta*) and will choose them easy occupations. (1962:292–93)

Furthermore, Junod suggests that where the authority structure of the compound stops, the indigenous seniority principle takes over. Those who have not been propositioned by the mine police "will probably receive a similar proposal from their older companions in the mine," who will then aid them at work.

The Taberer Report (1907; see also Harries 1990) confirms the Mozambican origins of "mine marriage" and its patriarchal character:

> It appears to have become a well recognised custom among the mine natives recruited from the East Coast to select from the youths and younger men what are termed *amankotshane* or *izinkotshane*.[6] An *inkotshane* may be described as a fag and is utilized for satisfying the passions. Any objections on the part of the youth to becoming an *inkotshane* are apparently without very much difficulty overcome by lavishing money and presents upon him. In some cases force and bullying are doubtless resorted to, but such extreme measures would appear to be the privilege of Native guards whose positions enable them to impose upon the

[6]Taberer, who was fluent in Xhosa, is here using an Nguni, rather than a Tsonga, form of "nkhontxana."

> young recruits with a minimum of risk of being reported to any European authority.

Philemon, reflecting on Shangaan practices in the 1950s, pushed the status hierarchy on the compound back to its most basic level, and insisted that only the izibonda could formally enter into mine marriages:

> Except the *swibonda*, others who worked there would do it without the *swibonda*'s knowledge because [otherwise] they would quarrel with the *xibonda*, even if it was not the *xibonda*'s boy, . . . because once you have a boy for yourself, it means that you expect the others to respect you as well. You put yourself on the same level with the *swibonda*.

Among Shangaans, then, the practice of mine marriage was firmly entrenched in the compound authority structure as opposed to workplace authority. Transgressions against the rules governing such relationships were dealt with in the indunas' courts. Philemon remembered that

> when a boy decided to fall in love with another man, especially in the same [room], there would be a fight, which [would] most likely be taken to the seniors, the indunas, who would fine the culprit by making him collect fire coal for, say, two months either for breach of contract or for "undermining" so-and-so's "husband." Even the indunas had their own boys. That was a known fact. In most cases the indunas were the first to choose "the best" from newcomers.

For other language groups on the mines, although indunas would certainly hear cases connected with transgressions of what all called *umteto ka sokisi* (the rules of mine marriage),[7] the black authority structure underground seems to have been more important in the establishment of sociosexual practices. Testimony is universal for all periods that black team leaders (ironically, the boss "boys" in the past) would come down especially hard on youngsters whom they fancied, letting up only when the young men succumbed to them. An old Mpondo described the situation in his youth as follows:

> On the first week I nearly ran away. It was very difficult to layisha [load] and the boss boy was really pushing me and told me, "You will agree." At first I didn't understand what he was talking about, and I asked another old man why the boss boy was so cruel to me. The old man laughed at me. He told me that the boss boy was after me as I was young and fat.

[7]For a tentative discussion of the origins of this name, see van Onselen 1982a:179–89.

Since the mine compounds were "ethnically" segregated but work teams were always integrated, cross-ethnic sexual relationships would have been initiated on the work sites. Because "homosexual" patterns were less well established among groups other than the Mozambicans (who contracted for much longer stints on the mines than any other group and thus were more likely to become boss boys), Mozambican boss boys apparently sought out partners from other ethnic groups. Boss boys with authority in the work situation, and the power to coerce, no doubt initially spearheaded the spread of mine marriages across ethnic lines. Eventually, the rights and privileges of the Mozambican boss boys were extended to other ethnic groups.

The element of coercion was less pronounced among Shangaans, whose young men seem to have been prepared for "marriage" even before arrival on the mine. Nonetheless, there is a certain ambivalence even in Philemon's account:

> It was a bit tough then. I mean that was not normal life. A newcomer was oriented into the mines in the most inhuman way. But I can only say that now because I am . . . looking at it in retrospect. . . . At first newcomers might have disliked it, but then they would internalize it. It was a way of life on the mines. . . . By the time a new worker arrived on the mines he had already been informed about what was going on there. He would then internalize it—accept it as a way of life and even derive a sense of security from it because he knew he wouldn't have to struggle about acquiring property—trousers, etcetera.

Initiation into mine marriages must have been considerably more traumatic for youths from other groups, especially in the earlier years. Few cases of "homosexual" assault ever found their way into the archives, but one that did (NLB 229, 583/15/145) leaves us with a sense of the importance of seniority and authority in the relationships among the workers. In August 1919, when a Sotho youngster named Moketi arrived at Brakpan Mines for his first contract, he was assigned to his own room, number forty-one, by Albert Mama, the mine policeman in charge of the Sotho section and the son of a chief from Mohales Hoek. Mama soon made his intentions clear. In a statement he made later, Moketi said:

> After I had been in the room about three or four days, native Mama, who had been speaking to me, commenced his actions on the fourth day. This native in his conversation asked me to be his wife. On the fourth day he came and slept with me under the same blanket. I allowed him to have carnal relations with me, because I was afraid of him, being a Chief, and [he] may do me some

> harm. We slept face to face and he placed his penis between my legs and emitted semen. He only did this once during the night. I reported this occurrence the next morning to two friends of mine of the same tribe, who reside in room number 34. . . . I did not shew them any marks of semen as I had wiped it off on my blanket. . . . From this time I continued to sleep with Chief Mama and almost every night he assaulted me in the same manner. He always acted in the same way and never attempted to commit sodomy.

About a month of such sexual activity was all that Moketi would bear, and he left his room, moving in with his friends in thirty-four. A group of Mama's followers came to fetch him back. "I went with them," said Moketi, "because I was afraid as they beat me with sticks." Mama was not among his abductors, however, and although Mama's gang returned to room thirty-four for Moketi's blanket, Mama and Moketi did not sleep together again. Instead, the next day Moketi and his incensed friends approached the compound manager. Mama was promptly dismissed from the mine with a month's salary in lieu of notice, although, in the words of the local native inspector, "the evidence [was] insufficient to warrant prosecution."

The parallels between the initiation into mine marriages and certain types of marriages at home, at least among some Nguni peoples, are too striking to leave unnoted. Philip Mayer (1978:27–31) reports that among traditional Bomvana and Gcaleka Xhosa-speakers, the majority of marriages are *thwala* marriages, or organized abductions.[8] Without consulting the woman or sometimes even her mother, the father arranges with the people of her prospective husband to have her forcibly abducted, taken to the new groom's homestead, held without meeting him until the initial *lobola* (bridewealth) payment is made, and then presented to him for sexual congress. These women have engaged in several years of *metsha* sex play with boyfriends, but they can hardly be expected to be in love with their husbands, no matter how much the latter may desire them. They ultimately submit as to "a fact of life": "Even if she is practically raped

[8]See also Hunter 1936:186–90, 531, who reports that in Pondoland thwala marriages were arranged with the woman's consent. Both Sean Redding and Malusi Mpumlwana have pointed out to me that the latter pattern may be more typical in the Transkei also, although Mpumlwana knows from personal experience of cases similar to those described by Mayer, and thwala marriages were mentioned in a majority of the older Mpondo and other Xhosa-speaking women's life histories collected by Vivienne Ndatshe at Vaal Reefs in 1990. Several older Xhosa-speaking women interviewed for Meredith Aldrich's (1989) study of intimate relationships gave graphic accounts of the trauma of their thwala marriages.

by her husband, the 'bride' gets up the next morning and prepares tea for his father as a sign of acquiescence. Women say they have to accept the situation and learn to love their husbands. They do not always find it easy" (Mayer 1978:28). The new wife does have an alternative. If she is desperate enough, she may fight back and run away to her own home to persuade her father to call the "marriage" off.

Even as women who have been through thwala may comfort themselves with the reflection that their husbands are good to them and send money regularly so that they can build up the homestead, so also the young men who agreed to be "wives of the mine" could say they did so for the money or the gifts, adding wryly "why should we worry since we cannot get pregnant." The difference, of course, is that many women finally resign themselves to their thwala marriages only after they have given birth to children.

Another sexual practice that paralleled rural custom was mentioned by some of the ex-miners in Pondoland. They spoke of established ukumetsha relationships in which parents would give their daughter a separate hut in which to metsha with her lover. In exchange the young man made protobridewealth payments, smaller than lobola, which ensured exclusive formal access to her sexual services but did not oblige him to marry her. This practice too might have provided a model for mine marriages, although such metsha arrangements were never referred to as "marriage" nor were the partners called "husband" or "wife."

One Mpondo man told Vivienne Ndatshe that when he started at Daggafontein Mine in 1940, his "boss boy, who was a Xhosa, treated him very nicely because he was in love with him." The boss boy offered him all his wages. He agreed because "he was on business" at the mine and "needed money desperately as he wanted to buy cattle and pay lobola for his wife and build his umzi." Some boys reportedly had two or three lovers, "which was very dangerous because these men might kill one another." They took chances because "they only did that for money."

So men became "wives" on the mines in order to become husbands and therefore real "men" more rapidly at home. Mine marriages were thus a part of the integrity brought forth by migrant cultures. Even as in thwala marriages among the Xhosa, attraction was necessarily on only one side in the beginning, although in both cases mutual affection might grow. Harries's Tsonga-speaking informants still recalled "the loving and deep ties that a husband often developed for his mine wife" (1990:330). Certainly, in both thwala and mine marriages, at least among the Mpondo, the junior partner bore the initial indignity partly out of necessity and partly out of interest in "building an umzi"—the true aspiration of every traditionalist Xhosa-speaker. Being a "wife" on the mine, for all its apparent gender reversals, eventually reinforced the potential for male hegemony at home. Indeed, Harries (1990:327–32) suggests that, for Mozambican workers, who worked long contracts on the mines, mine marriage constituted an important aspect of a young boy's passage to full masculinity.

Senior partners in mine marriages were presumably well established at home by the time they undertook the responsibility of having a "boy" of their own—or they were *amatshipa,* men who had abandoned country ways and become creatures of the mines and townships. At any rate, becoming a "husband" on the mines was one of the accoutrements of seniority in the mine system, a perquisite of success in the mine world, making somewhat more comfortable the hardships of the migrant life. Certainly, that was the view of the Shangaans—and also of most Mpondo, although it was by no means universal. Several Mpondo men interviewed by Vivienne Ndatshe stated that being on the mines was like going herding or fighting. One simply abstained while away from one's girlfriend or wife, which implied that sexual activity was "natural" in certain situations and abstention was "natural" in others.

It is important to stress, however, that "mine marriages" and abstention were not the only sexual options for black miners. As we have seen, compounds on the gold mines were never closed, so men who wished to leave on afternoons or weekends to shop or visit friends could always do so with a simple "permission slip" from a clerk at the gate. Another important reason for leaving the mine was to visit women in town. Miners often entered into fairly long-term liaisons with town women, who served them alcohol and provided sexual services in exchange for gifts, monetary or otherwise. One old Mpondo who had been a mine "wife" in his early years reported:

> I had an induna as my best friend who took me to the township. Again I had a boy, and the induna had one too. In the township we both had girlfriends. We left the boys in the compound when we went to town, but we never spent the night in the township. We just spent a few hours with our girlfriends and then returned to our boys. We loved them better.

It is important to remember that this man, when Ms. Ndatshe interviewed him in 1982, was married and living in an umzi in the country with his wife and family. Why did he prefer "boys" during his earlier years on the mines? That being so, why did he seek a town girlfriend at all? What did he mean when he said that they "loved their boys better"?

On the basis of the statements of other migrants, some of the answers seem to lie in a deep-seated and ambivalent fear of town women. Part of this was the simple and quite legitimate apprehension of being robbed. Several of the old men with town lovers asserted that they dared not go to sleep with them lest their pockets be picked. Others feared venereal disease. A deeper fear than any of these, I believe, was that of losing one's rural identity. The attractions of town women might seduce one into forgetting one's home, absconding, becoming amatshipa, or in Sesotho, *lekholoa,* "the one who stays a long time on the mines." In a society where rural marriage established an economic base for retirement the dangers of becoming amatshipa were the subject of many a cautionary tale. "Mine wives," after all, would always eventually "grow up" and become men, so that mine marriage had a natural limit, a "biological" terminus, as it were. Furthermore, town women might end up having children by the man, imposing on him all the responsibilities implied in African society by that fact.

Also important was the stability of mine marriage—its integration into a well-ordered system. Part of the attraction of arrangements with "boys" was surely their reliability, their assuredness, as opposed to the heady but risky attractions of town women who might seduce one away from umzi-building at home. The "wives of the mine" were on hand with their services on an everyday basis, important in a society where older men have a basic right to the services and benefits of domesticity. That senior men on the mines would return to their "boys" because they "loved them better" is thus understandable. Such "love" might become a permanent preference. There is evidence that in the long term "some men preferred boys." Next to alcohol and town women, informants in 1976 listed "homosexuality" as a major reason for men to abscond from home, abandoning wife and umzi for the urban scene. Such men either became fixtures on the mines, often puppets of mine management, or they left the mines for urban employment or to join urban criminal gangs.[9]

What of the white mine administration? How did whites view the *umteto ka sokisi?* The Tsonga-speaking informant, Philemon, reported that white miners themselves practiced ukumetsha with their *picannins* (black underground personal aides). Whether or not this was typical, the white compound staff certainly knew of mine marriages and turned a blind eye to them. Philemon was clear on that: "On all the mines it was the Law of

[9]For a graphic account of such urban gangs with a strong "homosexual" component in the early years on the Rand, see van Onselen 1982a, ch. 4; William Beinart's (1987) biographical essay on "M" touches on both mine and gang "homosexuality" during the 1930s as does a recent paper by Keith Breckenridge (1990).

Sokisi. The whole bureaucracy on the mines knew about it, and they did not oppose it anyway. . . . They helped to solve problems pertaining to it, especially the Compound Managers."

Although gold mine compounds were never closed, several Mpondo informants reported that on arrival at a mine new recruits would be told by the mine authorities, white officials as well as blacks, to stay away from town because of the danger of assaults and above all to avoid town women. "There are 'women' on the mine," they were informed. Because workers who drank in town on weekends might be good for little work on Mondays, it was in management's interest to keep them away from women and the alcohol they supplied. Besides securing steady productivity, management's condoning of mine marriages had an additional motivation as well. It helped assure the co-optation of black supervisors into their hegemonic roles on the mines.

Sex of the mine-marriage type did then serve the interests of the industry, as Charles van Onselen (1980:174–82) claims for other types of sexuality on the Rhodesian mines. Patrick Harries (1990:332) suggests that "by spending large amounts of money on their *nkhontxana,* the most experienced and skilled workers on the mines were obliged to renew their contracts, for it was unthinkable to return home empty-handed." What he overlooks, however, is that town women were even more expensive.

Compound managers had other reasons to tolerate the practice, for the moral economy ruled in this matter too. In 1916, a native inspector who suggested measures to stamp out "unnatural vice" cautioned that compound managers would be reluctant to enforce them for fear of wildcat strikes led by irate boss boys and black surface authorities (NLB 229, 585/15/145, 16/2/16). A report survives of at least one strike of the sort that he had predicted. On 20 October 1941, the South African police at Boksburg (NTS 7675, 102/332, 20/10/41) were called in to quiet a compound demonstration led by boss boys on East Geduld Gold Mine. Apparently, the Sotho compound police had brought to the attention of the compound manager the dances held by the Sotho:

> The Basutos are in the habit of holding dances in the compound during the night and . . . at these dances the young natives are dressed as women and squeezing and kissing are resorted to. Such dances are foreign to native custom and the compound manager warned the Basutos that these dances must stop. However, the dances were continued and twelve of the ringleaders and organizers of these dances were dismissed and sent to Johannesburg. They all admitted that they continued the dances and disobeyed the instructions of the compound manager. When the shift came up

> from underground in the afternoon, they heard of the dismissal of the twelve men. They then gathered and demanded their return else the compound manager and all the Basuto police boys must leave. They became rowdy and would not listen to anything the compound manager said.

Notice the solidarity of workers on behalf of the *umteto ka sokisi.* Note also that among the Sotho the support was from underground rather than from the black surface authorities. This fact confirms our account of the means by which mine marriages were spread among non-Shangaan groups. It is difficult to imagine Shangaan compound police objecting to dances involving mine "wives." Indeed, this report is the only one in the archives among 120 on disturbances from the 1940s.

Generally, "mine marriages" buttressed the self-esteem of black authority figures and afforded considerable personal comfort to both parties. Harries (1990) suggests that "the individualism experienced by men on the mines allowed them to fall in love to an extent that was rare at home, where the function of marriage was social and political rather than affective." In any event, mine marriages were rarely if ever challenged collectively and openly by blacks and seldom proscribed by the white authorities.

Young Men Who Refused

The Tsonga informant, Philemon, firmly believed that it was impossible to refuse. "There was no other way," he said. "One could hardly escape it. If somebody wanted you, he would hardly give up. I mean, he would go so far as sending people to come and propose to you on his behalf—until you agreed." And if all else failed, he would use witchcraft. Of course, unlike women and Shangaan youngsters, young men from other groups had not been socialized to the experience of subordinate sexual relations on their passage to manhood. As a result, many of them refused to participate in mine marriages. Approaches underground would also probably have been easier to fob off than those initiated in the domestic quarters. For a reluctant young man underground there seem to have been several ways of avoiding even the most ardent boss boy without being worked to the point of collapse. The first method of avoidance was simply to fight back; the second, to request transfer to another work section. One Mpondo informant used both those options:

> [I was working as a timber boy] when the boss boy sent me on the first day to *madala* side, the old part of the mine where nobody worked. Without noticing what he was after, I went there, and as I entered, he arrived and proposed love to me as a man does to a girl. I was very angry. I pushed him to the side and hit him. I left

> him there. He came back and tried to be rough. I hit him and knocked him down. The white staff asked what the matter was, and I told them the whole story. But they just changed me to another section and left the boss boy. I was very angry because I thought he deserved a punishment. Other miners told me that the whites knew about boss boys proposing to boys and they didn't care at all.

Another way of refusing to be an inkontshane was to call in the aid of one's home fellows, as did Moketi when he wished to be rid of Mama. This was a risky procedure, especially when one's prospective lover was of a different ethnic group, for it might precipitate a faction fight, as was reported to have occurred on Deelkraal Mine in 1979 (AIM 1982: Noyakaso and Mashwana).

The Origins and Social Function of Mine Marriages

Early evidence on inkontshane marriages in the mines attests that they were most common among Mozambicans. Junod (1962:493) suggested that the Tsonga had always preferred nkhontxana relationships because they feared venereal disease, but turn-of-the-century accounts of "undesirable Portuguese women" especially around the Transvaal coal mines, which were almost entirely manned by Mozambicans, call that assertion into question (NLB 261, 263; JUS 421, 3/1220/26). Mozambicans certainly held long contracts on the mines, however. In fact, in the very early years the Mozambicans actually brought young boys (*umfaans*) with them to serve them on the mines (SNA 46, 1540/02; NLB 229, 583/15/145, Randfontein South report; Harries 1990:322–24).

By 1916, several native inspectors reported that the practice of mine marriage had spread to members of other ethnic groups. Initially, young men from other tribes would agree to mine marriages with Mozambicans, many of whom were boss boys or mine policemen, for the money. We have seen that by entering a mine marriage a man might not only avoid the temptations of town but also double his wages and thereby reduce the number of his "joins" (six- or nine-month contracts). As one Mpondo exminer told Vivienne Ndatshe: "After nine months I had to go home. I had money and bought cattle. My father had been a mine worker. He was surprised at the money I brought and said to me that no matter what I might say, he knew why I had the money." Thus, many of those non-Shangaans who agreed to mine marriages despite the subordinate and essentially "feminine" part they had to play did so because they considered themselves at the mine "on business." The wages given them by their "husbands" would enable them to accumulate bridewealth sooner and thus begin to build an umzi. They agreed to play the part of "women" in sexual activity in order more rapidly to become "men" at home. Thus their sexual activity indirectly served to maintain the authority of the older men within the subsistence system at home. Luise White (1990) has demonstrated a similar function in colonial Kenya for certain types of female prostitution, whose practitioners also remitted money home to support their patriarchal rural homesteads.

I am not suggesting that the traditional system was retained unaltered. We have already seen how the status of married women improved. In addition, the wealth earned by younger men migrating individually to the mines gave them greater independence from their elders. It also inflated the bride-price, though, ensuring that as long as the bride-price was paid the traditional system of seniority would remain. James Kulani, speaking of Pondoland in the 1930s, expressed clearly the social logic of migrancy from the point of view of Mpondo elders:

> There were Xhosa women in the [urban] locations but *never* Mpondo women. The Mpondo women knew that they were not allowed to go to town and besides they were looking after the umzis while their husbands were away. The men arranged it so that clan-brothers are not all away at one time. Before he left, a young man arranged for help for his father and wife. Before they all went to the mines the *lobola* used to be paid by the clan-people who would get together and each contribute some animal, either give or lend. Now the young man does it all himself. Thus the old men are happy about youngsters going off to the mines.

Nkhontxana marriages, whatever their origins among the Mozambicans, fitted well into the umzi system, at least for the junior partners. The "homosexuality" that so distinctly reinforced the seniority system on the mines also served in more subtle ways to protect the seniority system back home. For Mpondo young men it reinforced their resistance to proletarianization; however much mine migrancy served the white political economy, young Mpondo participated in order to more surely secure their country interests. "Homosexuality" was thus an aspect of migrant integrity.

Much of the rush to permanent settlement in the cities in the 1930s and 1940s was by black workers from white farms. Rural homesteaders from South Africa and the High Commission Territories moved to higher-paying jobs in manufacturing but maintained their migrant patterns as long as they had *any* hope of building an umzi in the countryside. The mass migration of women to the cities from Basutoland during this period

(Bonner 1990) indicates wide-scale breakdown of the patriarchal rural homestead system at least in the lowlands there.

Pondoland and certain conservative parts of the Transkei remained substantial sources of mine labor, as did the more self-sufficient mountainous areas of Lesotho (and Mozambique for somewhat different reasons), but much of the labor force after 1950 was recruited in the tropical north. I have no evidence that black authorities on the compound and underground were able to talk or coerce youngsters from the far north into marriage, but my guess is that they probably did—and the young men submitted for reasons similar to those of the Mpondo.

Fully proletarianized South African youngsters, when they flocked to the mines in the early 1970s, however, vehemently eschewed any suggestion of homosexuality. The integrity of "homosexuality" within umzi patterns of accumulation and its part in country definitions of masculinity were quite foreign to them. Their attitudes toward town women were far less ambiguous. Thus, their sexual behavior was quite different. To understand these changes, however, we must first examine more closely the place of "town women" in traditional migrant cultures.

Availability of Town Women

At Luzupha in Pondoland, Vivienne Ndatshe spoke to an old man whose experiences with "town women" in the 1940s were typical of a number of the life histories she collected. When he was working his first contract in Johannesburg, he followed the imiteto of mine management and never visited the townships. He and his friends decided to remain in the compound, he said. But the beer in the compound was not tasty, and the women in town were most attractive. So on his next contract, which was at Venterspost, he accepted the invitation of a Sotho induna to come with him to visit his mistress (*ishweshwe*). When they arrived, another woman was also present. The thought crossed his mind that this had all been arranged for him:

> Luckily I had left my money at the compound and had little cash [remember the legendary stinginess of the Mpondo]. My friend bought beer and his ishweshwe gave us more. I was afraid to propose love, so I drank a lot to take the shyness away, and within an hour I had a lover whom I visited on the weekends thereafter. But I didn't forget my wife at home. I did not give the lover much money as I had little enough myself; I was saving my money at the mine office.

He had heard about prostitutes (*oonongogo*, sing. *nongogo*) but "had never practiced that" himself. He considered it "unhealthy for a human being." "Only dogs would do that," he said. However, "there were miners who liked oonongogo because one could go to them whenever he felt like it. If not, he could just stay away."

Four major themes emerge from this account that are echoed in other sources and for other periods from at least the turn of the century to the present. The first is the ambivalent attraction for town women as sexual beings. "Beware the breasts of the Tswana women" go the words of one Chopi song.[10] The second theme is the almost invariable coincidence of town women and the consumption of alcohol. A third is the differentiation in mine workers' minds between types of women. According to the above account, for instance, a mistress was a legitimate alternative to abstention while a man was on the mines, but prostitutes were "unhealthy for a human being." Paying for sex as an isolated act for its own sake seemed brutish to the informant—"only dogs do that." The fourth theme, which recurs frequently among Mpondo, is that miners were initiated into the mysteries of town women by mine-worker friends, often Sesotho speaking.

Another point often made in tales of town women is that they were available not only in the black townships but also on farms and smallholdings near the mines and in domestic servants' quarters of the white suburbs. In each of these alternative locales, alcohol and both prostitutes and mistresses may be found today. In addition, the mines themselves have always set aside a limited number of married quarters for senior and favored black employees. Here too archival records and observational studies indicate that resident wives or daughters of this black elite, or their guests, frequently lived as "town women." This is still the case today. Vivienne Ndatshe collected several life histories of such women at the Vaal Reefs village for married housing in 1990.

Ambivalence toward Town Women

As we have seen, even if town women were available, they were not always miners' first preference. The fear of becoming amatshipa and thus a creature of the mine or town cut deep among those who aspired to rural homestead proprietorship. Speaking from his experience of the 1950s, Ryna Dushu of Mantlaneni in Pondoland elaborated in his interview in 1984:

> If a person becomes amatshipa he stops sending money home and simply changes from one mine to the next without ever going home. Nobody knows where he is. Often such people return home eventually very poor, often ill. . . . Perhaps he gambles, chases

[10] I am indebted to Leroy Vail for this reference.

> women or drinks. His home fellows try to help but he rejects them, often violently, or he leaves the mine and goes to another. . . . If a wife is left she will not go to town, she may find another man or go back to her own home. The uncles will care for the old umzi for her son. If the man now returns he has very little power because his son is the owner of the umzi. If he is lucky his wife will come back to him, and they will be looked after by the young boy.

In 1976, across the mountains in Lesotho at Saint Marks Mission, T. H. Thabane interviewed such a man, who had been *lekholoa* in the 1950s and 1960s:

> As a young man who grew up in the mountains of Lesotho, he found himself suddenly ushered into a different society with a different life style, values, activities. He suddenly found himself living in a society of beautiful women who could use soap and water successfully, who used all sorts of cosmetics to make themselves beautiful and attractive, and who would choose good clothes that made them look really smart. He suddenly found himself living in a society . . . of people who could make entertainment and make life enjoyable to the full. . . . He slowly sank and became overwhelmed by its life and various activit[ies]. . . . He was in the midst of very pretty women, who he thought really loved him and really knew how to love. . . . He says they could do their job in bed. (AIM 1975)

He spent his money on town women, the old Sotho man continued, saying that "people from home bothered him about the misery of his wife . . . and letters from wife and parents bothered him." Thus at the end of his first contract he left the mine, telling no one where he was going. He signed on elsewhere, taking new lovers, fathering children by them, and then deserting them in turn. Eventually, he contracted tuberculosis and was laid off by the mines. His current mistress promptly threw him out, and he returned home with minimal compensation from the mine. By now the infant son he had left in the country was fifteen and refused to accept him. His rural wife had had four children by another man, but she nonetheless took him in:

> His wife, who suffered for fifteen years, is the one who must have the burden of nursing him as a dying man. Those who enjoyed the fruits of his sweat are far from him. He breaks into tears and sobs. He tells me that while he was stronger he used to gather young men around him and tell them his experience. He advised them

> and evangelized them. He is now very weak; his voice is sometimes hardly audible.

In every country district there are old men like this, returned amatshipa living out their final days in humiliation and abject poverty. Small wonder that town women, for all their undoubted attractions, were such a dubious temptation. In a system in which their future lies in what can be built up at home by their wives, even those who took town lovers usually tried to retain their rural links. There was less risk and greater integrity in loving "boys" than in pawning one's future with scheming town women—although "boys" too asked a price. "Boys" grew up, however, and unless one developed a permanent preference for "boys" as such, they apparently represented less risk.

Sexual activity, then, reinforces people's understanding of themselves and each other in terms of gender and power but always as defined within particular social and economic contexts. Sexual activity, which confirms our self-formation as "men" and "women," "intrusive" and "seductive," "powerful" and "weak," cuts across more general structures of power and meaning, sometimes affirming and sometimes contradicting them. Thus sexual activity may be part of the topography of resistance and co-optation not only in domestic struggles but also in sustaining more general practices of integrity and humiliation. Structural changes also affect sexual practices and gender statuses. Thus, next I examine changes in sexual meanings and activities on and around the mines after 1973 after first discussing what sex means to men.

Proper Sex and Prostitution

At least as early as 1902, authorities were conspiring to exert control over "loose women" brewing in the mine married housing. In 1913, for instance, Theodora Williams of the Anglican Mine Native Mission, told Commissioner Buckle: "Ninety percent of the boys [in the so-called married quarters] are not married. They bring in native women and these women being of low class bring in brandy. The decent class of boy complains because they have so often to live cheek by jowl with these bad lots" (NGI, 15/10/13:10).

For the mines at this period, the married quarters were a way of retaining competent workers, but at the same time some managers complained that they "corrupted the workers." The recruiter A. M. Mostert declared in 1914:

> At the Witwatersrand Mine, I had a location, and at the Glencairn Mine, and my efficiency was bad at both those places. The men

> were those big buck niggers and the women were in no sense their wives. The women make drink, and although these men were in your service, you never got anything out of them. . . . The men simply lived on the women who were making beer. They get hold of your compound boys and that is where the question of the young boy comes in. They decoy him to these locations and they give him beer and he meets the women and he becomes bad too and inefficient at his work. He prefers to lie round the huts. (NGI 27/4/14:43)

In 1931, A. J. Hoffman of the Johannesburg Criminal Investigation Department also testified to the link between brewing and prostitution:

> In allowing native women to brew beer, my experience has been this—that where native women have not been allowed to brew liquor, they are continually doing it now. But where the native women are allowed to brew and where it is sold by them . . . to the men, there is always a certain amount of prostitution carried on. Those native women who sell beer become prostitutes. (NEC:7652)

What "prostitution" meant in this context is unclear. A number of the African urban elite denied vehemently to the same Native Economic Commission (pp. 7445, 7929, 8346–47) that prostitution as a straightforward financial transaction ever existed among blacks. Were they merely wearing moral blinders or was there some truth in their protestations despite the police evidence?

To understand the dispute, we need to distinguish between different types of "town women." In addition to *ishweshwe* (pl. *amashweshwe*), which we translate as "mistress,"[11] and *nongogo* (pl. *oonongogo*), translated as "prostitute," there is a third category of town women—that of *isithandwa* (pl. *izithandwa*), best translated as "girlfriend." Whereas a man pays a fixed rate for a nongogo, he gives gifts to an isithandwa, and actually pays maintenance for an ishweshwe.[12] Miners who worked in the 1940s and 1950s insisted in their interviews that while women at the *she-*

[11]Women use *masihlalisane*, meaning "stay together," for male partners in such relationships.

[12]We provide the Xhosa nomenclature. Jochelson, Mothibeli, and Leger (1990:164), working with Sesotho categories, noted:

> Undoubtedly many men remain faithful to their spouses. Those who specifically seek sexual relationships, such as the men we interviewed, engage in relationships that may be broadly divided into three categories: cash transactions with prostitutes (*matekatse*); casual, short-term relationships with unmarried women (*baratani*) or married or divorced women (*linyatsi*; singular form, *nyatsi*); and longer-term though not necessarily permanent relationships involving domestic obligations for both parties, in which the man is referred to as *monna* and the woman as *mosadi*, or as husband and wife.

beens (liquor joints) may have engaged in sexual relations with customers, even several in one day, the transaction was not merely a financial one, at least not as the men related it.

Nor do the women tell a different story. Near Vaal Reefs in Kanana township in 1990, Vivienne Ndatshe interviewed several young women who were regulars in shebeens. One, an Mpondo from Port Saint Johns, who was quite typical, lived with a group of young women from the Transkei, sharing a backyard shack and receiving a steady stream of men. When Ms. Ndatshe asked her who paid the rent, she replied that they had different boyfriends who each paid something to help out since the women were not working. "So now you are prostitutes?" asked Ms. Ndatshe. "Not really, because we don't sell sex," she said, laughing. "Men just help us. They are our boyfriends." "But you said earlier that such friendships last only a day," Vivienne Ndatshe reminded her. "Sometimes longer than a day, if one is lucky," she replied, "paying us if there is no food, or buying beer for us." None of the group were married. Whether the women were oonongogo disguised as izithandwa or genuine izithandwa is not much to the point here. Men would no doubt have described the women as izithandwa who sometimes later became amashweshwe, and the women seemed to concur with that nomenclature.

For some time I surmised that many men rejected the very idea of prostitution because they were seeking mutuality with the women. I have a 1982 account of a shebeen in Thabong township at Welkom where Sotho traditionalists gathered to create a "home" atmosphere, drink home-brewed Sotho beer, and sing the songs of home. Any suggestion that female companionship was central to this type of activity for country men, however, overlooks the fact that the mutuality in this type of situation was with each other, not with the women. Women were available, the men had sex with them and that apparently met a need, but they regarded the women neither as true companions nor as prostitutes. The same pattern is found of course with "mine wives." Recall the Tsonga account of social gatherings that the "wives" attended in order to serve rather than participate. Mamphela Ramphele (1986:20) points to a similar phenomenon among Cape Town migrants:

> Preference is given to male company for drinking, gambling and other social activities, e.g., in Guguleto Hostel women are said not to be allowed to eat in the front rooms with men. This room becomes out of bounds to all females after the latter have placed food in front of their male partners or relatives.

Male-female relationships are not much different in rural marriages, either, although companionship seems to develop among couples in old age. The question remains, what do women mean to men?

I have the impression that what men value in satisfactory sexual relationships with women is the right and the power to initiate and control sexual activity rather than mutuality (although some sort of companionship might follow in old age). When we asked old men in Pondoland in 1988 whether women could actively and verbally "propose love to men," even as men did to women, seizing them and telling them they wanted "love" from them, they were puzzled by the question. Of course, women could act seductively and so convey their availability, they said, but "to propose love like men"—that was inconceivable. In this regard the passive "boys" in mine marriages were wives indeed.

Men appeared to enjoy the conquest of lovers more than companionship with them. Conquest implies the possibility of failure, as the isithandwa, unlike the nongogo did not sleep with everyone. One might guess that the reason oonongogo were so despised is that they did nothing to affirm a man's skill or prowess as a lover; they merely affirmed his wealth, but hardly even that, because the price was fixed. A nongogo presented no challenge. A statement from one of the 1976 mine participant observers seems to confirm this tentative judgment:

> One Saturday morning at work underground I listened to miners relate fascinating stories about booze, women and sexual intercourse with them. When they get to Thabong Township on a drinking spree, they also have women in their programme. After relating previous weekend experiences in the township, they would start giving each other certain hints and tactics for winning women in the shebeens and convincing them to have sex with them—"keep buying her some drinks until she is tipsy and she will agree to any suggestion you make . . ." They go even further to discuss sexual intercourse in the township. . . . Some of the miners listen with envy as they do not seem to be very successful with the women folk.

Primarily, then, to be an isithandwa a woman must lead a man to believe that he is seducing her. Of course, if she becomes his ishweshwe, there may be greater mutuality, but my impression is that their relationship then only involves a wider range of domestic services from the woman and regular support from the man rather than fuller companionship.

In most cases when Mpondo men spoke of going to town in the 1940s and 1950s to find women, they mentioned a friend, usually Sotho, who would accompany them and introduce them to their prospective sexual partners. Going to the bars and beerhalls near the townships was different. There men would go in groups and sometimes would find women. But finding an isithandwa or establishing an ishweshwe seems to have required a personal introduction. This was partly because most women in the Transvaal townships were Sesotho speaking (Bonner 1990) so language might have been an initial barrier for Mpondo. However, friend and family networks (along with ability to pay) seem to have been the deciding factors in initiating relationships between miners and town women, rather than language as such. As late as 1982, a small sample of mine shebeens in Thabong revealed that women running them invariably had a relative or boyfriend working on the mines. He would bring friends and casual contacts to drink at her house, and she would lay on women as well as beer. Since these were Sotho shebeens catering primarily to Sotho, language was not an issue. Perhaps the link with a male friend enabled miners to hold to their belief that the sexual relationship was more than merely financial, or perhaps such introductions assuaged somewhat the fear of the seductive power of town women.

Although there must always have been oonongogo around, their numbers seem to have been relatively small. In Welkom in 1982, for instance, where the male mine population numbered a couple hundred thousand, only about fifty oonongogo were at work in the bushes around the shopping centers, although others lived on farms near town. Nonetheless, sex for a fixed sum seems to be as much despised by the proletarianized "new" mineworkers as by rural migrants in the 1930s and 1940s.

Gift giving as remuneration for sexual intercourse remains much more acceptable to men's self-esteem, as was affirmed also in Ms. Ndatshe's conversations with women at the mines in 1990. The gift may in fact be quite generous. Once a relationship becomes established with the assumption of exclusive sexual rights to the woman (and her domestic services in return), the man expects to maintain her. In fact on paydays nowadays, "town women," and, increasingly wives visiting from the country, gather in substantial numbers at the mine gates to ensure their share of monetary "gifts" from their lovers or husbands.

Male-female role segregation ought not to surprise anyone acquainted with family history in the West.[13] Historically, in Bantu-speaking societies also, male attitudes toward sexuality stressed patriarchal dominance, although, as we have seen, male migration certainly strengthened the position of married women. Even in Schapera's (1971) extraordinary account of sexuality among the Kgatla, a careful reading shows that most of the affection and tenderness is on the woman's side. Sotho miners returning

[13]See for instance, Stone 1979, for the relatively recent development of companionate marriage among privileged classes in England, and Young and Wilmott 1957, for the continuance of role segregation among working-class English in the twentieth century.

home on busses and trains in 1976 were quiet and spoke with warmth of their children and homesteads, but referred to their wives only in comments about their fears of having been cuckolded.

Town Women and Country Wives

As long as a woman presided over an umzi in the absence of her husband, his obligation to remit to her was not merely moral but also in his own interest. However, after 1973, recruitment for the mines spread rapidly to nontraditional areas, and even in established mine-sending areas there is evidence that the number of traditional families is diminishing. The bonus reengagement scheme, obliging almost immediate reengagement (Crush, Jeeves, and Yudelman 1991:151–75), puts further pressure on the families since men are now away from home for longer periods than ever before.

Marriages of people without land who are entirely dependent on wages may be more genuinely companionate than in the old days. Indeed, young people increasingly exercise a romantic "choice" to which they had no formal right before. But companionate marriage requires ongoing mutual communication if it is to survive.[14] Migrants whose wives live in resettlement areas or rural reserves without imizi, however sincerely they may be "in love," run serious risks of marital dissolution (Sharp and Spiegel 1991).

A longer period at work, higher wage scales, and changes within the family structure have thus tended to place greater strain on marriages. It is important to note that traditional Xhosa and Mpondo families have in the past been some of the most stable under migrancy. The process of erosion of marriage took place earlier in lowland Lesotho and the Ciskei. In the 1970s, as the mines began to draw recruits from townships at smaller towns such as Grahamstown, marriages there had next to no defense against the ravages of migrancy. The effects of the gradual collapse of family life in the sending areas are twofold. On the one hand, more men from the mines tend to abjure mine marriages, seek out town women, and attempt to establish permanent relationships with them. On the other hand, more country women, no longer having ties with the land that bind them to the umzi, attempt to come to town, either to keep alive their relationships with mine-worker husbands or to set up as "town women" themselves.

[14]This, I think, is the major point being made by Mamphela Ramphele in her article cited above, although she assumes that such communication is necessary for any type of marriage. While communicative mutuality may sometimes have come to be part of a rural role-segregated marriage, it was hardly necessary there.

Many of the houses in townships near the mines have additions constructed by the owners to take in lodgers. Farm-worker villages also take in renters. Often such lodgers are visiting wives or mistresses of miners who pay their rent and maintain them there. Woman are coming to the mines in greater and greater numbers. The Chamber of Mines' policy of hiring South African labor has meant that a problem which has long been a concern of municipalities and the state is increasingly one besetting the mines. Nor is this a reversible process. More and more miners' country wives are coming to town to stay. The long-standing separation between town women and country wives is beginning to break down.

Although the trend is a fairly gradual one, as early as 1982 theological students found that more than a quarter of the mine-working husbands of wives interviewed in Qumbu in the Transkei had absconded. The erosion of family structures is even more advanced in Lesotho (Gay 1980, Murray 1981, Spiegel in Mayer 1980), although the opportunity to come home on weekends has apparently slowed familial disintegration there. Sotho theological students in 1981 reported marriages in generally better shape than did those doing research in 1976. Because country women move into the sprawling periurban developments around border-crossing points, however, to be available to husbands commuting from the mines every other week, weekend leaves have further weakened country homesteads, which might otherwise have continued to struggle to survive in the interior. Sotho families are increasingly nuclear, and older people are more desperate than ever despite higher mine wages. In-law conflicts between consumption-oriented wives and more frugal parents are a sign of the times. Sotho families without migrant sons or husbands are in deep trouble.

Wives from all the sending areas are now more ready to go to town to seek out their *lekholoa* husbands. Without fields or with less productive fields, and especially in bad years, they have to. Lowland Sotho women, who have felt those pressures longest, were legendary as the "town women" of the 1930s, 1940s, and 1950s (Bonner 1990). In 1963, the South African state declared Sotho female migrants illegal. That they still come is a measure of their desperation. The most striking change, however, is the increase in Xhosa-speaking rural female migrants in townships around the mines.

In 1990, Vivienne Ndatshe interviewed more than sixty Xhosa-speaking women living in backyard shacks or the mine married quarters at Vaal Reefs mine in the Western Transvaal. Not all of them intended to stay. On the whole, younger women (unmarried or recently married and better schooled) and those without rural imizi were more likely to want to stay in town. Although there is no invariable correlation between sustainable rural agricultural practice and geographical area, especially since the age variable cuts across regional differences, generally Mpondo women were most reluctant to settle in town and Ciskeians most agreeable to the idea. Access to viable agricultural land in the rural areas was the most important variable of all.

The story of a rural Ciskeian woman who came to town from an impoverished rural area captures all the major themes of similar stories by other migrant women: "I came to visit my husband who was not coming home, even on his leave. His parents sent me and told me to take my two children with me. I was thin and ugly and the children were poorly dressed." Many women who came to the mines from the most impoverished rural areas say they did so because their children were sick or hungry. Sometimes the problem was that the mother-in-law, with whom the young wife invariably resides, received money from the husband but did not share it sufficiently. In such cases the wife came to beg the husband to send money directly to her. Usually, however, the man stopped remitting altogether or sent money so infrequently that there was never enough to support the country household.

The Ciskeian woman's story continued:

> When he was called and found out I was there, he asked why I was there without telling him. He brought food for us. I gave it to the children. I was angry and at the same time scared. My brother was working here on the mines. I asked my husband if it was very far to where he worked. "Have you come to your brother or me?" he asked. I lied and said my mother gave me a message for him. My husband said nothing about where to find my brother. He took me to a house in the married quarters (*skomplas*) and I stayed there with the owner who was also from Ciskei.
>
> I had heard that my husband had another woman. Other women told me what was happening to our husbands when we stayed at home. There are women who don't stay long in the country but visit their husbands regularly. One woman said she would never stay at home for long. She and her husband would rather have no home in the country. She would not give him a chance with those town women. She also said she loves her husband and doesn't want to be separated from him by the job. . . .
>
> After three weeks my husband gave me money to go home. I went back to the country knowing to myself that I was coming back, but not to him. I told my mother-in-law what had happened and how her son treated me—even the money he gave me was too little. I loved my mother-in-law, but I had no choice because I was not married to her and she couldn't support me and the children needed school uniforms.

When I arrived home I went to see my own mother. I told her that I was going to work in Johannesburg for my children. I also told a friend, who decided to come with me. I left a letter on my mother-in-law's bed, so that when I had gone she could know where and why I left. I went with my friend to my brother in Stilfontein. He took us to Khuma [Stilfontein township] to a friend's backyard shack. The place was reserved for the friend's wife but she had gone back to the country.

My friend and I stayed there and looked for work in town, sometimes visiting my brother on the mine. We soon got boyfriends. It was not difficult to find a boyfriend. Miners love women. My boyfriend gave me money which I sent to my mother. Sometimes I sent clothes to my children. I wasn't going around much because I didn't want my husband to know my whereabouts.

Money is a temptation. I say this because another man really attracted me. He was a Shangaan. I left my old boyfriend for this man and am still staying with him. This Shangaan took me to Kanana and we have lost contact with my friend but I keep in touch with my brother. He tells me that my husband works in Carletonville now. When his mother told him that I have left, he went home and married another girl in the country. Now I feel free.

I sell beers around the mine now. We make good money. I support my mother and my children. I would rather stay here with my man than go back to the country. He is also no longer going back to his own country. He had a wife but does not correspond with her. He is very straight. From work he comes home. He doesn't care or tell me not to sell so I do what I like. We are busy applying for [a] house or we shall build our own. If I own a house I will bring my children here.

Although husbands do not usually reject their wives when the latter first appear at the mine from the countryside, many eventually do. Rejected wives apparently seldom move directly into prostitution. Instead, as with the case in point, they engage in a series of more or less permanent dependent relationships, quite possibly with remunerative sexual adventures on the side. Eventually, many (but not all) women end up in relatively long-term relationships with Shangaan men. Such "Shangaans," and here the women seem to be referring to "tropical" as well as Mozambican mine workers, have less bargaining power vis-à-vis South African women (Ms. Ndatshe was told that it is they who are most likely to frequent the haunts of the prostitutes), and they are thus less controlling and more generous with women willing to live with them. By the time a woman ends up with a "Shangaan," she is often engaged in some sort of small-scale entrepreneurial activity (most often beer brewing or retailing—sometimes with sex on the side—but also dressmaking or selling cooked meat and vegetables). Nonetheless, these women seldom seem to wish to be completely financially independent. Even if they can support themselves, women assume their right to assistance from the men with whom they live—presumably in remuneration for domestic and sexual services—and do not hesitate to leave them if such help is not forthcoming.

Another theme in these accounts is the importance of relatives. Many women mentioned relatives, especially mine-worker brothers, but also in-laws and mothers, in describing their decision to come to the mines to seek out their husbands. Only women fleeing from childhoods on white farms completely rejected their families of origin—and even they sometimes kept in touch with their siblings. Although conjugal relationships often failed to survive the wife's coming to town, a woman could fall back on other family ties, especially her brothers, who were often crucial for finding urban housing and making contact with new men. Furthermore, even persons who decided to stay in town at least kept in touch with parents (and in-laws if the marriage survived) and often left their children to be reared in the country.

It is difficult to estimate the numbers of these newly urbanized women. Given the uncertainty of South African township life and job insecurities, women without a viable umzi in the countryside did not necessarily want to give up their rural homes, although the majority were resigned to urban life or preferred it. Nokwandisa, a twenty-seven-year-old from Flagstaff, whose husband, a survey assistant, had bought a mine-subsidized suburban house at Kanana and whose children were at school in town, had her doubts about cutting her ties with the country:

> At home I have no fields and only a few sheep which are kept by a relative. [Nonetheless], I would like to have two homes. For the future we don't know what is going to happen in this country. If, because of politics, we some time end up with no place in the mines any more, we will have the place back in the country. Moreover, if we don't keep our home in Pondoland, people will laugh at us, and the chief will give our place to other people and we will have no land. That is why we keep both places. When I am here my health is much better than back in the country and I am happy to stay with my husband and children, all living together. But I also want to keep in contact with my husband's family.

For her, the country establishment was more like a second home than a viable economic option.

Much more common for women from Pondoland (and those areas of the Western Transkei and Ciskei where it is still possible to "build an umzi") is a firm affiliation to country life. For them, old ways die hard. Take, for instance, the case of Nolulamile, a twenty-two-year-old:

> Nolulamile has got two sisters and one brother. The elder sister and herself are married. Younger ones are still at school. She passed Standard III and left school because there was no boy to look after cattle. So she looked after her father's stock. She grew up with boys and was fighting with sticks on the veld. There were other girls who also looked after their parents' stock, but not as many as boys. . . . Nolulamile's father worked on the mines. Now he has stopped and stays at home to help his young son look after the few cattle remaining after the drought. In 1986 she married her country lover [and moved in with his large and prosperous family].
>
> Nolulamile is a real farm girl. She doesn't like to stay long on the mines, where people don't respect each other and where money is used every day. At home there is maize and other vegetables from the fields. She talked about wild vegetables which grow in the forest where you haven't planted them. If she could conceive and have children she would never come here, she said. When she is at home her husband sends money to her and she is satisfied.

Her story both depicts the tenacity and satisfaction with which country people with land hang onto their rural patrimony and also gives evidence of the modern strains on the umzi system. Nolulamile's father's lonely struggle to establish a viable umzi (even to the extent of having his daughter herd cattle, which would have been unheard of in the past, when brothers and clan relatives would have helped) contrasts with the wealth of the larger family into which she married.[15]

Nolulamile came to the mine to be with her husband in order to conceive. This is far and away the major reason women from traditional imizi come to the mines. By all accounts parents-in-law heartily dislike the idea since their daughter-in-law's absence deprives them of her company and her labor. However, mine management's policy of stabilization, with job security for black miners dependent on steady employment but with only short leaves allowed, makes it inevitable that wives will visit the mines. Proper medical attention at the mine hospital often keeps women in the area until they come to term and even for a month or two thereafter (and longer if the home area has a history of infant mortality).

[15]For an account of pressures on the homestead system in Lesotho, where, as in the Ciskei, underdevelopment is further along, see Murray 1981.

Nomkhonzi was only eighteen years old when she came for the first time to her husband on Vaal Reefs in August 1990 after becoming pregnant:

> [Nomkhonzi's] mother is a pensioner. Her father died in 1976. The only people still alive and helping her mother are the mother's brothers and their wives. Her brothers help her mother on the fields. They plough for her and their wives come at harvest time to help her. Nomkhonzi also goes and helps her mother.
>
> Nomkhonzi took a taxi from the country. Her husband told the taxi driver to bring his wife . . . to No. 6 Vaal Reefs where he works. Her husband then took her to Mandela Park—the site-and-service shanty-town where his clan-brother has a shack (*umkhukhu*). This man doesn't stay in Mandela Park, but lives in the compound. He lets the shack to his home friends' wives. Then when his wife visits she has somewhere to stay. There are two women now [October 1990] occupying the shack.
>
> Nomkhonzi will stay for a month after she has the baby and so will be going home in January or February 1991. Nomkhonzi doesn't like the house in town. She likes country life very much. "In town money is used too much whereas at home where we grow maize we don't have to buy much," she said. "Even if my husband does want to have a house here, I will never stay in it, but will visit. Or if we have a house we will let it to people visiting the mines."

Again and again in the accounts of visiting wives, rural social networks and the uncertainties of dependency on the urban monetary economy are given as reasons for giving priority to the country home. Nonetheless, several younger woman admitted to Ms. Ndatshe in 1990 that life for women is easier in town, so they rather enjoyed it, although some also were quite bored without the work at the umzi.

Near the end of her stay in Kanana, Vivienne Ndatshe summed up the different attitudes of older women whose husbands had access to land in the country:

> There are those who say they don't like to live in townships because their husbands might lose their jobs on the mines. Others say they want to have houses on the mines and at home. They prefer to go backwards and forwards until their husbands resign. . . . Yet others said if their husbands could build big nice houses [in the country] like those on the mines it would make a big difference because they wouldn't have to pay rent every month as they do on the mines. They would plant vegetables and they would have their own cattle on their own land. In townships peo-

> ple have big houses and little or no food or cattle. They buy everything. That's why most visiting wives are not really interested in staying permanently on the mines. One said she is happy to visit after working hard on the fields in the country. After hoeing and harvest time when the maize and other vegetables have been gathered in at home, then she visits her husband. "It's like when you are in boarding school," she said. "When its school holidays children go home to rest after studying hard. Even so for us, married women, we must rest near our husbands, as children rest near their parents."

It is to avoid dependency on wages, then, that women with access to land go back to the countryside year after year.

Some "superwomen" manage to have the best of both worlds. Usually, these are wives who rent homes in the mine village, the *skomplas,* at very low rates. Mrs. Regina Mkhazi, for instance, has ten children who go to school and live on their land in the country near Lusikisiki. She is in regular telephone contact with them. She goes home at the time of plowing and works with the children on their lands until the crops are in and then returns to her husband. In the *skomplas* she has her own sideline—she sells meat (sheep heads, which she buys from local farmers and resells to other residents). On weekends she also sells cooked meat to visitors at the shebeen next door (and perhaps manages to dispense a little liquid refreshment herself to regular customers). Although her husband originally married her by abducting her (*ukuthwala*), she is clearly very close to him. They show great fondness for each other. Nonetheless, at the end of her interview with Vivienne Ndatshe she returned to a theme that seems almost universal among country women. "Men are delicate [fickle?] people," she said:

> The women of Egoli [the "gold city," i.e., Johannesburg] are a temptation to our husbands. There are women whose husbands were taken away by these women of the township, or sometimes these women have run away from their husbands and come here to the mines to take our men away from us. And they do take them—some win them. So I want to be near my husband so that he will have no chance for these women. When he retires we are both going home and will stay together in our house at Lusikisiki.

Leaving aside the young women's need to conceive, then, two major themes emerge from the accounts provided by women with ongoing rural attachments. First, tension arises because of the uncertainties of urban life and mine employment and the struggle to maintain a viable rural existence. Second, country women fear the seductive potential of so-called town women. For country wives with viable imizi, it is the fear of town women that keeps them constantly moving between country and town. Labor stabilization policies, in combination with the collapse of the old encapsulating compound system and the existence of decent medical facilities at the mine, mean that the women are now obliged to migrate.

I do not seek to argue that there are no longer faithful husbands among mine migrants, but rather that, in structural terms, as the rewards for faithfulness diminish the attractions of town women surely increase. A vicious cycle operates here. As more men fail to support their rural families, more women are obliged to migrate to find men on the mines and thus provide a wider variety of options, and temptations, for the men that are there.

Even among traditionalist Mpondo the old arrangements with boy-wives are disappearing along with the integrity of tightly knit, home-based migrant cultures. At best, traditionalist country wives become superwomen with dual bases or risk losing their husbands by coming to the mines only to conceive. For more proletarianized workers, "homosexuality" is simply disgusting. For those men, town women are not alien or fearful, and serial or even parallel long-term relationships have become more and more common.

There has been a major shift in the expression of male sexuality and its functions for black miners in South Africa. If the "wives of the mine" were in the past a facet of more general resistance to proletarianization, the contemporary turn to town women and squatter families represents accommodation to the exigencies of total dependency on wages. Male sexuality, no longer retarding the proletarianization of both men and women, has now become an important reason for country wives to move to town. Whereas "homosexuality" on the mines had been both a source of rural resistance to the wage economy and also an accommodation to the migrant system, now "heterosexuality" challenges the migrant system even as rural society breaks down and the threat of AIDS, with the demise of ukumetsha, looms larger on the horizon (Jochelson, Mothibeli, and Leger 1991).

Conclusion

Whether we deal with traditional marriages, mine marriages, town women, or the recently emerging squatter "serial" marriages, the enduring expectation seems to be that mature men with authority in their social and economic spheres (and nowadays even younger men) are entitled to regular sexual activity. In the past, the gender of their partner was of less import than the older man's right to sexual congress and the young man's desire to establish an umzi. South African sexual politics, which took for granted male hegemony, was subsumed within the wider hegemonic system on the mines, paring "maleness" down to its essentials and endowing young men with temporary "wifehood." Stripped of any biological determination, "maleness" seems to have boiled down to two essential powers or rights, which enabled resistance to proletarianization on the wider structural level: first, the right to domestic services and, second, the right to be the active, initiating sexual partner. Sexuality, then, involved more than the physical act, extending to a range of personal services that more senior men were extremely reluctant to be without.

Mine marriages differed from rural marriages in one important respect, however. This is the matter of long-term reproduction, whether that be understood in its narrow sense of childbearing and rearing, or whether it encompass the entire process that is implied in the Xhosa notion of "building an umzi." Traditional rural male responsibilities for conception were such, however, that the reproductive sterility of mine marriages was viewed as an advantage: "At least one can't get pregnant." Even among the Tsonga, for whom inkotshane marriage was more closely integrated with the home system, such a relationship had a "biologically" defined terminal point—at which point, like the Greeks for Foucault (1986: pt. 4), they came up against principles of male assertiveness firmly rooted in popular consciousness. "Boys" always became "men," whether they took male or female partners.

On the mines the privileges of status conferred certain domestic rights. For many of the old men these no doubt filled needs for tenderness and companionship. Same-age groups of home friends apparently met each other's needs for companionship and mutuality; however, these friendships did not, given prevalent assumptions about "maleness" and seniority, provide for the expression of the self-assertion implicit in initiating sex, even as in role-segregated rural marriages. For that, and the accompanying domestic services, a man needed a "wife" or lover. Hence the seduction of "boys."

We have suggested as well that an additional attraction of mine marriage was its stability, its integration into a well-ordered and management-sanctioned system. At least part of the appeal of the "love of boys" was its reliability, its assuredness. Town women were not safe. If mine marriage and rural marriage were isomorphic (except with respect to reproduction), town women were different. Like extramarital affairs at home, they represented risk along with adventure. Men maintained town women through "gifts," monetary or otherwise, in exchange for services, sexual and domestic, without normative sanction, whereas the relationship with the "wife of the mine" was contractual, exclusive, an aspect of status and authority. Is it any wonder that senior men on the mines would return to their "boys" because they "loved them better?"

Proletarianization, when it finally came to the mines after 1973, destroyed the practical foundation for traditional male privilege. New "traditions" developed, which claimed the symbolic male authority of the old but which were actually based on men's access to wages and variations on the nuclear family system, rather than control of land as such. The result has been the profound modification of family structures and sexual practices. At the practical level, it has meant rapid disintegration of the migrant labor system and a massive migration of women to townships around the mines. Here some women have achieved a "male-dependent independence" that, while it continues to pay lip service to traditional male rights, actually undercuts the dominance of particular men over particular women. Others struggle to do double duty as both town women and country wives.

On the whole, loss of access to workable land and shortage of wage work for women have meant that women in general are more dependent than ever upon male largesse. Dependence on wage labor has meant a return to "heterosexuality" for mine workers, but the collapse of the umzi has meant the loss of the respect accorded to rural "women with manhood." Women as a class are trapped in the compliant "pleasures" of their "independence," while individual men exploit and are exploited by one woman after another in their search for sexual release and domestic stability. Male sexuality, for so long stabilized on the mines by the integrity of "homosexual" mine marriages and rural commitments, has become dangerously, perhaps fatally, heterosexual as AIDS begins to spread through South African society.

5 Convivialities

Drinking Patterns

The solidarity derived from communal drinking on the mines made it essential to that rural-oriented integrity that both sustained and was sustained by migrant cultures. Until 1962, despite the state's policy of total prohibition for Africans, black miners tenaciously insisted upon alcohol as a necessary accompaniment for informal sociability. Old men whom we interviewed, even those who otherwise insisted on their faithful adherence to mine rules, cheerfully admitted to illegal drinking. Whatever the regulations, consumption of alcohol was a right for adult men. Avoiding prohibition became a game for mine workers, and a source of innumerable entrepreneurial rackets on and around the compounds.

While the brewing and serving of liquor was traditionally a female pursuit, and men always preferred to drink alcohol produced and served by women, a blurring of gender lines occurred around alcohol, as with sexuality. On the compounds men brewed liquor for themselves and for sale to their fellows. Since gold mine compounds were never closed, however, more adventurous souls could venture forth to farm and town shebeens, to drink illicit liquor produced and served by town women.

Although the legalization of liquor sales to black South Africans in 1962 brought an end to compound brewing rackets, some men still preferred to drink in shebeens, where prices were higher but women served. Before 1973, there seems to have been little change in the sociable patterns of alcohol consumption by migrant peasant proprietors who had come to the mines to supplement homestead production. The radical change to a more proletarian "South African" labor force in the middle 1970s, however, introduced a new breed of black miners for whom "alcoholism" was a serious problem (Kruger and Rundle 1978). Whereas black mine workers for years had resisted state and management efforts to impose prohibition, members of the National Union of Mineworkers in the 1980s began to condemn drunkenness as demoralizing to worker solidarity. Local management also reversed themselves, now insisting on black workers' "right to drink" in the face of union boycotts of mine liquor outlets. Thus the meaning of drinking for both miners and management did an about-face after the recruitment of a different workforce in the 1970s. The consumption of alcohol, which for years had represented a crucial basis for worker solidarity in resistance to management, now came to be viewed as a means of management control.

Liquor and the Law

Charles van Onselen's (1982a) essay "Randlords and Rotgut" provides a graphic account of the social conflicts and systemic contradictions that led to a policy of total prohibition of hard liquor for blacks in the Transvaal by 1897. From then until 1962, the law prohibited the sale of intoxicating liquors to Africans. Beginning in 1903, however, the state permitted mines to serve allegedly nutritive low-alcohol African beer to their workers. Native Affairs inspectors indicated that most mines in 1909 served such "kaffir beer" once or twice a week (NLB 3, 313/09). This was still general practice in the 1940s (WMNWC, AMWU, 25/6/43:23). Indeed, for sixty years workers regarded a regular beer issue as their basic right. In November 1922, for instance, when visiting Shangaan dance teams at Randfontein Estates were issued compound beer, resulting in a shortage for regular workers, Mpondo rushed the beer kitchen in a group, and five combatants required hospitalization (NLB 197, 987/13/68, NA Inspector Randfontein, 17/11/22).

Since workers were able to leave the compounds during their free time, brewing policies of local administrations affected mine drinking. Municipalities after 1924 could adopt one or a combination of practices regarding kaffir beer for urban Africans. They could choose among total prohibition (as in Johannesburg), municipal monopolies in the form of "beer halls" (as in Durban), domestic brewing (as in Bloemfontein and Kroonstad), and a combination of domestic brewing and controlled local sales (as at New Brighton in Port Elizabeth). After 1937, however, unless municipalities established monopolistic beer halls or licensed individuals to sell African beer, they could not prohibit domestic brewing (Saffery 1940). Once it became clear that large profits could be made from beer halls, most towns opted to construct them. When the state took control over urban African affairs from the municipalities in the 1950s, beer halls (more euphemistically, "beer gardens") proliferated in urban areas. In 1962, pressures from South African liquor interests finally led the state to lift all controls on the sale of liquor to Africans. Within a year or two virtually all the gold mines had constructed "liquor outlets" (i.e., bars) inside the compounds.

I do not seek here to extend van Onselen's fascinating analysis of the struggles between different material and ideological interests during the long prohibition period, and the systemic pressures imposed on them by the pursuit of profit, but rather to look at the organization of illegal drinking among African mining men themselves and the place of alcohol in their lives. Prohibition never stopped African mine workers from imbibing stronger stuff than the watered-down compound issue. Compound brewing and alcohol purchased from illicit shebeens and municipal beer halls near the mines were always an important part of mine life. As we have seen, illegal drinking was an ingredient in the moral economy of the mine and helped support worker solidarity against proletarianization.

Management Attitudes toward Compound Drinking

While those missionaries and enthusiasts who confused temperance and total abstinence—or advocated total abstinence for "primitives" who couldn't hold their liquor—urged prohibition for "the natives," both management and black workers themselves held more nuanced and ambivalent attitudes toward alcohol. Management, of course, deplored the absenteeism that followed drinking bouts and yet was obliged to recognize worker demand for alcohol as a basic requirement of migration to the mines. Compounds that overlooked brewing were more popular with workers, so management had to walk a delicate line between the advantages of attracting employees, on the one hand, and the risks of high absenteeism and Native Affairs threats to revoke compound managers' licenses, on the other (for an early example, see TLC, paras. 548ff., 2,870, 4,401, 5,147, 10,228ff., 10,586ff.).

As early as December 1911, acting Police Commissioner Theo Truter pointed out that

> large quantities of kaffir beer, khali and skokian are being brewed in the different compounds and married quarters attached to compounds; . . . there is no doubt that the presence of large quantities of illicit liquor was well known all along the reef and was openly winked at by the Mine Authorities [because] it was thought that a large supply of beer would make the compounds popular. (NLB 38)

As an example of management dilemmas over alcohol, let us examine the "khali" scandal that was turned up by the Buckle Commission in 1913 and 1914. *Khali,* also called *skokiaan,* was based on a mysterious root said to have been derived from the San. It was pulped and mixed with golden syrup (sweet molasses), pearl barley, and water (NLB 367, 30/25/94, January 1926). The resulting mixture fermented very fast, being ready for consumption within an hour, according to one source, and certainly within two or three hours.[1]

Compound managers giving evidence before Commissioner Buckle sounded the alarm on khali. Both A. Spencer Edmunds of Geldenhuis East and G. A. Tandy of Princess Estate reported indiscriminate and widespread, indeed, virtually universal brewing of khali on compounds along the Rand. "One has only to look at the thousands of empty Golden Syrup tins strewn about in the vicinity of any Compound or Location and they tell their own tale," said Tandy.[2] Edmunds reported having stamped out khali in his compound but "at a great cost to the Mine—in 12 months my East Coast labour fell from 1233 to 703, a difference of 530 natives of the very best class" (NGI, 30/1/14:2–4; 3/3/14:1–6, GAT:1–2; 27/10/14:26; 30/1/14:11). According to M. Smith, the Native Affairs inspector on the East Rand:

> Liquor making . . . is a means of enticing East Coast natives especially to a Compound to allow promiscuous brewing of "Kali." Compounds that try to put down the practice are victimised by the other Compounds, whose policy it is to entice the drink loving labourers to leave the service of the former when time expired. . . . There have been several Chamber of Mines Circulars warning the Mines to put down the liquor making with a strong hand. . . . The ones who try to obey the instructions lose their natives and thereby incur the displeasure of their superiors. (NLB 136, 2756/13, 9/12/13)

Thus, while mine managers complained of loss of productivity because of khali consumption, they dared not act decisively against it for fear of losing workers in an already tight labor market. The Buckle report (paras. 515–18) actually recommended in 1914 that it be made an offense for any compound manager to be discovered with liquor in his compound. The Chamber of Mines agreed with this recommendation (NLB 115:31/7/14). However, the Association of Mine Managers considered it "obviously and grossly unfair to the Compound Manager" (CM, N5(a) NGI). The closer

[1]NLB 136, 2756/13/54: E. Meyer, Manager of ERPM, regarding Driefontein compound to SAP District Comdt., Boksburg, 27/4/16; see also NGI, S. A. M. Pritchard (DNL), and Pritchard's evidence published with the report of the Dominions Royal Commission, 6/4/14, paras. 2496ff. and 2555ff.

[2]According to Tandy's evidence, Shangaan and M'Chopi mine workers (who were the major brewers) insisted on an imported golden syrup called Lyles, rather than the local Natal variety, because it was stronger.

one came to the problem, it seems, the more tolerant one became of black miner drinking.

Recruiters feared that restrictions on brewing would affect their trade (NGI, 4/3/14:87–89), but industrial unrest on the Rand in 1913 and early 1914 gave the state, in the person of Director of Native Labour S. A. M. Pritchard, a chance to try to stamp out khali brewing. In the interests of "public safety" Pritchard forbade the import of golden syrup into the compounds. Figures for mine-worker drunkenness and absenteeism plummeted—as did sales of golden syrup in the concession stores around the mines. Pritchard was delighted and took steps to make permanent his state of emergency regulations. Although he could not prohibit the sale of golden syrup in normal times because of free trade principles, he sent a circular on 17 February 1914 to all mine managers (NLB 136, 2756/13), threatening to suspend their licenses if the compound managers did not immediately end all brewing on their compounds. At that point, virtually all compounds stopped workers from bringing golden syrup onto their premises. Many also disallowed any large (ten- to twenty-gallon) tins on their compounds. The decline in the sale and import of golden syrup continued, and the Transvaal Mines Traders' Association was up in arms (NLB 136, 2756/13, 6/3/14, 26/3/14, 22/4/14)—but to no avail, at least until the end of the war (NLB 136, 2756/13/54, Inspectors' responses to circular, 18/4/16).

The khali crisis was over, and, at least for a while, police raids on compounds turned up surprisingly little of the substance. Issues of compound popularity still continued to haunt the managers, however. An East Rand police report in January 1926, thirteen years after the khali scandal, noted:

> Apparently every endeavour must be made by the Compound Manager to make his compound popular amongst the natives. . . . I am informed that where a Compound Manager is exceptionally keen in putting down the liquor traffic in his compound and it becomes unpopular in consequence, he is told by those controlling him what is happening and he must take steps to make it more popular. (NLB 136, 2756/13, SAP Boksburg 29/1/26)

Khali was still being brewed in certain compound rooms or on nearby farms and townships under the alternative name of "skokian." Black miners also reverted to brown sugar and other additives to doctor up compound beer. The archives mention a range of adulterations, including eau de cologne (SNA 176, 2437/03, 29/9/03), concentrated essence of Jamaica ginger (*RDM*, 26/9/16), methylated spirits, carbide, "kaffir corn" malt (NLB 136, 2756/13/54, DNL circular, 22/8/21), sprouted grain and yeast (NLB 367, conference minutes, 5/9/24: 11–12; NLB 366, 45/26/110, circular from

SAP, Brakpan/Springs to compound managers, 23/2/26). As late as 1958, a farmer named Piet Bezuidenhout near the Welkom mines was seeking permission to supply sprouted grain to his workers in the face of sharp opposition from the township Native Advisory Committee (Welkom municipal archives, Native Advisory Committee minutes, 30/6/58).

The Role of Alcohol in Black Miners' Lives

Despite state legislation and missionary admonitions, most traditional African men viewed alcohol as an essential adjunct to sociability. At the same time, senior men did recognize that excessive drinking was a problem (Hunter 1936:357; NEC:3273, 3607, 3782), especially as migratory labor led to its spread among women and young men, the most productive members of traditional African societies (Guy 1990). By the 1970s, rural informants in Lesotho cited the temptations of alcohol as the most important of three reasons for migrants absconding (becoming amatshipa).

Traditionally, fairly heavy but socially controlled drinking was integral to African sociability (Mayer 1961:111–21). In the 1930s, Monica Hunter (1936:356–69) captured the rich fabric of country social interaction and the subordinate but crucial role of alcohol as follows:

> Pondo spend a vast amount of time visiting and gossiping. One seldom arrives at an *umzi* without finding some neighbour calling. As much work as possible is done in company. Men congregate at the chief's court to take snuff, and drink, and discuss the last fight, and the next adultery case to be tried. The trader's store is a centre to which young and old come to gossip and flirt, beg tobacco, and inquire as to the whereabouts of beer. Often a youth spends a whole morning at the store, talking to girls, chaffing with his contemporaries, and perhaps letting off steam in a stick-fight with a friend. . . . Meat feasts, dances and beer drinks are frequent between the harvest and ploughing seasons. During five winter months—June to October—I heard of seventy-three beer drinks, eight girls' initiation dances, three weddings, two feasts for the initiation of diviners, and a number of other ritual killings, within five miles of nTibane store. Many of the feasts lasted for two to three days. There was a young people's dance practically every weekend. Every festival is open to all who care to attend, and some travel ten miles to a beer drink or dance. In the season men and *amadikazi* [their lovers] often go on from one beer drink to another, sometimes not returning to their own homes for a week. Between November and May, when there is much work to be done in the fields and grain for beer is becoming scarce, there are few ritual feasts, but planting and weeding parties are frequent, and

> nowadays even pagans celebrate Christmas with a beer drink or fight.

This intense Mpondo sociability carried over into the mine compounds. Nyovela Manda's account to Vivienne Ndatshe is typical of several dozen others: "On Saturdays, miners were allowed to visit their home friends from other mines, or we were visited on our mines. We bought them beer and meat and sat in a semi-circle and talked about home events and our girlfriends as all the young men always talked. . . . That's how we enjoyed ourselves on the mines." Sakhile Mdelwa in Mfundzeni had a similar story:

> On the weekends I used to visit other mines. Every miner would visit his home friends in his free time. We talked about girlfriends and our families. If there were recent arrivals [new ones] from home, we were curious to know what was happening at home when they left. Sometimes we asked if our girlfriends had new boyfriends as we were away all those months. But no one would be cross about a girlfriend. They bought each other beer and sat in a circle, usually home friends alone.

McNamara's (1980) meticulous 1976 study, in which he phototracked drinking networks at an East Rand Proprietary Mines beer hall, found that persons from the same region and language group tended to drink together—in fact, one-half of the drinkers were from the same home village or rural "location." Such observations confirm accounts such as those above. However, several of Ms. Ndatshe's Mpondo informants mentioned drinking friendships with work mates that extended beyond ethnolinguistic boundaries. McNamara's study found that most such wider drinking sets included Shangaans. This observation is partially corroborated by Ms. Ndatshe's interviews with Mpondo, several of whom said that "the Shangaans are very nice." Such wider drinking groups did not have the same intimacy as home friend groups, however. "We had friends of other tribes, whom we had met at work," said Ndleleni Makhilane. "We visited each other on the weekends in the hostels. But our deepest friendships were with home friends." According to Mdelwa:

> We had friends from other tribes with whom we drank beer. We talked about the different customs and laws of our respective home lands and discovered if each other was married. Our greatest pride was our girlfriends and how many we had. We inquired whether our friends had their own imizi and if their parents were still alive. We also discussed our work and what had brought us to the mines.

Obviously, then, drinking sets on the mine compounds were not as closed as Mayer (1961:90–165) found for the networks of traditionalist *amaqaba* in East London in 1959, although like Mayer's Xhosa informants the Mpondo reported that the most exclusive home friend networks were among newcomers to the mines. Experienced workers, however, like Mpotsongo Mde, reported that Mpondo who roomed together were not necessarily from the same home area, but from all over Pondoland. Furthermore, their friends were often not home friends or even Mpondo, but underground work teammates.

> At first we would speak Fanagalo, but as the friendship continued we would learn each other's languages—especially Shangaans in this case. With home friends we would speak of home, but with work mates we spoke of how hard or how easily the work was going underground. We drank the beer supplied by the mines, supplemented by brown sugar. If we were found out, we would be punished.

Nor were Shangaans the only work friends mentioned. According to Sandiso Madikizela, for example:

> I was friendly with people from Basotho and other tribes who were work mates from the same team. We used to visit each other on weekends. When I went to a Basotho room, I was the guest of my Basotho acquaintance who would go to the kitchen and fetch food and meat and beer for me. . . . When we discussed our work, we spoke of the cruelty of the boss boy or the white man. We also talked about work if we were working in a very dangerous place and were scared.

Perhaps spatial separation of the compound from the direct impact of urban life enabled mine workers to engage in more loose-knit social networks than the Mayers' Xhosa without risking proletarianization.

Whatever the informal networks on the compound—and boundaries were not fixed—drinking was an integral part of them. For most miners the consumption of alcohol was indispensable to compound social life. Yet as we have seen, except for the low-alcohol compound beer twice a week, drinking on the mines, as well as in town and even in the countryside, was forbidden by law. Resistance to prohibition was taken for granted by both workers and management.

It is interesting to note that opposition to liquor controls was never taken up as a political issue by either the African National Congress or the Communist party in South Africa, presumably because the leaders of these movements shared a common petit bourgeois abhorrence of the evils of alcohol. The political potential of the liquor issue did emerge in debate in a meeting of the International Socialist League in Johannesburg on 11 October 1917, however (JUS 225, 3/527/17/1, Jali police spy report). About forty "natives" attended, a large number for the meetings of this proto-Communist organization. The focus of discussion was the Pass Laws, but someone asked "if the meeting also meant to help natives to sell Liquor." Another responded: "We must fight against everything and every law that is against us and when we get what we want we shall be able to obtain drink when we want it." No effort was made by the organization to follow up on this notion, despite the manifest importance of the issue in informal African resistance to state control.

Resistance to Prohibition

All our Mpondo informants readily acknowledged that supplementing the compound issue of beer with brown sugar was against the law. This particular umteto was regularly ignored in common practice, however. Workers would doctor the beer supplied by the mine and hide it for several days until it had "ripened" in containers that were buried either in the rooms or around the compound. Periodically, police raided the rooms and emptied the cans. The drains would run with beer, and the compound would be filled with the delicious stench of it. In an interview in 1988, Temba Gqumeni recalled with regret the waste of those raids. A police report about a raid on State Mines almost fifty years earlier said that "a river of skokian ran out of the gate whilst the Police were engaged in emptying the barrels, drums and other receptacles" (NLB 136, 2756/13, Sub-Inspector, Benoni to District Cmdt., Boksburg, 8/12/13). Resistance to prohibition had a long history on the South African mines as did the impotent determination of state officials to enforce it. Frequent police raids on compounds occurred, but it was difficult to pin the act of brewing on any one individual when rooms housed from fifteen to forty inmates. There were few prosecutions.

Generally, black miners did not dispute the obligation under law of the mine authorities to raid their rooms for liquor. Such arrangements, they said, were the umteto of the mine. One or two reports, however, indicate that in periods of tight labor supply or of mine-worker militancy against management, workers might take action to broaden the terms of the implicit contract about brewing.

The first case reported in the archives came within six weeks of a successful wage strike on Van Ryn Deep. On 31 January 1916, on the neighboring New Modderfontein Mine, about three hundred Mpondo held a meeting to plan a boycott of meat and beer and to picket the kitchen in protest against the compound manager's long-established practice of throwing out beer stored up in rooms (NTS 210, 277/16/473, SAP, Benoni to District Cmdt., Boksburg, 4/2/16; Acting DNL to Commissioner of Police, Pretoria, 11/2/16). According to the Director of Native Labour, a number of workers did boycott the beer issue for a couple of days until, in his words, "their natural inclinations . . . overcame their resolution . . . and the matter . . . adjusted itself."

The second reported instance, on 10 January 1943, was a full-scale riot at Nourse Mines (*Star* 10/1/43, 23/1/43 [Stop Press edition], 25/1/43 [Stop Press edition]; NTS 7675, 103/332, 11/1/43). About one hundred fifty Xhosa workers demanded "the right to brew beer in the compound" along with "an increased wage in lieu of rations." When Gilchrist, the compound manager, denied their request, they threw stones at him, marched to the kitchen and assaulted the cooks and the assistant compound manager, and then proceeded on to the beer room only to be met by the South African police, who arrested them. This affair was apparently inspired by the demand of the African Mine Workers' Union that workers be paid additional cash in lieu of rations and was a response to the quality of the food more generally. According to the courtroom testimony of the assistant compound manager, one Davidson, they pulled him "towards a pot of beans which [they] said were not fit for human consumption. The native held him with one hand and with the other tried to force some of the beans in his mouth."

Compound Brewing Rackets

Before 1930, and to some extent thereafter, Mozambican workers, with their many generations of migrancy, were among those most deeply involved in the informal sector of compound life. This was especially the case with liquor, since Mozambicans had acquired a taste for strong liquor at home and hence were particularly dissatisfied with the weak compound issue, whose alcoholic content varied from 5.6 percent to .87 percent with an average of 3.12 percent (NLB 158, 274/14/245). It had long been Portuguese practice to sell cheap metropolitan wine to its Mozambican subjects. Pinto Coelho's 1904 report on high mortality among Mozambican mine workers (SNA 244, 2912/04, 30/6/04) in fact advocated that they be supplied with wine for their health and to teach them moderation, for otherwise they would "seek oblivion in drunkenness, and . . . descend to the level of an animal." While Mozambican recruiters urged similarly, the Transvaal authorities refused to countenance such special pleading.

Historically, Mozambican miners have been canny businessmen. "East Coasters" migrated early to South Africa, to the sugar fields in Natal before the opening of the gold mines (Harries 1982), and they seem to have appreciated early the value of cash and consumer goods. Mpondo reported that their Mozambican friends laughed at them for investing their earnings in cattle. Unlike their South African fellows, Mozambican mine workers seem to have operated their homesteads like European peasant households with greater stress on cash incomes (First 1983). Evidence indicates that at least until 1930 Mozambicans predominated both in brewing "hard stuff" on the compounds and in selling it. For example, an East Rand police report on a December 1913 raid on Knight Central (NLB 136, 2756/13, 10/12/13) stated that "in four rooms occupied by Shangaans in the Compound about 1100 gallons of khali were found and 31 arrests made, no beer was found in any of the other rooms and there is no doubt that khali and skokian is brewed by the Shangaans and sold by them to the other natives in the Compound." In a couple of the faction fights involving alcohol and mentioned in the archives, workers had gone to a Mozambican room to get the liquor (NLB 207, 1721/14/48, 17/12/25; NLB 185, 1169/14/48, 9/7/14). Another worker, testifying about a friend who died as a result of a fall while inebriated, said the two of them had gone with two other Xhosa-speaking drinking friends to a "Shangaan" room to buy adulterated "native liquor."

Not only Shangaan rooms, but also certain mine compounds enjoyed distinct periods of popularity as centers for the supply of liquor, for example, Spes Bona compound in Johannesburg East (NLB 136, 2756/13, 18/3/14, 25/3/14, 28/11/14), West Driefontein compound on East Rand Proprietary Mines and New Primrose[3] on the East Rand around 1914 (NLB 136, 2756/13, 15/6/14 and replies), Langlaagte B on the Central Rand in the late teens (NLB 135, 2756/13/54, 10/8/17), and Witwatersrand Deep compound (NLB 136, 2756/17/54, 31/10/22) in the early 1920s.

Although not all reports specify the ethnic origins of compound beer dealers, whenever they do, they mention Mozambicans. As often, however, the reports mention that brewers had positions as mine police or cooks on the compound. Compound rackets, profitable entrepreneurial sidelines for Mozambican workers and black compound officials alike, frequently involved the sale of illicit liquor.

In his evidence to the Economic and Wage Commission in 1924, A. W. G. Champion, who had recently been employed as a mine clerk, alleged that the compound manager himself took a cut of the profits in liquor dealing, saying: "He permits this kaffir beer to be brewed and he gives what may be termed unstamped licenses to brew kaffir beer. . . . they

[3]For similar situations on other "Barnato" Johannesburg Consolidated Investment (JCI) compounds see NLB 198, 1504/14/80. JCI mines were notorious for illicit liquor at this time.

[the compound managers] make more than their salaries by selling jobs as boss boys and police boys'' (EWC, paras. 7790ff., 7851ff., 7955ff).

Such charges were difficult to substantiate since the state and management acted against compound managers only in the most egregious cases. Yet compound manager G. A. Tandy testified to the Buckle Commission in 1914 that ''in many cases police boys are in collusion with the brewers and get paid at the rate of about one pound for every tin of say 10 gallons brewed, and that is often the reason why some boys are so anxious to get police jobs'' (NGI, GAT 2). If his testimony is true, it would have been in the interests of prospective mine policemen to bribe compound managers.

Most evidence is indirect. For example, on New Primrose Mine in 1914, Compound Manager Bodley rehired as mine policeman a certain ''Waistcoat'' who had just completed six months' hard labor for liquor selling. Bodley would surely not have risked his license for nothing. Within months, a police raid found ''Waistcoat'' gambling in his room in which was stored eighty gallons of khali, obviously for sale (NLB 136, 2756/13, 15/6/14). On several mines, the head cook or a mine policeman was given the key to the brewing room and permitted to issue beer without supervision. Indeed, on many mines, free access to beer was a perquisite of the mine police force and their cronies. As late as our mine ethnography in 1976, when liquor was freely available at the mine bar, black compound police turned a blind eye to such illegal activities as *dagga* (marijuana) dealing in selected rooms.

Favoritism by mine police caused workers early on to take collective action demanding that mine police be appointed from their own ''tribe.'' Generally, however, black workers did not contest the right of indunas and mine policemen to brew liquor or to delegate the right to brew to particular rooms. Such arrangements, winked at if not actually supported by their white bosses, assured the availability of liquor on the mine.

Occasionally, resentments over liquor monopolies developed into ethnic conflict, however. On 31 January 1928, for instance, Portuguese workers on West Rand Consolidated refused their food and marched to the manager's house to demand the dismissal of the recently appointed head induna, who was a Xhosa-speaking Hlubi. The substantial increase in ''Cape'' labor on the mines during the 1920s and 1930s meant that the appointment of a Xhosa-speaking head induna was probably a new development. Mozambican boss boys led the demonstration (NLB 197, 987/13/68). They apparently resented ''the destroying of liquor in certain East Coast rooms.'' The compound manager himself reported that their protest ''was a deliberate attempt to master the liquor control'' and that the majority of the leaders ''came from rooms in which persistent attempts [were] made to carry on the manufacture of liquor concoctions." Reading between the lines, it appears that the new head induna had decided to break the Mozambican brewing racket by raiding rooms previously immune to mine police searches. The malcontents raised other issues against the new induna, complaining that their own induna was under his thumb. After wavering on the issue, management stood firm and arrested and repatriated eleven highly paid and experienced "East Coast Natives" not least because the compound manager feared collective violence from the majority "Cape" workers on behalf of "their" induna. A Native Affairs review criticized the compound manager for permitting the head induna "to raid the rooms for liquor without being accompanied by an European. . . . The East Coast natives, who . . . [were] particularly addicted to Skokian, resented *Natives* unaccompanied by any one in authority, entering their rooms and upsetting their liquor." Clearly, the matter of "rights" to brewing rackets was a delicate one on the compounds and was recognized to be so by the authorities.

Shebeens

The compounds were not the sole sites for brewing rackets aimed at mine workers, however. Mine locations, farm and township shebeens, and municipal beer halls were quite as important at different points in time. Sean Moroney's (1982) article "Mine Married Quarters" is a useful overview of archival material on mine locations including data on alcohol before 1920. We have already noted that a few skilled and trusted workers were housed by the mines (with their women—not necessarily their wives) in married quarters (*skomplas*) adjacent to the compounds. Such mine townships continue to this day to have a reputation for heavy drinking and access to women. Before 1920, those compounds that were well known for their liquor rackets were often also associated with infamous mine locations, which would be raided along with the compounds by zealous South African policemen. Moroney mentions Witwatersrand Deep location. He might as well have written of Van Ryn Estates or Langlaagte Royal locations. The skomplas was not the only place around the mines where mine workers could buy liquor, however.

Before urban townships sprang up around new mines, farm shebeens enjoyed privileged access to the large mine-worker market. In 1914, Jacobus van der Walt, member of parliament for Pretoria South, reported to the Natives Land Commission (NLC:267):

> [T]here are thousands of natives in my constituency, they mostly come from locations in the bushveld. They live in the neighbourhood of the goldfields from 6 to 8 miles away. . . . They sow lands

> mostly on the half share system. . . . The lands belong mostly to companies and rich people. It is very easy for a native to make a living there and that is why they congregate to a very great extent in that area. As a rule on Saturday nights the mine labourers go out on their bicycles to these lands and stop there during the week-end when they have beer drinks.

Such rural shebeens long outlasted sharecropping on South African farms.

Enforcing prohibition in the countryside was beyond the resources of the thinly scattered rural police force. Van der Walt added in his evidence before the Natives Land Commission:

> [T]his area is not protected by the town police and the rural police are too few in number to look properly after these natives, and numerous cases of stock thefts and even murder take place. Not only sheep and poultry are stolen but also the cattle given out by the Government to poor whites have been taken by these natives and slaughtered for these meetings.

The police argued that mine management bore the rightful responsibility for controlling forays of mine workers into the countryside. Thus, on 29 August 1916, the commissioner of police wrote to the secretary for native affairs urging that mine management passes issued to mine workers state their destination so that they could be kept away from "certain farms in the East Rand district which [were] hotbeds of illicit liquor traffic . . . [and where] liquor [was] buried on the veldt away from the houses" (NLB 210, 1875/4/72, 29/8/16).

New regulations did little to help, however. The manager of Sub-Nigel mine, for instance, reported in 1934 (TMGC:334ff.) that even though his mine refused the workers permission to visit Spaarwater farm, they went to shop at the store there. The property right of the store owner to trade with mine workers apparently could not be infringed upon. From the store, local "touts" would lead them to nearby settlements ("they spring up of their own accord like mushrooms, as soon as the boys come over with their money"), where "a good deal of illicit Native liquor, and prostitution, and other evils" abounded (TMGC:905).

In fact, the manager's investigations revealed that women came from Nigel township on Thursday to the farm huts, where they brewed for the weekend, and returned to town on Monday or Tuesday. Other rural shebeens on the Rand may likewise have been integrated quite early into the urban system, a system dominated in the 1930s by "regular Native skokiaan queens" from Basutoland, according to Graham Ballenden

(TMGC:602–3) of the Johannesburg municipality.[4] Each skokiaan queen, he said, "form[ed] a temporary attachment with a Mine Native" so that he would bring his friends to drink at her place. We have already noted this pattern in discussing contemporary sexual practices with town women at shebeens.

For mines in established urban areas, township shebeens provided attractions similar to the skomplas and the farm shebeens. However, there was greater variety in town, although town shebeens represented greater risks because of their urban clientele. More experienced mine workers, especially amatshipa voluntaries who signed on again and again, sought out the urban milieu. Such workers tended to congregate around the mines in Johannesburg municipality. Robinson Deep and City Deep, Nourse Mines, Simmer and Jack, and certain Crown Mines and Randfontein Estates compounds attracted such proletarianized (or lumpen proletarian) workers. On those mines the boundaries between compound and township were quite permeable, with many workers choosing to live in town and many more opting to drink there. Two townships—Prospect in central Johannesburg and Vrededorp in the west of the city—were renowned during and after World War I as places where mine workers both dwelt and drank. In 1919, a police report on Vrededorp read:

> Large numbers of natives are residing in this Location. They are chiefly employed on the neighbouring mines. These natives keep women here for the purpose of making and trading in illicit liquor. They are constantly being arrested and convicted, but as soon as one Liquor Den is closed others are opened. . . . On Saturdays and Sundays large numbers of natives visit these dens and are a nuisance to the European residents of Mayfair North, Fordsburg [neighboring suburbs] and Vrededorp. . . . I would estimate the number of natives, mostly mine natives living here, at about 1200. . . . The residents of Mayfair North . . . object very strongly to the large number of natives continually passing to and from the Crown Mines to the location. They are in many instances under the influence of liquor and insulting.[5]

[4]Bonner (1990) provides a detailed discussion of "undesirable Basotho women" in the townships on the Rand.

[5]SAP—Confidential 6/757/20/1/A, F. V. Lloyd, Sub-Inspector Western Area to Deputy Commissioner of Police, JHB, Report on "Malay Location, Vrededorp," 3/9/19; see also *RDM*, 2/3/20; NLB 309, 125/19/48, Minutes, 4/3/20, meeting with black residents, 25/3/20, DNL to SNA, 1/12/20; JUS 291, 3/215/20, Vrededorp Riots, 19/3/20. As late as 1931, white owners of concession stores around Crown Mines were complaining that liquor sales were cutting into their sales of legitimate merchandise (JUS 538, 7934/29/1 and following correspondence).

The very success of the Department of Native Affairs in obliging the mines to control compound brewing of khali in 1914 pushed mine workers out into the surrounding townships—especially on weekends.[6] Mine managers then confronted a new set of problems. On 22 August 1934, R. Develing, the compound manager of East Rand Proprietary Mines wrote to the municipal location superintendent in Benoni: "mine natives trek from here daily, especially over weekends and pay days, and in many cases absent themselves from work for several days. Others return to the compounds unfit for work either from assaults or being under the influence of liquor" (Benoni Town Council Archives, T240[7]).

Not only were many workers drunk or hung over when they reported for work on Monday morning, however. Others did not show up at all because of their arrest in town for liquor offenses. Conscientious policing of Prospect township in November 1916, for instance, so "seriously depleted Monday morning shifts" at Wolhuter Mine that the manager refused to allow his workers out without a special pass and then apparently "obstructed" the issue of such passes. This policy in effect incarcerated many Wolhuter workers within the compound. At once a deputation of merchants from trading stores around the mine visited the Native Affairs inspector to demand that the workers be allowed their legal right to patronize their shops and their eating houses (NLB 210, 1875/14/72, NA inspector's report on Prospect township, 25/11/16). In 1934, mine management was still facing the same dilemma. The manager of Sub-Nigel (TMGC:320) related despairingly: "they come back, especially at weekends, drunk, and there are a tremendous number of assaults, also convictions for liquor and so forth. That is my point really, why I stress the [need for] control."

Police attempts to prevent drinking by arresting mine workers in the townships, however, created as many problems for mine managements as did the aftereffects of the alcohol itself. As late as 1976 in Welkom, mine welfare officers would regularly bail out workers arrested in town on weekends for "drunk and disorderly" conduct and bring them back to work. Is it any wonder that mine and compound managers chose to wink at brewing rackets in their compounds or even at some adulterations of compound issue beer in worker rooms?

[6]See, for example, NLB 136, 2756/13, Manager, City Deep to DNL, 9/4/14, 17/6/14, 8/7/14, 17/7/14, regarding Prospect township and mine workers drinking and living there; NLB 40, NA Inspector, Boksburg to DNL, 12/12/14; Compound Manager, Wits Deep to NA Inspector, Boksburg, 21/12/14; NLB 137, 2756/13/54, NA Inspector, JHB-W, to DNL, "Drunkenness among [Mine] Natives," 1/6/15.
[7]I am grateful to J. Cohen for directing me to this reference.

At the same time, gold producers took every opportunity to attack municipalities for failing to control brewing in their townships (JUS 538, 7934/29/1, General Manager, Gold Producers' Committee, to Secretary for Justice, 17/9/29ff.). By the late 1920s and 1930s as mines closed down or combined in Johannesburg and began developing on the Far East Rand, centers of illegal liquor shifted to the East Rand townships of Benoni, Boksburg, and Brakpan (Bonner 1990). Boksburg early fenced off its location and forbade mine workers to enter, but Benoni location, the Benoni Indian Bazaar, and Power Street in Brakpan became latter-day Vrededorps and Prospects.[8] In the words of Leonard Cheeseman, an East Rand retailer giving evidence to the Trading on Mining Grounds Commission in 1934:

> Power Street is a business street with approximately thirty-eight shops. . . . They are in close proximity to State Mine and also to the Brakpan Location, and not very far from the municipal compound. Their idea of trade is entirely Native trade. Wherever there is Native trade of course you naturally get the skokiaan woman and so on—the illicit liquor selling. (TMGC:142)

Mine managers reporting to the same commission said they found the urban locations "very undesirable" (TMGC:345, 375ff.). Nonetheless, they were unable to prevent workers from "wandering about" on weekends. H. Wellbeloved of the Native Recruiting Corporation summed up the problem:

> They issue a large number of special passes over the week-end; but if a boy [black miner] really wants to go away, and you don't give him a special pass, he will go without it. He will take the risk of being caught. We don't really restrict the issue of special passes. . . . Take the Brakpan location: that is out of bounds. As far as the compound managers are concerned, they will not give their boys specials to go there, but they get there all the same. . . . The restraint is so slight that if any attempt were made to effect further control by the refusal of special passes [the workers] . . . would not stand for it. (TMGC:904–5)

Once again, on matters of importance to them, workers seemed relatively independent of management control. Municipalities were hard-pressed to control mine workers coming to drink, even in new well-policed townships,

[8]For Benoni and Brakpan locations, see JUS 538, 7934/29/2, Commissioner SAP to Secretary for Justice, "Illicit Liquor Selling: Benoni and Brakpan Locations." For Power Street, see NLB 136, 2756/13, letter to Assistant Magistrate, Brakpan, 18/12/27, and ensuing correspondence; and TMGC, 108ff. Phil Bonner (1990, 1991) tells the story of the East Rand at this time in graphic narrative detail.

such as Orlando (part of what later became Soweto). In fact, Graham Ballenden, manager for municipal affairs in Johannesburg in 1933, discovered that at least sixty mine workers had been rented houses in Orlando by claiming to be married to their "concubines," women from the slumyards in the center of town (TMGC:595–96). This arrangement benefited both the women, who were not entitled to a house unless they were married, and their mine-worker companions, who obtained the comforts of home life, a social center for drinking with their cronies, and possibly extra income: "The woman would make the liquor, and the [man] would go back to the mines and bring his friends—probably twenty or thirty of them over the weekend."

Supporting this account, several Mpondo informants mentioned Sotho friends in the 1950s and 1960s who had set up their lovers in town houses. Even in 1982, the social worker in the Welkom Anglo American Mine township (called Las Vegas by the locals) reported that many of the "wives" who moved into the new houses were in fact urban mistresses of the workers, rather than wives from the country. Ms. Ndatshe found a similar phenomenon at Vaal Reefs in 1990. The practice of claiming town women as "wives" to get the comforts of urban housing had not changed in the fifty years between Orlando in 1933 and Welkom in 1982, despite changes in the drinking laws, and it remained the same at Kanana near Vaal Reefs in 1990.

In summary, among those who came to drink at the shebeens at least one client would have close links with the shebeen owner. Shebeens had more to offer than simply alcohol, however. First, drinking occurred within a social context, and part of that context was certainly access to women. Second, men also came to the shebeens because they were convivial places to escape from the constraints of the workplace. Traditional mine workers seldom drank alone or with strangers. Drinking of beer, preferably prepared by women, was an aspect of male sociability, deeply rooted in those rural practices so eloquently evoked by Monica Hunter in the quotation at the beginning of this chapter.

After 1973

When prohibition ended for Africans in 1962, the gold mines at once established bars ("liquor outlets") on the compounds. This action brought about the demise of long-established compound brewing rackets and more informal adulterations of compound issue beer. Men no longer adopted the traditionally female task of brewing beer. Drinking groups no longer met semisecretly in compound rooms. Miners now could choose between the management-supervised liquor outlets or shebeens outside the compound. Shebeens, although more expensive, continued to draw miners because of their intimacy and the attraction of attentive women.

The new breed of more proletarianized miners who started to flock to the mines when wages increased after 1973 preferred manufactured "European" beer and earned more money to spend on hard liquor. Gradually, even the shebeens stopped brewing and began retailing mass-market beer and liquor, marked up 50 to 100 percent. Only one of the seven shebeens surveyed in Thabong in 1982, for instance, brewed traditional beer, and its clientele was older men from Lesotho. Furthermore, drinking networks were less likely to share a common commitment to peasant proprietorship. Men from pitifully overpopulated rural or urban slums no longer discussed and planned the building of the umzi as they drank together. With no productive future in the countryside, such migrants said that their numerous dependents "ate" their earnings. Men anticipating no future reward for the drudgery and the alienation of mine work and painful separation from loved ones were likely to find drink more a means of escape than a seal of solidarity. "Alcoholism" suddenly became a problem. One management study (Kruger and Rundle 1978) reported:

> [T]he hospital admission rate of men under the influence of alcohol at one of the mine hospitals in the Orange Free State has increased from 1.12 per 1000 per annum in 1973 to 10.7 per 1000 in 1977. This represents only the tip of the iceberg. The road accident and assault rates have increased in parallel.

In 1976, a participant observer in the Welkom Mine ethnography reported, for a period when mine wages in the Orange Free State averaged about R 97 a month:

> [T]here is a beer-hall in the middle of the compound which is full of people from Monday to Monday. Some people use more than R 3 a day, and the people drink in groups. The ordinary people drink Sotho beer while some few people who are a bit educated use brandy which really absorbs the whole money from [them]. Some of these people who always drink use most of the money that by the end of the week they have no money in their pockets and they forget to write letters to their families. . . . On Sundays the miners pay a visit to their friends who are in the other mines nearby. There they discuss matters relating to their homes. Some never talk about their homes. They just visit their friends in order to drink or to visit with them in towns where they can see the women.

Youth protests, originating in Soweto in 1976, spurred condemnation of the widening toll of escapist drinking in urban African townships. Radical township youth publicly denounced the alcoholic excesses of their elders as undermining the liberation struggle. Young people targeted beer halls and bottle stores as prime symbols of their parents' capitulation to white exploitation. In the middle 1980s some of their tactics eventually spilled onto the mines in the form of liquor outlet boycotts, led by militant young unionists.

The November 1985 liquor outlet boycotts at Vaal Reefs No. 1 compound are cases in point.[9] For both tactical and moral reasons, the local union chose alcohol as one of its rallying points. Because boycotting the liquor outlet did not directly affect production, management could not declare it illegal and seek a court injunction as they had just done with a widely supported go-slow. The workers believed that the boycott would nevertheless deal a blow to management profits. Furthermore, the new breed of workers tended to see alcohol as a strategy deliberately used by whites to keep blacks in submission. Supporters of the boycott insisted: "We are not here to drink, but to earn money for our families!" Such arguments won unanimous approval at the union meeting.

The first day of the boycott, 5 November 1985, the bar was empty. The next day a group of Mpondo workers marched into the liquor outlet, clad in sheets and heavily armed, and sat down to drink. Originally worn by iindlavini when they went to their dance contests, white sheets had become battle wear for Xhosa-speakers on the mines. This attire was meant to distinguish them from the Basotho, who wore blankets. The entire Xhosa-speaking mine-dance team crowded into a nearby room, fully armed, to offer reinforcement if necessary.[10] Nothing happened. The next day the bar was as busy as ever, with all the regulars back at their customary stations. The boycott was over.

Two weeks later, on 19 November, a second attempt aborted when the union ignored informal terms negotiated with the strikebreakers. Enthusiasm at the meeting for the second boycott had run so high that union leaders failed to allow a day to lay in a stock of liquor to tide the heavy drinkers over. White-sheeted men bearing arms broke the boycott again. Once again the new militants underestimated the importance of alcohol in the old migrant culture and the effectiveness of local management and

[9]This account of events at Vaal Reefs No. 1 is culled from evidence to the Bregman Commission (AAC/VR). More details on the affair are given at the conclusion of chapter 6.

[10]In fact the Xhosa dance team had officially been disbanded some time before at the insistence of the union head office, but ex-dancers continued to be housed in the same rooms and were regarded by their compound mates as dancers. The National Union of Mineworkers has long argued that ethnic dance teams have initiated faction fights on behalf of management.

mine security support for the conservatives. Compound police had twice condoned the serving of liquor to men carrying weapons. In retaliation, someone who was part of the township youth network threw a petrol bomb into the liquor outlet. For several days thereafter the strikebreakers roamed the compound and skomplas, allegedly in full view of management and accompanied by compound police, attacking shaft stewards. They seriously wounded one and killed two others. The shaft stewards had seriously disrupted their drinking, they said, and management had given them permission to root out these union leaders. Compound management clearly took advantage of divisions within the workforce over the issue of alcohol.

Drinking patterns were no longer a common ground for migrant solidarity and resistance to management. Traditionalist workers, including the Mpondo dance team, continued to assert their right to imbibe freely. Proletarianized workers with their activist leadership protested the evils of management-orchestrated alcoholic excess. Alcohol consumption, which for decades had brought migrant miners together, was now driving a wedge between them. Social drinking, which once had represented protest against management, could now signify collaboration with the enemy. Discussion of issues around contemporary mine-worker drinking brings us to the vexed question of violence among black workers themselves.

6 Faction Fights

Mine-Worker Violence

The topic of this chapter is not brutality underground or the structural violence built into the workings of the compound system as a form of hegemony. We have already examined those issues. Here I shall try to unravel changes and continuities in what management and workers alike called "faction fights," that is, violence among groups of workers themselves. "Violence" I define as action that causes or threatens to cause physical harm to another's person or property. I deal here with collective violence. Although acts of individual violence may precipitate collective violence, they do so only under certain conditions. Nor will explanations of individual violence necessarily suffice for collective violence. Faction fights were only partially products of management policies or the outcomes of the desperate misery of exploited men. On closer examination, most collective violence on the mines can be shown to have been strategic rather than merely primordial. Collective violence, I suggest, is the practice of politics by violent means.

White South African assumptions about faction fights tended to be stereotyped and couched in terms of "tribalism." The comment of a Welkom CID (Criminal Investigation Department) officer was typical. He said, "I don't know why they're beating each other to death, management doesn't know and I'm damn sure they don't know themselves" (Argyle [c. 1987]). Since data on faction fights rely heavily on police reports that tend to share such assumptions, one has to read and interpret those reports cautiously. Furthermore, since faction fights were regarded as in some sense a "normal" aspect of mine life, not all such skirmishes made their way into the newspapers or even the archives. For example, a police report about a 1910 Christmas fight between "Mxosas" and "East Coast boys" noted: "this is the fourth disturbance the Mxosas at this compound have caused during the year'' (NA 81, F164). There is no record of the other three, however. Indeed, only seven disturbances are recorded for 1910 (BBNA 1910:391–92). Four years later, James Millar, compound manager at Langlaagte B, told Commissioner H. O. Buckle that fights between ''Xhosa'' and ''Basutos'' were lessening (NGI, 27/10/14:35). ''On Block B four or five years ago we had faction fights once a week regularly,'' he said. In March 1914, James Douglas, deputy commissioner of police in Johannesburg, reported to Buckle that frequent but manageable trouble on the mines was ''due to faction fights . . . [that] often start[ed] by a paltry incident between two boys of different tribes'' (NGI, 6/3/14:2). On Boxing Day, 1913, the *Star* correspondent for the East Rand noted self-righteously that police precautions had prevented the usual Christmas compound riots—only to have to announce in the next issue a death and several injuries from a Boxing Day fight between ''Zulus'' and ''Basutos'' on Modder B Mine. In his report (NGI, para. 509), Buckle referred to African workers' ''ancient habit of faction fights.''

In the past, with rare exceptions, incidents of ''intertribal'' violence were thus taken by whites to be primordial and inevitable, precipitated by individual squabbles, no doubt, but unavoidable in dealing with primitive, ''uneducated natives'' (NGI, Douglas, 6/3/14). Policy was thus one of containment, and deaths from faction fights, like deaths from rock falls underground, were taken for granted. Rian Malan's *My Traitor's Heart* (1990) extends this conception of violence to white South Africans as well. While such treatment is more evenhanded and Malan's harrowing accounts are very powerful, nonetheless, just as with typical white South African accounts of black violence, he eschews other explanations in favor of primordialism.

Generalizations about the incidence of collective violence on the mines are difficult to make. McNamara (1985) has suggested on the basis of the Chamber of Mines archives and a literature review that there were two unusually quiet periods for conflicts on the mines. These were 1920–1940 and 1950–1970, somewhat more than half of the time between 1910 and the present. Of course, these periods of quiescence may have had to do with fluctuations of interest in recording faction fights, but additional archival evidence available to me does not disprove McNamara's essential position. I should modify his periodization slightly, however. On my evidence the relatively quiet years were 1921–1937 and 1947–1972, although data for the latter period are particularly scant.

What is striking about the archival evidence is how infrequently faction fights were recorded, even in the ''hot'' years. My search of the press and archives for 1938–1946 turned up accounts of twenty-seven faction fights.[1] McNamara's 1985 study lists eighty-eight between 1973 and 1982. When one considers the hundreds of thousands of workers, housed tribally, with supposedly different and hostile cultures, the infrequency of such conflict is surprising.

Faction Fights Described

We have seen that the solidarities and activities of compound life made it bearable for black migrant workers with access to land in the countryside. The social basis for maintenance of rural self-conceptions was the home-friend network, and miners would go to much trouble and take much pleasure in maintaining these rural links. Mine workers preferred, indeed insisted, on being housed near or with home friends, and management not only permitted but also encouraged such solidarities by housing people from similar linguistic regions together, although work teams were always mixed. This policy of ethnically segregated housing along with home-friend networks provided the social structural basis for faction fights.

McNamara (1980:310–20) found that personal acquaintance with home fellows might be extended to include people from the same region or even different but related language groups. Many mine workers whom Vivienne Ndatshe and I interviewed in Pondoland, where Xhosa is spoken, for instance, mentioned mine gatherings that included men from several Pondoland locations and even Xesibe and Baca miners. Similarly, Sotho and Tswana would hang out together, or Xhosa and Zulu. Thus, home-friend networks did not preclude wider friendships and could be quite varied. Ethnic identities themselves shifted, with ethnic boundaries defined as much by the numbers of home friends or common language speakers who happened to end up on any particular mine as on fixed or universal ethnic boundaries.[2] Moreover, if one was in a real minority, one might choose the most powerful group on the mine with which to associate oneself.

The ethnic identity of Baca workers is an interesting case in point. Baca, who speak Xhosa, developed a monopoly on night-soil removal; they specialized in cleaning out the bucket latrines. The other workers called them *sompungana*, meaning "shit carriers"—a sore point with the Baca. Baca

[1]Philip Bonner's recent work (1992) has turned up several more instances of "factional" violence among mine workers in the vicinity of East Rand townships. While these might have added five or six events to my list, they would not have affected the periodization, which Bonner's research essentially confirms, nor would they have much affected the numbers, which remain surprisingly low.

[2]For a nuanced account of the situational nature of ethnic identities and their implication in power relationships between men and women in the countryside in Northern Natal, see David Webster's superb essay in Spiegel and McAllister 1991.

were sometimes housed separately, which would have reinforced their own Baca identity. However, since often there were relatively few of them on the mines, they would then be classified and housed as Mpondo or Xhosa because of linguistic similarities. Again, it was a matter of numbers and management perceptions. In the early years, they were sometimes even housed with all "Cape Colony boys," which would have included Sesotho speakers from the northern Transkei and mixed groups from Herschel.

Reports on faction fights that reify ethnic distinctions along lines of housing blocks thus overlook differing meanings of "Xhosa" or even "Pondo" (who might include Xesibe and Baca, and who speak Xhosa). Similar distinctions may be made for such management categories as "Mozambican" and "Tropical." Even Sotho from Lesotho (often called "British Basuto"), sharply defined as they were by geopolitical boundaries, might be housed with "South African Basuto" (or Pedi or Tswana), who were themselves not unified groups.

Consider, for an example of the complexities of being "Xhosa," the police report about a fight at Venterspost compound, Randfontein, on 21 and 22 April 1940:

> The cause of the trouble originated underground the week before. Two Xosa boss boys assaulted a Pondo. The Xosas were charged with assault and released on bail. . . . The assault caused ill-feeling amongst the Pondos. During the afternoon of 21.4.1940, Xosas, of which one section [are] Bovanas, visited native huts on Panvlakte. The Bovanas assaulted 4 Xosas. The Xosas returned to the compound and thereafter attacked the Bovana section. . . . A Pondo took advantage of the turmoil to avenge the assault by the Xosa boss boys on a Pondo the week before and fatally stabbed a Xosa. . . . A Pondo was arrested. . . . A party of Pondos demanded the release of the prisoner. . . . [When this was refused] they replied that they would attack the Xosa unless the prisoner was released. Information was then received that the one affected section of the Xosas [Bomvana?], of the night before, had joined forces with the Pondos to attack the rest of the Xosas. (NTS 7675, SAP Krugersdorp, 27/4/40)

The Bomvana are a fiercely traditional Xhosa-speaking group from the southwest Transkei coastal area who are remembered by older Mpondo as fighters second only to themselves. The description of the fight itself is typical. The confusion of the policeman about "Xosas" arose from the fact that the Bomvana happened to be housed in the Xhosa block, but in their own section. Both they and the Mpondo speak Xhosa, but both were obviously ferociously independent of the "Xhosa" in this case. Lest any assume that the Bomvana and Mpondo were always allies, consider the following summary of a 1942 police report about a fight at Venterspost No. 1:

> Bomvanas returned to No. 1 compound from a beer drink and attacked Xhosas sleeping on the lawn in the compound (5/9/42). On Sunday (6/9/42) the Xhosas attacked the Bomvanas in retribution. Police from Randfontein restored order. However the Mpondo heard a rumor that three Mpondo had been stabbed by Bomvanas on a nearby farm so they attacked the Bomvanas in the compound, killing one and smashing everything in their rooms. Mine police were driven out of the compound and the compound manager who tried to pacify them had to retire under a rain of missiles. Police came and chased them to their rooms where they put up a violent fight. Eventually the Mpondo and Bomvanas were disarmed and the police collected a cartload of sticks, pieces of iron, hammers, etc. (NTS 7675, SAP Krugersdorp, 12/9/42)

Management ethnic assignations, artificial as they sometimes were, were nonetheless important in worker politics on the mines because of the way in which different types of jobs were allotted to certain groups and certain recreational activities were condoned for some groups but not for others. Take for instance the testimony of Ernest Cezula, who was on Crown Mines in the 1940s, and whom we interviewed in 1984:

> The Mpondo have a reputation for being trouble-makers but in fact that is because of their pride. They do fight often so as not to be looked down upon. On the job they value their independence—they don't want to be followed about and told what to do. Even the mine captain doesn't push them around if he wants to avoid trouble. Mozambicans and Sotho make good lashers because they don't tire easily—they have great endurance. Mpondo get tired quicker although they are stronger. Most of the machine boys are Mpondo, because they are strong. Some of the Sotho are jealous but they can do nothing because the Mpondo are so strong.

"Mpondo" became well-paid drillers (machine boys), then, because they had a reputation for physical strength. "Shangaans" were often boss boys. Sotho were supposedly excellent shovelers, which gave them access to well-paid shaft-sinking work (Guy and Thabane 1988). A 1938 report on a faction fight on Venterspost Mine during its early years stated: "In the early stages of the development of a mine it is customary for Basuto natives to predominate in numbers, natives of this race are arrogant and overbearing in manner and are inclined to pin-prick natives of other races if they are numerically stronger" (SAP, Krugersdorp, 17/3/38, in NTS 7674, 92/332).

Thus do Sotho pride and honor come to seem arrogant. Even in recent years, the point at which a newly developed mine comes into production and workers of non-Sotho origins are hired in substantial numbers is always a sensitive time. McNamara (1985:251–54) has an account of a fight at Deelkraal in 1980 that centered on this issue.

Explaining Collective Violence

Of course, violence in its immediacy and perturbation and bonding may even be enjoyable. There is one wonderful account (NLB 197, 1440/14/48) of a rollicking and obviously celebratory fight on Christmas and Boxing days in 1917 at City Deep and in Prospect township, with wild drunkenness and typically rough stick play. An account of a fight at Langlaagte B in July 1914 (NLB 185, 1169/14/48, NA JHB West, 9/7/14) also suggests the joy of fighting—this time by Sotho. Guy and Thabane (1987:447) comment on the testimony of Johannes Rantoa, who left the mines to hang out in town and fight with the MaRashea:

> There is an atmosphere of intense enjoyment in Rantoa's description of the fights in which he participated: the fight is something of a game just as football, in his accounts, has something of the fight. There can be no doubt that the exhilaration of physical combat gave relief in general conditions of severe social deprivation.

They go on to quote Rantoa:

> We were stronger than those people, there was not another reason [for fighting]. It was just the enjoyment of fighting and it was as if people were not satisfied during their time of herding. It was nice that thing of fighting each other like that, even though it was dangerous as it caused so many deaths.

Gordon (1978) writes of a faction fight on a Namibian copper mine as a "celebration of ethnicity." The practical integrity within migrant cultures, by stressing solidarities, may play into such violent "celebrations."

Such accounts stress the ritual nature of faction fighting before the 1970s. Despite their supposed prevalence, relatively few workers were actually killed in these fights, which may indeed explain their infrequent mention in press and archives. Young men in the Nguni and Lesotho countryside fought with sticks (Sotho also became expert stone-throwers in battles between villages), and some of the rules for such fights seem to have carried over into the compounds. According to the research of Percy Qayiso in the Mpondo countryside (Mayer and Mayer 1972:137), it was typical of Mpondo young men to stick fight inside the huts, and if a fight started "it [was] a common gambit to 'hit the lamp,' thus plunging the hut into darkness and confusion." Such fighting in the dark is often mentioned in mine reports of fights in which Mpondo were involved. On West Rand Consolidated, the day after a fight between Mpondo and Shangaans it was discovered "that Pondos, on the Sixth Level of the South Shaft of the property, had extinguished the electric lights and . . . assault[ed] the Shangaans" (NTS 7675, 102/332, SAP Krugersdorp, 27/12/40). Such accounts of fighting underground are extremely rare before the 1970s and 1980s, however.

McNamara (Mayer 1980:323) mentions the boredom of compound life and the effects of alcohol in reducing self-control as contributors to intergroup violence during the 1970s and early 1980s. However, such factors cannot explain variations in the frequency of collective violence, nor can the fun of fighting or its rural origins or its ritual aspects. Certainly, ethnic identifications, hypostatized by management housing and job assignment policies, were adopted by disparate home-friend groups of workers themselves both for wider mutual solidarity and to protect their occupational and recreational "territories." The rhetoric of violence is important in this context, since acts or threats of collective violence help to define the group committing the violence and also to define their opponents. Violence is almost always perceived as legitimate by the group committing it, whether as an expression of moral outrage or as retaliation for symbolic or physical violations of members of one's own group by "others."

During the 1920s, for example, Mpondo found many of the black supervisory (boss boy) jobs occupied by Mozambicans and by other Xhosa-speakers from the Ciskei and Western Transkei who had preceded them to the mines. The coincidence of a common language but different status on the mines was exacerbated in this case by the fact that Mpondo do not circumcise whereas Xhosa do. There are several reports of faction fights between them.

A typical example occurred on Central West Mine in December 1925 (NLB 207, 1721/14/48, SNC Krugersdorp, 17/12/25). The Xhosas (presumably boss boys) had apparently complained to the compound manager that the Mpondo were taking weapons underground. In the words of Charlie, a Xhosa: "We had a quarrel with the Pondos. We notified the Compound Manager twice before the fight. On the third occasion we became tired and started to fight." Members of both groups had gone on Sunday to a "Mtshangaan" room in the Xhosa compound to drink. Songolwane, a Mpondo, brought his stick with him. As he told the story:

> A Xosa tried to pull [my stick] away. [I] wanted to know why as it was [my] stick. [I] told the Xosa that it was an Umtata tree. The Xosa said to me "get away you 'Kwenkwe' Pondo." I asked the Xosa who was a Kwenkwe? I snatched my stick away and said you cannot have my stick because I am not circumcised. The Xosa held my stick with both his hands. I saw someone else strike the Xosa on his head. . . . After that the Pondos and Xosas fought. I fought as well. I was drinking "qedeveke"—we were all drinking "qedeveke."

Kwenkwe refers to a boy or uncircumcised youth; *qedeveke* is a home-brewed spirit famous for its "kick." The reference to "an Umtata tree" probably means that the deponent was from Western Pondoland, which borders Umtata. At any rate, a fight ensued. Someone, no doubt an Mpondo, extinguished the lights, and the Xhosa were driven from the room.

The Xhosa felt superior to the uncircumcised and irascible Mpondo "boy-men" who failed to carry on their bodies the mark of manhood. Circumcision still remains a contentious issue between "Xhosa" proper and the Xhosa-speaking Mpondo (and the Zulu, who also do not circumcise), especially if, as in this case, they are separately housed. According to the Mpondo that Ms. Ndatshe and I interviewed, when Mpondo and other Xhosa speakers were housed together, the room izibonda would encourage discussions of different customs in order to resolve the tensions—although "Ciskeians thought a little better of themselves as they said they were [real] men because of circumcision customs."

Collective violence is seldom merely moral or symbolic, however. It is generally instrumental as well. Although violence is a supremely useful rhetorical device, it is also a risky one and thus is more likely to be supported by group members when perceived real interests are at stake. In many of the cases under discussion, those interests seem to have been centered on self-defense against assaults by boss boys.

This motivation is explicit in yet another police account of a "Xhosa-Pondo" fight on Crown Mines X compound in 1938 (NTS 7674, 99/332, 10/6/38), on which we obtained further testimony from an old man in the country in 1984. On 9 June 1938, a force of police were called out to X compound. According to Jackson Yaca, an Mpondo participant who vividly remembered the event forty-six years later, the battle was caused by underground boss boys, most of whom were Xhosa and Sotho, who were "bothering the Mpondo, who did very hard work as lashers and timber-boys." There was also still widespread tension between Mpondo and Sotho-Xhosa on the "uncircumcised boys" issue. No doubt assaults underground by white miners and their boss boys, which were endemic anyway, were exacerbated by such attitudes. At any rate the Mpondo were never averse to exercising their power.

On that particular day in 1938, they held a meeting after work to discuss their treatment by the boss boys. Their leader was a machine driller from Lusikisiki, who was respected for his knowledge of mine ways. They went to the induna, who, being Xhosa, said Yaca, took no notice of them, so they went straight to the chief compound manager. According to the police report, the induna had approached the compound manager but the matter had not been "adjusted to the satisfaction of the Pondos." Yaca remembered that all the Mpondo "gathered at the office of the chief compound manager to complain of their treatment at the hands of the boss boys." When the manager asked them their problem, they all shouted their support for their spokesman. "The compound manager promised to investigate their complaints, but by this time they were so angry that they went to fight. . . . Then "khakis" [white policemen] came with batons to disperse them," said Yaca. The chief compound manager investigated the matter immediately and, according to the police report, dismissed two Xhosa boss boys to appease the Mpondo.

While collective violence both asserts instrumental goals, making a claim to the opponent about one's own rights and privileges, and reinforces group solidarity, it also sends a message to the dominant class (on the mines, management) about group identities and grievances. Not only did the Mpondo beat up the Xhosa in the case above but also the riot persuaded management to dismiss some of the hated boss boys. The message could hardly have been lost on other Xhosa boss boys on this mine. The efficacy of violence was explicitly affirmed by an Mpondo, Mtilisho Mdibaniso, in 1984:

> The compound manager would sack a man if he thought his case wasn't good, or he was a troublemaker in the compound. [I also] know of cases, however, where the compound manager would favor the Sotho because the Mpondo had a reputation for making trouble. The Mpondo accepted this because the manager's word was final. The Mpondo were very strong on the mines, however, so the manager was careful not to offend them too much. Their strength made him wary of injustice against them. The Mpondo were the miscreants on the mines—they were always fighting with the Sotho.

Thus did a reputation for belligerence help protect group interests.

In a similar case on the East Rand Proprietary Mines, on 27 December 1941, Barotse, relative newcomers to mine work, attacked Sotho. The Barotse claimed that continuous underground assaults were ignored by the compound manager (NTS 7675, 102/332, SAP Boksburg, 16/1/42). "The Compound Manager did not make it his business to see that their complaints received the attention of the Law [umteto?] as it should," so they told the police. The compound manager stated that it was seldom possible to get sufficient evidence for the courts to prosecute in such cases. The Barotse alleged in their turn that in that case the law was no good and did not give them a fair deal. They wished to deal with such assaults their own way. To the policeman who wrote the report, their demands simply confirmed his assumptions about primitive tribalism: "It was evident that the Barotsis, being a tropical tribe and owing to their undeveloped minds, did not or could not understand the procedure of the Law as far as prosecutions [were] concerned." The Barotse were given a warning, and no further action was taken.

Forty years later, in July 1982 on Kloof Gold Mine (McNamara 1985:255–56), workers from various ethnic groups rioted against Mozambicans because they had refused to participate in demonstrations against management on Gold Fields mines that year. Their violence was aggravated, however, also by the fact that Mozambicans dominated the boss boy jobs on mines in the area. In this "faction fight," Mozambican boss boys' rooms were burned down while other Mozambican rooms were left alone.

Such examples of violence against boss boys from different groups illustrate that faction fighting was and is rooted in more than merely symbolic solidarities. Often the most serious fights occurred on mines where there had been a large influx of new workers. On Modder B on 4 January 1926 (NLB 365, 28/26/48), for instance, following a massive Christmas faction fight, "East Coast Natives" killed six "Cape Colony natives" and one "British Sotho." Most whites believed that it was a typically "tribal" quarrel during the favorite fighting season. At that time, however, recruitment from the Cape was picking up, and on Modder B, Mozambican numbers had been limited by the recruiting organizations, much to the chagrin of management, who preferred the more experienced Mozambican workers. This shift in numerical balance, which represented a long-term threat to the more numerous Mozambicans, was almost certainly part of the problem (NLB 365, 28/26/48). H. S. Cooke, the director of native labor, who himself undertook an immediate review in this case, found that the compound manager had disarmed the Cape workers but not the East Coasters. He suspended the compound manager on the spot. Such careful investigations were few and far between, however. More frequently, matters were left to the South African police and the compound authorities to sort out, with the threat of further factional violence the major incentive for mine officials to ensure fairness.

A full explanation of faction fights cannot rest upon assumptions about presumed group solidarities alone but must also take into account the capillaries of power and configurations of interest on and around the mines. The category of "tribe" tends to obscure such factors. Certainly, to understand "factional" mine violence, one needs to know when the different groups arrived on each mine, the specific work they were assigned, with whom they were housed, how large a complement they formed on the mine, whether or not they were assigned their own compound policemen or induna or both, their prior experience of mine or other wage labor, and who controlled the various rackets in the compound—meat, alcohol, "boys"—and the shebeens and eating houses outside. Thorough investigation must be undertaken on a mine-by-mine basis. McNamara's analysis (Mayer 1980) of the impact on one mine of the arrival of Zimbabwean recruits from the rural slums of Harare in 1976 is an excellent example. At issue is not a reductionist denial of the importance of "ethnic" solidarities but rather an insistence on their historical contexts, their shifting character and relativity in response to changing local conditions. This point holds for any social scientific explanation that relies on the notion of "ethnicity," whether in Yugoslavia, Russia, Somalia, India, or even Canada (Johnstone 1990).

Rural Roots, Ethnicity, and the Organization of Faction Fights

We have seen that faction fights were important as assertions and confirmations of "ethnic" solidarities among mine workers. Often they would break out along already established ethnic lines, usually when one group believed it was being unjustly treated or its perceived interests were threatened. Sometimes such fights would be organized by the older men of a particular group. One black ex–mine official recalled how some fights got started in the 1940s, 1950s, and 1960s:

> A young man from one of the tribes, usually Sotho or Pondo, would get into a fight and get beaten by one from another. He would run away and say that he had been attacked by a gang from the other group. The next day the Pondos would have a caucus and say, "Come and look at this young man who has been beaten." Such meetings would be called by the older men from the tribe on the compound.

Retired Mpondo mine workers, interviewed in the 1980s, asserted that they, the Bomvana and the Sotho, were more likely than other groups on the mines to indulge in violence. Management representatives I spoke to were inclined to agree. I attempted an analysis of recorded faction fights during this century in relation to the proportional representation of participants in the total mine labor force at the time. I also counted those who initiated the fights on record, where this was noted in the reports.

The data are too slim to be fully convincing, but the results are interesting. They seem to confirm the belligerence of Mpondo, Xhosa, and Sotho as well as the Mozambicans' reputation among white management and Mpondo for being "gentle," "soft," and "very nice people." Mozambicans did fight if sufficiently provoked by Cape or Sotho workers, although they tended to engage in stone throwing rather than hand-to-hand combat. In one case, they employed explosives smuggled from underground against Mpondo—much to the disgust of the latter (NLB 197, 1440/14/48, NA Randfontein, 20/11/22). "Tropicals," especially Malawians, appear to have been quite violent, especially when their numbers were increasing on the mines, although I cannot claim this with certitude because of incomplete information. How may we account for the differences that do emerge?

Figures for total workforce participation can be misleading, especially for the smaller groups. An apparently high level of Swazi militancy during 1910–1920, for instance, may be explained by the fact that in 1910 almost half of the entire Swazi gold mine workforce was housed on the Cason compound at East Rand Proprietary Mines (NA 81, F164, NA inspector report, 6/1/11). With one exception, all recorded Swazi participation in faction fights before 1973 was on this compound, where they were favored by management (NLB 197, 1440/14/48, event of 25/12/14). Indeed, a high concentration of any group on one compound probably exacerbated already existing tensions, as would a rapidly changing proportion of different groups.

Part of the explanation for ethnic strife lies in the relative size of a particular group or sudden increases in the recruitment of certain groups who thus became numerous but were locked out by the seniority system from better-paid and less strenuous work. Members of such groups were also liable to interpret boss boy brutality in ethnic terms. Conflict was heightened with influxes of inexperienced but better-educated mine workers—as was the case with the recruitment of Zimbabweans and Xhosa speakers after 1973.

A somewhat higher incidence for initiating collective violence by Cape (especially Mpondo) workers than by Mozambicans cannot be explained in any of the above terms, however. True, new groups of "Tropicals" (including Malawians) began to move in by the late 1940s (Crush, Jeeves, and Yudelman 1991) and may have threatened established workers. Perhaps after 1947, Cape workers became objects of violence rather than instigators of it. Nonetheless, there does seem to be a tendency for Cape workers (and to a lesser extent Sotho) to resort to collective violence. Social practices in the rural areas from which they came may account for their different behavior.

Until the middle 1970s, the rules for faction fighting on the mines seem to have been derived from the mores of cattle-herding boys in Transkei and Lesotho. Our interviews in Pondoland confirmed the observations of Guy and Thabane in Lesotho:

> All our informants have stressed the importance of their boyhood herding to the development of their characters. It was then, in the struggle for dominance within herding groups, in the physical privation, in the rivalry amongst different groups, that the fighting skills, the physical toughness and the aggression which one needs to deal successfully with the world were developed. (Guy and Thabane 1987:445)

S. J. Jingoes's account (1975) of his youth in rural Lesotho is filled with stirring tales of battles between stock-herding youngsters of neighboring villages over grazing rights to their stony fields. One understands after reading his account why Sotho are renowned and feared on the mines for their stone throwing.

In traditionalist Transkei, fighting was also the norm for young men and boys. Indeed, male toddlers were cuffed by their mothers into setting upon each other almost as soon as they could walk (Mayer and Mayer 1970:165; Hunter 1936:160). As with the Sotho, however, traditional Xhosa youthful male violence was supposedly abandoned with the transition to manhood symbolized by initiatory circumcision. Young men settled squabbles with sticks, but responsible adult men talked things through, relying on the consensual order provided by imiteto.

Young boys while herding cattle learned to fight with sticks (and to fight fair) from somewhat older boys. In their later teen years they formalized such practices in battles between regional youth groups. Individuals might get carried away in the heat of battle, but hitting an opponent when he was down was deeply deplored. Thus, even though stick fighting was rough play, it was play nonetheless, with its own rules. When they become men, traditional Xhosa were supposed to put away such childish things and learn the imiteto, the laws and discipline of manhood.

Throughout all stages of life, Xhosa rural practices were subject to careful regulation by peer groups. On the mines, however, such controls might be lifted in the hurly-burly of mine life—especially when confronted with its real inequities. Sotho informants insisted to me: "We don't fight after we have been circumcised." However, one Sotho man on President Steyn Mine told the joint National Union of Mineworkers/Anglo American inquiry into mine violence: "Treat us like boys and we'll behave like boys" (Leatt et al. 1986). An Mpondo ex-miner told Ms. Ndatshe in 1982:

> There were faction fights but they were very rare. I don't know really what caused them. All I know is that Mpondo and Sotho were like herd boys. They were used to fighting boys of the other side. Sometimes it was a simple challenge—the Mpondo said they could defeat the Sotho, or the Sotho would swear at the Mpondo.

Some of the literature on the Mpondo suggests that Mpondo men may have been socialized to violence as a basic attribute of their manhood. When the Mayers' research worker, Percy Qayiso, himself Mpondo, returned to Pondoland having studied Xhosa youth groups, he was shocked at the lack of respect for law and the recourse to violence among the Mpondo. Whereas among the traditional Xhosa, respect forbids circumcised men to hit each other, Qayiso found that "Pondo ideology [was] quite different." In the words of Iona Mayer, based on Qayiso's research:

> [The Mpondo allow] even mature men to "settle by blows," and indeed [judge] it more manly to hit back when offended, than to submit or run away. The only man whom respect forbids a *man* to hit are his own father and senior kinsmen. Here youngmanhood is spoken of as the most pugnacious age of all, like boyhood among the circumcised peoples. In local terms, then, the "cheeky" youth who makes as if to hit a man is so to speak claiming a new adult equality with him. (Mayer and Mayer 1972)

Can such differences explain the Mpondo reputation and record of fighting on the mines? If controls on young Mpondo men were weak even at home, the roughness and brutality of mine life may well have reinforced their pugnacity.

As we have seen, however, all the older Mpondo men in the Lusikisiki district that we interviewed in 1988 about violence insisted that physical strength and fighting ability had nothing to do with true manhood (*ubudoda*). Ubudoda, they said, had to do with one's ability to administer a household, settle disputes within it, decide differences between family members, and ensure peace and productivity. Manhood, for older Mpondo, thus is a moral concept associated with one's effectiveness as a family head more than one's prowess as a warrior. Fighting ability, especially strategic sense, might ensure esteem from a young man's peers, but for adult men it was irrelevant they said. Furthermore, it was universally agreed that men went to the mines in order to earn the wherewithal to build a homestead where they could practice the integrity of this moral conception of manhood. Again and again, Mpondo ex-miners insisted: "We were on the mines for business." Thus, although the Mpondo may show greater tolerance of adult male pugnacity than the Xhosa and Sotho, they do not morally approve of violence to settle disputes. Arguments for the rural socialization of young men to violence thus need to be supplemented by the notion of a more general regression to "youngmanhood" when they go to live in the compounds away from their local elders and women.

Although differences in socialization and the tendency to regress may help to explain the choice for violence on the mines, I am not convinced that they are sufficient explanations. As important for understanding Mpondo proclivities to collective violence, in my opinion, is social organization. To the best of my knowledge, the Mpondo (and perhaps the Baca and Xesibe) were the only major group who adapted their youth organizations to mine life. Sotho workers might seem to be an exception to this generalization. In the early years of recruitment from Lesotho, minor chiefs would recruit gangs of their own adherents who would work on the mines under their personal supervision. Such arrangements surely made for firmer home-group solidarities and may help explain the high level of Sotho involvement in faction fighting during the 1910s. However, such alternative sources of authority both at work and in the compound were quite unacceptable to management once the immediate recruiting crisis of the period prior to the establishment of the Native Recruiting Corporation (NRC) was over in the late teens (Jeeves 1985:157–60; see also NLB 197, 1440/14/48, NA Randfontein South, 28/4/15). Furthermore, from the 1920s to the early 1960s, the pattern among Sotho was to leave the mines after a contract or two and settle into the urban scene, where fights among Sotho MaRashea gangs were a feature of the post–Second World War years (Guy and Thabane 1987; Bonner 1988).

For the Mpondo, however, both traditionalist igubura youth organizations and indlavini groups were in existence on mine compounds at least through the 1950s and 1960s. Virtually every informant interviewed in Lusikisiki district who went to the mines before the 1970s was a participant in igubura or indlavini activities, and many of them continued such gatherings on the mines. Indeed, as we saw in the first chapter, Beinart's evidence suggests that indlavini groups were formed by young men with minimal schooling who had been migrants. Furthermore, all commentators on indlavini activities stress their internal discipline and the violence of their dealings with nonmembers. Indlavini from the same regions were not necessarily on the same mines but the existence of such organizations typically provided for Mpondo a wider circle of trust and solidarity than did home-friend networks among other groups. Mpondo ethnic assertiveness was thus more firmly grounded in organizational networks than were the more fluid ethnic identities of other groups. Charges by the National Union of Mineworkers these days that ethnic "dance teams" are frequently leaders in faction fights further suggest the importance of organizational factors. We have already had cause to note the importance of organized Mpondo drinkers on Vaal Reefs No. 1. Our tale will return to them again and again.

Factoring in rural-based social organization by some migrants on the mines still does not explain why Mpondo and other Xhosa speakers and Sotho so readily participated in collective violence. Together, however, with rural socialization of youthful violence and the tendency to regress to youthful behavior, these three factors seem necessary for an explanation of group differences in recourse to violence. Sufficiency, of course, requires analysis of conditions on individual mines at particular times. While full evidence for particular cases before the 1970s is difficult to obtain, McNamara's (1985) excellent and thorough account of conflict between 1973 and 1982 comes close to the ideal. We will thus turn to an examination of his findings.

Sotho-Xhosa Faction Fights in the 1970s

Collective violence on the South African gold mines before the 1970s was handled by a combination of authorities, and where local mine management paternalism was insufficient, the formal authority of the South African police was invoked. The informal authority of management-appointed and worker-accepted "tribal" black officials, and the existence among some worker groups of migrant organizations and cultures with their own rules for fights, both encouraged and contained violence along "ethnic" lines. In the context of such rules before 1973, as we have seen, local and particular rather than industrywide issues tended to generate conflict.

With the dramatic rise in the price of gold in the early 1970s, the gold industry, for both strategic and moral reasons, decided to raise wages substantially. In 1973 there were more workers from Malawi (109,731), Mozambique (83,390), and the combined ex–High Commission territories of Lesotho, Botswana, and Swaziland (101,671) on the gold mines than workers from within the borders of South Africa itself (81,375). The perilousness of such dependence on foreign labor was dramatically demonstrated in 1974, when President Hastings Banda decided to withdraw all Malawians from the mines as their contracts expired. The number of Malawian workers on the mines dropped from over 100,000 in 1973 to fewer than 500 by 1976. At about the same time, the changeover of governments in

Mozambique cut the Mozambican labor supply almost in half, and a threatened insurrection in Lesotho led to massive repatriations there.[3]

Armed with the new wage scales and aided by the collapse of homeland subsistence production and the mechanization of white farming, the Chamber of Mines mounted a massive and successful recruiting campaign within South Africa and Lesotho. As a temporary measure, they also recruited urban labor from Rhodesia (Zimbabwe). By 1983, the Sotho labor complement on the South African gold mines had increased by one-half, to 95,731, and South African labor had gone up threefold, to 239,065 (mostly from the Transkei and Ciskei, but also from white farming and urban areas). The ethnic complexion of the mine labor force thus changed radically and very rapidly with the recruitment of a more proletarianized labor force.

Almost at once, in 1974, ethnic strife between Xhosa- and Sesotho-speaking workers broke out on Welkom Mine in the Orange Free State. Unlike similar disputes in the past, however, the dispute on this mine spread quickly to others. The incidence of disputes with management also increased. Rapid systemic changes between 1973 and 1982 brought with them changes in the nature and incidence of collective violence both among workers and against management. One might have expected greater conflict with management as a more proletarianized workforce was recruited from within South Africa, but what explains the increase in so-called tribal violence?

McNamara isolated eighty-eight "intergroup clashes" on the mines between 1973 and 1982. In 38.6 percent (thirty-four cases) of these, local workers, including Sotho, Tswana, and Swazi, fought with "foreigners," mostly from Malawi, Mozambique, and Zimbabwe. Conflicts including Malawians occurred largely during the period between Hastings Banda's announcement that migrant labor from Malawi to South Africa would be phased out and the actual return of Malawian workers. Apparently, Malawians, anxious to get home quickly (perhaps eager to find jobs in what all knew would be a tight labor market), picked fights in the hopes of being deported—as did Sotho for a short time in the middle 1970s. Mozambican and Rhodesian workers were recruited from urban areas in their home countries to replace the departing Malawians. Their involvement in intergroup struggles stemmed much more directly from their proletarian status.

What is most striking about intergroup clashes during this period is that over 40 percent (thirty-seven of the eighty-eight cases) involved con-

[3]Crush, Jeeves, and Yudelman (1991) provide a full discussion of changes in the mine labor force.

flicts between Sesotho (sometimes allied with Tswana) and Nguni-speaking workers. Such ethnic consistency on the part of mine "faction fighters" is unique in the history of the mining industry and has lent credence to primordial interpretations. Even McNamara (1985:217) writes of a "feud"; however, he also provides several other interpretations that conform quite closely to the conclusions of my historical research. Three explanatory factors seem particularly convincing.

The first important issue is not directly mentioned by McNamara although it is implicit in much of his analysis. This is the question of proletarianization. As we have seen, by raising wages and actively recruiting "South African" labor from townships and rural slums in the middle 1970s, the South African mining industry did not merely increase the "South African" proportion of its labor force. For the first time in its history, it hired large numbers of fully proletarianized, if still migrant, workers, although this extremely rapid process of proletarianization was uneven, and was still proceeding into the 1990s, with pockets of "traditional" workers continuing to live by the old migrant values.[4] The impact of the new workers on the industry has been volcanic, however. They are better educated, with urban tastes in dress, music, and entertainment (and styles of violence, for that matter), and far more intolerant of crowded living conditions and mistreatment at work and in the compounds. They tend to regard their blanket-garbed fellow workers as country bumpkins and to reject the authority of illiterate indunas and mine police, as well as Sotho and Shangaan team leaders (formerly called boss boys). The Zimbabweans hired off the streets of Harare to replace the departing Malawians in 1975 were forerunners of these new workers on the mines.

Men entirely dependent on wage labor for their livelihood, working to support dependent families in far-flung rural slums—if they had not already abandoned them for town women—are not inclined to sit around within the compound and share stories of rural life with home fellows. Instead they look for excitement away from the mine in local shebeens, or they drink to get drunk every evening and on weekends in the mine liquor outlet. These new mine workers are no longer insulated from the liberation struggle going on in South Africa—many of them are in fact part of it. Paternalistic mine authorities do not impress them. They expect due process and proper worker representation.

Proletarianization did not mean that conflict over wages and labor conditions would not be interpreted in ethnic terms. The new workers, the large majority of them Xhosa speaking, when they first began to come to

[4]For figures on new workers as a percentage of total recruitment from various territories between 1971 and 1982, see McNamara 1985:245.

the mines in the early 1970s, did not come to the well-paid jobs with ample authority to which they perhaps expected their education entitled them. Instead, they were allotted the lowest-paying jobs in the most marginal mines, subject to all the constraints and assaults on their dignity that mine work in South Africa has implied over the years.

The second big issue in understanding Sotho-Xhosa faction fights follows from the first. Sotho tended to dominate the better-paying jobs on the Orange Free State mines, leading to Xhosa resentments over wage differences and treatment on the job. McNamara (1985:211) produces figures demonstrating that on a Free State mine in 1977 experienced workers from Lesotho came to dominate supervisory job categories. With the departure of Malawians, Sotho became team leaders or boss boys, machine operators, and winch and locomotive drivers. Even the easier unskilled jobs in timber support and maintenance became predominantly Sotho on the Free State mines, whereas Xhosa speakers were relegated to the most menial underground ("lashing") jobs. Sotho dominance of better-paid and less arduous work was one result of 1963 South African legislation that forbade Sotho from working in South Africa except on the mines. Thus Sotho mine workers on the Free State mines (like Mozambicans in the Transvaal before them) worked longer contracts on the mines and returned more regularly, building up seniority. Furthermore, the earlier pattern of proletarianized Sotho working one or two shifts on the mines and then moving into secondary industry was hampered if not stopped altogether by the 1963 legislation, so that the process of proletarianization of Sotho mine workers started a decade earlier than that of South Africans.

We have already noted a tendency for ethnic conflict to break out between established groups and new arrivals to the mines. This is not only because of pay differentials but also because assaults by team leaders underground were regarded as a normal part of mine work. Thus in the early 1970s, thoroughly proletarianized (i.e., wage-dependent) and better-educated Xhosa-speaking workers were recruited for the most strenuous and least well remunerated jobs on the Free State mines and subject to pressure from largely Sotho supervisors underground. Little was needed in the way of precipitating factors to pitch Xhosa speakers into faction fights with Sotho.

The same situation applied to Rhodesians from Harare recruited for Transvaal mines in 1974 and 1975, although in their case the fights were with Xhosa speakers and Mozambicans as well as Sotho, presumably because Sotho monopoly of well-paid supervisory positions was a Free State phenomenon (McNamara 1985:142–85). Indeed, in 1982, when wide disparities between supervisory and unskilled wages were exacerbated by a new round of wage increases at the end of June, especially on mines (mostly in the Transvaal) controlled by the Gold Fields and Gencor groups, a series of outbreaks of violence against Mozambicans occurred. These were interpreted by management and the press alike as straight "tribal" fighting. In fact, however, as McNamara (1985:311–19) demonstrates, the real issue was antagonism against team leaders, 60 percent of whom were Mozambican on one typical Transvaal mine (with a 20 percent Mozambican labor force) in 1981. Thus, on the Transvaal mines, Mozambicans shared the Sotho monopoly of team leader jobs. Interestingly enough, the 1982 "anti-Mozambican faction fights" were conducted by an alliance of Sesotho and Xhosa-speaking workers, despite their supposed "feud" on the Orange Free State. Once again the context of "ethnicity" must be stressed.

Of course, not all "new miners" in the Free State were Xhosa speaking, but they were predominantly so, and ethnic solidarities and collective violence arise in response to majorities. Resentments of newly recruited and more proletarianized Xhosa-speaking mine workers were reinforced by a further development, especially on Anglo American mines, which made up the majority of Orange Free State mines. This was the introduction in 1973 of the Paterson job-grading system, which "attached special value to decision-making and responsibility" in calculating wages. Historically, machine drillers (because of the bonus system for numbers of holes drilled) were the highest wage earners on the mine. Furthermore, their work was universally regarded by mine workers as the most arduous and dangerous of all. Typically, although not exclusively of course, such work was undertaken by Xhosa-speaking Mpondo, who were also, as we have seen, one of the best-organized groups on the mines. Under the Paterson system, team leaders began receiving higher wages than machine drillers. Massive wage increases between 1973 and 1975 rewarded black supervisors even more (McNamara 1985:214–15). Thus the introduction of the Paterson scale at the same time that largely Xhosa-speaking "new workers" were being recruited for the mines provided an already established Xhosa-speaking leadership cadre from the machine drillers, who had resentments of their own and a history of resorting to collective violence to achieve their ends.

The question of leadership is the third explanatory factor raised by McNamara's analysis of faction fights during the 1970s. Typically, "new workers" rejected the established black mine authorities as not representative of their interests. However, McNamara (1985:222–26) cites four cases between June 1975 and July 1976 in which Xhosa-speaking indunas on Transvaal mines apparently fomented ethnic violence in the face of shifting ethnic composition of the workforce on their mines. Indunas were traditionally given a high degree of discretion by management. In these cases they seem to have feared loss of influence as more Sotho moved onto their mines or, in one case, an Mpondo induna sought to establish greater influence as more Mpondo workers were recruited to his mine. Such developments serve to remind us of the complexity of the structural changes that occurred in the 1970s. Once again, whether reactive or proactive, it was Xhosa-speaking (and in two of the four cases, Mpondo) indunas who were willing and able to initiate collective violence, and they did so in the old way, by handing out sticks.

The nature of violence on the mines has begun to change, however. Before the 1980s (and even to some extent during the period of transition in the 1970s), despite the frequency of collective violence, its ritualized forms and traditional methods meant that deaths were relatively infrequent. More recently, new methods of fighting, more typical of slum streets than country cattle-herding, have led to wide-scale slaughter. The Johannesburg *Weekly Mail* for 23–29 January 1987 declared that during the preceding year 113 black mine workers had been killed by other black miners on South African gold mines. The mines included Kloof, Vaal Reefs, Western Deep Levels, Kinross, President Steyn, and Beatrix. The list did not include a death at East Rand Proprietary Mines in April (*Star*, 21/4/86) and one at Grootvlei in December (*Sunday Times*, 21/12/86), which bring the total to 115. While these figures pale in comparison to the (originally police- or Inkatha-based) carnage in contemporary Natal and the Transvaal townships, they are large compared with earlier experience on the mines.

In response to the unrest, we have already noted that some mining houses have begun to rationalize white and black managements at the local level, gradually replacing paternalistic authority with bureaucratized supervision and armed security forces along police lines. As a result, on Anglo American mines, indunas have become "unit supervisors" without ethnic responsibilities and local compound managers have been disempowered. In addition, Anglo American, the wealthiest of the mining houses, permitted, even encouraged, the founding of the black National Union of Mineworkers (NUM) in the early 1980s. The corporation's intent was to create a labor conciliation system that would oblige the NUM to control and discipline its own members. However, disputes on the mines had deep structural and historical causes that could not be controlled or removed by the creation of a trade union. If anything, the NUM, by empowering its members in local contestations, has made matters worse for old-style local management patriarchal control. Furthermore, the coming of the union has not at all overcome the incidence of collective violence along "ethnic" lines.

Unionization and Ethnic Strife: The Case of Vaal Reefs No. 1

The union's problems from mobilizing an ethnically divided labor force, especially when extensive new recruitment patterns are being established, have an interesting precursor in 1946, where a call for a strike by the African Mine Workers' Union (AMWU) led to ethnic strife between "Xhosas" and recently arrived "Tropicals" at No. 1 compound, Western Reefs (a predecessor of Vaal Reefs), which was still in the process of being opened up. A police report from Klerksdorp stated that on 4 April 1946 the compound manager asked for assistance, declaring that "trouble amongst the three thousand natives in the compound had started at 7 a.m., that a riot was developing and compound property was being damaged." Police were rushed to the scene and found Xhosa and Tropicals confronting one another. On seeing the police, the workers returned to their quarters and "three scotch cart loads of jumpers, sticks, knobkerries, pieces of iron, stones and bricks were removed from the rooms." The police concluded that there were two major reasons for the disturbance: three cooks had distributed rations unfairly, and three mine policemen were ill-treating workers of other tribes. All six of the offenders were dismissed (NTS 7686, 262/332, SAP Klerksdorp, 6/5/46). Further inquiry by the inspector of native laborers and the NRC, however, revealed a more complex situation. According to the inspector's report, "the Xosas approached the Tropicals and it was agreed that they should not feed at a particular meal time as a preliminary protest in connection with some agitation about applying for ten shillings per day wages and to feed themselves. The Xosas, however, did feed and the Tropicals became annoyed" (NTS 7686, 262/332, NA Klerksdorp, 3/5/46).

The ethnic confrontation reported by the police on Western Reefs in 1946 thus grew directly out of the AMWU demand for ten shillings a day, which was also to motivate the strike later in August (described in chapter 7). Ethnic divisions in this case meant that a hunger strike degenerated into a full-scale faction fight. Indeed, the 1946 strike was remarkable in that ethnic strife did not occur on other mines, perhaps because their labor forces in the 1940s were quite stable, especially on the more established mines, with entrenched job allocations that were relatively satisfactory or at least acceptable to all ethnic groups.

The National Union of Mineworkers, when it established itself on the mines after 1982, was not so lucky. It was obliged to organize a changing and differentiated workforce in which class and ethnic divisions sometimes coincided but often cut across one another. Workers were divided along class lines, between the older traditional miners with their roots in the countryside and more fully proletarianized recent recruits. The allocation of jobs, which followed such class lines, also potentially coincided with ethnic divisions. These might be manipulated by local management or security forces to build up resentment against the union. Organizing on such contested and shifting terrain, in the face of contradictory management strategies of control, posed problems of great complexity for the union. Furthermore, closer identification of a "South Africanized" labor force with the liberation struggle in the country eventually obliged the NUM, along with other members of the Congress of South African Trade Unions (COSATU) to take a stand on political issues, despite the risk of dividing the mine labor force (James 1991).

For several years after the founding of the NUM in 1982, its immediate successes in curbing unfair dismissals and in confronting safety issues led to widespread support. Initially, it targeted team leaders but soon learned that this was a shaky strategy since team leaders were in intercalary positions that forced them to choose between their responsibility to management and their identification as workers. The team leaders' identification as workers was further threatened when management on many mines provided separate and superior housing for them and built special messes where clerks, team leaders, and other black supervisors could dine in finer style. The union thus shifted its attention to machine drillers, which inadvertently meant a shift from organizing mostly Sotho to concentrating on Mpondo. In both cases, however, the union was organizing older, more established workers. With the formation of COSATU in 1985, and the NUM's explicit support of its strategy of "political" or "social movement unionism," the union has moved into more controversial terrain in which support from the new breed of mine workers has become increasingly important. At the same time, support from more traditional miners, although they remain members, has become less overt.

An extended examination of a "Sotho-Xhosa faction fight" on Vaal Reefs No. 1 compound in March 1986 will complete the argument of this chapter as well as point up a number of new developments in the explanation of "ethnic violence" during the 1980s.[5] While many of the old divisions in the workforce still exert their influence, they have now been overlaid by new struggles between local unionists and local management.

A convenient beginning for the events on Vaal Reefs No. 1 compound is the killing in mid-February 1986 of four Sotho team leaders on Vaal

[5]For an alternative account of the events on Vaal Reefs No. 1, see Shanafelt 1989.

Reefs No. 5, which, like No. 1, is located in the East Division. On 24 February, Mgedezi, an NUM shaft steward on No. 5, was arrested along with four others by the South African police in connection with the team leader killings. Early on the morning of 25 February, NUM shaft stewards went from room to room on No. 1 to urge workers to stay away the next day in sympathy with Mgedezi. There was a total strike on all three shafts in East Division.

A group of NUM pickets gathered at the No. 1 shaft gate. However, "Seven" Mojakisane, a Sotho gang supervisor who was renowned among the workers as a traditionalist of great integrity and was also known to be a MaRashea, decided to go to work. He later gave his reason as follows:

> [S]ome of my Sotho people were already killed and I was not afraid to be killed. I said to myself I would be the same as the other Sothos who were already killed and the strike was also not legal. . . . I was also told that [one of the team leaders who had been killed was from my home district] and had fought viciously in defence of himself. (AAC/VR:5120, 5103)

Having deposited his belongings with a friend in the white quarters, Seven returned to the compound and walked to the shaft area to report for work, ignoring a request to attend an NUM meeting from Thabang, the dynamic Sotho shaft steward. At the Training Centre he picked up a couple of dozen newcomers to the mine, who had allegedly been threatened by management with dismissal if they did not accompany him (AAC/VR:4286). They went from room to room together, dressed in their work clothes, donning blankets and arming themselves (AAC/VR:5116). They then marched through the picket lines and went underground. No others went to work that day. However, the consensus had been broken, and when they went to work the next day, again armed and blanketed, everyone followed their example. The influence of the Mosotho shaft steward, Thabang, seems to have been crucial in the decision to avoid confrontation, else "there would [have been] violence and the name of the trade union would [have been] smeared" (AAC/VR:1508).

Shortly thereafter Seven took thirty days leave at the suggestion of management. Of course, no action was taken against him or the others for going underground armed, although that was strictly against the regulations. Mlamli Botha, the outspoken Mpondo shaft steward, expressed his disgust in no uncertain terms, saying that it was "the first time in the history of this mine to see people with all sorts of dangerous weapons, passing next to Management, going straight to work with all those weapons" (AAC/VR:1504). The point to note is not just the integrity and consistency of both Seven's position and that of the shaft steward but also their incommensurability. Seven's outrage at a strike in support of the killings of Sotho home fellows who were also fellow underground supervisors was as deeply felt as Mlamli Botha's disgust at Seven's management-supported and armed strikebreaking.

While Seven expressed himself in unavowedly ethnic terms, however, Botha's deepest resentment was aimed at management, as well it might have been, for there is ample evidence that on this mine at least, local management and mine security exploited traditional ethnic solidarities to their own advantage against the union. When ethnic conflict erupted on the mine, however, senior mine management washed its hands of responsibility, either claiming the inevitability of primordial "tribal" sentiment or, more frequently, blaming the union.

I do not wish to be misunderstood here. Actions of local NUM shaft stewards and activists were certainly provocative on this compound, but, beyond calling abortive meetings, local management did not seriously try to negotiate with the local union structure. Instead, it used ethnic solidarities to try to arouse hostility against union activists. Here management was aided by the fact that the Sotho induna, who was also head induna on the compound, apparently felt his authority threatened by the new shaft steward system. Indeed, he had gained his position as head induna five years before when the then head induna, a Xhosa speaker, had sought to mobilize the Xhosa against a Sotho influx on the compound and had been demoted to ordinary induna for his efforts (AAC/VR:5184). Thus, there was already bad blood not only between indunas and shaft stewards but also between the indunas appointed to represent Sotho and Xhosa on the mine. As yet another complication, head office management in Johannesburg was in the process of eliminating the induna system as an ethnic system altogether (AAC/VR:3735–40). This proposal posed a further threat to old-style indunas and local management who relied on them.

To return to the narrative, perceived senior mine management inaction in the Mgedezi affair continued to rankle NUM shaft stewards at the Vaal Reefs East Division. On the weekend of 1–2 March, they met and decided to propose to the workers that they engage in a short-day strike, working only four hours a day (roughly half-time). Black miners on No. 1 shaft began such a strike on Wednesday, 5 March. During the afternoon, union activists paraded around the compound carrying the NUM flag, dancing and singing songs of defiance. On the night of 5 March, the indunas' cars were damaged by commercial explosives hurled into the locked building where they were parked. The following day, four elderly mine clerks who elected to work a full day were dragged from their offices by the militants and roughly forced to parade about with them, carrying the flag.

Management, understandably furious at the short-day strike and the accompanying rowdy behavior, obtained a court order against the strike, closed the shaft on Friday, 7 March, and obliged workers, in the presence of armed security personnel, to sign a document reaffirming their conditions of employment and their willingness to continue working on the mine. On Saturday night, 8 March, presumably in retaliation, a bomb was exploded outside the bedroom of the Sotho chief induna. Compound rumor attributed the bombs to two sources: Thabang, the militant Mosotho shaft steward, and Machain, the Xhosa induna. Indeed, Thabang was believed to be in cahoots with Machain (AAC/VR:2737). There were those who said that Thabang, who was a dynamic leader in the union and among the Sotho, coveted the Sotho induna's position (AAC/VR:4550). This was clearly nonsense in any formal sense, not least because the position itself was being phased out, but it does demonstrate the popular respect accorded to Thabang by a substantial number of Sotho. Indeed, as we saw in chapter 3, shaft stewards were taking over many of the indunas' traditional functions on the mine—representing workers in individual grievance cases, for instance, and caring for their general welfare (AAC/VR:3939–43).

Be that as it may, a group of traditionalist Sotho at once set up an armed guard over their induna and declared themselves ready to settle with Thabang and Machain and the Xhosa (AAC/VR:2736). Thus opposition to the union came to be identified in popular worker belief—or at least in the eyes of local management—with the Sotho on the mine. By implication, Xhosa speakers were perceived by local whites to be NUM supporters. According to one witness, in fact, a group of conservative white miners were loudly and openly associating Xhosa speakers with the expansion of the NUM on the mine (AAC/VR:4339–41). That they perceived Xhosa speakers as unionists is the only possible explanation for the subsequent behavior of local management and mine security.

On Monday, 10 March, everyone went to work. However, that night—or Tuesday morning at 2 A.M. to be precise—a group of about twenty Sotho, armed and wearing blankets, stomped around the compound, blowing whistles and calling the Sotho to arms. Workers emerged sleepily from their rooms, apparently puzzled by the commotion. Since in this hostel workers were housed ethnically by room but blocks were arranged by work group, the rooms of the various ethnic groups were scattered throughout the compound. The armed Sotho announced that they wanted the head of Thabang, the charismatic Sotho shaft steward perceived by many as a direct threat to the Sotho induna, and they named other Sotho shaft stewards as well. They also said they were after *amapantsula,* fancy-dressing urban toughs, who now work on the mines (AAC/VR:4319–24).[6] According to another account, as a result of the whistles, many Sotho milled about shouting, "Let us go and attack Xhosas." Eventually, close to one hundred had gathered with their blankets and their weapons outside the Sotho induna's room (AAC/VR:995).

Someone, probably the Sotho induna himself, called security, who entered the compound in two armored vehicles (Hippos), told the now wide-awake workers to go back to their rooms and to bed, shot off one or two tear-gas canisters for effect and put a guard on the compound gate. The induna called off his warriors from their declaration of war. For such it was. No one slept that night. Sotho, Xhosa, and Mpondo alike spent the remainder of the night feverishly making weapons that they might defend themselves in the battle they knew lay ahead (AAC/VR:1000, 1693–98). Underground that day, also, time was devoted to weapon construction. Welding torches were used to produce weapons from metal found underground, and no mine policeman dared to disarm workers emerging from the crush at the shaft head.

Mlamli Botha, the Mpondo shaft steward, accompanied senior Xhosa-speaking black compound officials, including the induna and the subinduna, early in the morning to report to the hostel manager, "Tsotsi" Maritz, about the ruckus of the night before. They wanted the indunas with two representatives from each group to meet to iron out the matter. Maritz sent them to a clerk to make formal statements but did no more. Mlamli Botha, realizing that nothing would be done, went off to town to Orkney and bought himself a serrated sword. In the afternoon, when people came up from work, a delegation of two shaft stewards, one Sotho, one Xhosa, went to Maritz to request permission to use the hall for an emergency meeting about the whistle blowing of the night before. After a lengthy wait while Maritz talked to the Sotho and then to the Xhosa induna, permission was refused. Maritz told the shaft stewards that he knew that the trouble was simply a matter of rivalry between the indunas and implied that he had sorted it out (AAC/VR:4332–34, 4553–55). Meanwhile, union "comrades," activists waiting outside the compound office, dispersed as the Sotho warriors began to congregate outside the head induna's room across the way. Maritz went home.

By eight that evening the two groups had lined up facing each other, the Sotho in their blankets, many of the Xhosa in white sheets. Asked who made up the "Xhosa," Mlamli Botha replied: "When I say Xhosa, I mean the Xhosa-speaking people. It might be Pondos, Bacas, Bomvanas,

[6]The witness who mentioned this final demand was himself *amapantsula* and also a "comrade," a youthful political militant.

Xhosas, but they are Xhosas. Also from Ciskei" (AAC/VR:1003). The Sotho leaders blasted their whistles, and their group attacked. They were a distinct minority since many had chosen not to join the fight, and the Xhosa pushed them out of the compound. At that point, security arrived in four Hippos and, openly promising aid to the Sotho, advanced into the compound firing rubber bullets at white-sheeted Xhosa workers. The Sotho war group returned to the compound behind the Hippos, hurling stones to accompany the security bullets. The fighting Xhosa were hemmed into one corner of the compound.

The Sotho looted and rampaged through Xhosa rooms, smashing lockers and stealing and destroying belongings. A Sotho and a Swazi mine policeman led the security guards from one Xhosa room to the next, so that security could roust the inhabitants out for target practice with rubber bullets. In the rush to escape the bullets, people "were just getting into rooms that they could come across near them, so that it was just a mixture in the rooms. Sothos and Xhosas mixed" (AAC/VR:4561). The number of fatalities resulting from the clash is vague: one man was reportedly hacked to death in his room in the presence of the mine police (tribal representatives) (AAC/VR:1837–41), and apparently one Sotho was killed in the original rout from the compound. Many from both groups were seriously wounded. Ethnic divisions were by no means set in stone, however. Thabang, the Sotho shaft steward, was rescued by a group of Xhosa and smuggled out of the compound. Sigayi, a young Xhosa-speaking "comrade," was chased by the security force's rubber bullets into a Sotho room, where he was promptly loaned a Sotho blanket and allowed to spend the night (AAC/VR:4344–46).

It is particularly striking how little eagerness both sides showed for the fight. Mlamli Botha said of the Xhosa speakers that "we were ready for anything" and admitted that he had personally participated in the fight "to defend myself because I was attacked" (AAC/VR:1696–99). When asked why he returned with his weapon rather than staying in town or elsewhere off the mine, he replied: "I knew that that thing was not only directed to me alone . . . it was directed to all the Xhosa-speaking" (AAC/VR:1761–62). There was no joy in this expression of solidarity, however. When Commissioner Bregman asked him directly whether he would have been disappointed had there been no fight, he answered simply: "I would have been exceedingly happy" (AAC/VR:1710).

Matsepe Mokheti, a Sotho worker on the night shift, went down that evening unsure whether there would be a fight, until a white shift-overseer came eager with the news. Mokheti at once told his work mates, Sotho and Xhosa alike. One of the consultants to the Bregman Commission asked him later whether there was "a change of atmosphere underground[.] Whether [he] continued working just normally, or whether now there was tension or something like that?" Mokheti replied: "We continued working normally until the end of the shift. [Then, because the cage came up late] we started preparing ourselves underground and we took roof bolts to make weapons. . . . we did this jointly. We were even helping each other as to how to make weapons." His interlocutor was astounded: "But Xhosas helping Basuto? And Basuto helping Xhosa? How does it come about that you did not desert or fight there and then?" "There was a suggestion from one of the Sotho chaps that these Xhosa should be fought here underground," said Mokheti, "[but] one of the guys opposed this and said it would be illegal and [you] could be sent to jail if you fight underground." "So instead you decided to help each other to make arms?" "Yes, until the cage came" (AAC/VR:2749–51).

On coming to the surface, they found their night-shift fellows, ethnically mixed and by now fully armed, locked together in the crush office at the surface. Shortly thereafter they were released, but the compound gate was manned by security who would not let them in. There was no sign of fighting. They stood there a long time, that mixed group of night-shift workers with their weapons at rest. Finally, at about five in the morning they were disarmed and allowed into the hostel.

Mokheti was asked why they were so eager to get into the hostel. Did they want to fight? He responded simply: "We were hungry because we were from work and we wanted to go to the kitchen. . . . we had already heard that there was no fighting going on." When asked if they would have joined in any fighting, he said: "I believe that if we found that there was fighting going on we were also going to fight" (AAC/VR:2755). However, Mokheti's entire testimony hardly depicts primordial thirst for blood. Instead, like that of Mlamli Botha, it implies unenthusiastic acceptance of the taken-for-granted and mutually assumed responsibility to follow through on the obligations of one's group membership.

Once inside, the night shift finally separated, the Sotho going to their folk and the Xhosa to their own. The hostel manager, "Tsotsi" Maritz met them at the gate and guided the Sotho to the kitchen, saying as he went that they should fight the Xhosa if they came. "He was really encouraging the fight," said Mokheti. "He assured us that security was going to help us [with tear gas] if the Xhosas were defeating us. . . . He said Xhosas were troublesome people. They are the cause of strikes" (AAC/VR:2758, 2761). The Sotho night shift got special food that day, but Xhosa speakers went hungry.

After the Sotho night shift had eaten, all the workers were shunted out to the sports stadium and the general manager of the East Division announced that the fight had really between tribal supporters of the two indunas. The indunas solemnly shook hands. No one queried "Tsotsi" Maritz's behavior. Nor was any action taken against security, although at a meeting on 14 March between senior East Division management and ministerial delegations from Lesotho and Transkei, four security officers were named as having taken sides (AAC/VR:KVD45). The two whistle-blowing Sotho battle leaders were acquitted in the local magistrates court of any wrongdoing.

Local compound management and mine security had learned a useful lesson that they would apply again. It is surely no coincidence that the state police discovered "black-on-black" violence at about the same time as this outbreak at Vaal Reefs (Haysom 1986). Traditionalist black miners learned that violence against perceived union supporters would have the support of management and the security forces. Prior to the grand reconciliation in the stadium, senior management met with delegations of six Sesotho- and six Xhosa-speaking workers; only one in each delegation was an NUM member. Their representativeness was highly questionable. To management's delight, the Sotho delegation declared:

> [T]he four hour shifts [go-slow] resulted from the people having two leaders, namely the Union and Management. They said that Management approved union meetings, which were used as a platform to instruct people not to go underground. When people object, they are called impimpis [informers]. They said that the union leads by force and Management leads by talking. They asked Management to help the people to go to work.

The general manager responded warmly, apparently totally unaware of how much things were changing on his mine and how widespread was genuine support for the union. Perhaps he learned later, when the mine exploded into a much larger "faction fight," how much his outdated industrial relations practices and his subordinates' recourse to violence really cost in terms of human life and industrial productivity.

What is so fascinating, and at the same time so appalling, about this case study is how wrong modern mine management at all levels was about collective violence and ethnic conflict—that it was primordial and uncontrollable—and yet how effectively they were able to foment it when necessary. Here senior officials avoided assuming responsibility for brutalities that they condoned in practice. Furthermore, senior management and union leadership alike tended to hold each other responsible for actions of the other's subordinates when they clearly had no intention of disciplining their own. Given the rapid growth of the union, its popular democratic principles, and the constraints under which it is obliged to operate, and given management's claims of firm control, it seems to me that management must bear the primary responsibility in such cases. Yet they eschew such responsibility in the interest of an imposed order that simply sets the scene for renewed conflict. I suspect that similar conclusions could be drawn about the role of the de Klerk government and the South African police in contemporary "black-on-black" township violence.

The material in this chapter has ranged from early examples of collective violence on the mines mentioned briefly in archival records to a detailed account of a full-scale event whose ramifications persist to the present day. In referring to all this material—and the argument becomes more convincing as more detailed testimony becomes available—I have not had to fall back on primordial explanations rooted in aggressive instinct or violent emotion. Individual violence may sometimes have such libidinal roots, and people certainly identify powerfully with perceived group interests and solidarities, but collective violence has a logic that implies strategic choices, brutalized and brutalizing maybe, but directed toward sensible, and sometimes moral, purposes. Indeed, violent strategic choices are often made out of moral outrage at entrenched injustices that are often themselves violently enforced. It is the long-range consequences of violence, rather than violent acts themselves, that make the strongest moral case against collective violence as a strategy. In the Vaal Reefs case, the majority of the workers seemed better aware of that risk than either management or militants. The consequences of ritual collective violence were less heinous in the past because management or the South African police could usually be trusted to intervene to restore order, and traditional workers respected their intervention. In the particular conjuncture of the 1980s, however, with worker organization finally coming to the mines, certain levels of management and mine police and security, as well as the South African police, seemed to be willing to risk disorder in an attempt to smash the union's threatened new order. If this is indeed so, their purposes were well served by twisting traditional ethnic solidarities, which preserved personal integrity in the old migrant culture, to new ends.

7 Solidarities

Practices of Unionization

Any notion that management exercised total control over black miners' lives should surely have been dispelled by the foregoing accounts of migrant cultures and informal worker organization. That is not to deny management's overall structural hegemony. On the mines between 1910 and 1970, the moral economy enabled worker resistance to local inequities but as part of a wider political economy of capital accumulation and management control also left untouched fundamental relations of domination and exploitation. Mining executives greatly feared the costs (both monetary and political) of black migrant mine-worker unionization and opposed it vehemently. Many state officials, especially in the South African police and the Department of Mines, shared such fears (Yudelman 1983, Moodie 1988).

The role of the South African police in scattered protest and demonstration strikes under the moral economy of the mine before 1973 was discussed in chapter 3. As we have seen, both workers and local management regarded such demonstrations as a semilegitimate redress. Sometimes workers would lend emphasis to their demands by smashing windows and raiding the kitchen, but usually damage was minimal. When such affairs did get out of hand, they were dealt with by the South African police, whose authority was seldom seriously challenged by demonstrating workers. It was as though the presence of the police meant that the matter had got "the ear of the government," which was perceived by workers to be relatively impartial and certainly very powerful. In most cases, police action was quite restrained—firearms, for instance, were hardly ever used. The point is that the demonstrators were not challenging the constituted order (nor were they seen by management or police to be doing so), but merely trying to set it to rights as they saw it. Management seldom completely ignored collective action by black workers, and the coercive arm of the state tolerated it while keeping it in line. The moral economy of the mine thus extended to include the state police.

The establishment of the African Mine Workers' Union (AMWU) and its rapid growth among black mine workers after 1943 completely changed the rules of the game—at least as far as the Chamber of Mines and police were concerned (Moodie 1988). Under the moral economy, black mine workers fought vigorously for the integrity of their life-worlds within a total system that offered a measure of protection for their rural production base while allowing mine owners to extract surplus value from their labor-power. They came to the mines for what they perceived to be their own purposes, to earn wages in order to complement the labor of women and children in rural homestead production. Higher wages would have enabled greater investment in their home economies, but leaving mine work and the compound existence for such higher wages exposed them unprotected to the temptations of "town." Hence the quid pro quo of the migrant system, whose hold was always most tenuous when rapid inflation or severe drought eroded investment prospects at home.

In the 1920s and 1930s devoted Communist party organizers had attempted to found trade unions among black mine workers, but with scant success before the 1940s. African unionization in other sectors of the economy began to take off in the late 1930s, however, and, under conditions of high inflation and low rainfall during the war years, black mine workers did begin to join the AMWU, despite adamant opposition from the Chamber of Mines and almost all departments of the South African state (Moodie 1988). In 1946, more than seventy thousand black mine workers came out on strike. It was the first widespread and unified black migrant industrial action since 1920 and the second in the history of the South African gold mines. The organizing efforts of the AMWU and the defeat of the 1946 strike provide a case study of the limits of the moral economy and the extent of state and management hegemony on the mines during the decades between 1910 and 1970.

The suppression of the strike by violent police intervention exposed the coercive framework of state and management hegemony. Equally interesting for this study is the fact that the strike took place under the aegis of a union at all. According to the conventional argument, migrant labor systems inhibit union organization (Crush 1989). How did the newly established AMWU overcome such systemic limits? To what extent was the apparent increase in mine-worker militancy in the 1940s the work of the new union, and how did it fit into the existing moral economy of worker resistance? I shall address these questions by analyzing the origins and operations of the AMWU and by describing worker action during the strike.

The collapse of the AMWU after the 1946 strike signaled the end of black unionization on the mines until the establishment of the National Union of Mineworkers (NUM) in 1982. Having examined the strengths and weaknesses of the AMWU, we shall turn to the different organizing methods and the new socioeconomic context that enabled the NUM to establish a more lasting presence on the mines.

The Establishment of the African Mine Workers' Union

On 3 August 1941, Guar Radebe, a member of the Communist party and the shadow "minister of mines" in the Transvaal African Congress, called a large conference to "establish on the widest possible basis a representative Committee for the special purpose of catering for African Mine Workers, taking up their grievances, and organizing them into a Trade Union" (Xuma:ABX 410609b). Thus began the first successful effort to establish a trade union among black miners. By the middle of 1942, the Committee to Organise African Mineworkers had become the AMWU with J. B. Marks as president. Moscow-trained, Marks's unique combination of energy, effrontery, and eloquence brought the AMWU to the notice of large numbers of black gold miners, and his leadership posed a vital challenge to the Chamber of Mines and the state, especially on the issue of wages.

J. J. Majoro, an ex–mine clerk who had been working at organizing miners for the Communist party for several years, had become secretary and began to work systematically at recruiting mine workers. In an interview years later, Marks remembered that by 1942, largely because of Majoro's efforts, the AMWU was "able to get quite a number of good contacts on the mines" (Carter-Karis Collection 2:XM42:94:11). During the first year of Marks's secretariat, however, the union grew slowly because meetings were held in the urban townships rather than near the compounds on mining grounds. Contacts would be made surreptitiously "underground, by night, crawling and that, hiding," to avoid risking a confrontation with the compound authorities.

There is fragmentary evidence that the party made some progress, especially on mines near Johannesburg like Crown Mines, Robinson Deep, City Deep, and Nourse Mines. The workers on these mines were more likely to be proletarianized, dependent on wage labor, and engaged in urban rackets like illegal brewing, hawking, and other informal sector activities that they could run from compounds near the city. These were also war years, when migrants, especially from Lesotho, came to the mines or stayed on to avoid being "volunteered" for the draft. Indeed, in the absence of skilled whites, most of whom were serving in the war, better-educated and experienced black workers found promising job opportunities on the mines.

On 2 January 1943, workers on Robinson Deep Gold Mine in the heart of Johannesburg, where the union was well organized, held a compound meeting to request higher wages and threatened a strike if their demands were not met (NTS 7681, 166/332). The union's lawyers also defended strikers arrested a few days later at Langlaagte Estates. On 9 January, Majoro wrote to the minister of labor requesting a wage determination for black mine workers (NTS 2224, 442/280). Soon afterward the state appointed the Witwatersrand Mine Natives' Wages (Lansdown) Commission, a decision incorrectly read by the union as a direct response to its demands (Moodie 1988).

Most of the union's success in the early years was because of Majoro's contacts among black mine clerks. The union's statement to the Lansdown Commission on mine wages in 1943, for instance, clearly demonstrated its commitment to the interests of mine clerks and other senior and more proletarianized workers.[1] The document strongly urged abolition of the color bar, which prevented black advancement in supervisory and clerical jobs, and abandonment of the migrant labor system. Under the heading of housing, almost as much space was devoted to conditions in the married quarters for clerical and supervisory staff as to the compounds themselves. None of this was of much interest to the majority of rural-based migrants. The document made little mention of underground safety and no demands regarding relations in production. The union did urge that workers be allowed to do their own cooking, either with mine-supplied raw meat (a distinct preference for rural migrants) or through wage increases to permit workers to buy their own food. AMWU demands, like those under the moral economy, thus concentrated largely on compound rather than workplace issues. Since the Lansdown Commission was a wages commission, the 1943 AMWU document did demand increases. Challenges on wages were especially threatening to management at this time because the gold industry was in a profit squeeze in the 1940s and 1950s prior to the opening up of the Orange Free State mines (James 1987). Nonetheless, the Lansdown Commission did grant black miners a small wage increase, although it was less than wartime inflation and was paid by the state out of the tax surcharge on mining profits.

[1]The text of the AMWU's statement of evidence to Lansdown has been reprinted as an appendix in Allen 1992:428–70. An original is in the Corey Library at Rhodes University, which also has other fragments from the commission's evidence, including the deposition of the South African Communist party.

By its own account the union had only eighteen hundred members in May 1943 (TUCSA:Dc 18). Since there were about three hundred thousand black mine workers at that time, secretive methods of organizing through mine clerks were clearly not reaping wide-scale worker response, although these early members probably always constituted a hard core of the faithful. Early in 1944, Marks decided, as he said later, "to take the bull by the horns, . . . to trespass on mine property and hold a meeting of the workers":

> The first meeting was held outside the Robinson [compound], Randfontein, on a Sunday. Saturday evening we took out a leaflet calling the workers to the mine, about five to six thousand workers [attended]. Needless to say a large number of police were present too. I addressed the meeting. That was the kickoff. They didn't arrest. I take it they wanted to see how far we could go. . . . We had now penetrated the mines. After that we were able to have these meetings which we were having for seven days of the week, from Sunday to Sunday, every afternoon. And never attended by less than two or three thousand people at the mines. We were able to set up committees as we went. . . . The union had become quite powerful. . . . It was growing by leaps and bounds.

Marks had made a brave and momentous decision. After years of covert work, largely among clerks and amatshipa (absconders), the union was suddenly appealing openly to all black mine workers. The response was tremendous. The police came to every meeting—they would allow miners to enlist in the lights of their cars in exchange for the final tallies. Mine management also sent their spies. They took careful notes on the speeches, and some of these found their way into the Native Affairs files.[2] Workers flocked to join the union. Robert Mahlati was a clerk at East Camp D'Or then. He remembered when interviewed in 1984 that

> Marks would come and he would use the stadiums, football grounds. In those days there was no security branch and it used to be the South African police—a sergeant and a couple of people to take notes—who would come, although the mine police would also take notes. All the miners would just go there, the compound manager wouldn't stop them. . . . Marks was going from mine to mine and the mines were very many in those days—over 60—so you would never know when he was going to be coming. People seemed to know, I don't know who told them, but this meeting was not far from the compound. Ordinary underground miners

[2]Unless otherwise noted, AMWU speeches are quoted from police or chamber spy reports in NTS 7248, 224/326.

> were members—even clerks were paying their sixpence. . . . Virtually the whole compound would go to the meetings.

Why did the speeches of Marks and Majoro have such appeal in those exhilarating early months of 1944? What were union officials saying that brought people out to hear them, despite the opposition of the compound hierarchy, and to part with their hard-earned shillings and sixpences (one shilling to join, sixpence a month thereafter)? Who came out and what did they come to hear? What did the AMWU people actually say?

The Rhetoric of the AMWU and the Moral Economy of the Mine

If police reports on the speeches are in any way representative, union activity was spread across the Rand with special concentrations at Randfontein Estates in the west and Brakpan Mine in the east. Nonetheless, most of the Mpondo to whom we spoke in 1984 had never heard of the AMWU, nor had most of the senior black miners interviewed at Vaal Reefs that same year, although virtually everyone knew of the 1946 strike (and they all knew of the NUM, which had been founded barely two years before, in 1982). Similarly, William Beinart (1987:296) tells the life history of an Mpondo who later became an African National Congress activist and who was on the mines in 1946 but knew nothing of the union until he and his fellows were given "pamphlets telling [them] about the strike." Clerks whom I interviewed at Vaal Reefs in 1984, however, knew of the AMWU, as did the few underground workers who had been on mines near towns such as City Deep and Robinson Deep. The Mpondo stated that those who "went to meetings" and were strike leaders in 1946 were amatshipa, those who had "forgotten" their country homes. Core support for the AMWU thus came from those mine workers who had been most fully proletarianized, separated from rural production and dependent on wages, sometimes supplemented by income from various rackets.

The strategy of the union, however, was to reach well beyond this minority of proletarianized amatshipa to the rank and file of rural migrants. To do this, the AMWU would have had to graft its own ideology onto the moral economy of the mine and speak in the language of the various migrant cultures so that the moral outrage which inspired local compound demonstrations could be channeled in more "progressive" directions. Time and again in their speeches, union officials appealed to their audiences to change their methods of protest: "The days of resisting were past when buildings were destroyed, or they went to the kitchen and spilt the food, they now had to put forward their complaints in some other way. There was only one way, that was organisation and unity, through the medium of Trade Unions." At the same time, whenever there was an extemporaneous outburst on a mine, the union sought to intervene, paying for the legal defense of those charged and seeking to keep workers on other mines informed about what had occurred.

The difficulty was that the old moral economy of the mine was essentially defensive. It was also typically restricted to local situations and ultimately geared to rural projects. Thus the union needed great sensitivity and skill to gain a foothold within the moral economy and then universalize its message to all miners on a more proactive basis. One can sense in the speeches a searching around for issues that would unite the miners in moral outrage at management hegemony itself. Union officials believed that mine workers needed to see through the taken-for-grantedness and sense of inevitability of their exploitation in such a way that they could act against it decisively and effectively. The way to achieve this breakthrough in consciousness was to seize upon the opposition that the workers already exerted, albeit informally, in the moral economy and try to enable them to channel it in ways that challenged the hegemony of the whole system.

Of course, worker accommodation to management hegemony was not absolute. It was precisely the potential for opposition that required alertness from the managing classes and ensured their prompt recourse to coercion when worker challenges got out of hand. In fact, if the ruling group wanted to maintain its hegemony, it had to accommodate itself both to demands of the moral economy and to other determinants in the political economy and the natural environment, all of which continually impose new pressures and limits on action by both dominant and subdominant groups. Management strove to particularize such adjustments, or to apply them consistently from mine to mine, and to offer concessions, when forced to make them, as acts of paternalistic benevolence rather than responses to worker demands.

On the South African gold mines during the 1940s, the basic migrant labor system was taken for granted by workers and management as the only proper way to mine gold in South Africa. It thus formed part of the mise-en-scène in which the drama of moral economy resistance was fought out. To suggest the abolition of the migrant labor system itself, as the AMWU did in its submission to the Lansdown Commission in 1943, represented the point of view of only a small minority of mine workers. Such a suggestion ran counter to the material basis of migrant integrity in rural production and to the unequal equilibrium established, resisted, and reasserted by struggles in terms of the implicit contract enforced under the moral economy. To what extent, then, was the union's leadership able to appeal to more traditional mine workers?

AMWU speeches reported by the police are interesting, not only because of what they emphasized and what they left out, but also because of how their emphases varied over the seven- or eight-month period in 1944 when union organizers were freely addressing large meetings in the immediate vicinity of the mine compounds.

A typical speech by James Majoro at Rand Leases Gold Mine on 31 January 1944 dealt with most of the issues stressed during the first three months of intensive recruitment. Addressing a crowd of over three hundred close to the compound, Majoro said:

> We have come here today to tell you workers of Rand Leases that you are proper men and workers and therefore you must be treated as such. . . . Today you find your "bosses" underground earning as much as two pound five shillings per day, not because the Chamber of Mines loves them, but because of their strong trade union that speaks for them. The Compound Managers also have an Association of their own. Ordinary delivery boys in towns today are paid two pound ten a week. They, too, have formed their own Unions that speak for them. What have you mine workers, the hardest working people in the country? You are herded into compounds, you sleep in cement "coffins," you receive the disgraceful sum of one shilling and eight pence a day, and you are given dirty food.

Almost every AMWU speech throughout the entire period from January to August 1944 raised the issues of bad food, weak beer, concrete bunks, and poor wages. Again and again the police and mine spy reports listed the main points of AMWU speeches as "better wages, better food, and better living conditions." During the early period (January through March), comparisons with white mine wages and with urban black wages were also fairly common, until the publication of the Lansdown Commission report gave the union a yardstick by which to measure wage demands for black miners. Again and again union organizers insisted that the reason for wage differentials between black miners and others in secondary industry was lack of unity and organization among mine workers. In the early period, 43 percent of the reported speeches mention an appeal for unity and organization. Thus at Rand Leases on 31 January, Majoro continued: "I am speaking to you as an experienced mine worker, I have been kicked and ill-treated underground like any one of you. I say to you that you are being treated like this because you are not organized."

At Rand Leases four months before, in September 1943, 350 underground workers had staged an underground sit-down strike. To suggest that that rather unusual event was unorganized seems more than a little naive, but Majoro of course was speaking of union membership and equating that with organization. There is little evidence that AMWU activity on the mines extended much beyond recruitment meetings addressed by union officials. "Organization" during the 1940s seems to have meant little more than representation by professional union organizers to management.[3] The union thus sought to identify itself with the successes of informal extemporaneous resistance but apparently made little effort to institutionalize it on the compounds or in the workplace.

The union's greatest claim to effectiveness was the appointment of the Lansdown Commission, although, as we now know, this was a response to strikes by power station workers rather than the appeals of the AMWU (Moodie 1988). Majoro spoke of Lansdown to the Rand Leases workers in January 1944:

> When we first started this Union, we told the Government of this country that our people are suffering on the mines. . . . The Government informed us that representatives of the Chamber of Mines had stated that the African mine workers are more than satisfied. . . . We refuted these allegations, and the Government agreed to appoint a commission of enquiry to investigate the conditions on the mines.

Majoro's speech continued with a theme that was mentioned in about a quarter of the January and February speeches and in the AMWU statement to Lansdown but then dropped almost entirely. This was the question of adequate family housing for all married black mine workers. The union was essentially urging the abolition of the migrant labor system, which was not a major issue for the large majority of mine workers. The argument on this point was largely derived from the experience of the clerks and amatshipa to whom the union appealed in its early years.

Majoro concluded his 31 January speech with a rousing entreaty—that *did* seize the attention of his listeners—and a warning:

> I say to you that the time is coming when you will no longer ask but tell the Compound Manager what you want. (Prolonged cheers.) A strike is a formidable weapon only when it is well organized, so before you hear from us continue to do your work honestly and respect your employers.

[3]For a discussion of the highly effective informal migrant worker organization on the power stations, and efforts by union professionals to horn in on the act and claim to "represent" them, and indeed, water down their demands, see Moodie 1988.

Whenever an AMWU speaker mentioned the possibility of a strike or defiance of management, he would always cover himself in terms of the law, since War Measure 145 had made strikes illegal, by adding that workers should wait until the time was ripe. The recently defeated underground sit-down strike on Rand Leases must have added a certain poignancy to Majoro's statement on this occasion. Even in this period of relative freedom for union spokesmen, there is no evidence of any specific links between what union officials said at the various mines and particular local grievances under the moral economy, not to mention underground work issues. Majoro's speech at Rand Leases, for instance, while it made reference to the strike there four months before, ignored the specifics of that forceful example of collective action underground. (Indeed, we still do not know the reason for that unusual and resolute action.) In this regard, Majoro was conforming to the limits of the moral economy, whose expression of moral outrage (on the gold mines at any rate) seldom included issues at the point of production.[4] Expressing defiance of the compound manager, however, certainly got Majoro impressive audience response.

Constant references (in 38 percent of the speeches in March and 57 percent in April) to the Lansdown Commission and the union's part in getting it appointed and giving evidence before it, paid off at the end of March 1944, when wage raises were implemented as a result of Lansdown's recommendations. Marks at once leapt to seize the credit. In several speeches from this period, Marks responded with indignation to compound managers' suggestion that they initiated the raise. The recruitment drive took off faster than ever. Marks's effrontery became delightedly blatant. His ebullience was evident even in a policeman's report of a speech he gave on 4 May:

> [Marks said] the natives were to respect their Compound Managers, but should not be afraid of them. As African people they wanted their rights. They wanted decent wages, food and good accommodation. Some Compound Managers had an oppressive policy. Each time he met a bully Compound Manager he felt like taking his jacket off and also kick[ing] him in the backside. The Government believed in cheap native labor. The natives had been robbed of their land and forced to come to the mines. The conditions on the mines were most unattractive and for this management were responsible. When the Natives stood together they [would] get what they want.

[4]The coal mines were different in this regard. One of the unsolved puzzles of mine worker collective action during the late 1930s and early 1940s is why this should have been the case.

This speech achieved an effective amalgam of defiance of unjust compound administration with general condemnation of state collaboration in rural exploitation. It also drew together condemnation of management for the deplorable conditions on the mines and an appeal for worker solidarity and union organization.

Marks seems to have been rhetorically the best skilled of the AMWU officials, combining in a vivid way grievances paramount in mine experience (especially compound manager despotism) with general condemnation of the cheap labor system in the political economy of South Africa. The question remains to what extent Marks and his union succeeded during its brief spell of relative freedom (and in its undercover work before and after) in grafting their point of view onto the life-worlds of ordinary miners? In a famous passage, Gramsci (1971:198–99) insisted that if a new radical theory is to be accepted in such a way as to become effective it must build upon "the 'spontaneous' feelings of the masses [which] have been formed through everyday experience illuminated by 'common sense,' i.e., the traditional popular conception of the world."

> Between [radical theory and popular common sense] there is a "quantitative" difference of degree, not one of quality. A "reciprocal" reduction, so to speak, a passage from one to the other and vice versa, must be possible. . . . Neglecting, or worse still despising, so-called "spontaneous" movements, i.e., failing to give them conscious leadership or to raise them to a higher plain by inserting them into politics, may often have extremely serious consequences.

Marks certainly believed that he was building an alliance between what he called "the principles of collective bargaining" and the traditions of black mine workers. In 1949, speaking to the Botha Commission, he said of black miners that while "they may not understand . . . trade unionism in its very strict sense, . . . the principle that they come together to bargain collectively . . . has been very well taken by them" (ILC:12136–37). He added: "Their old tribal organizations very readily respond to such a thing. They realize that if they would stand together and ask for something, they are more likely to get it than going individually."

Although Marks thought that he had managed to tap traditional sources of worker resistance on the mines, it is doubtful whether he and Majoro really understood the moral economy of the mine and its underpinnings in compound social networks. AMWU top officials apparently relied upon a rather general notion of "getting the confidence of responsible men in a tribal group" (Carter-Karis Collection 2:XM42:96/1). However, the izibonda, as we have seen, were room representatives rather than "tribal" representatives as such, and, according to Mpondo, they were the most important compound leaders. Marks and Majoro actually asserted to the Botha Commission that the izibonda were no more than management stooges, insisting, quite incorrectly, that management appointed the izibonda without any consultation with roommates (ILC:12144–45, 12130, 12134). No doubt, union members on the mines themselves were much more aware of how things actually worked. Certainly, the 1946 strike demonstrated that informal worker organizations were happy to support union demands if those coincided with their own interests—and workers were undeniably united and educated by such demands, especially for higher wages but also for better food.

From time to time the police, who were concerned about the AMWU speeches but could not persuade the attorney-general to proceed against the leaders, called in Marks and Majoro and confronted them with copies of what they were supposed to have said. These occasional interrogations do not seem to have scared Marks or Majoro into toning down their rhetoric. Instead, they began publicly to attack the African "Judases" who were reporting on their meetings. In a period when the Chamber of Mines was assiduously refusing to reply to union letters, but obviously carefully reading spy reports, speeches at the compounds often began to be aimed at the chamber and the government as well as the workers. This double audience does seem to have altered Marks's rhetorical presentation. On 31 May, for example, Marks said: "If the employers did not listen to their demands, it should be squeezed out of them by taking them by the throat. In the olden days natives fought with sticks. Today they were fighting with their mouths, but if the employers would not listen they would fight with sticks."

Compound managers tried to fight back, the bold ones confronting Marks to little avail and others instructing their mine police to rip up notices of his meetings. Marks reveled in the give and take, taunting the compound manager of S. A. Lands (more often called "Sallies") Mine, as follows:

> Some of the Compound Managers did as Mr Moore did here, only they are a little braver than himself because they run away from the meeting, but Mr Moore runs away [from] a paper. He instructed his Police Boys to take away all papers at the gate. Why is he afraid of the papers? Why are you not afraid? Let us get the reason why. The paper says we want higher wages, decent food, good treatment and good accommodation. This is what Mr Moore is afraid of.

As the union moved jubilantly toward its annual meeting at the end of July 1944, Marks seemed confident that it could achieve its goals without a strike.[5] The 1944 AMWU annual conference was a triumphal affair, attended by seven hundred delegates from every mine on the Witwatersrand and about thirteen hundred rank-and-file members, who all crowded into Inchcape Hall in Johannesburg. It must have seemed to the union that nothing could stop its march to recognition.

The Defeat of the 1946 Strike

In fact, the Chamber of Mines mustered the full power of the state and property laws against the AMWU. By Proclamation 1425 of August 1944, organizations were forbidden from holding meetings on mining grounds without permission. Since virtually every compound was surrounded by miles of mine-owned open land, the new ruling virtually banned union meetings in the vicinity of the mines.

Proclamation 1425 was a severe blow to the AMWU. Union organizers had relied upon mass meetings outside the compounds to enroll members and to collect subscriptions. They had also done little to encourage local shaft-based worker organization. After August 1944, when Proclamation 1425 was announced, the police who had always haunted the meetings of the union began to disperse workers who gathered. Confrontation tactics with management, at which Marks was so skilled and which had so impressed black miners, could no longer be used. The chamber issued strict instructions to mine management to have no dealings at all with the union, because it was feared that any contact, even opposition, might give the organization credibility. Once more, loyal members were obliged to sneak away to secret meetings in Johannesburg. Clerks, who had access to telephones, again became pivotal but were obliged to be more secretive than ever.

No doubt the work of the union could proceed on mines such as Robinson Deep, City Deep, and Crown Mines, which were situated in or near towns and many of whose workers were proletarianized amatshipa anyway. Jackson Yaca at Durban Deep in the 1940s, told us in 1984 that he "heard from the people who went to the bars [in town], that there were people who went to the meetings in Johannesburg. It was those people at the bar who came with [the strike demand in 1946]." Most of these organizers were amatshipa. But the recruiting methods used in the first eight months of 1944 to lure many thousands of ordinary black miners into the union were no longer effective. Especially on the Far East Rand (Benoni, Boksburg, Brakpan, Springs, and Nigel), the AMWU was essentially

[5] At the height of the war in Europe, with Communist Russia fighting for its life, Marks, who was a devoted party member, was hardly likely to encourage a strike that would hurt the Allied war effort.

banned from contact with the workers. Basic grievances remained salient, of course. Members who could get to AMWU meetings in Johannesburg vented their grievances from the floor (*Guardian,* 17/5/45; NTS 7248, 224/326, Chamber spy report of 14/5/45 and SAP to DNL, 16/5/45):

> Delegate after delegate complained of the conditions on the mines, the inadequate pay, the rising cost of living, the expense of clothes, the hard working and living conditions. Every delegate emphasised that unless the government did something, the African mineworkers would find some way to do things for themselves. (*Inkululeko,* 28/5/45)

Worker grievances began to spill over onto the mines themselves, especially those near towns. On 19 May, about two hundred workers met with Miller, the chief compound manager at Crown Mines, to demand cost of living allowances as recommended by the Lansdown Commission.[6] He told them that they had signed contracts and were legally bound to fulfill them. Furthermore, since the government had set their current pay scales, the decision was out of the hands of the mines. On 20 May, several of the Crown Mines people went to Marks to tell him what had happened. Miller sacked them forthwith.

Food for the mines had become a major concern for mine management during the last years of the war. The nationwide food shortage was mentioned in the annual Chamber of Mines presidential addresses in 1944, 1945, and 1946 as a major problem. Management understood only too well the importance of adequate supplies of food in the moral economy of the mine. For many traditional contracted mine workers, low wages were to some extent offset by the ample diet—especially a generous supply of meat. The state food controller's insistence that the mines serve canned beef in the place of freshly cooked meat had provided the union with useful leverage on several mines during its "open" period in 1944, and food shortages continued to be a cause around which collective worker action, whether extemporaneous or union organized, took place. Mentions of food by protesting gold mine workers increased from nine in 1938–1942 to twenty-seven in 1943–1947.

It was thus surely no great surprise to management when, on 16 July 1945, workers (almost certainly union members, mostly wage dependent) at No. 5 shaft, Crown Mines (C compound), went on duty without drawing

[6]Unless otherwise noted, reports on mine worker actions in 1946 are from NTS 7248, 224/326.

any rations from the kitchen.[7] At 4:30 in the afternoon on 18 July, the Crown Mines workers held a meeting on the mine sports field that was attended by about two thousand mostly Xhosa-speaking workers. At the meeting,

> it was decided to continue not to accept food from the kitchen and to go on as they had been doing, i.e., to buy their own food, until Sunday when they would call the Compound Manager and demand payment in cash for the week's food which they had not consumed. If no redress, they would continue to refuse the mine rations for a month.

The next morning, on 19 July, about half the six thousand workers at Crown Mines X compound refused their food. (The remainder, mostly Sotho, "stated that they were not going to go without their food.") The hunger strike was thus spreading, undoubtedly aided by the fact that workers were apparently able to get as much bread and maize meal as they wanted, as well as some meat, from local concession stores, despite the state's claim that there was a shortage of those foodstuffs. The food controller was brought in to harass the stores, and the miners were running out of money, so by the evening of 19 July, workers on both C and X compounds were "feeding normally."

The total failure of the hunger strike on Crown Mines must have caused the AMWU officials to rethink their approach to the adamantly intractable chamber. By the beginning of 1946 it was clear to Marks that if the union did not offer firm leadership extemporaneous action by black miners would occur only sporadically and ineffectually on different mines from time to time as in the past (*Inkululeko*, 28/1/46). The question was, What could the union do about it? As their membership rapidly eroded and worker resentment about food shortages and inflation grew, Marks and Majoro began to consider a general miners' strike. Marks surely suspected that the chances of successfully calling a large-scale general strike were slim given the restrictions on organization. Even if the union did successfully call a strike on all the gold mines, its leaders must have wondered how widespread or effective it could be, especially on the East Rand, where the AMWU was stretched especially thin. Nonetheless, the intransigence of the Chamber of Mines and the state was inexorably pushing union officials and their active members toward a work stoppage that might shake the

[7]According to the DNL's report, the protesters included all the surface workers (2,265), 260 contractor's employees living on the mine, and 1,133 underground workers. Surface workers and contractor's employees were much more likely to be proletarianized amatshipa.

chamber out of its complacent disregard of union representations. Perhaps only too aware of their weakness, however, AMWU officials proceeded cautiously.

At the annual mass conference of the AMWU on 14 April 1946, Marks noted:

> [T]here are rumours around the mines that we are about to come out on strike because of shortage of food. These rumours are being spread by the White Mine Workers. We are not going to go on a blind strike, but if any of you want to strike you should report first to the officials of your Union and we shall be on the spot. When Europeans strike they do not smash in offices and machines on the Mine, they just refuse to work until they get what they want. That is how we should act too.

However, L. C. Joffe, one of the invited speakers and an active Communist party member, added:

> I am not telling you that when you go out [of] here you should go and make a strike, but I do say that you should prepare yourself first if you want to make a strike. I believe that one of these days you might be compelled by your suffering to act and I assure you that the Communist Party will stand with you until you get your elementary rights. The Chamber of Mines is very much afraid of the African Mine Workers' Union. You are brave men—good fighters—make your Union strong so that you can speak with one voice from the Cape to Tanganyika, from Portuguese East Africa to South West Africa. The Gold you dig from the mines is yours. Why should you let people who do no work take it away from you? Unite to fight for your rights. Forward Comrades. Long live the African Mine Workers' Union.

The temperature of the rhetoric was heating up. That both featured speakers (L. C. Joffe and Issy Wolfson) were committed Communist party members perhaps underlined the union's new determination. Their presence certainly implied that the Communist party's wartime reluctance to upset gold production had disappeared with victory.

The most intense militancy apparently came from the two thousand mine workers in the audience, however. The level of enthusiasm was high. According to the *Guardian* (25/4/46):

> Enthusiastic discussion took place from the floor, where nearly all the delegates—the great majority of those present being underground workers—stated if the Union were unable to secure redress of the miners demands through making representations to the au-

> thorities and the employers, the only alternative would be to take action by withholding their labour.

Perhaps the size of the crowd was due at least in part to an item on the agenda circulated on the mines beforehand: "A minimum wage of 10s. per day." The conference did pass a resolution demanding "adequate and suitable food" and a minimum wage of ten shillings a day, and those present pledged themselves "to struggle for this demand with all [their] might." Marks's closing remarks reveal how tenuous he thought the union's hold over its members was. "I thank you very much," he said, "and you can leave the whole of your affairs in the hands of your leaders and only do what they tell you."

The workers were apparently not willing to leave their affairs in the union's hands. On the next Saturday, 20 April, black miners at X and S compounds on Crown Mines (where the AMWU had its largest membership) held meetings demanding minimum wages of ten shillings per day. In addition, workers on S compound, which had not been involved in the earlier hunger strike, wanted the right to feed themselves. Miller, the chief compound manager, refused to consider either demand, and he brought in Native Affairs officials to remind workers that strikes were illegal. Nonetheless, "as a protest the night shifts on the two shafts concerned refused to go underground on Tuesday night" (*Guardian*, 2/5/46). After that, however, work proceeded as usual.

In a statement issued afterward, Marks acknowledged that "this event must be regarded more as a demonstration than a serious strike." However, he then went on to warn: "a very grave situation is developing on the mines due to the mounting discontent of the workers. If the authorities continue to refuse to even listen to representations made peacefully by our Union, I'm afraid there can only be one result." Once again, Marks was announcing the growing impatience of his constituents and the relative moderation of the union. But once again, he stressed that there was a limit beyond which the union would have to agree to a strike.

As though to underline his warning, in the next ten days there was a sudden rash of meetings and strikes on compounds, largely on the West Rand, demanding ten shillings a day (NTS 7686, 259/332, Memo 1/5/46; *Guardian*, 16/5/46). On the weekend of 27 April, workers called compound meetings on Rand Leases, Randfontein Estates, and Luipaardsvlei Mines. The native commissioner, A. J. P. O'Connell, was summoned to each location to announce the illegality of strikes and that both state and management were obdurate in their refusal to consider any raises. At Rand Leases, two of the leaders told O'Connell quite openly that

> they, and others, had called a meeting of the Natives in terms of a decision taken at a meeting of the African Mine Workers' Union held in Johannesburg on the 14th instant. The decision to demand 10s. a shift was reached after the Union meeting had been exhorted thereto by two Europeans. They frankly stated it was their intention to stop work that night if their demand was not met.

During the week after 28 April, workers actually came out on strike on Rand Leases, Durban Roodepoort Deep, Luipaardsvlei, and Randfontein Estates. Several thousand miners were involved. Picketing of the night shift often commenced such actions, and in two cases workers broke ranks on the way to work and defied management with arsenals of rocks atop mine dumps. The police were called in and charged the strikers. Police records note ninety-seven arrests.

What are we to make of this first wave of "ten shilling" demonstrations? First, they were not organized as the full-scale strike was to be in August. The AMWU conference on 14 April had not called for a strike (although the level of the rhetoric was certainly high). Instead, it had suggested the possibility of a strike if further representations to the state and Chamber of Mines failed. Thus, these early actions could rightly be dubbed "protest demonstrations," all of which followed initial confrontations with state officials and senior mine management. Where actual stoppages occurred, they came about as a direct result of O'Connell's and mine management's dogged refusal to consider any of the workers' demands. It was because the initial meetings were held in the evenings to avoid interfering with the normal working of the mine that so many of the actual strikes commenced with violent, or allegedly violent, intimidation of the night shift. This first strike wave was a series of extemporaneous disturbances on closely adjacent mines, rather than a centrally organized affair.

However, although these first strikes were extemporaneous, they did not express merely local grievances. They had a common theme, and their inspiration was Joffe and Wolfson's support at the April AMWU meeting for the demand of ten shillings a day, fueled by drought in the countryside and food shortages on the mines. Again and again, workers confronted O'Connell with the statement that white men had authorized black wages of ten shillings a day. Although workers may have used Wolfson's and Joffe's speeches to justify their demands to O'Connell, the speeches themselves may also have inspired them to cross a certain psychological "threshold of inevitability" about wage levels. This was probably especially true for the least proletarianized workers and gave additional force to the demands once the breakthrough to make them had been achieved.

All the evidence implies, however, that the leaders of these early demonstration strikes were experienced older men, many of them "time expired" and, in Mpondo parlance, amatshipa. The articulateness of their demands implied a fairly sophisticated acquaintance with trade union practice. In fact, the willingness of the workers on the West Rand to appoint spokesmen and their leaders' willingness to speak up were two unusual characteristics of these demonstrations. It implied the spokesmen's assurance of the righteousness of their cause, but it also implied a certain faith in the willingness of the authorities to recognize their right to withhold their labor according to international trade union principles. Such outspokenness was not heard again on the mines for decades because of the regularity with which such spokesmen were fired by the mines. Even in the 1980s and 1990s, representatives of NUM often faced victimization in the retrenchment practices of local mine managements. The older process, long established in the moral economy, by which leaders hid behind mass demonstrators was designed to avoid victimization. In fact, in May 1946, the union was far too weak to protect its West Rand leaders from victimization, and the state was unwilling to do so. As a result, the hold of the AMWU on the West Rand, where it had been quite strong, was effectively broken after these April demonstrations. During the great black miners' strike in August 1946, no mines on the West Rand participated at all, except for brief stayaways on Robinson and Battery Reef compounds at Randfontein Estates.

The first meeting of the AMWU after the West Rand protests, on 15 May 1946, was badly attended and a somber and resolute occasion (GWU, Dbc 2.1., evidence of Sergeant H. G. Boy at the trial of J. B. Marks and others, 2/9/46). Gone was the excitement of the previous meeting, for everyone now knew what they were up against. "We are wrestling with a giant," said Marks:

> At your conference you took decisions and very important decisions, and you did not take the decisions because you wanted to; you took them because circumstances forced you. You have approached the mine authorities in a [disciplined] manner and put your demand to them and in every case where you asked for fish you got a serpent.

When the meeting was thrown open to the floor, several workers spoke in favor of the union. Then a Xhosa named Moustache from Randfontein Estates, a well-dressed man among his blanketed fellows, perhaps a clerk, rose to say:

> What are we to do to get this 10s. a day. I say only one thing: if I have the right there must be unity among us that when we stop

> work it must be done by all of us at the same time and date, and would be very pleased if this will penetrate our feelings.

Marks called for a resolution, which had to "come from the floor," Moustache spoke again:

> This is now the point I am after. I say only one thing can help us; that we at this meeting strike from East to West, and when we take this action it must be done on one day and within the law. I think this is the only way to succeed in our demands. Before we do that we take a decision and leave it with Marks so that he can report it in full to the Government and the Chamber of Mines. We shall stipulate a time limit for our demands, and if we agree on this decision, we will state a day and time. We are cowards and do not make our demands. I move that we should strike.

A Sotho speaker, also from the West Rand, seconded the motion, saying resignedly as he did so, "We may agree here but once away we forget." The vote, by show of hands, was unanimously in favor.

Marks was careful in closing the meeting to insist on thorough report-back procedures at the local mine level. He also sought to avoid the disarray that had recently occurred on the West Rand. Nothing should go off half-cocked this time:

> As Chairman of your Union I am going to guide you; you have come representing your mine workers; you have the duty to go back and tell them what happened at this meeting; you make this coming Sunday one of mass meetings from East to West, that if the Chamber of Mines does not accede to your demands you will withdraw your labour on a date. On this occasion you must not misunderstand me; you are not going to tell your manager, you are going to tell you own people what happened here.

The union officials had set the great report-back meeting for Sunday, 4 August 1946. When a mere four hundred miners showed up in Market Square, Newtown, that day, Marks and Majoro must have been quite unsure of their course. They explained how they had approached both the state and the chamber and had been ignored as usual. As always at these meetings, there were many speakers from the crowd, and then Moustache once more got up and proposed a strike for 12 August. The police climbed onto the running boards of their cars in order to better watch the vote. It was overwhelmingly in favor of striking. At that, Marks turned to the crowd, and, as he said later:

> I explained to them what a strike would involve, sacrifices would have to be made, to refrain from falling for any provocation, to be

> non-violent. To do nothing else on the day of the strike but to remain in their rooms. That's what I put to them. And many other things naturally, as a leader would put to people who are going into battle. . . . They were ready, they were ripe for it. (Carter-Karis Collection 2:XM42:94)

The following Sunday, 11 August, nighttime temperatures dropped below freezing. Striking workers made several unsuccessful attempts to stop the night shifts from going down, and police were called in for isolated acts of stone throwing. This was not to be a repeat of the West Rand debacle, however. The next day, seven mines were shut down completely; on five others, substantial bodies of workers struck work. The 1946 black miners' strike was on.

Figures for the strike are confusing. Police, Native Affairs, and press reports do not agree, either internally or with each other. The Department of Native Affairs reported twenty-one out of forty-seven mines on the Witwatersrand had been affected, eleven wholly, ten partially, with 73,557 out of 287,376 black workers actually involved and more than one thousand arrests and 1,248 injuries as a result of police action with nine black miners killed. Sixteen hundred white policemen were involved, and the police borrowed sixteen troop carriers from the army to render them more mobile as they rushed reinforcements from mine to mine.

The quietest area was the West Rand, which had had its action in April and where the police used force right from the outset. After their April experiences, West Rand workers no doubt had little stomach for collective action. On the East Rand there was no experience to serve as a guide. To a man, the workers on several mines there refused to appear for work on Monday, 12 August, remaining quietly in their rooms as Marks had instructed them. A reporter who toured the area

> found the strikers treating the occasion as a Sunday, except that a few were making purchases at the concession stores. They sat or lay about in blanketed groups, sunning themselves behind compound walls out of the wind. Others strolled along veld paths smoking and talking. At one mine, weekend musical programmes were being given through loudspeakers. Many of the giant sheave wheels which crown the headgears were still. The only signs of abnormal conditions were the frequent lorry-loads of armed police arriving in the area from the training depot at Pretoria, from Johannesburg and elsewhere. (*RDM*, 13/8/46)

On the Central Rand, where a substantial proportion of the workforce were amatshipa, there was some picketing and the strike was less orderly and unified, but many workers on the compounds stayed away for some of the time over the next five days.

The strike was broken by the South African police with the cooperation of the Native Affairs department. Police action was violent and vicious, especially at Sub-Nigel (where police used firearms) and West Springs, in response to remarkably disciplined passive resistance (particularly on the East Rand). By Wednesday, 14 August, the police and mine management seemed to have developed violent and effective techniques for strikebreaking. On that day at Rose Deep Mine, for instance, two thousand workers went on strike for the first time and gathered on the mine dump outside. By 9:30 A.M. they had returned to the compound, where they were addressed in typical terms by the native commissioner, who told them they were breaking the law and advised them to return to work. "They were however in a truculent mood," he reported, "and disinclined to be advised. The assistance of the Police became necessary [and] sixty-three natives sustained superficial injuries. . . . [Next day] all the labourers returned to work."

More details are available for Nourse Mines, Robinson Deep, and City Deep, three heavily unionized mines in the central area that struck work for sustained periods of time. At each of these mines, on Monday, 12 August, "a small number of Natives . . . [had been] singled out and ordered to report for work within half an hour failing which they would be prosecuted." These tactics had little effect except that on each mine partial strikes became total the next day. Events at Robinson Deep may be used to describe police strikebreaking techniques (and union resistance) at these inner-city mines. Close to Johannesburg, the Robinson Deep Mine, with City Deep, was one of the most effectively organized on the Rand. On Tuesday, 13 August, about six hundred workers went to work, but the remainder remained firmly and quietly on strike despite twenty-four arrests (*RDM*, 13/8/46, 14/8/46). That night the compound manager went around the entire compound with the induna, "starting at room 1." Johannes Mabaso (interviewed in Pondoland in 1984) remembered: "When he came in the workers threw their porridge at him and told him to 'fuck off' unless he had the money. He went all over the compound with the induna. Someone else, who was drinking beer, poured it on the induna."

The next day, 14 August, the police decided to use force to break the strike. Early in the morning, management officials awakened the compound and ordered the inmates to work. Predictably, their instructions were ignored, so about two hundred uniformed men were sent to rout people out of their rooms. A detachment of police drew up in the compound with fixed bayonets and revolvers. Another group remained outside the gate to shepherd workers along to the shaft head. The balance of men were set to clearing the rooms with batons. One of the strikers was interviewed by Michael Scott shortly after the events. He remembered: "Many hundreds of people were attacked by the police. It was the police who started the fighting. The people were not armed with sticks. The police came after three days. They were using sticks. The people were sitting in their rooms when the police came and assaulted them" (GWU, Dbc 2.1, 7/11/46).

According to press reports, several of the rooms resisted as well as they could, giving others the chance to flee the compound. A clerk, Emmanuel Ralengau, told Michael Scott:

> On Wednesday at 6:30 a.m. the Compound Manager went round from room to room telling all the boys to go back to work. They refused. Coming back from the lavatory I overheard two senior policemen saying that they were going to bring many other policemen to chase the boys out. I followed the two police officers out of the Compound to see what was going to happen. I saw that the other police were all lined up there. There were three groups that went inside the Compound and one group was left by the gate. In about five minutes the boys were chased out. The group of police which was posed by the gate then assaulted the boys with short sticks. The boys then ran away to the "dams" [mine dumps].

According to the press, once outside the compound the strikers, breaking through the police guard, formed a semicircle and began to stone the police, who had to take shelter behind parked cars. Armed police were posted at the compound gates to prevent any further exodus, and then an armed detachment was sent outside. The stone throwers fled to three dumps covered with loose stones and gathered piles of missiles at the tops of them. The police simply cordoned them off and left them up there for the day, while they drove the others off to work. After 10 P.M. some of the strikers came down in twos and threes from the dumps, but many slept up there (*RDM*, 15/8/46). Some of the strikers had been chased underground on the Wednesday. As Johannes Mabaso recollected almost thirty years later, when the police chased them underground, they were "so frightened that even the surface people went down. Some had no shoes, so they just had to wait at the station. That day no proper work was done because the wrong people were in the wrong places. The bosses underground just said: 'Have a rest.'"

The next morning, Thursday, 15 August, the police returned three hundred strong and surrounded the entire dump area containing the roughly twelve hundred strikers who were holding out. Ralengau gave Michael

Scott an insider's account of what happened (GWU, Dbc 2.1, 7/11/46) that is essentially confirmed by press reports (*Star*, 15/8/46; *RDM*, 19/8/46):

> Some boys were sent [by the police] to speak to the strikers who were sitting on top of a mine dump. They pretended they were members of the Union and wanted to hold a meeting about the strike. By this means they persuaded the strikers to come down from the mine dump which consisted of stones and pieces of rock and to go to another dump which was made of fine sand and where there were no stones. The police then charged them and dispersed the strikers. Some of those who ran to the top of the dump were assaulted and knocked down. They overbalanced and came falling head over heels right down to the bottom of the dump.
>
> A group of strikers set out to report to the [AMWU] head office in Sauer Street what was happening at the mine and in the Compound. But two lorries of police were sent after them. They caught them and chased them back hitting them with batons. When they got back the senior police addressed them. They said: "You have been asking for ten shillings a day haven't you? The only things you will get are what you have got . . . ," pointing to the cuts and bruises and the others who had bandages on them. No one made any reply. It was after this that the boys decided to return to work.

Marks and several other leaders of the union had long since been arrested. Had the Robinson Deep men made it to Sauer Street they would have found AMWU headquarters deserted. By this time the police were engaged in mopping up.

What can we make of the strike from the workers' point of view? How was it organized, and why was it so much more successful and widespread than anybody thought it would be? Who actually participated in the strike, and why? To begin with the last question first, most reports on the strike are surprisingly free of ethnic references. However, when "tribes" are mentioned, they invariably say that Mpondo or Sotho were actively involved in the strike or mention "Shangaans" or "Tropicals" as willing to return to work. Thus we can probably conclude that although involvement in the strike depended mostly on informal organization at the local mine level the most enthusiastic participants were from the Eastern Cape or from Lesotho. There is no evidence that any particular job categories of black miners were more actively involved in the strike than others. Those who remembered the event thought that all categories were equally involved. This was hardly surprising, given that the central focus of the strike was wages rather than work conditions.

With regard to organization, Marks was aware that a successful strike would have to tap into the black miners' informal networks, centered on the moral economy. Thus he ensured that the participants set a date a week after the meeting for the strike. He knew, he said, "from long experience in the work of the mines" that he had "to allow for a week to declare a strike" after the decision had been made.

> That was to allow the workers to report back. You must always, if you work on the mines, allow a Sunday, because on Sundays they travel extensively, they visit friends and I knew they were all going to talk about a strike on Sunday so I had to allow a Sunday to be in between the meeting and the Monday, the 12th of August. (Carter-Karis Collection 2:XM42:94)

The union had to rely on its members to get the news of the strike date into the mines because union officials were forbidden access to workers. The week's delay was also important because the union had to arrange to deploy all its available support from the Communist party, the African National Congress, and other black unions on the Rand in order to print and distribute strike leaflets around the compounds. Edwin Mofutsanyane, interviewed in 1984, remembered that

> it was difficult to get to these people so, in order to provide them with information about what was happening, we had to do something so we distributed pamphlets. It was done in many places. We divided our people—they used to go with cars and leave their cars and walk to a place to let these people know what is actually happening.

The pamphleteering was important. Again and again in our 1984 interviews, old men who had been on the mines at the time recalled the "papers" that appeared in the compounds the week before the strike. Many of them carried such "papers" when they confronted management. It was as though having something written overcame their sense of inevitability about wages, which, of course, was reinforced by written contracts. Having an alternative document seems to have enabled them to cross the threshold from complaints among themselves about low wages to collective strike action. One man's testimony pulled together themes expressed by several others:

> I can remember that day very well. It was Sunday. When I came back to the compound from wherever I had visited, the men in the room showed me a paper and said, "There's a letter." I took it and read it. It read thus: "Every man should be paid ten shillings a day, he should live in good conditions and eat good food." It or-

> dered all the men to get together to a meeting. They met and decided that on the following day, a Monday, they were not going to work. When the gong went I tried to leave because I was expected to work with the shift-boss. The men stopped me. I joined the strike. I did not go to work. Later in the day, the underground manager came. He said: "Hey, get to work." We answered him: "We are not getting there, we want that ten shillings which you yourself wrote us a letter about." He denied writing the letter: "When I give you money, I don't give you a letter—I'll give you the money and I'll tell you. I do not know who wrote that letter." We answered: "We don't know either, it is you who write." He went away. The following day, on Tuesday, we did not go to work. Round about nine a.m. the police came. They drove us by force. . . . Who wrote the papers? Later we learned that these papers were circulated by the union—we did not know the union. No one knew its name.

At least three themes emerge from this account. First, the impact of the pamphlets was important. These stated worker demands in writing and could be construed by some to have been issued by management and used by others to confront management—"It is you who write." As another worker put it: "Papers were distributed all over. No one quite knows where the papers came from, but they were about the strike. Those who could not read went to those who could and they said we should have ten shillings and the idea spread round like magic. Because of these papers not a single person went to work."

The second theme is the general lack of acquaintance with the union, especially on the East Rand, except among clerks. Even at Brakpan Mine, which was the best organized by the union of the East Rand mines, a worker reported: "It was only those people who could read who told us all these things—that on such a day we should expect to be paid ten shillings a day, and if we were not paid we should not go underground, but who was behind it we do not know. Obviously there must have been a union only we did not know about it, we just saw letters circulated and read to us." This ignorance on the East Rand of the very existence of the union was so general and widespread that one cannot but believe it was genuine. How then was the strike organized? We need to turn to informal networks within the compound ("meetings") if we are to understand what occurred in August 1946.

The third theme, then, is that of informal organization. Although the "papers" and the secret activities of union members may have precipitated the strike, it was the workers' own organization on the compounds that followed through on their lead. Testimony from two old men in Pondoland gave convincing detail on how workers on the East Rand arranged the strike among themselves. Unsurprisingly, the procedures were similar to those adopted for demonstrations and disturbances for protest within the moral economy. Mpotsongo Mde was at Van Dyk, which held out longer than any other East Rand mine. Mobilization started, he said, with papers that were placed in their rooms on Friday and Saturday. The educated ones read these papers to their mates. The people in the room thought that the papers came from the white Mineworkers' Union, which was indeed out on strike the week after the black strike had been suppressed.[8] Mde continued:

> We knew we were breaking the imiteto because we were told to go underground, but the papers were talking about money—the money for which we had left our homes to come and work on the mines. Our only ambition was money. We didn't care about anything except that money—ten shillings would have made it much better for us. On the Sunday when we were drinking with men of the other tribes we were talking about the money, saying: "Hm, we are going to be better paid." In the room we were talking about this, having meetings about it—we decided in the rooms, not outside when we were drinking with others. In each room, two men were deputed to go to all the rooms with the message: "Tomorrow, no work. Monday, not going to work." So everybody in the compound knew. The men we chose were men whom we trusted: it was the izibonda and their assistants. When the manager was telling us to go to work, he was addressing the whole compound and we all refused then and there. When we went back to their rooms we spoke of the strike, telling each other that if we stayed away the manager would give us the money.

The role of the izibonda was confirmed by Mafukusa Mfusane, who was on Nigel mine, which went on strike on the Thursday for one day only. They went on strike, he said, because they heard when they visited other mines that people were on strike for ten shillings. It was a room decision, he remembered:

> On the night before the strike, all the people in the room decided to strike. There was no compound meeting. In the morning we woke up as usual and dressed for work but we did not want to go down so [we] sat at the shafthead. . . . The izibonda went from room to room telling the people that on such and such a day we

[8]This is the only hint that I found in any of my interviews or in the Department of Native Affairs files of the strike of white mine workers that took place around the time of the black miners' strike and was settled by negotiation.

> will get dressed but we won't go down to work. The rooms made the decision and then it was discussed at a meeting of the izibonda. I was the one who told my isibonda to tell the other izibonda that people must not go down. No one told me but we heard from the other compounds, and then we discussed it in our room—we were older in our room—and we told the isibonda to tell the others. The isibonda was an old man, but it was his responsibility to take the message. . . . We sat on the surface and the manager . . . phoned the police, who came and asked why we wanted to strike. We said together that we wanted ten shillings. The police said they didn't understand and one person should be appointed to speak for us, but we said together: "We all say that," because we feared that if we nominated one person he would be sacked or jailed.

These accounts are perfectly consistent with what we know of extemporaneous work-stoppages on mines throughout the period before 1974. They provide convincing reasons for the solidarity, peaceableness, and restraint of the 1946 strikers on the East Rand, whose behavior conformed closely to the moral economy of the mine. They were sure that they were in the right, even if they did break the formal imiteto, to demand decent food and better pay in an inflationary period. Thus, in many respects, the strike on the East Rand was simply a coordinated protest demonstration. There was apparently little picketing, no formal leadership, and little, if any, union involvement in the grass-roots organization of the strike. Except perhaps on Sub-Nigel, if police reports about war dances at a distance are to be believed, workers on the East Rand did not fight back, despite substantial police provocation. Even mass marches on Johannesburg were perceived by the workers themselves to be peaceful protests without aggressive intent. Such an interpretation of the strike on the East Rand explains both the extraordinary solidarity of the strikers and their willingness to return to work when it was all over. Mpotsongo Mde concluded his story of the strike at Van Dyk in the following terms: "We never struck again. We are still waiting for that money. We never spoke about it amongst ourselves in later years—nobody ever talked about it. We had been defeated."

The East Rand strike was thus an indigenous affair, rooted in the moral economy of the mine, with all the strengths and weaknesses of that type of collective action. One Mpondo ex-miner showed a glimmer of awareness of this when he said at the end of his account of the strike: "Everyone was talking about it but after a couple of weeks none spoke of it because nothing happened; we got no money. All we used to speak about was work and then go home. We did tell our sons, but they were not particularly interested because we didn't get money—if those soldiers were beating our sons nowadays, they would fight back."

On the West and Central Rand, where the union was much stronger and many more workers were fully proletarianized, the patterns were rather different, and some people did fight back. We have already discussed the April disturbances on the West Rand, with their actively militant picketing, their spokesmen willing to be identified and openly admitting their union commitments, and their confrontational tactics with management. Similarly, cadres of workers on City Deep and especially Robinson Deep were willing to fight for the right to withhold their labor. There the strike was organized, not by the izibonda, but by openly active union members, who were able to keep in contact with each other and with headquarters by meeting in the Syrian bars and eating houses in town. Ordinary Mpondo workers on the inner-city mines feared them. In 1984, Zebron Nqabayi described his experience on City Deep:

> I didn't go to the meetings myself—I just heard gossip about them. In my room there were people going to the meetings and in the whole compound it was a mixture of people [different tribes] going to those meetings. I myself was afraid. Even the clerks were beaten by people if they wanted to go to work; . . . the clerks didn't go to the meetings, they went to their rooms, else they would be beaten. Most people at the meetings were amatshipa, because they had been there a long time. They pushed these new ones into what they wanted—they had power over the new ones. At the beginning of the strike [these amatshipa] ran outside and stayed in the mine-dumps, watching if any person or tribe would go to work. They were armed with sticks, stones and whatever they could get (also jumpers). They came back into the compound at suppertime for their food, ate, and then returned to the dumps. At night they came back to sleep.

On the Central Rand then, the strike was organized by unionized workers with militant proletarian consciousness. Aggressive methods of mobilization had their price, however. Union members on the West and Central Rand, by ignoring the indigenous isibonda room networks, split the workforce. The amatshipa had lost touch with the moral economy of the mine and the local and communal sense of outrage that it could evoke. Robinson and City Deep union activists did hold out longest, in fact, but only by striking fear into their fellow workers as well as fighting the police. In response to overt aggression by the police, it was these committed union cadres who resorted to violence, against both police and work mates, whereas the more "tribal" migrants on the East Rand showed extraordinary solidarity in the face of police and management threats but abstained from violence even when confronted by extreme police provocation.

How then are we to explain the solidarity of the strike on the East Rand? At the level of conscious action, the strike may be viewed as resulting from acceptance of the validity of union demands by workers operating in terms of the existing moral economy of the mine. Although the trade union implant was rudimentary, without the AMWU, mine workers might have continued to accept their low wages as hegemonic necessity. Union activity, busy as it became in 1944, could not have hoped to mobilize seventy thousand black migrant workers, however, without drawing upon the moral economy of resistance that was part of black miners' lore and practice. The potential for resistance, persistent, largely nonviolent, but righteous over local infractions of an unwritten code, was gathered by the union into a massive coordinated effort on behalf of ten shillings a day. This mobilization for better wages in an inflationary economy, definitely union inspired, was also helped by food shortages, given the centrality of the right to good food in the moral economy.

The primary intent of the 1946 strike, however, was for higher wages. Again and again, when asked why they had struck work, old men would reply: "Money." As they sat in their rooms instead of going to work on the first Monday, they spoke of the ten shillings and how they would use it. They certainly needed more money. The raises granted under Lansdown in 1944 had not brought real wages to the 1936 level (Wilson 1969:46). Drought persisted in much of the countryside in 1945 and 1946. Black mine workers needed no agitators to point out their dire straits. Thus, although it was initiated by the African Mine Workers' Union, on most mines the strike was organized according to the mine workers' own established but informal means of redressing grievances.

There was never any suggestion from our Mpondo informants in 1984 that the future of the migrant labor system itself had been at stake. Of course, they were homestead proprietors, who had returned home to realize their rural investments. Most South African–based black proletarians simply left the mines after the 1946 defeat, leaving the way open to substantial increases in mine labor from tropical central Africa, where rural bases were still viable (Crush, Jeeves, and Yudelman 1991).

The defeat of the 1946 strike reestablished management hegemony within the migrant economy. Mine workers returned to the implicit contract set by the moral economy to guarantee protection against arbitrary management power and to establish a measure of equity within the parameters of management hegemony. The migrant system spread its net wider and wider into the tropical north in the 1950s and 1960s, but it prevailed with surprisingly few modifications until the great crisis of the 1970s (Jeeves and Yudelman 1986). To pick up the issue of unionization, we must thus turn to the 1970s and the possibilities opened up by changes in the migrant system during this decade.

Challenges to Mine Management Hegemony

Any attempt to understand the resounding successes of the contemporary black miners' union, the National Union of Mineworkers (NUM), founded in 1982, must begin with the rise of the price of gold on international markets that began in the late 1960s (James 1991:18–22). The gold price (fixed since 1949 at U.S.$36 an ounce but rising gradually after 1968 and rapidly after 1972) had imposed severe cost constraints on gold mining in the 1950s and 1960s. By 1972, however, profits were double what they had been in 1970, and by 1973 they had trebled. Black mine wages increased only one-third during the same period.

Nineteen seventy-four was a year of labor supply crises for the industry. In 1972, only 25 percent of black mine recruits (for a labor force totaling more than 350,000 workers) were from within the borders of South Africa; the rest were foreign (29 percent from the old High Commission Territories—mostly Lesotho, 21 percent from Southern Mozambique, and 24 percent "Tropicals"—mostly from Malawi). In May 1974, after the fatal crash of an airplane carrying Malawian recruits, Malawian president Hastings Banda withdrew all Malawian labor. By 1975, "Tropicals" made up only 3 percent of mine labor recruits. At the same time, the revolution in Mozambique cast doubt on the Mozambican supply, which fell to 6 percent of total new recruits by 1976 (Crush, Jeeves, and Yudelman 1991:234–35). Suddenly, the bottom had fallen out of the mine labor supply. Foreign labor had been favored because it was willing or able to work in the mines for very low wages under the old migrant system. The wage dependency of the majority of South African workers meant that they simply could not support their families on mine-workers' incomes. To attract them back to the mines, even in a recessionary economy, the mines had to raise wages. Average cash wages for black miners were increased 61.5 percent in 1974 and 67.8 percent again in 1975 (McNamara 1985:288). The 1974 increase more than doubled the 1972 base salary, and the 1975 increase raised it three-and-a-half times.

Although mine wages were still below those in manufacturing, they attracted workers from South Africa's rural resettlement slums and South African and Zimbabwean townships—as well as additional supplies from traditional sending areas in the Transkei and Lesotho. Numbers of new recruits from the South African hinterland skyrocketed in 1975, 1976, and

1977, with more than one-third of them novices. Novices also made up about a quarter of the new recruits from Lesotho and Mozambique in 1974 and 1975. Numbers of Zimbabwean workers (all novices, mostly from urban areas) increased from 3 in 1974 to 18,653 in 1977, before dropping again to 112 in 1982 and none in 1985 (McNamara 1985:245).

Absorbing so many novices into the industry would have been bad enough for the mines even if the new recruits had been traditional rural proprietors. What made things worse for both management and more traditional workers who wanted to maintain their powers under the old migrant system was that a different kind of individual responded to the appeal of higher wages. Not only were the new mine workers who came from rural slums and urban townships better educated and completely wage dependent, but many of these "novices" had had previous experience in secondary and tertiary industry (60.1 percent in manufacturing, construction, and public utilities; 49 percent in commerce, transportation, and services) (Crush, Jeeves, and Yudelman 1991:130). The new workers were thus not merely proletarianized but also some of them might well have had experience in unionizing industries before coming to the mines. They were certainly less tolerant of mining conditions than more traditional migrants. Thus the average length of stay on the mines for workers from South Africa (and even Lesotho) dropped off during the years of transition as the number of desertions and broken contracts increased (McNamara 1985:246).[9]

The result was several years of chaos for the mining industry, which certainly did not leap eagerly into the era of organized labor. On the one hand, many of those novices who remained as migrant mine workers had different assumptions and aspirations from traditional migrants. On the other, a substantial proportion of the more experienced migrant workforce—especially from the Transkei and the Lesotho interior—continued to try to live the old migrant cultures. Social conflict was virtually unavoidable. We have already dealt with the outbreak of "ethnic" violence. Here we shall examine black miner struggles with mine management and the Chamber of Mines.

McNamara, based on his extensive access to chamber and mining house reports, estimates that there were 158 worker-management confrontations between 1973 and 1982. He summarizes his findings as follows:

> At least 20% of the conflicts comprised 50 persons or less, but there were also several conflicts (10% of the total) which com-

[9]During this same period, the abolition of the Masters and Servants Act in 1974 did away with the clause that made desertion a criminal offense for black workers. This change exacerbated the trend toward briefer mine stays.

> prised over 1000 workers, a few of which involved up to 4000 men on particular mines. . . . Of the total number of conflicts, at least two thirds (106) affected the work routine and collectively resulted in the loss of a conservatively estimated 120,000 man shifts. 40% of the encounters were also associated with physical violence, 16 of which (10% of the total) resulted in death. A total of 36 workers lost their lives, mainly as a result of security action, but also partly through inter-worker violence. An estimated 467 injuries were also recorded. Roughly half (74) of the total number of recorded conflicts were characterized by the discharge and repatriation of workers (on both a voluntary and involuntary basis). During the ten-year period under review, close to 10,000 workers were repatriated back to their homes in the aftermath of confrontations with mine management. (McNamara 1985:360)

Such figures represent a massive escalation of conflict from the days of the old moral economy, even at its height in the 1940s. Furthermore, earlier conflicts with management had tended to take place on the compound after work hours. The new pattern of contestation had a much more serious effect on production. In the analysis that follows, we shall rely heavily on McNamara's benchmark study.

Mine wages had been a nonnegotiable aspect of the informal moral economy of the mine. As we have seen, the AMWU failed to change this pattern. Occasional increases, when they occurred, were set by the Chamber of Mines without worker input and were applied universally across the entire industry. By the 1970s, however, the chamber was divided on wage issues. Anglo American, the largest and wealthiest mining house, pushed for immediate and substantial wage increases once the price of gold started to climb. Other mining houses, particularly Gold Fields and Gencor, were much more reluctant to move precipitously.[10] It took the shock of 1974 to pitch the chamber into substantial wage hikes, but these were not applied evenly across the board. Predictably, workers reacted vehemently to wage differentials between adjacent mines controlled by different mining houses, which unilaterally decided increases within a fairly wide range. Some of the most serious disturbances of the 1970s and early 1980s may

[10]Because Wilmot James's recent book (1991:92–96) gives a useful account of the struggle within the Chamber of Mines between Anglo American and the other mining houses, we shall not deal in detail with this aspect, important though it certainly is. Besides systemic reasons like the wealth and future longevity of Anglo American mines and the breadth of its involvement in South African manufacturing industry, one should note the contingent fact that the nationalization of the Zambian copper-mining industry had brought back to South Africa senior Anglo American mining management with direct experience working with black unions.

be explained by this factor alone, which would have been cause for collective action even under the old moral economy.

In June 1974, for instance, Harmony Mine, which is owned by Rand Mines and is fairly close to the complex of Anglo American mines in the Orange Free State, announced wage increases substantially lower than those of neighboring mines (McNamara 1985:301–5). On Tuesday, 4 June, the evening that increases were put into effect, workers from Mozambique and Lesotho held a meeting in the dance arena to plan a strike. Six of them were arrested by mine security, but strike rumors continued to circulate. On Saturday, 8 June, strike notices were distributed, and a group of ventilation workers was arrested. That night another meeting was held in the dance arena, and a strike was mooted for Monday, 10 June. Early next morning, six of the strike organizers were arrested and handed over to the South African police.

On Sunday evening, five hundred men gathered in front of the compound offices, armed with sticks, dancing, shouting, and blowing whistles. They wrecked the liquor outlet and set it and the boot store on fire, smashed the compound offices, and destroyed company service records. Mine security plied tear gas on the demonstrators, who withdrew to the compound and destroyed the indunas' residences. Two other hostels were drawn into the conflict, and the South African police intervened ineffectually, killing five workers.

On Monday, 10 June, about one thousand workers refused to go underground, shouting from the crowd that they wanted wage equity with other mines. The Chamber of Mines met hastily in Johannesburg and implemented increases immediately. Work resumed on Tuesday, 11 June, after the new rates had been marked on the black miners' tickets. This affair could as easily have taken place in the 1940s, except that the brunt of the organization seems to have fallen to experienced Mozambican and Basotho team leaders rather than the izibonda.

That wages were being raised on all the mines, but not equally, immediately brought wages into contention along moral economy lines. Similarly, eight years later in 1982, when wage increases on Gold Fields and Gencor mines were only half as much as on Anglo American mines, almost all the mines controlled by either Gold Fields or Gencor erupted into violence. In one week from 1 to 7 July:

> 48 work shifts were lost or seriously affected on ten mines [of the Goldfields and Gencor groups], of which 15 were night shifts. Nine men were killed (6 of them by security action) and 13 sustained gunshot wounds. Over 3,000 men were repatriated and at least eight hostels were extensively damaged. (McNamara 1985:315)

Although we have few details about how Gold Fields and Gencor miners organized in 1982, worker behavior made it clear that differences between wage increases awarded by the different mining houses were at the heart of the action (McNamara 1985:311–19). Once again, moral outrage at inequities between neighboring mines had inspired militant protest demonstrations.

A further aspect of some of the 1982 wage demonstrations revealed another way in which the mining industry in the 1970s had broached the uneasy equilibrium of the old moral economy. Most of the strikers were from the lower levels of the workforce, namely, lashers, loco drivers, and drillers. Few team leaders participated in the 1982 strikes. This fact is understandable, since their relatively high wages on Gold Fields mines were increased by 15 to 20 percent, whereas humble lashers received no more than 9 percent increases. Since Anglo Vaal and Rand mines (for its older mines, Durban Deep and East Rand Proprietary Mines) gave only 13 percent (about the same as or less on average than Gold Fields and Gencor) but spread the increase equally across the different job categories, wage differentials between job strata still seem to have been as important in inspiring worker outrage as the overall percentage increase in 1982.[11]

Workers struck, then, not only because of wage differences among mining houses but also because of increasing economic stratification of the black mine labor force, with especially large increases for team leaders (once boss boys). The latter issue had led to moral outrage among certain categories of worker, especially machine drillers, as early as 1973. In fact, the first large strike of the 1970s took place on Western Deep Levels, an Anglo American mine near Carletonville, around this issue (McNamara 1985:295–301). At the same time that it had begun to increase wages in the early 1970s, we have seen that Anglo American also introduced a new job classification system (called the Paterson scale), based on "scientific" assessment of levels of responsibility required in various job categories. This was management's latest effort to reorganize underground production. At last the old "leading-hand scheme" was going to be funded by substantially higher remuneration for team leaders. For the first time boss boys were paid higher wages than machine drillers, whose piece-work opportunities had always made them the best-paid workers on the mines and whose work was certainly the most dangerous and strenuous. Winch drivers and loco drivers also began to move toward parity with machine drillers, and machine drillers were more closely integrated into the stope team.

[11]One might argue also that workers were aware of the profitability problems of the Rand Mines and Anglo Vaal Mines involved. Certainly, few of the Gold Fields mines had profitability problems.

They thus had to do a wider range of jobs in the stope and fell more directly under the authority of the team leader.

In August 1973, two hundred machine drillers at Western Deep Levels refused to go underground and met with management to complain about their reduced status and relatively lower wage increases. Management, who described them as "rather trade union conscious," whatever that meant in 1973, were determined to stand pat on the new rates. When this position was communicated to the dissident machine operators on 11 September, it was received riotously, and eighty workers moved off to a nearby hill to discuss their options. At 7 P.M. they came down to the shaft head and tried to prevent the night shift from going underground. Stones were thrown, and the South African police were called in. After an unsuccessful baton charge and tear-gas attack, the police fired warning shots to no avail. When a policeman was hurt by a stone, the police began firing into the crowd, and in the ensuing running battle the liquor outlet and meat store were looted and burned. Twelve miners were killed and twenty-eight injured (McNamara 1985:295–300).

The Carletonville affair seems not to have been very different from the typical moral economy disturbances that had been occurring on the mines for at least the past half-century. One cannot but sympathize with men who had worked and bribed their way into the most dangerous but best-paying underground work for blacks (on the deepest and most dangerous mine), who suddenly found their position upstaged by management fiat. This was the first of a series of disputes on several different mines about wages and bonuses, indicating yet again that the moral economy had been extended in the 1970s to include issues of remuneration (McNamara 1985:306).

So far, beyond this widening of the terms of the moral economy, the methods and purposes of black collective action on the mines were not radically different from those of earlier years. The same might be said for a massive riot at President Steyn in 1978 over food supplies (McNamara 1985:339–40) and several confrontations about pay deductions for death benefit insurance, introduced unilaterally without consultation by management and poorly communicated to workers (McNamara 1985:324–28). That such demonstrations tended to be led by team leaders and machine drillers, who were the most traditional and experienced workers on the mines, lends credence to assumptions about continuity with the old moral economy.

Other aspects of the Carletonville affair at Western Deep Levels in 1973, however, do imply new methods that were to become more frequent during the following decade. That a group of workers fled the compound to the mine dumps and descended to picket the night shift sounds familiar to one acquainted with the details of the 1946 strike. Such methods in the 1940s, however, were explicitly not those of traditional migrants but rather of the most proletarianized and unionized members of the workforce. In fact, typical moral economy disturbances seldom interfered with mine production (although serious ones might escalate into work stoppages) so there was no need for picketing.

There are only two recorded sit-downs underground on the gold mines before 1970, on New Kleinfontein in 1941 and Rand Leases in 1943. Complaints about production matters, most often delays in hauling, involuntary overtime, and incorrectly marked tickets, tended to be raised at compound demonstrations. Mpondo told us that since they were "on business" on the mine they were reluctant to lose a day's pay. There is no historical record at all of black gold miners refusing to work because of dangerous conditions underground or an unpleasant work environment.

McNamara (1985:328), however, found that 31 percent of the worker-management conflicts between 1973 and 1982 raised workplace issues. Those dealing with assaults and overwork were minor compared with contestation over safety issues and delays in hoisting. Often they involved sit-down strikes underground. Half the sixteen cases dealing with safety issues involved urban black Zimbabweans who had been recruited in haste after the withdrawal of Malawian migrants and who may be seen as bellwethers of the most radical of the new miners who were being hired from South Africa. Urban "Rhodesians" lasted only two years on the mines (1975–1977), but with their superior education, flashy dress, violent homophobia, and liberation politics they were not unlike many of the younger new South Africans who later came to be known on the mines as "comrades" because of their identification with youthful militants in South African township struggles.[12]

The Zimbabweans became famous for their lack of respect for mine authorities, both white and black, surface and underground, and for their confrontational style. Even during periods of relative quiescence on the mines, Zimbabweans would go on strike when fellow countrymen were killed underground, often insisting on a period of mourning. Sometimes they refused to work in places they regarded as unsafe, and they frequently challenged white miners' assumptions of racial superiority. In addition, the Zimbabweans had their own ethnic identity, although this meant that their direct influence on fellow miners from other groups was relatively slight. As an indicator of issues that would have to be addressed as more

[12]For Rhodesian recruits in the 1970s, see McNamara 1980, 1985:142–186; for township recruits, see James 1991:72–79.

and more educated and proletarianized South Africans began to come to the mines, however, their experience is quite significant. Their example helps explain why safety, for instance, which had never been an issue under the moral economy, was so important for the NUM when it began to recruit on the mines in 1982.

A series of disturbances around hoisting (besides the Gold Fields and Gencor wage riots) nudged the Chamber of Mines to recognize black trade unions in 1982. Hoisting disputes raised old issues in new ways with much more direct impact on production than any previous moral economy protests. Twenty-five such disputes took place between 1975 and 1982—with fifteen in 1981–1982 (McNamara 1985:350). Late hauling had been a complaint among black mine workers since the Buckle Commission in 1913. But in the 1970s and 1980s, to express their discontent with the practice, they began to resort regularly to a technique rare before 1975, namely, the underground sit-down strike. It is significant that this and other methods began to be widely used in 1975, as soon as the more proletarianized migrants began to settle in on the mines.

McNamara (1985:330–33) describes in detail a strike called on President Steyn in that year. On Wednesday, 22 October 1975, an underground fire had slowed production, so management pushed for blasting to take place as early as possible each day. Hoisting schedules were revised so that white miners could be lowered and raised earlier than usual. No effort was made to communicate these changes or the reasons for them to black workers, although as a result blacks were kept underground for long hours. On Friday, 24 October, at 73 level, the hoisting of the black shift was interrupted when a handful of white miners pushed in front of the waiting blacks and were taken to the surface. Irate, the black workers refused to take the cage when it returned. Instead, they took black officials hostage and retreated to the shaft telephone, inviting blacks on lower levels to join the strike. A deputation of white personnel officials (direct descendants of the old *fokisi*) were stoned when they descended to negotiate with the strikers. The compound manager (stating that the problem was a matter for underground line management) refused to go down with his indunas to speak to the workers.

Meanwhile, the strikers telephoned the surface and threatened to push loaded ore trucks down the shaft. A riot squad from mine security was sent down to bring the men up but was forced to retreat under a hail of stones. The strikers commandeered the underground pump station and started to pump water down the shaft. Management cut off the water supply and, at the request of a spokesman from the strikers, sent down the Sotho induna and a couple of black compound policemen to parley with them. They received the induna's exhortations in total silence.

It was not until the next morning that the strikers phoned the surface and requested to be hoisted. No action was taken against the men, who marched off to the kitchen for a meal, but management promptly adjusted the hoisting schedules and resolved to inform workers fully about any future changes in routine. The strike had been completely effective. Similar sit-downs occurred again and again during the late 1970s and especially the early 1980s. Since they interfered with production, such strikes got management's urgent attention. Moreover, hoisting delays quite often were associated with racial preferences for white miners and were deeply resented by the new breed of black worker. Racial insults and assaults underground were sharply curbed by such worker action, since white miners earned production bonuses from black work. Nonetheless, the explicit racism of white workers and the adamant resentment of it by the new black miners continued to present a headache for production management.

The Establishment of the NUM

By 1982, even the more conservative members of the Chamber of Mines were agreed that some form of effective communication between workers and local management was absolutely essential to quiet the dissension that kept surfacing and interfering with gold production (James 1991:92–96). Earlier efforts to establish liaison committees had failed dismally since production management tended to use them simply as channels of downward communication and as a result workers distrusted them. Thus, in 1982, the chamber decided to grant access to unions who wished to recruit black mine workers. To obtain the right to such access, a union had to have its constitution vetted by the mining houses. In return, management allotted aspirant unions an office on the mine and the use of a telephone.

Despite these unprecedented managerial concessions, until the coming of the National Union of Mineworkers, several nascent unions made no headway on the mines. The NUM was established in August 1982 by the black consciousness–oriented Council of Unions of South Africa (CUSA). Cyril Ramaphosa, a young labor lawyer in CUSA's legal department, from his student days "a gifted administrator" (Chikane 1988:39), was released to serve as general secretary of the new miners' union.[13] He remembered the events during an interview in 1984:

[13]Besides the standard secondary sources, which will be cited when used, and Bregman Commission evidence, this account of the growth of the NUM depends on interviews with several participants, including Cyril Ramaphosa himself at the NUM offices in 1984, and, in Lesotho in 1988, Puseletso Salae, an organizer on the West Rand, Jack Mpapea, an early shaft steward and eventually branch chairman on Vaal Reefs No. 4 shaft, and Ramafola Molupe, a team leader on Stilfontein Mine.

> [B]etween the end of 1981 and the beginning of 1982 . . . two CUSA unions in their organizing campaigns in companies which are close to the mines had come across miners and these miners had expressed a wish to join their unions. [The CUSA unions that had been approached] did not have the know-how to cater for them—they enrolled some of them, but they realized that it was pointless to even to try to start organizing them because they were just not geared for this type of industry. So the whole thing started being discussed in CUSA and . . . the unions within CUSA committed themselves to assist with the organization of a mine workers' union. The CUSA executive then asked me to leave the legal department and be in charge [of organizing] the mines.

One of the individuals who had approached CUSA was Puseletso Salae. Sotho, with a high school education, Salae had been working for TEBA (The Employment Bureau of Africa, the latest manifestation of the Chamber of Mines recruiting organization, previously the NRC and WNLA) since 1975 as a fingerprint expert. After a period of training and work in Johannesburg, he was transferred to Vaal Reefs No. 6 shaft, which was his base for five years or so. He moved constantly from shaft to shaft on Vaal Reefs checking and classifying fingerprints. A warm and friendly individual, he built up an extensive network of acquaintances on all the shafts and compounds of the vast Vaal Reefs complex. He was also trained to use computers on Vaal Reefs, and when TEBA in Johannesburg decided to computerize, he was brought back to assist in the process. He discovered to his disgust that he was expected to train the whites who would eventually become his supervisors.

A friend took him to the CUSA offices, where he met Cyril Ramaphosa. He still remembers that first meeting:

> I told him my story. He said, "No, we don't have a union here for people who are working in the mines, and we are unable to help you unless you can help us to form a union in the mining industry. . . ." Ultimately [after several meetings], my friend and I got some pamphlets from Ramaphosa and we tried to distribute them at TEBA secretively, giving them to people, sometimes at night, sometimes at work, asking people to join the union. But we were caught and we were all dismissed. When we got to the offices at CUSA, Cyril had already made some arrangements and he told us, "Gentlemen, let us start working together. You are now the organizers of the union." I started in NUM at that time.

Ramaphosa remembered that the real organizing effort started in October. There were five organizers in the beginning. Three had worked on the mines. At first they decided not to ask the Chamber of Mines for access to the mines, but by the end of September they had learned, as had J. B. Marks so many years before, that organization was virtually impossible without access to the mines. On 19 October, the chamber granted the NUM access to its mines, promising office space but severely restricting recruitment activities like outdoor meetings, meetings in hostels, and distribution of pamphlets (Thompson 1984:159). Nonetheless, according to Ramaphosa, by the first annual conference in December 1982, the union "had about 14,000 members and the conference was attended by about 3,000 miners from the Free State, the Western Transvaal and the Klerksdorp area." By 1986, NUM had 79,340 paid-up members, 83 percent of them from Anglo American mines and 10 percent from Gold Fields mines.

According to Ramaphosa, while the union concentrated its efforts on Anglo American mines and a few Gold Fields mines, this "was not really by choice."

> [W]e were just reacting to interest. . . . In Anglo American the company had itself developed a lot of structures allowing workers to air their views and so forth. . . . Their industrial relations policies were actually fairly good. . . . On the other hand, Gold Fields mines were probably the worst in terms of the treatment at work and the residential places . . . and the pay.

Thus the union found most of its support from workers at either end of the spectrum of treatment—at Anglo American, where workers were already accustomed to speaking their minds and at Gold Fields, where conditions were really bad.

In his 1984 interview, Ramaphosa identified three issues as central to the union's recruitment strategy: wages, unfair dismissals, and safety. From the outset, then, the NUM concentrated on work issues. At first, the promise of collective bargaining about wages was less attractive to workers because "they could not believe that such a thing as negotiating wages with the bosses would ever be possible." Safety (especially increased compensation for injuries) had some appeal, but attention to unfair dismissals was fundamental.

By the early 1980s, the labor supply crisis of the 1970s was over for the mines, and, almost for the first time in their entire history, there was a glut of applicants for mine jobs. In the past, workers dismissed from one mine could almost always find work at another. The increasing oversupply and the introduction of a system of computerized blacklisting suddenly meant, from the early 1980s, that dismissal from one mine likely meant dismissal from mining employment altogether (Crush 1992). Unfair dismissal at once became a major issue. Early on, the NUM had taken up the cause of workers dismissed from Kloof Mine after the 1982 riots and had managed to use the law to get them reinstated. "It was a victory which we were able to boast about with potential members," Ramaphosa remembered.

Salae, who virtually single-handedly organized the entire Vaal Reefs complex with its ten shafts, also remembered the issue of dismissals as central to his recruitment strategy:

> There were a lot of complaints. People were dismissed at that time, they were dismissed almost every day. I remember at Vaal Reefs people were coming by to my office almost every day, early in the morning you'll find five people in a shaft, "I've been dismissed." "I was late at work, five minutes late." Some would say, "No, it is because I was from Lesotho, I was supposed to report on Monday and my wife was sick. Here is a letter from the doctor. I'm trying to show this letter to my boss, he doesn't want to listen to me and he says I should go out of the hostel immediately." Sometimes people were dismissed because they were making arguments with their supervisors, or perhaps the induna doesn't like him, and other petty matters. I managed to get more people to join the union because all the time I was going out to fight management over dismissals and I managed to win cases all the time. The men would go around and tell other guys, "I am back! I went to the union office and I am now back." Then all the men in his room would come and join the union immediately.

At first a large majority of the members (at least from the Free State) were team leaders. They chose to be members, said Ramaphosa, because they were very vulnerable at work, with much responsibility and visibility. The union also concentrated on them initially because they thought that recruiting supervisors would bring in the entire team. Within six months, they learned such a strategy was flawed because of the new divisions in the workforce that had been brought about by the introduction of the Paterson scale and larger increases for team leaders. As a result, Ramaphosa said, they redirected their recruiting efforts at machine drillers, who were "the real power behind the throne" and "more influential in any gang because they did the hardest piece of the job and everybody else depended on them for production." Of course, as we know, they were also the work category most negatively affected by the introduction of the Paterson scale. They "joined as a group because they felt that if they were united the union would be able to assist them in increasing their production bonus and so on."

Salae gave a detailed account of how the union's organizational growth was managed at the local level on Vaal Reefs. At first, as with the AMWU forty years before, the primary goal was simply to sign up members. "There was little effort to follow up in the early stages," he said. "We just signed people up." His contacts among the black clerical and personnel staff, dating from his years at No. 6 shaft as a fingerprint specialist, stood him in excellent stead at the beginning:

> I decided to start at Number Six shaft because I had been staying at Number Six. I spoke to Ramaphosa and we visited Vaal Reefs on Sunday before I started there. We met some other guys, mostly clerks and a senior trainer, whom I knew there. We had some discussions with them, sitting in the car. . . . They were aware and very much interested. I started at Number Six because then I would be able to start with those people who were waiting for me there.

Recruitment was a communal effort:

> Fortunately, when I started they were able to help me a lot, they were recruiting people and also helping me to distribute pamphlets and arranging secret meetings for me to meet with people outside the hostels, maybe in the location or the churches. Despite being given an office, I was not allowed to hold meetings inside the compound at that time. Later on when they saw that we had a lot of members they said we could meet inside the hostels. They gave me a hall, inside the training center at Number Six. Then I had to collect people from far shafts, bringing them to Number Six where we had the only hall. People were reluctant to spend their money on travel to such meetings which they did not understand. So I contacted head office and asked for funds to rent busses to bring people to Number Six. The hall was quite tiny, holding no more than 200 people, so I had to explain to them in a series of groups, with someone outside signing them up afterwards. . . . I had a receipt book. . . . I would say, "Pay for two months." At that time we didn't have any stop-order system.

Personal contacts again helped spread the news:

> A senior PA [black personnel assistant] at Number Four shaft who was living at Number Six and other workers were also staying at Number Six . . . heard about this union and they told the other people at Number Four shaft. Then the PA helped me a lot. He sent other people from Number Four and at the end of the day he would sometimes come with 200 membership forms, properly filled in. It was primarily the clerks and the PAs that were signing

people up. . . . There was a PA on Number Two, a Xhosa guy, very interested in trade unions, who met me at Number Six and took some forms and signed up other people at Number Two.

Anglo American had given the union an office at each of the ten shafts on Vaal Reefs. Local shaft managements kept the keys, and Salae had to appear in person each day to pick them up. Initially, the union could not afford to give him a car so he was dependent on public transport and hitching rides with company drivers. He would move from office to office, opening it up and then sneaking out to the next shaft. Local off-duty clerical and personnel staff sat in the office and signed up members. Each evening, Salae would make the rounds again. Without the help of his contacts on the mine, the union could never have grown as fast as it did at Vaal Reefs.

Such wide use of interpersonal networks made for a different style of organizing than that of the AMWU in 1944. It was also different from anything management had ever known. They had expected union officials to do all the union work. As Salae said, "Management was not happy that I opened the office and went out. They would go and lock the office. They said, 'No, tell the people that they must move out of this office. They are not employed by the union. The union must come and sign you up.' So I would [have to sneak out]."

Unlike the AMWU in the 1940s, right from the beginning the NUM organizing strategy involved building local structures at the workplace. Ramaphosa was insistent on this:

> We were already organizing structures at this early stage. As we organized people we would call meetings and get the workers to elect their own shaft stewards. It meant that the leadership on the mine was beginning to come up more and more. As they elected their leaders we felt that it was necessary to put some of them through basic training, which would amount to, say, a one-day seminar on how to recruit and what a union means. We would then organize organizing committees on the mines themselves and we found that workers responded very positively.

Salae provided more detail on how this local shaft-level organizing operated. Although his early goal was to increase numbers in order to get recognition for the union from the company, he did not neglect local structures. In fact, he relied on such structures to supplement his own personal networks at Vaal Reefs. He explained:

> I was trying to talk to the people, to have very few people, maybe three or four. When I left the shaft there should be a committee

> there. Soon they would form a shaft committee. They were helping me a lot, those people. A shaft committee would consist of seven people. This was before the shaft stewards, but at least there was a committee. Once such a committee was formed, those who were on night shift would meet me at the office, so that I could come to the shaft and open the office so that they could sign people up. Then I would move to another shaft and open the office, disappear again, until I got to a new shaft where I would stay the whole day explaining to people about the union.

Small informal committees could certainly help with recruitment, but the union organizer was the only one entitled to represent workers before management tribunals on matters such as dismissals or assaults. As the union grew, it became increasingly impossible for one or two organizers to undertake that kind of grass-roots representation, and yet it was upon such strategies that the union's support was based. The next step was logical, given the history of the independent trade unions in South Africa in the 1970s, although it would have been completely novel if the AMWU had attempted it in the 1940s. Representative functions were given to worker-elected officials, called shaft stewards on the mines. Jack Mpapea, who was eventually chief shaft steward on Vaal Reefs No. 4, gave a succinct account of the new procedures:

> As the time went on, the NUM head office decided that the power that was in the hands of the organizer should be given to the shaft stewards. That is, the union approached management that there should be what you call the shaft steward of the men. The people should elect democratically their own representatives. They must be signed up—recognized by management. [Then,] if anybody had a problem as a worker, he must take his shaft steward to represent him.

This was a new umteto with a vengeance. Once management agreed to the shaft steward system, the induna system rapidly became redundant (at least in its representative functions), and a new regime ruled the compounds, an NUM regime. Mpapea explained:

> With the establishment of the NUM, of the union, to represent the workers in the mine, there's a great difference because now, if ever there's a problem, . . . you are allowed to sit down and given a chance for a hearing. . . . In a hearing [about a work problem] there's a mine captain and the PA and the accused, with his representative called a shaft steward from the union. . . . Inside the hostel . . . you would be called to the hostel manager, with your representative, and the induna would be there also. [This was

> different from the old days] when you were called alone and there was nobody representing you. [Then it] was only the induna and the compound manager. . . . [Now] with the presence of the union, nobody can accuse you without your representative. The representative all the time, we find, is the shaft steward. He must be there all the time. It doesn't matter whether the issues are related to the workplace or to the hostel.

I did not speak to a single contemporary black mine worker, including James Ramarobi, the recently retired Sotho induna on No. 1 shaft at Vaal Reefs who had been the figurehead for traditionalist attacks on shaft stewards, who denied the merits of such a representative system for workers. However much they might resent or regret the rowdiness of particular union "comrades," or the political radicalism of many shaft stewards, all black workers had nothing but praise for this "representive" aspect of the union's work in combatting unfair dismissals. Here the NUM struck a chord that echoed with traditional and new workers alike, because it performed a useful and necessary function on the mine, dealing with a galloping new problem. If any one factor can explain the incredibly rapid growth of the union, this is it. Black workers all welcomed the establishment of a representative democratic presence to enforce new, more equitable, imiteto on the mines. The structure of management hegemony had been altered fundamentally.

Before turning to a brief discussion of union politics in the broader sense, we must try to examine more closely exactly what representative democracy meant to mine workers, because it differs significantly from the conventional model predominant in civil society in the West. While management has had great difficulty understanding how such grass-roots democracy operates among African mine workers, all the workers themselves, whether traditional rural proprietors or proletarians, seem to agree on its meaning and purpose.

Democracy and the Union

This discussion is based on 1986 testimony to the Bregman Commission at No. 1 shaft on Vaal Reefs. In the course of the cross-examination of Mlamli Botha, the Mpondo shaft steward, about the liquor outlet boycott, a puzzling matter of procedure was raised. It was never properly answered, or at least not answered to the satisfaction of management's lawyers, who kept returning to the issue, which also troubled Commissioner Bregman himself. The question was about the representativeness of union decisions—to what extent were decisions made at union meetings binding on all workers when there were 4,500 workers in the compound but the meeting hall could accommodate at most 700 to 1,000 persons?

Except in the case of the election of shaft stewards, there seems to have been no procedure by which those who did not attend the meetings delegated authority to those who did. Meetings were simply announced in the compound and those who wished to do so, and were able to get in, attended. Nonetheless, in Mlamli Botha's view, decisions made by workers at such meetings were "binding and . . . regard[ed] as law" (AAC/VR:2232). Botha clearly meant that assent by those present at such meetings established their decisions as imiteto. As he said, "If the majority of the people, this vote, says we have got to do this thing in this way, even if I say that . . . the end would be the ways of death, I . . . have no power on my own to sway the majority if they have decided and resolved that this is the direction we [should take]" (AAC/VR:2084).

He described the decision to boycott the liquor outlet as follows:

> The liquor outlet boycott was not organized by the shaft stewards. [Rather they] presented to the meeting the predicament they were faced with with regard to the dismissed five workers. The workers at this meeting said that if Management [was] unable to assist by rescinding its decision to expel the five then it must be given a stick, it must be punished by us not patronising the liquor outlet. This became acceptable to the general meeting and then the boycott started that way. . . . When the decision to boycott the bars was taken, those people were still around in the compound. Although they had been dismissed they had not left the compound. The boycott was aimed at persuading management to negotiate about the dismissal of these workers while they were still around in the compound. (AAC/VR:2463–64, 2212)

The strategic point is well taken. One of the advantages of a migrant labor force from management's point of view was that dismissed workers would leave the premises once their appeal had failed and redress then became difficult for the union. Workers in this case felt that they needed to act fast. Counsel for management tried to argue that the meeting had been bludgeoned into the decision to boycott by the shaft stewards' rhetorical power. Thus the Xhosa sub-induna, a management witness, was asked (AAC/VR:2797): "So would it be fair to say that if a meeting decides to institute a boycott of the liquor outlet, that that decision had been sponsored by the shaft stewards?" He refused to take the bait: "Always it is usually the workers who raise up a suggestion. . . . The shaft stewards tell the workers at the meeting what they have been discussing with the management, and the workers may have questions." The shaft stewards may have had a certain veto power over decisions of the meeting, because, as the sub-induna pointed out, "they were elected to be [the miners'] representatives," but all the witnesses, when asked about the decision to boycott the liquor outlet, concurred that this was based on a suggestion that came from the floor of the meeting.

The question remains, however, why the decision at the meeting was binding on those not present. In terms of Western conceptions of democracy, it ought not to have been. What is most interesting, however, is that the Mpondo who broke the boycott clearly believed that it *was* binding on *them*. According to Mlamli Botha, they found it necessary to make all sorts of excuses for having broken the umteto of the meeting.

Soon after the six Mpondo boycott-breakers had entered the bar, unchallenged by the compound policeman, although they were wearing sheets and fully armed with swords and sharpened sticks, Mlamli Botha, who certainly had no lack of courage, went in to speak to them with the other Mpondo shaft steward. They seemed alert, Botha said, but "just happy, . . . singing their own [drinking] songs" (AAC/VR:1076). He asked them to meet with him the following Sunday at the union office in the compound. They came, the entire Xhosa-Pondo dance team, about seventy persons, and met with Botha and other responsible compound elders.[14] "We were six shaft stewards," Botha reported, "two Pondos and four Sothos [as well as] . . . other Pondo elders in the hostel so that these would be also there when I [was] talking to these Pondos." Botha was clearly determined to bring the full brunt of the authority of the old moral economy to bear on the Mpondo boycott-breakers.

His account of the conversation that followed makes fascinating reading:

> I specifically asked them what was the motive behind their going to the liquor outlet armed. I asked them why they had to be armed. In reply they said . . . they were armed because they wanted to see who was going to attack them, according to them. I asked them whether there was any rumour that whoever went to the liquor outlet was going to be assaulted. Now I did not get an answer to this. I warned them that they must be careful what they [were] doing because here we did not come to fight, we have come to work. (AAC/VR:1080)

The latter statement, of course, was a good point to make to traditional Mpondo. As we have seen, it is one they constantly make to each other, in regard not only to fighting but also to all other activities on the mine.

[14]Later, Botha remembered them as numbering thirty: "They were filling our office" (AAC/VR:2069a).

Botha continued: "I also advised them that if anybody did not like what was said in the meeting he must please voice it out in the meeting so that it can be solved—discussed and solved." In response, they raised a series of other grievances. "It was useless to obey the law," they said, because they had not been compensated for losses incurred in a faction fight in March 1986, and they were tired of rumors going around that they were going to attack other Xhosa speakers for assaulting Matyaba, an Mpondo personnel assistant who had tried to run Transkei Bantustan elections on the compound (AAC/VR:2071). In addition, they expressed the time-honored Mpondo grievance: "The other Xhosa group relegate[d] them as inferiors or as young men because they [had] never been to the circumcision school" (AAC/VR:2071a). As far as Mlamli Botha was concerned, these grievances were no more than smoke screens to cover up that "they had made a mistake by breaking the boycott." "It is natural," he said, "for some person to raise another issue in defence of his action" (AAC/VR:2231).

The shaft stewards and the elders dealt patiently with all these grievances to the best of their ability and then returned to the matter of "breaking a decision of . . . the workers" (AAC/VR:2225). Here the boycott-breakers had no defense. According to Botha:

> [They] told me that they would never again go around in the hostel with arms and if [it] could please be relayed over to the other people . . . that they were asking for forgiveness, saying that they have realised that they had erred. . . . They said if we could, please, in the subsequent meeting ask for forgiveness from the other people [and] that they must forget now about this behaviour in the liquor outlet. (AAC/VR:1083)

Apparently, they also elicited from Botha and the other shaft stewards present, including Ernest Kang, the Sotho chief shaft steward, an agreement that in the event of future boycotts there would be time to stock up liquor before the boycott became effective (AAC/VR:2064a). It was this agreement that was not adhered to when a second boycott was called. We shall return to those events in the final chapter. Meanwhile, we must try to understand why the decisions of a meeting with a minority of workers present could be agreed to be binding on all workers, including those who hated the decision. A particularly powerful understanding of the implications of consensus seems to be involved.

In our conversations with Mpondo mine workers, what we would call consensus was evoked in two analogous contexts. Several men who had been iindlavini described for us the process by which they "elected" their leader, their chief, or *impathi*. "We would talk among ourselves," one of them said, "and then we would agree on who should be the leader." I asked him what would happen if even one man held out for someone else. "We would talk some more," he said. If complete agreement could not be reached, "we would simply choose someone else." He and his fellows could not conceive of choosing a leader who did not have the support of every member of the group. "Election" necessarily involved what we in the West would call "achieving consensus." A negative voice implied a veto right. Of course, the matter would never be brought to the vote among the iindlavini, and all sorts of arguments and group pressures could be brought to bear, but the overall impression one gets from these accounts is of a genuine effort to arrive at a general "sense of the meeting" to which all could accede.

The elections of room izibonda were similarly described by workers. Furthermore, while our participant observers were on Welkom Mine in 1976, an isibonda election was held in the room of one of them. That was the room in which five or six of the inmates were members of a *dagga*-dealing gang. They had originally met while in jail together and on their release had drifted to the mines, where they arranged to be roomed together. They were an ethnically integrated group, but their leader was a particularly dynamic Sotho. Our observer was sure that he would be a shoo-in for the vacant position of isibonda in the room. Instead, he and his mates participated in the election of another, rather quiet and steady individual, who was not even a gang member, for the job.

In both these instances, a similar insistence on consensus seems to have been at work. The obverse of such an understanding of democratic process is a powerful sense of the binding quality of decisions once they have been reached in this way. Persons who are given ample opportunity to raise objections are expected to abide by the outcome of the meeting if they remain silent. On the one hand, of course, there is potential for coercion if individuals remain silent because of group pressure, but, on the other hand, to persons who stress the need for consensus, a close vote looks like coercion to the minority who has been outvoted. In such a conception, a compromise that accommodates the minority is much preferable to reliance on a bare majority. Open discussion is designed less for bringing matters to the vote than for negotiating a consensus. By all accounts and in my own experience, discussion among African decision makers can go on for hours on closely argued issues before a consensus is reached.

Local union leaders at Vaal Reefs testified at some length before the Bregman Commission about how shaft stewards were elected. According to Mlamli Botha:

> First there is the nomination by a member from the floor. Then secondly there must be a seconder to that name. Then the chair-

> man is going to announce now the election itself on that one name. And then an election is conducted on that one name. . . . The chairman is going to start by asking for people who vote for the particular candidate to raise their right hands. Then a count is taken. After the count . . . he is going to ask the very same assembly of people to vote against the same name . . . and it will be a different set of individuals who will be raising their right hands against the same name. Then the numbers of the votes are compared and the higher number is taken which will determine whether he wins or loses the vote. (AAC/VR:2386–87)

Notice the importance of public affirmation of the negative vote and the voting on each individual in turn. Since a steward and an alternative are to be elected and there are seldom more than two nominees, one might expect that voters would be asked to vote once and the candidate with the highest number of votes would then be declared elected. That is explicitly *not* how these NUM local elections proceed, however. The NUM shaft steward who was brought before the commission to confirm Botha's account gave the following explanation of the importance of the negative vote (AAC/VR:2390–91). Commissioner Bregman asked him specifically: "What about the point raised by Mr. Botha that you first . . . look for votes in favour of the person and then you look for votes against the person? Is that the procedure that was adopted?" The response was emphatic: "Yes. Maybe there are people who disagree. Because when you are elected you must be somebody who is voted by all the people, not to say that maybe I elect you because I like you or because you are my friend."

Again the stress on the ideal of consensus, "you must be somebody who is voted by all the people." Presumably, the force of the negative vote can be important in such elections. The method seems cumbersome, and one may well wonder how it actually works in practice, but workers do seem to have been happy about the outcome. Not a single witness to the Bregman Commission, however conservative, complained that union representatives had been unfairly selected. Furthermore, workers generally seemed to think that shaft stewards carried out their responsibilities as well as they were able in representing them to management.[15] Objections by more conservative workers (and even some moderates) to the militant actions of certain shaft stewards were bluntly voiced to the commission and in fact had been violently expressed on the mine at the time, but no

[15]In one transcript of evidence by Matsepe Mokheti, a generally reliable Mosotho witness, it seemed initially that he was unhappy about shaft steward representation of his grievances (AAC/VR:3642–45). The evidence is certainly confusing, but it is my impression that his chief gripe in the end had to do with management procedures rather than shaft steward actions.

one suggested that any shaft steward had been unfairly selected or that decisions made at union meetings were unrepresentative of worker opinion.

Indeed, the Xhosa sub-induna, who was a lowly managerial official and himself apparently involved in the deadly hunt for shaft stewards, laid the blame for the lack of a "healthy work relationship between management and the shaft stewards" firmly at the feet of management, saying that "management delays in responding to . . . anything ventured by the shaft stewards" (AAC/VR:2858). In evidence to the Bregman Commission, at any rate, only white management witnesses and their counsel were outspokenly critical of shaft steward elections and the local union's handling of report-back meetings.

Meanwhile, compound management tended to rely for its decisions on the deliberations of a hand-picked consultative committee of "trusties," indunas, mine police, and clerical staff, who were increasingly out of touch with compound dynamics or simply did not perceive it as in their interest to give management accurate information. Consultative committees had simply become, in the words of a Transkei government representative to the Bregman Commission, "a top-down conduit pipe" for management "to get the feeling of the people" (AAC/VR:3596–98). The same committees could "then remit to the people" management's instructions without dealing with arguments from shaft stewards. "Elsewhere in the world," he said, "grievances . . . are handled by a representative body":

> I take it that the attitude of management was that shaft stewards were rather contentious people to deal with and they could not possibly be used as conduit pipes because they would come with this and raise that and possibly influence workers. . . . But now you get a conflict situation where the NUM knows itself as a representative of the workers and it will be having its own members in that work situation who will have to be represented by NUM again.

The problem was that management, not the workers, still felt "that there [were] non-NUM members who [were] workers in the same situation" and "that it has got to attend to the grievances of those people."

Thus, although from the point of view of the great majority of workers, including the most traditional Mpondo dance-team members, who could be persuaded to hunt down shaft stewards and kill them, decisions made at union meetings were representative and binding on all compound inmates, when management found such decisions embarrassing and obstructive to their goals, they could claim nonrepresentativeness. Rather than conscientiously seeking out and negotiating directly with union representatives, local compound management on this particular shaft of Vaal Reefs apparently preferred either to work around the local shaft stewards committee by appointing consultative committees or to actively foment strife along ethnic lines in order to break union solidarities.[16]

Workers and Politics

The whole matter of the union's policies was complicated on the local mine level because on certain issues, especially matters of national South African politics, workers differed among themselves. The black trade union movement in South Africa, which reemerged in the 1970s and established itself with a strong focus on shop floor organization, was obliged, because of the despotic nature of the South African state (Greenberg 1987:9–25), to wheel and engage in the political struggle (Lambert 1987). The result is what Eddie Webster calls "social-movement unionism," concerned "with labour as a social and political force, not simply as a commodity to be bargained over" (1988:195–96). At the national level, the NUM has been outspoken in its support for this recent political trend in the black independent trade union movement, condemning apartheid, advocating international sanctions and disinvestment, and embracing the political ideals of the African National Congress Freedom Charter (James 1991:109).

At the level of local mine management, political pronouncements by senior NUM officials have predictably been ill received. Union activists are seen as wild and uncontrollable revolutionaries. Local union officials themselves are ambivalent. Evidence to the Bregman Commission again provides the deepest insights, for example, the evidence of Mlamli Botha, the Mpondo shaft steward, this time regarding external political influences on mine life (AAC/VR:2178–87). Was there "a significant degree of political consciousness and perhaps political activity in the hostel?" he was asked. Botha struggled to express himself clearly and fairly. He dealt first with white miners: "One will always find that the white workers here on the mines, they are always against the black people. Then in retaliation the blacks also become against them." He elaborated:

[16]On page 510 of the Bregman report, advocate Bregman is critical of the local representatives of the NUM for failing to turn up for meetings with compound management. It seems to me clear, however, that compound management made no more than a pro forma effort to keep in touch with union representatives. Apparently, the shaft stewards' committees met regularly with production management, and when shaft stewards were really needed (as in the Porky Rheeders affair [see footnote 18]), management found them soon enough. The truth of the matter is that negotiation has never been part of compound managers' training, nor is it institutionalized in compound organization. The Bregman record makes it quite clear that union meetings with compound management were essentially top-down affairs in which union representatives were expected to bring information in exchange for receiving orders.

> So you will find that underground there [in the case of] some of the white employees on their hats it is written "AWB" [Afrikaner Weerstandbeweging, the militantly conservative Afrikaner organization]. . . . that is what brings a lot of discord amongst the black workers and the white workers on the mines. . . . The writing means nothing, but the education that he has received from the AWB that you must always be against the black man, that he will definitely take to the work situation and implement it fully. . . . They are being educated to be against a black man. . . . if you teach a person to do this he will definitely carry out and implement it fully. . . . The NUM [itself] has got its own education; the education that I know as a leader in the NUM I must carry out and go according to the education that I have received from NUM.

For all the increased protection for black miners from assaults underground during the past two decades (and it is substantial and undeniable), Botha's general argument about white racism will come as no surprise. But Botha did not stop at his condemnation of the AWB. He developed the thought and applied it to blacks also:

> Although I may not have a thorough knowledge about this AWB, . . . it does appear that there is a fountain or a well where they get . . . a bad type of education which is dirty and which says that they must be against the blacks. The same applies to the black people. It does appear that they also have got a well where they get a knowledge which is very bad which they . . . form . . . against the whites.

What "well" was Mlamli Botha referring to here? A trenchant and loyal unionist, he was certainly not referring to the NUM, whose education had eschewed racial and ethnic division. He raised the notion of "very bad knowledge" for blacks in the context of discussion of the political consciousness and practices of black township militants of the United Democratic Front (UDF), those known throughout South Africa as "comrades," or *amaqabane*.

For all his political savvy, forceful sense of justice, and deep commitment to the union and what it stood for, Botha remained profoundly rural and Mpondo in his personal identity. Thus, his perspective bridged the growing gap between rural conservatives and proletarianized political radicals on the mines. His union commitment was mine based, and he shared the disdain felt by many of his more conservative mine-fellows for the politics of liberation in the cities of South Africa. Later in his evidence, Botha clarified the meaning of his unease about black politics in a nuanced and lengthy discussion of a certain group of amaqabane on the mines (AAC/VR:2359–47).

The "spirit of comradeship," Botha said, usually emanated from black townships and had no ethnic character. However, he was not willing to commit himself to the suggestion that all comrades were of urban origin. Indeed, the two individuals who were specifically identified, or identified themselves, as "comrades" in the Bregman evidence were from the Ciskei and the Western Transkei, underdeveloped areas of the Xhosa-speaking Bantustans. One has the sense that while the "comradely" style was originally urban, on the mines it had its roots in young men from rural slums who consciously adopted urban attitudes.

According to Botha, the amaqabane distinguished themselves by their enthusiastic singing of union and other political songs at meetings and around the hostel, drumming up support for the union, and waving a white flag emblazoned with "NUM" and the emblem of the union. In addition, he said, comrades loved to wear T-shirts, not only of the NUM and COSATU but also of the UDF and AZAPO (Azanian People's Organization, a black-consciousness equivalent of the nonracial UDF), and they wore the badges of various political organizations. They encouraged support using methods similar to youthful township comrades, although, in Botha's opinion, "the comrades in the [mine] hostel [were] not as radical as the ones in the townships."

Singing at union meetings, led by the comrades, was important for union solidarity, said Botha, there was no question about that:

> We, as blacks, we always sing songs to motivate or to . . . add colour to an occasion. . . . That is our attitude as blacks. Singing songs, especially after meeting, . . . is a symbol, it is an indication of approbation. . . . There are church choirs, young men who have got quartets and choir leaders—church choir leaders—besides the congregation at large. The role of those people, because they lead in singing, is to make church service attractive and . . . the Comrades play a similar role in the union in the hostel because they encourage attendance, they make the union meeting more attractive by singing.[17]

Botha allowed that the comrades were "enthusiastic members of the Union and they enjoy[ed] support," but that "sometimes they overstep[ped] their marks in other respects."

It was this overstepping of the mark that perturbed Botha and gave the union a bad name, he said. He denied management's perception of a formal link between the comrades and the union organization as such. "The

[17]For further testimony on the importance of singing in ordinary African life in South Africa, see Moss 1990:65–66.

branch has got nothing to do with the comrades," he said. "The branch is the responsibility of the shaft stewards. [The comrades] are not known to have been elected by anybody in the hostel." Thus, for Mlamli Botha, the question of election, of accountability to a constituency, clearly distinguished union activity from that of the comrades. That is not to say that there was no overlap, even in terms of leadership: "There are shaft stewards who are always among the comrades when they sing there"—a group of five or six shaft stewards, who "doubled up as comrades." Other shaft stewards might join in at random "carried away by the song," but "the election of shaft stewards [was] not the business of comrades," and Botha very much doubted that "comradely" persuasion could have swayed a union election.

Botha first noticed the comrades in August 1985, he said, when the UDF had called a boycott of stores, and young miners outside No. 1 hostel accosted people returning from shopping in town and scattered their purchases on the road. On that occasion, however, the NUM branch chairman, Thabang, the charismatic Sotho shaft steward on No. 1, actually challenged the comrades:

> Mr. Thabang was speaking after the spilling of grocery incident at the bus rank. He told the meeting that the Comrades were not needed because of their mischief. He said the incident of spilling people's groceries would cast the union in an unfavourable light because the union would be accused of such activities. . . . The wrong activities of the Comrades subsided after this speech by Mr. Thabang.

"The wrong activities of the Comrades" may have subsided after Thabang's intervention, but, according to Botha, the comrades' mischief picked up again in 1986. As an instance, Botha cited how, during the four-hour strike, elderly black clerical officials had been roughly forced to sing and march around the compound, carrying the union flag. Another worker remembered that these respectable old men had been "made to run through the hostel being assaulted, beaten up, . . . full of blood" (AAC/VR:2690–91). They had had to be hospitalized. Others who broke the strike, he said, were brought to the meeting, where they apologized for their strike-breaking with all sorts of excuses (AAC/VR:2676). Thembinkosi Sigayi, one of the leaders of the gang of comrades in the frog-marching of the old men, was quite unrepentant when he told the commission of the event (AAC/VR:4295–4307), but he did admit that the workers' meeting had agreed that there should be no intimidation. The elderly black mine officials, he said in a deliberate understatement, willingly marched with his group of "workers," insisting here on identifying his comrades and himself as "workers." The old men knew they had "offended" and were thus being "punished" by "us workers"—although, he added, they did say afterward that he and his comrades were "illiterate" and knew nothing. This remark, which recalls decades of arrogance by educated mine clerks over their illiterate charges, is increasingly misplaced these days, of course, especially with regard to the "new miners." Even though it was said on this occasion under extreme duress, the attitude it bespoke may have lent a certain edge to the "comrades' " intimidatory action against these *amanene.*

In fact, the militancy of the comrade element on the compound presented the local union organization with a dilemma. On the one hand, the amaqabane disrupted compound life and gave the union a bad name, not only with management but also with its own more moderate members. On the other hand, they were useful as enforcers of decisions made at union meetings. Wilmot James (1991), for instance, makes much of their importance in holding workers firm during the 1987 strike. James's account relies heavily on management's records of the strike, however, and overlooks the uneasiness of union stalwarts such as Mlamli Botha about the comrades' intimidation tactics.

Botha, in his testimony to the Bregman Commission, certainly refused to condone such "comradely" behavior. He spelled the problem out metaphorically as follows:

> You know you do something with good aims and intentions, just like constructing your house and plastering it, and yet unaware that there will be beetles coming in and eating it away, then you find your house collapsing because of those beetles. . . . [Similarly, although] . . . it would appear . . . [that] the Union was formed with good intentions, because of the incidents involving comrades which have happened here, . . . the Union is not doing the right things because of these comrades. (AAC/VR:2373)

Once again, it is important to notice the importance of accountability and democratic discussion for Mlamli Botha. In these areas the comrades fell short. But so did management.

When management used a court order to break the go-slow strike that led to the intimidation of the elderly clerks, for instance, and then forced workers to sign reaffirmations of their contracts at gunpoint, Botha's first question to the official in charge addressed whether "there [had] been any meeting prior to the signing." The reply was that management had the power to do anything it liked (AAC/VR:1030). Botha was outraged. He agreed that it was "reasonable that at least they should go to work legally, as required of them by the contract," but he insisted that "a document of that nature should have been debated—there should have been consultation and negotiation about a document of that nature" (AAC/VR:1546).

Management, in other words, was acting coercively, and, said Botha, "the majority of the workers felt dissatisfied about the decision," emphasizing that they signed "for the sake of signing [and under duress] because really the management never called them before the steps of declaration [were] taken, never called and discussed with them the significance of the declaration" (AAC/VR:2549). The insistence on democratic discussion and mutual agreement was firmly entrenched in the ranks of union leadership on No. 1 shaft, and it ran directly counter to bureaucratic despotism as well as all other forms of intimidation. The whole debate harked back to an insistence on proper order, agreed imiteto, the loss of which meant arbitrary domination, whether by management or comrades, and elicited moral indignation. Mlamli Botha turned the tables on management in his typical clear-thinking fashion:

> The management has never referred to the existence of comrades because I do not think they . . . explicitly know about the existence of comrades. But they have always complained about people with bad influence. Ever since the beginning of 1986 they have been talking about bad influence, bad influence including the incident of [the bullying during the four-hour strike], including the faction fighting. . . . It is an on-going complaint that there is a bad influence, whereas we know, of course, that there has always been a [white] bad influence on the Mine. In fact [in] one of the incidents I will quote . . . Porky [Rheeders] is part of the bad influence which exists in this Mine. (AAC/VR:2379)

Thus Botha made a neat transition from the bad behavior of comrades to the "bad influence" of whites, whom he had mentioned at first as those who had originally brought "politics" to the mines.[18]

Botha would perhaps have been closer to management perceptions if he had said that they did not mention comrades because they assumed that the entire union leadership on the mine were comrades. This management misperception was a serious mistake (Botha estimated that only five or six of the forty-five shaft stewards on Vaal Reefs No. 1 were actually comrades), although Botha himself admitted that at the time of his testimony "this [had] spread around. The comrades [were] all over [on the mines]" (AAC/VR:2376).

The collapse of the induna system has left black miners with a fairly unvarnished view of white management despotism. Management can no

[18]"Porky" Rheeders was a white mine overseer who was very free with the word *kaffir* and other insults to black workers.

longer hide behind the power of their "inaccessibility," leaving indunas and their cohorts to bear the brunt of worker resentment. Nor are workers willing to aim their outrage merely at those "bad" white individuals whose racism is an overt aspect of their self-presentation to blacks. Instead, management is targeted for its failure to control such "bad" whites and for its total inability to distinguish between the relatively small but vociferous "comrade" element on the mines and the large majority of deeply committed but nonetheless "responsible" union members.[19]

The 1984 Black Miners' Strike

To balance the lengthy case study of the AMWU and the 1946 strike, we will examine the NUM's mode of operating in similar situations. Since adequate discussion of the defeat of the 1987 strike, when 330,000 workers were out for three weeks (Crush, Jeeves, and Yudelman 1991:200) would take at least another chapter,[20] we shall deal here with the threatened wage strike in 1984, which was called off at the last minute because of management concessions. Our account relies upon interviews with NUM members and a head office executive in the Anglo American Corporation.

In 1983, the NUM signed a negotiation agreement with the Chamber of Mines just before the June wage-announcement deadline. Although the union had come in with a demand for a 30 percent raise, the chamber rushed it into settling for about 14 percent. There was a backlash from workers, who had expected more from the new union. "That really put the pressure on for 1984," said Cyril Ramaphosa. "The 1984 strike was planned in 1983. There was a lot of bitterness, not only amongst members but amongst ourselves as well as officials, and we knew that we had to have a showdown with the Chamber in 1984."

In 1984, the NUM initiated negotiations with huge wage demands but soon settled down to a firm demand for a 25 percent increase. The chamber countered with 8 percent, and then 10 percent. At that point the NUM declared a dispute and held a national strike committee meeting that voted to strike, and the union started on the tedious process of going through the motions preparatory to a legal strike. Ramaphosa insisted that all the organizers attend the negotiating sessions. He also included in the negotiating team the chairmen of the branch committees in each region and

[19]The tendency to elide the union and the comrades is widespread among white South Africans. In fact, the most serious weakness of Commissioner Bregman's own report is that he makes the same mistake, despite having sat through days of testimony from Mlamli Botha.

[20]Chapter 7 of Wilmot James's recent (1991) book is indeed devoted to a discussion of the 1987 strike. I myself am working on a book-length study of the event.

the regional chairman and his secretary. Ramaphosa was spokesperson. Negotiations broke down finally in September 1984, and the union prepared for the final strike vote. Jack Mpapea, then chief shaft steward from Vaal Reefs No. 4 remembered the occasion vividly:

> The first step the union took was to collect all the shaft stewards in one place . . . with the negotiating team that had been meeting with the Chamber of Mines. They started reporting to the workers that, "You have been demanding this and this and this and the Chamber of Mines is prepared only to give you this." Those figures were shown on the board that the wages would be this and this after the increment now. [The local representatives] were not happy as workers there in that meeting.

The local representatives demanded more money, or a legal strike, said Mpapea, and were told that they had to organize a report-back to their members. This request created severe logistical difficulties since Vaal Reefs management still did not allow union meetings on the compounds, but they persevered:

> We decided to hire halls in the nearby townships, sometimes using the churches, collecting all the workers on the weekends. . . . We hired buses also to take all these workers from the hostel straight to the location or township, where we briefed them fully about the strike, about wages—reporting, giving them the feedback from the negotiating team.

There was overwhelming support for a legal strike at the meetings held on 14 September. A strike was called for 17 September.

Ever since the August strike-committee meeting, the union had been preparing for the strike:

> Everybody knew the 17th was D-Day [said Ramaphosa], which was very good for us because even those workers who had not joined the union had already got the message that nobody goes to work. Management, on the other hand, was trying to dissuade workers from going on strike, by threatening dismissals, loss of benefits, etc. But the workers could not be [dissuaded].

At the last minute the Chamber of Mines offered a 14 percent raise. "After preparing for a strike, after mobilizing the workers for a strike, . . . on Sunday Cyril was phoned and we were all told to go to the Chamber of Mines at one o'clock that day," remembered Salae.

The strike was called off until the workers had considered management's offer. This was the greatest test for the young union. Mobilizing mine workers for their first legal strike ever had been a major achievement, but cajoling them back to work until they had considered the new offer would be even more difficult. The union guaranteed that its members would go back to work. That, said Salae, was a blunder. "We started moving now to the head office and prepared a pamphlet," he continued, "telling the people that they must go back to work" and that the union thought the 14 percent raise "a better offer." Organizers and shaft stewards had their work cut out for them:

> We were many that attended, because all the shaft stewards were collected at head office. . . . Some had to move as far as Welkom mines, at least three hours drive, some to get to Vaal Reefs, and the East Rand. At Vaal Reefs, I remember it took me five—no seven—days speaking to the workers. They were not prepared to accept the offer, saying, "No, no, you are a sell-out, you've sold us out." The workers were very angry, I remember at Number Three shaft, two shaft stewards ran away, they went out of the hostel, straight to Johannesburg. They were afraid to stay in the hostel. Workers were not even prepared to listen to anybody. . . . I had to move from shaft to shaft, through that night, during the day, during the next night, and the next day. . . . None of the shafts at Vaal Reefs went down that night. After two days, Number Five agreed, Number Eight and Number Nine. Then we were left with Number Two, Number One, Number Four and Number Six shafts. They refused entirely, they said, "No!" They were not prepared to go to work. . . . I had to go myself and speak to the workers and I managed to win them, to persuade them to go back to work.

Overall on the various mines, fifty thousand workers came out by Monday morning. Although the union was working desperately to talk them back to work, police intervened violently on several mines and by the end of the week, when all were back at work again, ten had died and about five hundred were hurt (Friedman 1987:366–68).

The Anglo American executive whom I interviewed spoke with admiration of the way in which union officials worked day and night to get its members back to work. The NUM was able to demonstrate clearly to management and to other workers the depth of its support and its ability to demobilize even its most radical elements. "Afterwards," observed Mpapea, "most of the Mpondo, even the Shangaans, started joining the union. They were then aware that the union [was] powerful and [successful] in its legal strike action. So most of the people, Zulus as well, started joining the union." The shaft steward system, which had kept workers in close contact with their union representatives, and the sense on the mine that the union represented a new order, proper imiteto, was paying off. Perhaps management was surprised by the massive support workers gave the union in 1987, but they should not have been after 1984.

Matters were complicated for the local union, certainly, by the turn to social-movement unionism in 1985. Such a stance was less problematic for union members on Vaal Reefs, however, than an outbreak of intense ethnic conflict that flared up on the mines in 1986, and, as we shall see, was not unrelated to management strategies. We return in the conclusion to the complex events at Vaal Reefs No. 1.

Conclusion

Within the limits of one particular South African industry, this book has touched on many notions central to contemporary social theory. Personal integrity and social responsibility, power and authority, communal identity, political resistance and accommodation, masculinity and femininity, collective violence and nonviolent contestation, all have informed the account of the particularities of this historically and institutionally bounded case. Different narratives from a wide range of sources have also unearthed a series of "genealogical" changes in the substantive meanings of each of these terms over time and in different socioeconomic contexts.

Social analysts must always find a compromise between retaining the distinctive voices of their subjects and achieving a wider theoretical understanding of people's stories and the events they describe. Although theoretical concepts afford an unusually powerful set of explanatory tools, their use inevitably entails a selective reading of evidence. While trying to remain faithful to the tone of black miners' accounts of their lives, I have set them in a theoretical frame that I hope will be useful to contemporary South African mine workers as well as to a wider readership. If the book has measured up to my intent, my theoretical perspective should be clear to the reader from its concrete application in the preceding text. In this conclusion I give an explicit summary of the theoretical ideas that have guided my analysis. Then, in a final case study, I conclude the story of the struggle on Vaal Reefs No. 1 in 1986 and pull together several of the themes that run through the text.

The question of the relationship between agency and structure is central to contemporary social theory. Marx stated the problem succinctly when he noted at the beginning of *The Eighteenth Brumaire* ([1852] 1974) that human actors "make their own history, but not of their own free will; not under circumstances they themselves have chosen but under the given and inherited circumstances with which they are directly confronted." Social analysis has tended to divide between those who stress structural constraints on human action and thus explain events as transformations of structures, and those for whom interpretation of actors' intentions is sufficient to explain events.

Voluntaristic theories of power, for instance, follow Machiavelli in suggesting that all power is ultimately strategic. Strategy may be defined as the pursuit of advantage by individual or collective actors. On the South African mines both underground and in the compounds, for instance, strategic power is exerted "informally" by migrant men and their supervisors over each other in the midst of the processes of production and reproduction.[1] However, one goes too far in suggesting that all power is strategic. Strategies, after all, operate according to the particular purposes of groups and individuals within and around rule-defined structures already established through prior practices. Structures are experienced by actors as directing and constraining them, as providing access to resources for action and also as setting limits to action. One may, of course, subsume formal structures within the discourse of strategic relationships by positing structures as the congealed outcomes of strategies and resistances, but this is a somewhat clumsy procedure (however historically accurate), since structures do form a part of actors' direct experience, and, besides, actors are themselves socially formed. In the case of the South African gold mines at least, strategies presuppose prior informal moral commitments and agreements both among workers and between workers and management. In addition, structural rules and procedures provide formal access to resources for actors in the situation, however much informal strategies may seek to circumvent them. Mine strategies have taken for granted rules and solidarities implicated in both the formal structures and the moral economies of particular mines at different times and the resources that can be mobilized by different groups at different historical moments.

More convincing than thinking of all power as strategic is to conceive of formal power, or social structure more generally, as allocating rights and resources unequally within particular historical structures among differently socialized actors who then make the best (or worst) of their positions and situations by strategic maneuvers. Social structures, so understood, certainly have their origins in purposive action, but once they have come into being they constrain future action. Once structures have been established, dominants' maintenance of control as well as subdominants'

[1]Reproduction here refers to those domestic and other services that "deliver the worker with his lunch box to the factory gate every morning."

resistance involve strategic action within established but contested patterns of social interaction on changing historical terrain. In this view, structures define the uneven, unequal, and shifting terrain upon which actors struggle for power. Actors experience structures as formally or informally patterned rules of conduct, more or less firmly sanctioned, which exist outside of them, both constrain and empower their social practices and distribute material goods according to regular procedures.

Anthony Giddens has sought to link structure and agency by elaborating a notion of "structuration," which suggests that social structures are always in process, made up from "social practices ordered across space and time" (1984:2). Thus, for Giddens, structures are precipitated out of social interaction, formed through the strategic activities of agents and their unintended consequences. At the same time, however, the conditions for social action, and the very self-formation of actors themselves, depend upon the workings of prior social structures. Social structures, then, give rise to actors who reproduce or re-form them more or less effectively depending on the availability and accessibility of necessary resources, their own self-formative experience, their native ability, and new and existing social networks.

Structures, as Giddens describes them, thus constrain and empower social actors as they pursue strategic goals. The Mpondo who broke the liquor boycott on Vaal Reefs No. 1 because they wanted to drink nonetheless respected the lawfulness of the union decision even as they contravened it. They clearly felt a need to rationalize their defiance of the imiteto of the union. Actors experience the constraints of social structures, whether as institutionalized moral obligations or material limits, consciously and directly. At the same time, they are also empowered by moral and material resources available from structural forces, even as Seven Mojakisane was empowered by local management support, by his traditional Sotho integrity, by his reputation as a MaRashea and fearless warrior, and by the weapons he had in hand, when he and his blanketed fellows broke the strike in support of Mgedezi, which started the trouble at Vaal Reefs No. 1 in February 1986.

The moral economy and migrant cultures empowered black workers on the South African gold mines before the 1970s, but at the same time collective action according to the rules of the moral economy confirmed a wider overall system of management hegemony of which workers had only a partial consciousness. The practices of actors and the possibilities and limits of social structures exist on the same plane, that of social interaction. Actors are "accountable" in Giddens's language (1984:30) because they can give reasons and justifications for their practices, whatever the unintended consequences. Most of the events described in this book take place on this level of self-conscious social interaction, where agency and structures reciprocate.

This book also attempts a deeper level of explanation, however, employing abstract analytical concepts that lie outside the immediate experience of social agents. "Proletarianization" is the most obvious of such notions used throughout the book. The notion of "system" is useful to introduce arguments at this more abstract level. Many years ago, David Lockwood (1964:245) made what he called a "wholly artificial" distinction between "social integration" and "system integration": "Whereas the problem of social integration focuses attention upon the orderly or conflictful relationships between the *actors*, the problem of system integration focuses on the orderly or conflictful relationships between the *parts* of a social system."[2]

Systems transcend actors in a manner best explained according to a logic whose elements are analytical units formally related to one another rather than social practices as such. Systems analysis cuts across social practices and institutions by uncovering forces that set limits and exert pressures upon social structures and strategic practices alike. The systemic mode of explanation introduces an analytical shorthand to explain complex "causal" patterns whose effects elude interpretation in terms of institutionalized social structures and actors' intentions and their consequences. Crises at the system level operate behind the backs of actors, altering the terrain of contestation even as actors strive to devise winning strategies with every available structural resource. Thus, in the early 1990s, the National Union of Mineworkers, even as it struggled to improve black wages and conditions of work in response to management and white worker structures and strategies, was tethered by the current crisis of accumulation in the gold industry as a whole.

Although one could, I suppose, break down the operations of social systems into myriad structured social interactions and their intended and unintended consequences, that would be a laborious and ultimately frus-

[2]Jurgen Habermas (1989) picks up on Lockwood's distinction between system integration/conflict and social integration/contradiction. Conscious of the different logics of systems analysis and social life-worlds, he separates them, but then, in what seems to me to be a serious category mistake, rediscovers them hypostasized in different and differentiated concrete social institutions. Habermas thus excludes social or life-world analysis from economic and political institutions and systemic analysis from education and the family (Frazer 1989:113–43; Ingram 1987:115–34). He then frets about how, in modernity, systems colonize life-worlds. Lukacs's Weberian reading of Marx's theory of alienation as reification thus returns in a new guise to center stage in Habermas's notion of "the colonization of the life-world."

trating task since the operation of the system as a whole transcends its individual parts. While social structures coexist with actors in Lockwood's "social" realm of concrete interaction in the life-world, "systems" are analytical constructs devised by observers to specify the limits and pressures imposed upon structures and actors by the logic of their own operation within particular historical epochs. Systems "exist" through the consistency with which their parts relate to one other within explanatory wholes that have their own internal principles of reproduction and transformation. Capitalist commodity production and exchange, with its internal contradictions and crises, is an example of such a system.

Systemic logic, as I understand it, however, is never ineluctable or inevitable at more concrete levels of social analysis, although it points up powerful limits and pressures on social interaction. Indeed, systems summarize the logic behind those "given and inherited circumstances" around which actors "make their own history."

While I am working with a particular, generally Marxist, type of system analysis (although, like Gramsci and Michael Burawoy,[3] I seek to retain historical contingency), there are other system theories. For example, the normative functionalism of Talcott Parsons was formulated with more universal claims than the version of Marxism that undergirds the argument of this book. "Family system theory" (Hoffman 1981) has revolutionized therapeutic practice. Piaget (1971), in a fascinating account, postulates a series of systemic structures characterized by "wholeness," "transformations," and "self-regulation," which operate by the intercalation of the movements of their elements. For Piaget, elementary systems become the units of more complex systems. Although Piaget's (1971:98–99) notion of social system, which "like causality in physics, is a theoretic construct, not an empirical given, . . . [belonging] not to consciousness but to behavior," is analytical precisely in Lockwood's sense, it is also more deterministic than I believe history permits us to be. Like orthodox Marxism and Parsonianism (or, for that matter, orthodox Freudian symbolic analysis[4]), Piaget's "structuralism" implies a determinism whose "laws of transformation" refuse agency or contingency. For all their internal con-

[3]The work of Michael Burawoy (1979, 1985) provides a rendition of a similar problem complex to that set forth here. His distinction between relations *of* production and relations *in* production returns us to Lockwood's differentiation between the systemic and the social. I am not sure, however, that Burawoy's notion of "production politics" distinguishes sufficiently clearly between systemic and social problems in political analysis.

[4]It is fascinating to observe in the authorized version of Freud's (1953) *Interpretation of Dreams* how Freud's methodology shifted from hermeneutics to determinism as his "system" of analysis became more rigid.

sistency, such systems operate in only the most general way in historical applications, especially over long time spans, as abstract principles of integration and contradiction, equilibrium and crisis. In practice, systemic logic is discernible only as distorted (but seldom controverted) by the structured vagaries of social practices and organized agencies firmly located in time and space.

System Crises in South African Gold Mining

Perhaps it is dangerous to try to draw out the general systemic theme that informs this entire book. When this research began, however, I intended to explicate the process of proletarianization on South African gold mines. The work is still framed by that attempt, embedded in Marxist system logic, although the foregoing chapters have revealed social developments more complex and uneven than I expected at the outset. I hope to have demonstrated that although traditional migrants to the mines confronted systemic pressures toward proletarianization some of them were able to resist because they still possessed viable material bases rooted in an alternative political economy of homestead production. Mine managements after the Anglo-Boer War resisted systemic pressures to hire proletarianized workers, for reasons of necessity at first and then as a matter of convenience, since they had invested in a monopsonistic migrant recruitment structure that brought them cheap, if not reliable, labor supplies, and they were able to set up production processes that enabled capital accumulation with a racially divided workforce. Contradictions at the system level, leading to the gradual underdevelopment of the migrant labor supply areas close to the mines, were avoided by spreading recruiting nets wider and wider into tropical Africa.

In the end, political developments in the African hinterland, coinciding with price fluctuations in the international gold market, led to a sudden, if uneven, process of proletarianizing the mine labor force as a whole. Systemic changes on the mines came about not as a result of the gradual dispossession of African proprietors in South Africa, since the mines had been able to avoid the effects of that by hiring rural homestead proprietors from tropical Africa to the north, but rather because of a radical shift in mine recruiting practices made possible by a rise in wages. In the past, black South African workers who had been unable to resist the forces of proletarianization simply left the mines for secondary industry and other urban occupations or got involved in mine rackets because they could not survive on mine wages alone.

Hiring them back in the 1970s by increasing wages meant that the mine compound, without changing its physical aspect at all (if anything, compounds were improved during the 1970s), shifted from being, for traditional migrant workers, a haven against proletarianization (however harsh), to being, for the new migrants, an unbearably oppressive institution of outright exploitation. South African gold mining was thrust into a crisis of legitimacy, or at least a crisis of hegemony,[5] with rapidly deteriorating system integration, threats to capital accumulation, and increasing social conflict. Substantial investment in compound improvements and the rationalization of compound authority had little effect on the problem. Liaison committees were clearly not doing the job. Heavy investment in productive equipment was not bringing about adequate improvements in productivity. Thus, granting access to African trade unions in 1982 was a logical, if somewhat risky, attempt to solve a severe systemic crisis.[6] Management efforts to confront such crises posed political questions, both at the system level and in specific structural contexts.

The concept of power has different applications in system analysis and social structural interaction. The work of Claus Offe (1984 and 1985), for instance, provides good examples of both systemic and social operations of power. On the system level, as Offe points out, the establishment of the welfare state both resolved a crisis of legitimation for capitalism and led to an eventual fiscal crisis of accumulation for the state. Of course, in the last instance, capital accumulation has to be the bottom line for an industrial concern—as, indeed, it is for the capitalist state. I have already argued that the mining industry in the 1970s faced a serious hegemonic crisis. In the 1980s, the focus shifted, for, with a low price for gold on the world market, profit margins were cut drastically.[7] Tens of thousands of

[5]The notion of legitimacy, derived as it is from Max Weber, has always seemed to me to be fundamentally ambiguous. On the one hand, legitimation implies approval, the acceptance by members of the essential validity of a political order, "the ultimate grounds of the validity of a domination" (Weber 1968:953). On the other hand, Weber (1968:213) recognizes that an order may exist that lacks approval by the subjects and yet wherein the ruling class and its administrators legitimate each other. More useful, I believe, is Gramsci's notion of hegemony, which I have adopted in this book. Here the approval accorded by the shared "ultimate ground" of a dominant ideology is replaced by the consent attained by a "common sense" that conceals from ruled and ruling class alike the true nature of the hegemonic system. The notion in the United States that an individual's failure to succeed is his or her own fault would be an example of such hegemonic common sense. The implicit contract of the moral economy on the South African gold mines, for all its militancy, would be an example of hegemonic common sense there.

[6]I am inclined to agree with James (1991), as opposed to Pycroft and Munslow (1988), that, at least for the more conservative mining houses, this was as much a move of desperation as a Machiavellian scheme for co-optation.

[7]That the price of gold soared from U.S.$35 an ounce to around U.S.$800 an ounce before dropping to its present level of about U.S.$350 an ounce exacerbated the

black workers were laid off. The industry went into a full-scale accumulation crisis that profoundly affected the terms for resolution of the hegemonic crisis of the 1970s.

While analysis of proletarianization and system crises enables one to outline some of the systemic pressures and limits on social practices described in this book, nonetheless, such an abstract analysis does not arrive at a "structure, objective, independent of human will . . . which can be measured with the systems of the exact sciences" posited by Marx and repeated by Gramsci (1971:180). Even an overall systematic drive to accumulate capital does not imply a single, logically consistent path for historical development. The way in which system contradictions are worked out is not set in advance and does not proceed according to an ineluctable pattern.

Hastings Banda's decision to withdraw Malawian labor from the South African gold mines in 1974, for instance, precipitated a crisis whose systemic causes lay elsewhere—in the underdevelopment of the black South Africa labor supply areas. Nonetheless, without Banda's action, the Chamber of Mines might have made different decisions, and without the rise in the price of gold, it would have had to. Even at a system level, then, history intervenes both through events and the impact of wider systems. Abstract systems are concretely specified only through historical contingencies and particularities.

Thus, the analysis of systems abstracts from life-worlds to describe a general tendency of determinations whose actual course, and indeed outcomes and effects, must be fleshed out by the contingencies of historical decision and social interaction. It is here that organizations and moralities, identities and solidarities, strategies and lost opportunities, come into play. Here we return to the dialectic of structure and agency that takes place in the realm of the social. Social practices, however strategic, are never completely open. They are limited by their environment, that is, by patterns laid down by prior events that limit access to ideal or material structural and personal resources. Discussion of political practices as structuring order and informing strategic action on the mines becomes unavoidable.

Powers

Management control in the compounds demanded constant vigilance on the part of those who exercised formal power there, white and black offi-

---

problem because the industry had committed itself to levels of new development and capitalization that assumed that the price of gold would never again be below U.S.$400 an ounce.

cials alike. At the very least, collective demands by workers and the need for stability obliged managements to adhere to the rules that they had made and the formal and informal contracts they had negotiated, but the existence of such codes also meant ongoing struggle over their implications and interpretations in particular situations. Alcohol, meat, sexual practices, various economic exchanges and services, sidelines and rackets, all were subject to contestation.

Management structures and strategies necessarily sought to maintain control. Ideally, for managements, their control would be taken for granted by themselves and their subordinates, as hegemonic common sense. As a matter of fact, most subdominants chose to avoid rather than resist the overt effects of management hegemony by living in alternative but not directly antagonistic life-worlds. Where, as on the mines before 1973, the hegemonic class was obliged to accommodate alternative cultures with specific integrities and particular gendered patterns of self-formation, a moral economy developed, an implicit contract or pattern of consent perceived as morally binding by dominants and subdominants alike. Members of the dominant class who challenged such a mutually accepted moral order invariably risked moral outrage. Moreover, fellow dominants often felt such outrage as much as subordinates. And since there was always the possibility that moral outrage might precipitate counterhegemonic insight, challenging the consent implicit in the operation of hegemonic structures, dominant classes tended to treat the moral economy and demands made in its name with great respect, however despotic the coercive power upon which they could draw if they had to. Moral outrage has always provided excellent motivation for resolute action. Collective action in the name of the moral economy thus became a major strategy for mobilizing resistance to local inequities, while at the same time it also reinforced overall hegemonic assumptions and structures. The moral economy of the mine structured the social order of the mine compound in a manner that enabled both management and migrant homestead proprietors to realize their practical strategic purposes.

In the 1980s, new forms of ethnic collective violence, reinforced by the uneven proletarianization of the 1970s, became so destructive of production, and challenges to management control so disruptive, that unionization seemed preferable to chaos. The decision to permit unionization thus signified a genuinely organic crisis for management hegemony. It is important to stress that hegemonic compromise, if it is truly to resolve organic crisis, demands genuine concessions by the ruling class. Anglo American head office appeared to be seeking genuine, if limited, reforms and a measure of power sharing with the union. Leaving aside for the moment the question of whether union leadership was willing to settle with Anglo top management (and on what terms), a much more telling question seems to be whether local management—especially lower-level local management—was willing or able to permit the level of power sharing demanded by a new, more representative order that included the union, especially with local involvement in underground safety and discipline and compound control. The NUM and Anglo American signed a "code of conduct" in 1990 setting out procedures for future confrontations on the local level. Such agreement at the top, however, is no guarantee that there will be enforcement on the local level—by either side.

One final extended example from Vaal Reefs No. 1 in 1986, although it took place before the 1987 strike and the adoption of the code of conduct, will point up some of the moral and strategic problems that actual implementation of the union and mining-house code of conduct may cause on the local level. At least on Vaal Reefs, local management seemed to have assumed that a representative union would be little more than a means of downward communication, like the already existing consultative committees and izibonda meetings. Of course, such a sweetheart union would have failed to resolve managements' hegemonic crisis. No doubt, Anglo American's top management wanted the union to provide genuine representation for militant and alienated workers in order to work out compromises in the interests of productivity. In fact, the new union order, while it challenged many of the old prerogatives of mine management, made no effort to replace management's technical administration of gold production. Rather, NUM local branches sought to work in cooperation with management to achieve production goals while at the same time challenging management despotism in the name of new imiteto, defining a new order, democratically established by the workers and collectively negotiated with management.

On Vaal Reefs No. 1, at least, local management took unkindly to this union threat to its authority and feared what it perceived to be the risks associated with cooperation with the local branch of the union. They identified the union entirely with the actions of its militant left wing, and at the same time that the shaft stewards of the NUM claimed to be working seriously at establishing a new, more just and democratic order on the mine, certain sections of local management (most notably hostel management and the mine security forces) co-opted traditional integrities and ethnic rivalries in the interest of breaking what they perceived to be the union threat to managerial prerogatives. In response to what they perceived as mob behavior by union militants, there is evidence that local hostel management deliberately encouraged mob behavior by their own conservative trusties. That management hegemony on this mine was already disintegrating added to the urgency and brutality of their strategy.

The central events in our account are two serious Sotho-Xhosa "faction fights" on Vaal Reefs No. 1 that took place within a couple of weeks of one another in November and December 1986. On 22 and 23 November, thirteen persons died, and on 6 December, nine were killed.[8] While I shall try to show that ethnic tensions were secondary to and fomented by hostilities between the local branch of the union and local management, the story touches on many of the themes of the foregoing chapters, pointing up their relevance to political struggles at the grass roots. Simply put, the local branch of the union tried to establish a more democratic moral economy in the face of effective management disruption of the union effort. There can be few more graphic examples anywhere of what Giddens might call an attempt at structuration and its sabotage by "de-structive" social practices in the name of an ancien régime.

I have already discussed the tendency for management on Vaal Reefs to attribute all political violence on the mine to "the union." An important instance was the "Matyaba affair" at No. 1 hostel, when a group of rowdies, carrying the flag of the Congress of South African Students, broke up management-sanctioned elections for the Transkei government and beat up an Mpondo mine official (widely regarded by workers as a management stooge) who was supervising the elections. While some of the "comrades" involved may have been members of the union, opposition to the elections was apparently not union sanctioned at all, being regarded by union stalwarts as an affair for Transkeians alone. Nonetheless, management blamed the union for the violence, and the South African police arrested three union members (including one shaft steward) and put them on trial. They were acquitted for lack of evidence.

Local management's tendency to blame the union for all political intimidation by mine workers was deeply resented by union officials. Especially when management used its own security forces or called in the South African police, the use of force evoked a deep sense of moral outrage in union stalwarts. Two incidents on Vaal Reefs No. 1 were mentioned by black union witnesses to the Bregman Commission as instances of management despotism. The first had to do with the conservative white mine official, "Porky" Rheeders, to whom the Mpondo shaft steward, Mlamli Botha, was so deeply inimical. What really worried Botha in the Rheeders

[8]These fights were in fact the occasion for the appointment of the Bregman Commission, a private commission of inquiry set up by the Anglo American Gold Division. Our account relies entirely upon evidence gathered by the commission, which is uniquely rich in testimony about contemporary mine life.

case was management's failure to discipline the official adequately for explicit racism. The story is a simple one, harking back to similar stories told over the past century on the South African gold mines about intense black worker outrage about hoisting delays. Complaints about delays in hoisting blacks from underground are as old as deep-level mines themselves. Since workers are paid for hours spent at the work sites rather than surface to surface, it is understandably a sore issue.

In this case, on 4 July 1986, mine overseer J. A. Rheeders, otherwise known as "Porky," "stopped [black] people [on 59 level] from getting to the lift while they were knocking off. He said to the workers that 'this is not a lift for the kaffirs [niggers], this is a lift for the whites' " (AAC/VR:1041) and proceeded to the surface with the cage almost empty. When the cage returned, the black workers refused to be hoisted, saying that they wanted the "kaffir lift." White officials who went down were totally unable to break the sit-down strike and had to call in representatives of the union to negotiate with the workers. Three shaft stewards went down and eventually, after gaining some concessions from management, were able to get the workers at 59 level to leave the mine. Meanwhile, other union activists, furious that the drinking set on the mine had gone to the bar as though nothing had happened, burst in on the liquor outlet, grabbed beer from the drinkers, and spilled it on the ground, saying: "You are enjoying yourselves in the bar while other people are . . . not [yet] out of the Mine" (AAC/VR:1781–83).

Two days later, Meshack Lange, the shaft steward who had done all the mediating in the negotiations and essentially talked the striking workers to the surface, was detained under a state of emergency and held by the South African police. Outraged workers demonstrated in front of the hostel manager's office. In Mlamli Botha's words:

> People were really angry about this because Porky who started the whole thing was not arrested under the state of emergency whereas the shaft steward who came to assist . . . was consequently arrested. . . . I believe he was arrested since he made the workers listen to him [so that] management was of the view that he was also responsible for inciting the workers to refuse to go from underground. (AAC/VR:2189)

In addition, said Botha in disgust, although he had heard that management had censured Porky Rheeders, they did so in private, out of the presence of the shaft stewards at the inquiry.

In this case, the conception of management despotism held by Botha actually did not apply, in my opinion. Senior management had gone to great lengths to hold an inquiry. In time-honored fashion, Rheeders found a couple of white miners to perjure themselves for him. Judging from the inquiry's minutes (AAC/VR:KVD49), Porky Rheeders's witnesses were manifestly lying, but ultimately it was the word of white against black. Perhaps the section manager should have found against Rheeders; however, in light of the conflicting evidence, he did not do so. Nonetheless, Rheeders received a severe reprimand, which was noted on his record. In addition, the general manager of Vaal Reefs wrote to the local police asking for Lange's release: "this man's detention has caused serious industrial unrest at our No. 1 Shaft and the inhabitants of No. 1 Hostel have asked me to take up the matter on their behalf" (AAC/VR:KVD51). The police refused to cooperate.

It seems to me, as it seemed to the workers at No. 1, that Meschack Lange's detention two days after the Porky incident can hardly have been coincidental. It is unlikely, however, that senior mine management asked the state police to arrest Lange, as Mlamli Botha believed (AAC/VR:2192). It is much more probable that Rheeders, who was a prominent conservative member of the small white community in the area, used his personal influence to initiate the detention. Union members failed to distinguish between different levels of management and between formal and informal relations with the local police in their understanding of the Porky affair. That workers were convinced of senior management's involvement, however, demonstrates how completely black miners were committed to a total despot theory of management power by the middle of 1986.

The second case illustrating local union convictions about management's despotism does indeed provide an example of it. Furthermore, it led to what local union officials believed were several totally unjust dismissals. Indeed, the first liquor outlet boycott of 5 November grew directly out of this case.

At eight o'clock in the morning of 8 October 1986, the section manager on No. 1 "received information that employees were going to refuse to come out of the mine" (AAC/VR:KVD59).[9] Accordingly, he dispatched mine overseers to the various levels on the mine to clear the mine of

[9]Nowhere in the commission's record is there evidence of any effort to discover whence he received this "information." Mlamli Botha alleged that the section manager was acting on the basis of rumors with little foundation in fact and that he should have approached the union at once to verify his "information." Given the consequences of the section manager's action, it is surprising that the commission did not try to find out why he acted as he did. At any rate, the event demonstrates how much more difficult it became for management to act unilaterally on the basis of "information" from compound trusties. Besides, with the breakdown of the induna system, such informants were increasingly less likely to have reliable information anyway.

workers and to take note of any who refused to come up. That the section manager was willing to disrupt production on the basis of rumor demonstrates how rattled management must have been by the Porky Rheeders sit-down strike. At 66 level, several workers boarded the cage reluctantly, and others remained behind. When they refused the command of John Mills, the mine overseer, to enter the "Mary-Anne" cage (a small cage used for transporting officials in and out of the mine) he had ordered especially for them, he summoned mine security officers, who eventually batoned the workers into the cage. Once aboard, one man was viciously assaulted on the suspicion that he had been involved in the attack on Raymond Matyaba at the disruption of the Transkeian elections a month earlier. On the surface, the grievously wounded man was rushed to the hospital. The remainder of the group of mine workers from 66 level (twenty-six in number) were marched past waiting guard-dogs into a van and taken to security headquarters. Only sixteen of the twenty-seven turned out to be NUM members. The men were charged before the section manager, and twenty of them were found not guilty of disobeying the orders of their superiors. Seven were found guilty and dismissed from the mine on the spot. They appealed to the production manager, who reprieved two of them but sustained the discharges of the other five.

Mlamli Botha represented some of the accused at the disciplinary hearing presided over by Fulscher, the section manager. He pressed their case strongly, with typically astute arguments and his characteristic sense of justice and outrage at arbitrary power:

> I asked Mr. Fulscher whether a worker could be taken out of his job even before his time has come for him to get off. To which he said on this particular day he had arranged that people should knock off early. I asked Mr. Fulscher whether prior he had told the people about this to which he said "No," he said that it was only his own right. I asked Mr. Fulscher as people were striking underground according to him with which shaft steward did he go down in this incident. He said he did not call any shaft steward. I reminded him about the July incident when he had called a shaft steward to underground when people were refusing to go out. I asked him why then not this time. . . . [I]n terms of the spirit of the agreement we have with management if there is any problem with the workers they should go through the shaft stewards. . . . He did not give an answer. I asked him [whether he considered it just] to do this type of thing. He just said that I am dismissing these people because they refused to get to the lift. I wanted to know what type of evidence did he have because it was work time when he forced these people to the lift. People at Station 65, their

> lift begins at quarter to three to take them up. You, at half past eleven at work time you are taking them up, you are telling them to go to the lift. He did not even answer, he just said "I am dismissing these people." Then I told him that you are exercising your own right and that is illegal. (AAC/VR:1058–59)

To Mlamli Botha, management was behaving most arbitrarily. The "laws" that Fulscher was contravening were the new imiteto of a mine with an active union presence. Whatever rumors he might have heard about a threatened underground sit-down, Fulscher should have checked with the shaft stewards before taking action, Botha believed, as had been done in resolving the Porky Rheeders affair. The men refused to board the cage at John Mills's command, said Botha, "because of the manner in which the security was forcing them to go and board the cage . . . [and besides] this happened at a time when they were supposed to have been working" (AAC/VR:1946).

Furthermore, the handful of men who were actually dismissed were all "comrades" (AAC/VR:2428), militants who were openly associated with the union and thus liable to victimization by management because of their singing and dancing in the compound. In Botha's opinion, it was their close identification with the union, rather than their refusal to ride the cage as such, which distinguished them from those nonunionists who had behaved similarly underground but who were acquitted. Thus the dismissals could be construed as a direct assault on union structures and activities on the compound.

There can be little question that production management at No. 1 had been severely shaken by the Porky Rheeders sit-down strike underground. Like the four-hour go-slow that had preceded the March faction fight, the Porky affair had affected mine production. No doubt management thought it had the potential to be far more disruptive in the future since it had demonstrated management's impotence without union cooperation. It must have seemed to production management that union solidarity might once again, as in the case of the four-hour strike, threaten their control of production. This time they were no doubt determined to act forcefully without union participation, for in the sphere of production, mine management is openly and avowedly despotic—invoking "safety" as the last line of defense of their authority. Little wonder that Fulscher was edgy and acted arbitrarily in dismissing suspected sit-down striker union "comrades" without strong evidence.

When the production manager dismissed their appeal, on 31 October, the shaft stewards asked "Tsotsi" Maritz, the hostel manager (AAC/VR:179–81, 1065–66), for permission to hold a meeting on 4 November for "feedback." Mlamli Botha told the Bregman Commission what occurred there:

> We talked to the people as they were upset. We told them that some of them, the workers, had been dismissed as a result of this [Fulscher] incident. We told them further that we tried to represent them to the management to our best, but our appeals were fruitless. We told them now we have come back with this report and we are now waiting for your mandate as you are the people who elected us. . . . We then waited for their mandate. . . . The hall was full, in fact there was even some over-spilling. . . . The people said in that case then we will boycott the liquor outlet, because they did not come to the mine to drink. And that is our own way of punishing the management until it succumbed . . . so that they can . . . cancel the dismissals. (AAC/VR:1066–69)

Thus began the first liquor outlet boycott, described briefly at the end of chapter 5 as evidence of changing attitudes toward alcohol. A more detailed examination of the events of both liquor boycotts (and their consequences) will reveal much about the strengths and limits of contemporary worker resistance to management, divisions among the workers themselves, and management strategies in the face of union struggles to establish a new order on mine compounds in the 1980s.

The November Liquor Boycotts

Perhaps the first point to make about the liquor outlet boycotts at No. 1 is that they were a last-ditch strategy devised by workers out of weakness rather than strength. The most effective way for workers to impress management is to withhold their labor—to strike. "Illegal" wildcat strikes, or even protest assemblies as under the old moral economy, were no longer an option, however, since workers were under a court injunction, and with "legal" strikes one has to show one's hand so far in advance that they are not very effective in redressing local injustices, especially unjust dismissals. In the 1980s, the NUM took several precedent-setting dismissal cases to the Industrial Court (Benjamin 1987), but such cases take years to be resolved while perceived injustices multiply at the local level.

Workers honestly (and erroneously) believed that the liquor outlets earned substantial profits for mine management. Many younger men also self-righteously urged abstention for the drinkers' own good. To those who spoke up at the meeting, then, a liquor outlet boycott would kill several birds at once. Perhaps the heavy drinkers were too busy at the bar to come to the meeting to state their case. Nonetheless, as we have seen, the Mpondo rebels took the decision of the meeting seriously and broke the boycott somewhat reluctantly. Their explanations to Mlamli Botha lacked the conviction and integrity of Seven's earlier strike-breaking action. Nonetheless, their armed action successfully broke the first liquor boycott of 5 November.

Unfortunately for union solidarity, Mlamli Botha was writing his standard seven (ninth-grade) final year examinations immediately after the first bar boycott was broken. Thus he could not attend the meeting that called for a second boycott, on Wednesday, 19 November, which was agreed to without any discussion of the Mpondo conditions. When Botha returned to his room that evening from a day of writing his exams, he was met by a deputation of "elders," consisting of an Mpondo elder, a Baca elder, "and a Bomvana youth," representatives of three of the most belligerent, conservative, and least proletarianized groups on the mine. According to Botha:

> They told me that the liquor outlet had been boycotted. . . . They got me while I was getting out of my room, saying to me that they had been looking for me for quite a time to tell me this . . . [because] there was something that they were not satisfied with. . . . They said they were not satisfied with the boycott, with the closing of the liquor outlet without having been given an opportunity to air their views. . . . [Indeed, they insisted] that I should see to it that the boycott was broken so that people could gain an access to liquor. . . . They complained that . . . at the meeting to boycott the bar for the second time, it was not spoken well of them because of the manner in which they had broken the first boycott; and they were further given a warning [by some workers at the meeting] that if they would break the boycott again some action would be taken against them [indeed, that their lives would be at risk]. (AAC/VR:1086–88, 1998–2006)

Such threats were distinctly at odds with the agreement entered into by the Mpondo with Botha and the other shaft stewards "that whenever there was a general resolution whether it be a strike or a liquor boycott, it should be given a day's grace before it is implemented."

Botha, under pressure to complete his examinations, told them to wait five days, until 24 November, when he would attend to their complaint. The Mpondo elder responded that "as they were keen to go to the liquor outlet they would take up arms and go to the liquor outlet." Botha asked them why they needed to be armed. "You as an elder," he said to the Mpondo, "what sort of example are you setting?" Turning away from Botha, the Mpondo elder said: "All right, we will see what we will do on the 24th about this matter."

It is necessary to stress the import of this meeting with Botha. After the Mpondo "dance team" had broken the 5 November boycott, Mlamli Botha had met with the boycotters and Mpondo and other Xhosa-speaking elders and had persuaded them to apologize at the meeting for their action, as long as the union agreed that future liquor boycott calls would allow drinkers a day to lay in a stock of liquor. Now, the elders themselves were coming to him to complain that the union had not kept its side of the bargain, even though Botha had conveyed to the chair and secretary of the local union branch the message from the Mpondo: "If you take a decision today you skip a day and then you implement" (AAC/VR:2061a). Indeed, the union chair and Mlamli Botha had agreed that "at the next general meeting [Botha would] be given a chance to address the people and explain to them the problem that was faced by the Pondo people, [which had] made them break the earlier liquor boycott." By its precipitous action in ignoring the Mpondo request and simply belaboring the Mpondo at the meeting, the local union succeeded in alienating not only the toughs of the Mpondo dance team but also the entire Mpondo (and much of the Bomvana and Baca) community on the mine.[10] In retrospect, the local union had made a most serious strategic error. At the very least, even in Botha's absence, the other shaft stewards should have raised the terms of their agreement with the Mpondo drinkers for discussion at the meeting.

This time, the Mpondo felt no moral obligation to respect the boycott call, meeting or no meeting. The only sanction now was a threat of coercion from union militants. That threat the Mpondo were happy to meet in their own belligerent style. On Friday, 21 November, armed and clad in the white sheets that constituted Xhosa battle-dress, the Mpondo dance team once again marched into the liquor outlet (unhindered by the mine police) and broke the boycott a second time. Within an hour, a motley group of regular drinkers from various groups on the mine were back at their favorite tables in the outdoor enclosure near the bar.

[10]On Vaal Reefs No. 1 at this time there were relatively few Mpondo—no more than two hundred—but they had not been simply absorbed into the Xhosa-speaking community. Rather, in typical Mpondo style, they maintained an organized identity as Mpondo. Mlamli Botha, for instance, was no traditionalist and shared the union's disdain for the *mtshongolo*, or dance teams, but he seems to have known his Mpondo home fellows quite well. When Matyaba (whom Botha despised in his role of management informer and constant and outright critic of the union) was assaulted after the breakup of the Transkei elections, for instance, he came round in the hospital to find Mlamli Botha praying at his bedside. When Botha was cross-examined on his apparent hypocrisy, he responded simply: "It is not that he was my friend, Sir. Why I went to the hospital is because we come from the same place—he is on my side. . . . [He calls me] home boy" (AAC/VR:1421, 2128).

It is important to note that although they felt justified, in the eyes of the other workers (who knew nothing of the shaft stewards' promise to delay any future boycott for a day) the Mpondo had contravened a community decision, they had broken the respected union umteto. In the words of Sotho worker and ordinary union member, Matsepe Mokheti: "Then the Pondos went to the bar while the rest of the workers had not allowed anybody to go to the bar. . . . And there was no meeting held that the bar is opened. . . . After the decision had been made [the Mpondo] never raised any complaint against the decision which was made to boycott the bar" (AAC/VR:2652, 3675). Mokheti admitted that there was disagreement among the workforce about liquor boycotts: "A certain section of the people was not happy that the boycott had been broken, but there was yet another group which was very happy because all they wanted was to drink" (AAC/VR:3676). Decisions made by union meetings were not always popular, then, but were adhered to, partly out of respect for the consensus, partly in agreement with the larger goals being pursued by the union on behalf of the community, partly from concern about the public condemnation that was sure to be measured out to those who contravened the decision, and partly, of course, from fear of active intimidation.

Clearly, the threats of intimidation would have been far less effective if they had not been made in accordance with the "law" or decisions (the imiteto) of the meeting. As we have noted before, the members of the local branch of the union, whom management regarded as unruly "agitators," were by far the most representative group on the mine, earning respect and representing just and proper order for the large majority of workers—including even the least proletarianized among them. Furthermore, for most workers, local management had lost any shred of legitimacy and maintained its hegemony by notching up the level of coercion to extract the barest consent from most of its black employees. It was in the distinct interest of local management to try to rid the mine of those "union agitators" who were undermining its authority and, in its opinion, leading the majority of workers astray. The discontent of the Mpondo and other heavy drinkers certainly represented potential divisions among workers within the compound, barely papered over by union imiteto, although we should note that a similar liquor boycott at No. 9 compound lasted for many weeks.

As we saw in the previous chapter, "Tsotsi" Maritz had tried to use Sotho ethnic solidarities to break the union in March. When that effort backfired, no action was taken against him nor were security officials implicated for their part in fomenting it. Maybe Maritz really did believe that the Mpondo position represented that of the silent majority of workers at No. 1. At any rate, Mpondo grievances against the union surely represented an opportunity for a local management intent on union breaking.

The Hunt for Shaft Stewards

Between six and seven in the evening of 21 November, the day the Mpondo from the rooms of the dance team "opened" the bar at Vaal Reefs No. 1, someone—almost certainly a shaft steward with "comradely" sympathies (AAC/VR:2353–58)—lobbed a petrol bomb over the roof of the bar and into the drinking enclosure. The trousers of a Sotho drinker caught fire but were soon extinguished. The armed Mpondo at once burst out of the liquor outlet and, having terrorized the audience in the cinema nearby, began a systematic room by room search for shaft stewards and other union activists. That night, Ernest Kang, the Sotho chief shaft steward, was beaten up by the armed group.

The other shaft stewards and union militants changed quickly out of their union T-shirts, and most of them chose not to sleep in their beds that night. Mlamli Botha, for instance, slept in the mine married quarters (the *skomplas*), having been called by a friend while underground on the night shift. His friend warned him that the Mpondo were on the warpath, met him when he emerged from the mine, and provided him with an armed escort to safety in the married quarters. The next morning, Botha returned to the compound to lodge a complaint about the shaft steward hunt with "Tsotsi" Maritz, the compound manager (AAC/VR:1222–24). He told Maritz that he had not slept the previous night and asked for protection. Characteristically, according to Botha, the compound manager responded evasively and in a manner certain to encourage fighting:

> [H]e was unable to offer any protection, I should just defend myself. I asked him . . . "If you do not offer any protection, do you actually believe that the shaft stewards are responsible for these incidents?" He said that he does not blame the shaft stewards, [it] is only the Pondos that are blaming the shaft stewards, and he said that there was nothing he was going to do for me.

Several witnesses reported that the "Mpondo" (by now supplemented with other Xhosa-speaking toughs) claimed that they had immunity from management in their harassing of shaft stewards. Certainly, all witnesses agreed that the entire black compound staff chose to ignore the shaft steward hunt going on in full view for a couple of days. In fact, at least three hostel police actually joined the Mpondo gang in the search for shaft stewards. Matsepe Mokheti's evidence is most clear on this point, although it was supported by the evidence of at least two other witnesses. In an interesting interchange, Mokheti testified as follows:

Q: Tell us how you know that the Hostel Manager was aware of the hunt for the shaft stewards?

MOKHETI: Because I was standing next to the boot store . . . while Ndlovu was still chasing Tankiso. . . . [A]t that time [the compound manager] was still standing in front of his office in the compound office block. . . .

Q: Was Ndlovu alone or was he with a group of people?

MOKHETI: There was just a few because some of the other people were on the other blocks chasing Mahamba. . . .

Q: Did Ndlovu catch Tankiso?

MOKHETI: I do not know whether he cought hold of him because I also ran away and took a different direction.[11]

Q: And do you believe, or are you sure that the Hostel Manager saw this chase?

MOKHETI: Yes, I saw him standing with his Mtetelelis [black personnel staff] outside the office. . . .

Q: Were there other inmates around there just witnessing the occasion?

MOKHETI: Yes, they were standing there witnessing and Mahamba even shouted that he should be supported: "Workers support". . . [but] he never got any assistance, they just looked at him.

Mokheti not only claimed to have seen the compound manager with his staff watching the hunt for shaft stewards, but he also said that compound policemen had joined the Mpondo in the chase. To Mokheti, this implied official support:

Q: Now you have mentioned, and of course these names have also been mentioned in evidence, that [three of the hostel policemen] were in fact in the group of the Pondos and Bacas who were searching for shaft stewards? Now these are considered in the hostel by the inmates to be men of the law, that is officials, being hostel police. You will agree with me that those are the people least expected to be joining forces with a dangerous group as the Pondos and Bacas searching for shaft stewards.

MOKHETI: Yes, according to the law, . . . [t]hey were supposed to have reported it. (AAC/VR:3968–77)

[11]In fact, according to a union representative on the commission: "Tankiso was caught and wounded. . . . He was stabbed with a spear at the back" (AAC/VR:3970).

Once again, the "law" is mentioned in the evidence to this commission. This time it was the old "law" of management, which management itself was contravening. Indeed, one might make the case that the notion of what is lawful, and, the different levels of agreement and dispute about what is lawful, was an important theme uniting the testimony of all the different compound dwellers on No. 1, whatever their affiliations. It seems clear from worker evidence to Bregman that the threat to order on the compound was neither random factional ethnic hatred, nor union agitation, but rather local compound management and its black cronies, who chose to contravene their own imiteto in the interest of reestablishing their control of the compound.[12] Its own structures of authority, already in tatters, were simply ignored by management in this instance.

Maritz, in fact, told the commission that he was not in the compound that Saturday afternoon at all but at home. An unreliable witness, he did say that he was called three times by his black staff, who reported that the Mpondo were fighting in the compound, but he did nothing. Mine security patrolled the compound in their armored vehicles several times but claimed they could not pin anything on anyone, since Maritz permitted workers to wander around armed with sticks in his compound. Herman Fouche, the head of the mine security force, confirmed in his evidence that he had been to No. 1 compound several times on the Saturday. He went to the liquor outlet:

> Well immediately a group of about fifteen of them came forward, I introduced myself to them, I told them what I am doing there. I asked them what is the problem in the liquor outlet because I received a report there is a fight, is anybody injured, what is going on. And they told me to leave them alone, they are just drinking there, paying with their own money, not the money of the National Union of Mineworkers. . . . [Some of them were wearing

[12]Nine months after the events here described, on 17 August 1987, in the midst of the three-week long 1987 strike, a shaft steward at Vaal Reefs No. 1 mentioned in a handwritten message to the NUM head office:

> Mr. de Graeve [the shaft personnel officer] stated that the blacks won't go on strike because he organised the faction fight instead. . . . He is also refusing to re-employ people who were dismissed during the faction [fight] which took place in December 1986. He is also claiming to be the manager at Vaal Reefs East and Mr. Dicks [who was general manager at the time] has nothing to do [that is, he has no authority]. . . . The Section Manager Mr. J. Fulsher [*sic*] claims that the NUM members . . . cannot get promotion as long as they are still members. (CTH, Reel 1, C3)

The note also named other members of local management as intimidating workers on strike. Apparently, nine months later, local management was still celebrating its success in breaking the union by fomenting the 1986 faction fights and reimposing its own despotic imiteto on the compound.

> sheets, and] there were a few of them with sticks which did not bother me much because it is quite common on this mine that black people traditionally carry sticks with them. (AAC/VR: 410–25)

The white sheets did bother Fouche, however, and he called out the mine security's armored vehicles to tour around the compound. The Xhosa-speaking sub-induna, who was himself a participant in the hunt for shaft stewards, told Bregman that white security guards in those patrolling vehicles had instructed workers standing around to "kill the shaft stewards" (AAC/VR:3052–71).[13] Several witnesses agreed with him.

The Sotho worker, Mokheti, had heard that the plan to eliminate the shaft stewards was originally hatched right after the failure of the first bar boycott and initially included dance teams from both the Mpondo and Sotho groups (AAC/VR:3932–46, 3953–55). If so, it is difficult to imagine that local management was not aware of what was going on and did not at the very least agree to look away. Dance teams were widely regarded as management men by union supporters on the mines, and the armed groups who roamed the compound were undoubtedly claiming management sanction. Apparently, they said they had six days' dispensation from management to clean up the shaft stewards. It is unlikely that the Mpondo elders who were put off by Mlamli Botha on 19 November did not go to management with their complaint. Even if there was no earlier plot with management, as elders they would almost certainly have fallen back on the old authority structure when the union let them down. Maritz was either extraordinarily incompetent or, at the very least, knew what was going on and chose to look the other way. Indeed, both his testimony and that of the workers inclines one to believe that he was both incompetent and devious.

Whatever the overt involvement of local white management and the mine security forces, there can be no doubt that black representatives of the old induna system were deeply implicated in the Mpondo dancers' effort to rid the compound of the shaft stewards who threatened their own power as well as that of white management. Furthermore, if the Xhosa sub-induna and several other black witnesses are to be believed, they definitely acted in the conviction that local management would protect them.

[13]Actually, in his evidence the Xhosa sub-induna said that the instructions from the security vehicles were issued on Friday night, but this directly contradicts the evidence of H. H. Fouche, and Saturday evening seems more likely to have been the time this occurred, especially given Mokheti's account of similar instructions that same night from security after they had fetched the body of Patrick Masela, who was killed in an incident discussed below.

Months later, Mlamli Botha reported: "we are told that at the work situation where these dancing [Mpondo] work, they [have been bragging] that it is nice to murder somebody . . . and [they have not been] arrested or apprehended by the police" (AAC/VR:2077a).

The dancers' comment "it is nice to murder somebody" refers to an assault that occurred on the night of Saturday, 22 November. Two men were killed, Patrick Masela, a Xhosa speaker from the Western Transkei, who was not a shaft steward but "was always among [them]" and led the songs at union meetings, and Alton Mhlamvu, a Zulu-speaking shaft steward who also sang with the "comrades." Mhlamvu was killed in the street in the skomplas, the mine village for married couples, and there is little evidence about how he died. We know more about the killing of Patrick Masela.

Masela's wife was actually visiting the mine at the time of his death. She was staying at the visiting wives center in the skomplas, when "a mob of people" came there on Saturday "with the intention of getting to grips with her husband and herself":

> [They] were scattering all other residents of the hostel in different directions, . . . actually chasing all people on their way to the [skomplas]. . . . As she was standing not far from the entrance to the centre she also turned around running . . . and in [the] process she fell. . . . Shortly before that her husband had been running towards her away from the [armed] mob. . . . [He ran] past her, past the gate to the centre, and away into the middle of the [skomplas]. . . . Some moments later when she was in Room 4 at the centre [where she and Patrick Masela were staying during her visit], this group came back [but] did not find her there. . . . [They] did not walk into the house, but made enquiries from neighbours. (AAC/VR:3633–38)

Masela, perhaps to protect his wife, eventually made his way back to the compound and settled down in the bed of a friend who was a Bazalwana (a Xhosa-speaking group of ardent Christians) in a Bazalwana room and went to sleep, perhaps thinking that the "room of prayer" might serve as a sanctuary (AAC/VR:3680–96). Unfortunately for him, none of the praying Christians were in the room when he was discovered by a hostel resident who immediately went to fetch the armed hunters. Apparently, Masela, cornered on the stairs, fought back vigorously, but he was battered to death in a most gruesome fashion. Maritz and Fouche came with an ambulance to take away the body. White security men moved about from room to room, ostensibly investigating but instead, according to Matsepe Mokheti, "asking us why we were not chasing the shaft stewards" (AAC/

VR:3693–94). Some answered, because "they are our representatives," but most made no reply. That night Mokheti did not sleep. Instead, he said, he was "sitting, watching [for] what [was] going to happen."

November 23: Faction Fight

Shaft steward searches in the skomplas must have continued that night, because Alton Mhlamvu was later killed in the street there. No doubt few of the compound residents slept very well. Like Mokheti, they were waiting. Next morning, on Sunday, 23 November, the groups of Xhosa speakers who had been hunting for shaft stewards left through the back gate of the compound, near the liquor outlet, for one last thorough house-to-house search of the skomplas. They were armed and clad in white sheets and said as they left that "all people who 'tete' [speak with clicks], that means all Xhosa speaking people," should join them (AAC/VR:3706). Those who stayed in the compound, they said, would be dealt with on their return.

Apparently, at this point the "Mpondo" hunt for shaft stewards took on a consciously ethnic dimension. Sotho were explicitly excluded from the last stages of the attack on shaft stewards. The reasons for the shift are somewhat obscure, but the Xhosa mine policeman who participated in the shaft steward hunt, when asked to explain it said simply: "I do not know why the Sothos did not attack the shaft stewards because the incident started at the liquor outlet" (AAC/VR: 2958). Thus perhaps Xhosa speakers resented the fact that they had been left to do the dirty work for the entire multiethnic band of drinkers whose peace had been disturbed by the petrol bomb, or perhaps they were unhappy that they had been left to break the liquor boycott alone. Also, perhaps it was Sotho-speaking "comrades" who had disrupted the drinking in October when management violently hoisted everybody early. In addition, of course, Sotho looting of Xhosa-speakers' lockers during the March faction fight, described in the previous chapter, still rankled with the Mpondo, who now had management support and were no doubt determined to right that perceived wrong.

Some other Xhosa speakers followed the leaders to the skomplas, numbering by the end about four hundred persons. Back in the compound, the *amapantsula* (urban "spivs" [James 1991:72–75] who worked on the mines and had no ethnic allegiances) began to slip away out of windows, a sure sign that ethnic violence was about to begin (AAC/VR:2892–93, 3772). The Sotho armed hastily (AAC/VR:3747–3828, 2889–2973). At this point, they were joined by the many Xhosa speakers who had chosen not to go to the skomplas and who therefore also felt threatened by the return of the vengeful Mpondo-led mob. Having set a guard at the liquor outlet gate, this armed group ("most of the Sothos . . . a big group") waited silently just inside the main gate of the compound for the return of the "Mpondo." "There was no whistle blown, we were standing there . . . only standing there, guarding," said Mokheti. "When they entered the hostel they found us standing next to room 16. . . . We wanted only to see whether it [was] true that we were going to be attacked together with the Xhosas that remained with us" (AAC/VR:3742, 3749).

Returning from the skomplas, as they came through the gate, the vanguard of the Xhosa-speaking group saw the armed and largely Sotho crowd standing and waiting. At once, one of the Mpondo sounded on his horn, the Sotho responded with a whistle, and the two groups ran toward one another and met in a flurry of action. Two Xhosa speakers died on the spot, and the "Mpondo" withdrew, encircled the compound, and entered again at the liquor outlet gate, which one of the mine policemen[14] opened for them. At this point, for reasons that are obscure, the Xhosa who had been left in the compound switched sides and drove the Sotho out of the hostel.

The mine security officers arrived and placed their armored vehicles at the hostel gate, effectively keeping the Sotho from retaliating. Fouche, the chief security officer, entered the compound and found armed and white-sheeted Mpondo immediately inside the gate and a motley group of Xhosa speakers farther back. For the rest of the night, members of the mine security patrolled the compound and escorted out to the Sotho group other workers who had barricaded themselves into their rooms when the fight started. Meanwhile, the Mpondo systematically raided the lockers of the Sotho. According to Fouche:

> [W]e heard noises in various rooms. Breaking open lockers, that was the sort of noise we heard. . . . [T]hey did it most professionally I would say because they had a guard outside warning them when we are nearing the room and they just ran away into the group. At that stage I was of the opinion that this is some criminal, purely criminal element, who is taking the opportunity to enrich themselves while everything is in chaos. . . . [So] I went to this Xhosa/Pondo group—because there were no ways that the security force I had inside could protect each and every room. You again need an army for that. We tried. But I then went to the Xhosas and Pondos and said "Now listen, whilst you people sort of

[14]Apparently, he was a Mosotho who had been an assistant induna and was much respected. Some Basotho were out to get him afterward, but others believed that he had been assured by the Xhosa sub-induna that the Xhosa would not fight (AAC/VR:3816).

> see yourself in control of the hostel inside [in comparison] with the Sothos, I would like you to help us to stop these criminals from stealing other peoples' belongings." I was then told by the Xhosas and Pondos that "Oh no, we are just taking back what was taken from us during March." (AAC/VR:485–89)

In the morning, when everyone was marched by security to the adjacent soccer stadium, the Sotho were understandably upset about having been locked out of the compound and having had to hear their lockers being smashed for much of the night. They also feared that their antagonists, disarmed in the soccer stadium, would have hidden weapons in the hostel to use at a later date. Eventually, however, they reluctantly agreed to make peace. Everyone was searched on the way back into the compound, and the next day, while workers were underground, security and the mine police broke open locked lockers and searched thoroughly for weapons. Fouche gave graphic testimony:

> We have found weapons—now this is all sorts of weapons varying from sticks to pangas—in the lockers we have found, where the lockers were pushed against the wall, there we found weapons. We found weapons hidden away in the chimney of the stoves of the rooms. We found weapons under the top of the stainless steel tables in the room, especially pangas, the sharp end, the point of the blade was stuck into the opening you know where the table and the frame meets. . . . Where there were, for instance in the rooms where you have got these wooden poles going across, on top of that we found. Under the beds, under the mattresses we found. On the toilets, at the urinal, the flushing bin on top has got little small self-tap screws on, we removed the screws and opened and found many many pangas lying in the water, in the flush there. . . . Where there were double stories with the gutter running on the top, we took it out of the gutter. We took dangerous weapons off the roofs. We monitored the ground and we saw where the ground has been disturbed and we dug there and we took out weapons. Overalls hanging in trees, hanging on the washing-line we found weapons hooked onto the hanger, inside the trousers of the overalls. We found weapons hidden away in the arena. Weapons in long grass. (AAC/VR:509–19)

Security filled more than one dump-truck load with weapons found in and around No. 1 that day. For twelve days, an uneasy calm descended on the compound.

December 6: Faction Fight

On 5 December, a different faction fight, this time between the Mpondo and a combination of Xhosa and Sotho, started on the neighboring compound at No. 2 shaft. It seems that the Mpondo dance team initiated the conflict on that compound as well, but there are few details. Refugees poured into No. 1 compound. On the night of 6 December, a fight started in the liquor outlet at No. 1, apparently because a Sotho accosted an Mpondo wearing a shirt he claimed had been taken from his locker on 23 November. At once, the Xhosa and Mpondo attacked the Sotho in No. 1 compound and drove them out through the main gate. The Xhosa speakers conducted mopping-up operations throughout the compound. Nine persons were killed, seven of them Sotho and one Tswana and one Baca. The Sotho had been taken by surprise. They were scared to return to the compound, and when management gave all who refused to work the ultimatum of going home, it was Sotho who availed themselves of the opportunity. Two-thirds of the seven hundred–odd workers who resigned were Sotho, whereas only about 7 percent of the Xhosa speakers left the mine.

The Bregman Commission heard insufficient testimony on the 6 December affair at No. 1 to enable careful analysis.[15] We have only two full accounts of the events, those of Fouche (AAC/VR:525–50) and Matsepe Mokheti (AAC/VR:3845–22). While neither could explain how the fighting began, episodes from the stories of each of them once again cast doubt on primordial explanations of such "tribal" strife.

Mokheti reported that although the Sotho were not happy about the way security had handled the 23 November affair, they certainly had not expected trouble on 6 December. When the Mpondo attacked, some of the Sotho were asleep, others were in the change houses—"we were divided, we were scattered." People ran away, jumping walls and diving through windows. Mokheti, who was cornered in the quadrangle at Section 13, watched a compatriot being butchered. Another was already lying dead beside him. Mokheti himself escaped by slipping down a side passage—and then he got away only because of the kindness of one of the Mpondo:

> I managed to go through that passage because one Pondo called Goduka stopped these people from attacking me and then I was able to manage to go through that passage. . . . I believe they would have killed me. . . . [Goduka was not a personal friend of mine, but I did help him] by sewing his pair of trousers and [he] did not have any money so [I] told him to forget the debt. . . . [He] went through that passage with me and . . . he instructed me to run. . . . I ran. . . . [Indeed] because I was terrified I knocked against a drum which was full of coal [and] I fell. . . . There were no people

[15]Perhaps, knowing the Sotho resentment, the Xhosa speakers had planned a preemptive strike. As is so often the case with the history of faction fights, the evidence is simply insufficient to understand the motives for the fight.

> chasing me from behind but now in the direction of the kitchen there was a group coming. . . . They were in pursuit of me. . . . I pulled my blanket and I started running . . . in the direction of the Skittle Alley where I found a group of Basuto there . . . who were walking in the direction of the main gate. (AAC/VR:3851–53)

Thus did Mokheti's "sideline," and the generosity with which he practised it, save his life. Never a coward, once he was out of the compound, he joined the group of Sotho workers who went round to the liquor outlet gate and started to throw stones over the roof at the Xhosa speakers within.

This account of Mokheti's rescue again provides an example of the contextual nature of collective violence (see chapter 6). Fouche, the security officer, who fully accepted primordial accounts of "tribal" violence, was astonished, however, when those Sotho who had opted to resign from the mine were escorted into the compound to collect their belongings:

> I assured [the Mpondo] that these people do only want to fetch their belongings, they are under our protection and anybody attacking them has got to deal with us. I also warned them that if I see but one weapon I am going to arrest the person. And I told the Sothos which I was about to take in to lay down their arms before they go in which they did. And I told them how we are going to do it. . . . I told them that they must always keep me in eye, when I stop they must stop, and when they come to a room they must tell me so and we will take some security officers to escort that three or four people to that room and this actually happened. When we entered the hostel I did not see one weapon, I did not see people moving around. As a matter of fact they were all sitting. . . . And I really could not understand it, up to today I cannot understand it. When those Sothos went out of that hostel they greeted some of the Pondos and Xhosas with their hand when they walked out with their belongings. Do not ask me why, I just cannot clarify it. They were friends, they were really friends in the hostel when we took them in. . . . [A] man coming out of the room with his . . . goods in a bundle in a blanket over his shoulder, he will go to a man who is sitting in the hostel who must be a Pondo or a Xhosa, talking to him, shaking hands and leaving. I saw a lot of them doing it. (AAC/VR:547–48)

After all the fuss about lockers being broken into, Fouche was not willing to take any chances this time around. As soon as he was in effective occupation of the compound, he announced that anyone breaking into a locker would be shot on the spot. He need not have worried: "I was then told by the Pondos 'Do not worry, we will not do it. We already had our revenge,' and they did not do it" (AAC/VR:546). For all their fearsome and brutal power, the Mpondo still acted with their own idea of integrity, according to what they perceived to be just.

Conclusion

That is an appropriate moment to leave Vaal Reefs No. 1, because what is perhaps most interesting about the Bregman testimony is the extent to which, even in the midst of the chaos of "tribal" or "racial" strife, a wider sense of social order prevailed. Collective violence, in this case, and I would submit in almost all cases, is not free-floating, uncontrollable, or indiscriminate. Instead, as I have argued at length in chapter 6, it is focused, strategic, and deliberate, for all the powerful sense of solidarity that fuels it.

What is most surprising about the South African mine evidence, however, is the cogency of the sense of order that continues to structure compound life. Compounds have been presumed to be tinderboxes for conflict rooted in the alienation of the "inmates" (Leatt et al. 1986). The increase in alcoholism on the mines certainly implies that conditions are worse than they used to be before the 1970s, but recurring mentions of "law" in testimony from mine workers themselves indicates that there are countervailing factors. In fact, perhaps the most important everyday function of the National Union of Mineworkers is to generate "laws" (imiteto), which hold workers accountable and bind them to a common purpose, at the same time that it represents their interests to management. Management reactions are increasingly seen as despotic and arbitrary, "lawless" in both policy and practice. The law of the union, on the other hand, is representative because it is generated from the "meeting," and respect for the decisions of the "meeting" extends even to those who dislike their effects.

Of course, the consensus form of participatory democracy, which worked so well in selection of izibonda and in election of iindlavini "chiefs," can suppress dissent and lead to intimidation by larger groups. On the one hand, those of us whose own practices presuppose an intense degree of individualism have to be careful not to overlook the communitarian sense in which African mine workers may willingly (if not always eagerly) accept decisions that they personally dislike for what is perceived to be the common good. Solidarity and "laws" establish important settings for strategy in the struggle for power and have always done so on the mines.

On the other hand, a stress on decisions of "meetings" as "lawful" also has the potential to paper over real structural (even systemic) divisions and differences of interest that may emerge later as dangerously disruptive—especially in situations where outside powers consciously exploit such divisions to further their own interests. Division is an important strategy in the maintenance of control. However, management was beginning to discover that the exacerbation of ethnic divisions on the mines could have seriously deleterious effects on production. It is clear from minutes of meetings held with branch and national representatives of the NUM after the 6 December fight (AAC/VR:11/12/86; 14/12/86) that top management panicked at the massive loss of experienced Sotho workers who chose to leave the mine. Indeed, with the decay of the old compound manager-induna system, as a matter of policy and of fact, the union has become management's only recourse as its downward communication system disintegrates. Workers (whether or not they were paid-up members of the union) regularly rejected unrepresentative consultative committees and the contemporary isibonda system as means of representation.

Anglo American top management wanted a working relationship with the union. However, such a relationship implied a different and much more democratic philosophy of line management at the local level than had ever existed on the mines before.[16] Power sharing, which is time-consuming and may interfere temporarily with production, does not come easily to mine managers accustomed to absolute rule and even less easily to local white and black officials and security officers—not to mention their buddies in the South African police. But the old days when management could impose imiteto and force workers to strategize within the parameters of management authority have gone for good—if they ever existed in pure form. Unionized African mine workers have created new imiteto among themselves. These new "laws" are entrenched in the (more or less) open debate of union meetings, which empower shaft stewards to talk back to managers and demand compromises from them. As we have seen, such a democratic style is anathema to old-style local managements (many perceive it as revolutionary agitation), and they do their best to manipulate latent divisions to disrupt the union. The problem for local managers is that if they are successful in using conservative workers to challenge union organization the resulting chaos makes rational management impossible.

Anglo American's intransigence in the face of the massive 1987 strike may be seen as an effort by the Anglo head office to establish the limits of a new, acceptable hegemony. In the words of Bobby Godsell, group industrial relations consultant at Anglo American: "Though [the 1987 strike] was indeed a conflict about wages, . . . it was not only a conflict about wages. I think both sides saw this as a strike that was about power

[16]There was one brief period after World War I, when the white unions shared some power until management forced the 1922 strike.

as well'' (Benjamin, Jacobus, and Albertyn 1989:99). While the new hegemony might accommodate a union culture that was determined to be vigilant on unfair dismissals and safety issues and with its own imiteto, and that might even permit a level of codetermination, management could not afford (and was certainly unwilling) to allow full-fledged ''workers' control.'' In fact, however, the intervention of a new systemic contingency—the collapse in the price of gold—will probably be as effective as NUM's strike defeat in setting the limits for the new hegemonic compromise. This development may well have strengthened management's resolve in breaking the strike. For management, it was perhaps better to force direct confrontation in order to establish the rules for a new hegemony than to continue to make concessions in the face of the growing accumulation crisis.

After the 1987 strike, union membership went up substantially on Anglo American mines (Crush, Jeeves, and Yudelman 1991:189) according to management figures. According to the union, local management constraints on union activity in 1988 were tighter than they had ever been (NUM 1988). An initiative for a more cooperative hegemony (legitimation in the form of a code of conduct) came from top management in 1990. Only time will tell whether it has had the clout to make it stick at the local level. In 1991, both management and union were sobered by the impact of continued poor gold prices. On the systemic level, representatives of the union were arguing for major restructuring of the industry (Leger and Nicol n.d.). No restructuring will work, however, unless the union's imiteto (or at least a new cooperative set of rules) can replace the despotism of local management. Structural reforms are mere talk unless they are implemented on the level of agency. To initiate reform, the companies need strong principled union leaders, new men of integrity. But these were precisely the men who were being discarded through selective dismissals and retrenchments. Mlamli Botha became chief shaft steward at No. 1 before management fired him, for instance.

The union may not be able to guarantee peace and order on the compound—nor should it, given its charge to represent workers boldly—but the despotic alternative will lead to simmering disorder and poor productivity. On the mines, ''boys'' have finally become men. Will white management be able to adjust to the new order, or will it simply abandon the opportunity of cooperation in the name of control?

The question is bigger than the mining industry alone, but the mining industry has historically been a bellwether for the rest of the country. It seems to me that the events at Vaal Reefs No. 1 might well help us understand the violence in Natal since the mid-1980s and the violence in the

Transvaal townships in the 1990s. In both these cases, conservative Nguni (in the Inkatha case, Zulu) rural elders and migrant hostel-dwellers seem to have initiated the violence, with the collaboration of the KwaZulu police in Natal and active encouragement from, if not the sanction of, the South African police in the Transvaal. In a very real sense, Inkatha avowedly represents the old order in South Africa, with its homeland leader indunas and its ethnic police—and its rural-based integrity now directed against an ANC-inspired order in the name of an old order whose time has come. As on the mines, there is something tragic about the way in which migrant cultures, which for so long provided insulation against the temptations of proletarianization, now wreak violence and disruption in the name of order (Haysom 1986). The greater tragedy is that initially in response, but now in random violence, in many townships urban "comrades" are terrorizing ordinary people in the name of "discipline." One may hope that, as on the mines, they too will recognize the authority of democratically decided "law," the imiteto of grassroots "meetings," when and if democratic rights are granted to black South Africans.

If this book has achieved its purpose, it has demonstrated beyond doubt that black mine workers have always presented a challenge to those who have hired them. Of course, part of the challenge in the past was moot because they needed each other, those fierce proud men of the countryside and their gold-tipped employers, but the challenge remained because most mine workers simply refused to be lackeys on tight leashes. Now the men of the union are replacing the men of migrant cultures, but many remain men of integrity, with shared understandings of democratic processes and a new moral order established by the achievement of consensus in public meetings.

What then may we say about "integrity?" My use of the notion of integrity has grown out of my own reflection on black miners' accounts of their lives. I have since discovered a parallel social scientific use of the term, by Kenelm Burridge in *New Heaven, New Earth* (1969), in the context of an analysis of millenarian activities:

> Qualities of integrity . . . are secreted in the modes of exploitation of material resources, in the ways in which such exploitation is accorded approval, esteem, influence and power; they are demonstrated by prescribed behaviour in selected areas and arenas of social life. When integrity is ill-defined, or unattainable, qualities of conscience—upon which a moral order ultimately depends—become correspondingly vitiated and random. When this happens the bases of power become random and unordered. When assumptions about power are in doubt, when the redemptive process is in

> doubt, when the prestige system is in doubt, then integrity is in doubt. And when integrity is in doubt, a new man—born of new assumptions, a new redemptive process, and a new prestige system—becomes necessary. (Burridge 1969:96)

Migrant cultures, I argue, historically maintained for mine migrants their integrity in Burridge's sense. The crisis of hegemony that came about on the mines with the shift to proletarian labor and the demise of migrant cultures was also a crisis of integrity—hence, perhaps, the millenarian overtones in support for the National Union of Mineworkers, and the note of bewilderment with which some of the old men of integrity were eventually moved to defy the union.

Contemporary workers who are completely dependent upon wage labor, who perhaps migrate to the mines from tiny, unproductive lots in rural slums, have no "home" in which to practice tiro, no umzi to build. They are simply workers. For them, because wage labor is their life, the conditions of work and relations at work, both with management and with fellow workers, take on a different meaning. For them, the National Union of Mineworkers is much more than a means to a rural end. For them, the trade union *is* a home of a sort.

There is plenty of room for misunderstanding between rural proprietors and the rural and urban dispossessed. An urban young man told Catherine Campbell (1991:12) in Durban (totally misunderstanding the integrity of migrant cultures and the moral economy that they supported):

> On the farms [meaning rural homesteads] they think they have got nothing to fight for. They have their own cow, their own space, their own chief. And they think that they have got everything they could dream of—such a person knows nothing about their rights, about the needs of black people—such is content to be an oppressed labourer.

For those traditional migrant homesteaders who continue to work on the mines, however, political strikes and demonstrations, instead of being an expression of workplace solidarity may seem an interference with the seizure of wages for their rural projects (although all workers stand together in supporting the NUM on its opposition to arbitrary dismissals and retrenchments). There was an authenticity about Seven's strike-breaking activities, for instance, which emerged again in the Mpondo exacting only what they perceived to be their fair share of loot from Sotho lockers. Nor was the manner in which the Mpondo defied the second liquor boycott on No. 1 totally disrespectful of the authority of the union meeting.

Now that the material basis for migrant cultures is finally disappearing (but unevenly, with all sorts of consequences) the NUM has a high calling and responsibility. Its members look to it not only to improve conditions and wages (mmereko), but also to inspire a meaningful communal culture, a set of rules (imiteto), to replace the one being lost. Trade union organization in South Africa, if it is to be true to its members, must nurture and struggle for worker integrity that is counterhegemonic within the system of wage labor itself. If the union's notion of socialism does not include this deeper moral meaning, then it is being untrue to the history of migrants' struggle. Testimony from many union members evinces a fierce loyalty to their organization, a practice of integrity that goes well beyond material interests to a union culture that defines social responsibility in new terms.[17] In this sense, the National Union of Mineworkers is indeed a redemptive organization, not only redefining what it means to be a man but also seeking wider worker solidarity in the name of a new, specifically democratic, social order on the mines.

There is an irony here, because the new manhood of union solidarity is accompanied by a new conception of womanhood whose greater dependency points to a brittle fragility in the new male integrity. The old men knew that they achieved their purposes only in partnership with women who were faithful to their complementary goals. There was mutual respect. It is much less clear how the new order defines manhood in relation to women. According to Mamphele Ramphele (1989), the old patriarchal order is invoked to establish a new, more despotic patriarchalism, with the erosion of women's old material base in rural production. New patterns of gender differentiation and new experiences of alienation for both men and women now seem implicit in migrancy (Sharp and Spiegel 1991). Because of these ramifications, the NUM militantly opposes the migrant labor system.

A new struggle has broken out on new terrain, however similar it looks to the old. In the old days, young men might become "women" on the mines, but there was mutual respect among men and between men and women because they shared common goals and complemented each other, however unequally, in achieving them (or "sold out," became amatshipa, and settled down to mine or town ways). In the new life-worlds on the mines, men are bound to one another through the union, but women, whether in town or country, have become simple dependents of the men, whether they exploit their sexuality in marriage or a series of relationships. The complementarity of traditional male and female roles, ruled

[17]For an account of a union cooperative that evidenced the practice of such integrity in a Natal manufacturing industry, see Bonnin and Sitas 1988; see also Iris Berger's accounts (1992) of the early years of the Garment Workers' Union and the Food and Canning Workers' Union after the Second World War.

though it was by patriarchy, has given way to much more overt conflict and mutual exploitation. The new politics of production has given rise to a new family politics that implies a more nuclear family and a crisis of hegemony for male domination. Here again, as with the wider crisis of low gold prices for the mining economy, AIDS may present a wider reproductive crisis for men and women alike in South Africa. Here, however, we move well beyond the scope even of this wide-ranging book.

Glossary of African Words and Technical Terms

African personal assistant (PA) Black official. Position created in the middle 1960s to investigate underground complaints. High school graduate (also called *masiza*).

amanene Members of "respectable" class, usually salaried with a high school education.

amapantsula Youthful urban "spivs" or flashily dressed "toughs."

amaqaba Xhosa for traditional individuals, non-Christian with slight if any schooling (often translated as "red blanket" or "red"; also *nombola*).

amashweshwe Plural form of *ishweshwe.*

amatshipa Nguni for those who have abandoned country ways, absconded to urban life.

baba Sotho for father (term of address as in "papa").

boss boy Black supervisor of underground work team (now called "team leader").

comrade Youthful militant, usually township based.

dagga Marijuana.

development Process of opening up new haulage tunnels underground.

face Front of stope.

fanakalo Nguni-based pidgin used to give commands at work.

fokisi (Afr. *fokkies*) Underground controller or overseer of black labor.

gangisa Tsonga for *ukumetsha.*

hanging Roof of stope.

haulage Underground tunnel from shaft to stope.

hlobongo Zulu for *ukumetsha.*

home boy Someone from one's own home district. Usually rendered "home fellow" in the text.

igubura Mpondo age-set for traditional young men (*amaqaba, nombola*).
iindlavini Plural form of *indlavini.*
imikhukhu Plural form of *umkhukhu.*
imiteto Plural form of *umteto.*
imizi Plural form of *umzi.*
impathi Chief.
impimpi Informer.
indlavini Member of age-set for young men (Mpondo, Baca, Xesibe) with elementary education and Christian church attachment who has retained aspiration to rural homestead proprietorship.
indoda Xhosa for man.
induna Head black official in the compound; one induna would be appointed for each "tribal" group. (Now called "unit supervisor"—technically merely an administrator without ethnic function.)
inkontshane See *nkhontxana.*
inkosi Nguni for lord, chief.
ishweshwe Xhosa for mistress, a regular female lover to whom a man pays some support.
isibonda Elected room representative on compound.
isithandwa Xhosa for lover.
izibonda Plural form of *isibonda.*
izithandwa Plural for *isithandwa.*
jumper Metal bit one to four feet in length used to drill rock.
kaffir A slang insult, equivalent to "nigger."
khali Powerful brew made in illegal stills.
layisha (Eng. lash) To load or shovel rock underground.
lekholoa Sesotho for one who has abandoned country ways or absconded to urban life.
lifela Free-style songs composed by Sotha men and women to give expression to the experiences of everyday life.
lobola Nguni for bridewealth.
maqabane Militant activists; "comrades."
marewu A porridge-like beverage with a yeasty flavor.
masiza Black personnel assistant (PA).
maximum average system Agreement between mining houses enforced by recruitment agencies that dictated that average black wages on individual mines could not exceed a fixed maximum.
mmereko Setswana for wage work (from the Afr. *werk*).
morena Sotho for lord.
muti Medicine.

nkhontxana Tsonga for lover (also used as adjective for relationship).
nombola Equivalent to *amaqaba.*
nongogo Prostitute, woman who sells herself for money.
oonongogo Plural form of *nongogo.*
pangela To work for the whites (Xhosa). Derived from the root to "seize" or "grab."
picannin Literally, "small boy." A black man who works as a personal attendant or aide for a white miner.
police boy Black policeman appointed by management to maintain order on the mine (answers to *induna*—now called "tribal representative").
shaft sinking Process of drilling vertical shaft to open up a deep-level mine.
shebeen Informal bar, or a home where alcohol is served for profit.
sibonda Tsonga version of *isibonda.*
sjambok Rawhide quirt.
skokiaan Powerful brew made in illegal stills.
skomplas (Afr. *skoonplaas*) Mine quarters for married senior black mine staff and their wives (real or otherwise).
stokisi (Afr. *stokkies*) Mine lockup (literally, "stocks").
stope Opening into the ore-bearing rock from haulage.
thwala Xhosa for marriage by abduction.
tinkonkana Plural form of *nkonkana.*
tiro Setswana for fulfilling work, communal labor.
tram To move rock in trucks along haulage underground.
tsotsi Black urban gangster.
ubudoda Nguni for manhood.
ubufazi Nguni word for womanhood.
ukumetsha Xhosa for youthful sexual practices involving ejaculation between the thighs without penetration.
ukuthwala Marriage by abduction.
ukwakha To construct in the sense of building for posterity (Xhosa). *Ukwakha umzi* (to build the *umzi*) corresponds in many ways to the Twana notion of *tiro.*
umfaan Young boy.
umkhukhu Shack.
umteto Nguni for rule, law, proper procedure.
umteto ka sokisi Rules for homosexual relationships.
umzi Nguni for homestead, rural agricultural small-holding, rural household.
xibonda Plural form of *sibonda.*

References

ARCHIVAL SOURCES

Central Archives, Pretoria
Commission Evidence (K-series)
Economic and Wage Commission 1925–26 (EWC)
Industrial Legislation Commission 1949–50 (ILC)
Low Grade Mines Commission 1919–20 (LGMC)
Low Grade Ore Commission 1931 (LGOC)
Mining Regulations Commission 1924–25 (MRC)
Native Economic Commission 1930–31 (NEC)
Native Grievances Inquiry 1913–14 (NGI—fragmentary)
Trading on Mining Grounds Commission 1934 (TMGC)
Department of Justice 1912–48 (JUS)
Department of Labour 1926–48 (ARB)
Department of Mines and Industries 1916–48 (MNW)
Department of Native Affairs 1910–52 (NA and NTS)
Department of Police 1912–48, including confidential (conf.) files (SAP)
Government Native Labour Bureau 1902–34 (NLB)

Corey Library, Rhodes University, Grahamstown
Witwatersrand Mine Natives' Wages Commission 1943 (WMNWC—fragmentary)

Special Collections, University of the Witwatersrand, Johannesburg
Garment Workers' Union (GWU)
Trade Union Congress of South Africa (TUCSA)
Xuma Papers (Xuma)

Cooperative Africana Microform Project,
Center for Research Libraries, Chicago
Carter-Karis Collection

African Collection, Sterling Library, Yale University
Evidence to the Bregman Commission 1987 (AAC/VR)
Archives of Cheadle, Thompson, and Haysom 1983–90 (CTH)

NEWSPAPERS

Guardian (Cape Town)
Inkululeko (Johannesburg)
Rand Daily Mail (Johannesburg)
Star (Johannesburg)
Weekly Mail (Johannesburg)

BOOKS AND ARTICLES

AIM (Agency for Industrial Mission). 1976. *Another Blanket.* Roodepoort: AIM.

Aldrich, M. J. 1989. *Intimacy: A Developmental Perspective.* Doctoral dissertation, University of the Witwatersrand, Johannesburg.

Allen, V. L. 1992. *The History of Black Mineworkers in South Africa.* Vol. 1. Keighley, W. Yorkshire: Moor Press.

Alverson, H. 1978. *Mind in the Heart of Darkness.* New Haven: Yale University Press.

Alverson, M. 1987. *Under African Sun.* Chicago: University of Chicago Press.

Arble, M. 1976. *The Long Tunnel: A Coal-Miner's Journal.* New York: Atheneum.

Argyle, J. 1975. Faction Fights and the Problem of Explanation in Social Anthropology. Paper delivered at the annual conference of South African Anthropologists.

——— [c. 1987]. Explaining Faction Fights. Typescript.

Beinart, W. 1979. *Joyini Inkomo*: Cattle Advances and the Origins of Migrancy from Pondoland. *JSAS* 5, 2.

——— 1980. Labour Migrancy and Rural Production: Pondoland circa 1900–1950. In Mayer 1980.

——— 1982. *The Political Economy of Pondoland, 1860–1930.* Cambridge: Cambridge University Press.

——— 1987. Worker Consciousness, Ethnic Particularism, and Nationalism. In *The Politics of Race, Class, and Nationalism in Twentieth-*

Century South Africa, eds. S. Marks and S. Tripido. London and New York: Longman.
——— 1991. "The Rise of the Indlavini." In *Tradition and Transition in Southern Africa,* eds. A. D. Spiegel and P. A. McAllister. Johannesburg: Witwatersrand University Press.
Benjamin, P. 1987. Trade Unions and the Industrial Court. In *South African Review,* vol. 4, eds. G. Moss and I. Obery. Johannesburg: Ravan.
Benjamin, P., R. Jacobus, and C. Albertyn. 1989. *Strikes, Lock-Outs, and Arbitration in South African Labour Law.* Cape Town: Juta.
Bennett, T. W., D. J. Devine, D. B. Hutchison, I. Leeman, and D. van Zyl Smit. 1989. *Policing and the Law.* Cape Town: Juta.
Berger, I. 1992. *Threads of Solidarity: Women in South African Industry, 1900–1980.* Bloomington and Indianapolis: Indiana University Press.
Berkowitz, L. 1982. Violence and Rule-Following Behaviour. In *Aggression and Violence,* eds. P. Marsh and A. Campbell. New York: St. Martins.
——— 1986. Some Varieties of Human Aggression: Criminal Violence as Coercion, Rule-Following, Impression Management, and Impulsive Behavior. In *Violent Transactions: The Limits of Personality,* eds. A. Campbell and J. J. Gibbs. Oxford: Basil Blackwell.
Bonner, P. L. 1988. Family, Crime, and Political Consciousness on the East Rand, 1935–1955. *JSAS* 14, 3.
——— 1990. "Desirable or Undesirable Basotho Women?" Liquor, Prostitution, and the Migration of Basotho Women to the Rand, 1920–1945. In Walker 1990.
——— 1992. Backs to the Fence: Law, Liquor, and the Search for Social Control in an East Rand Town, 1929–1942. In *Liquor and Labor in Southern Africa,* eds. J. Crush and C. Ambler. Athens: Ohio University Press.
Bonnin, D., and A. Sitas. 1988. Lessons from the Sarmcol Strike. In *Popular Struggles in South Africa,* eds. W. Cobbett and R. Cohen. London: James Currey.
Bozzoli, B. 1991. *Women of Phokeng.* Portsmouth, N.H.: Heinemann. London: James Currey.
Brecher, J. 1972. *Strike.* Boston: South End Press.
Breckenridge, K. 1990. Migrancy, Crime, and Faction Fighting: The Role of the Isitshozi in the Development of Ethnic Organisations in the Compounds. *JSAS* 16, 1.
Bulmer, M. I. A. 1975. Sociological Models of the Mining Community. *Sociological Review* 23.
Burawoy, M. 1972. Another Look at the Mineworker. *African Social Research* 14.

——— 1979. *Manufacturing Consent.* Chicago: University of Chicago Press.

——— 1985. *The Politics of Production.* London and New York: Verso.

Burridge, K. 1969. *New Heaven, New Earth.* New York: Schocken.

Campbell, C. 1991. Learning to Kill? Masculinity, the Family and the Current Political Violence. *JSAS* 18, 3.

Chamber of Mines. 1943. *Evidence to the Mine Native Wages Commission.* Johannesburg: Chamber of Mines.

Chikane, F. 1988. *No Life of My Own.* Braamfontein: Skotaville.

Comaroff, J. L., and J. Comaroff. 1987. The Madman and the Migrant: Work and Labor in the Historical Consciousness of a South African People. *American Ethnologist* 14.

Coplan, D. 1987. Eloquent Knowledge: Lesotho Migrants' Songs and the Anthropology of Experience. *American Ethnologist* 14, 3.

Crush, J. 1987. Restructuring Migrant Labour on the Gold Mines. In *South African Review,* vol. 5, eds. G. Moss and I. Obery. Johannesburg: Ravan.

——— 1989. Migrancy and Militance: The Case of the National Union of Mineworkers of South Africa. *African Affairs* 88.

——— 1992. Surveillance on the South African Gold Mines. *JSAS* 18, 4.

Crush, J., A. Jeeves, and D. Yudelman. 1991. *South Africa's Labor Empire.* Boulder: Westview.

Davies, R. 1979. Capital Restructuring and the Modification of the Racial Division of Labour in South Africa. *JSAS* 5, 2.

Delius, P. 1989. Sebatagomo: Migrant Organization, the ANC, and the Sekhukhuneland Revolt. *JSAS* 15, 4.

Dennis, N., F. Henriques, and C. Slaughter. 1956. *Coal Is Our Life.* London: Tavistock.

Deutsch, S. 1987. Women and Intercultural Relations: The Case of Hispanic New Mexico and Colorado. *Signs* 12, 4.

Dubow, S. 1989. *Racial Segregation and the Origins of Apartheid in South Africa, 1919–1936.* London: Macmillan.

Epstein, A. L. 1958. *Politics in an Urban African Community.* Manchester: Manchester University Press.

First, R. 1983. *Black Gold: The Mozambican Miner, Proletarian and Peasant.* New York: St. Martins.

Ford, A. S. 1944. Scientific Management, with Particular Application to a Witwatersrand Gold Mine. In *Association of Mine Managers of the Transvaal, 1942–1945.* Johannesburg: Chamber of Mines.

Foucault, M. 1979. *Discipline and Punish: The Birth of the Prison.* New York: Vintage.

——— 1980. *The History of Sexuality*.Vol. 1. New York: Vintage.
——— 1986. *The Use of Pleasure*. New York: Vintage.
Fraser, N. 1989. *Unruly Practices*. Minneapolis: University of Minnesota Press.
Freud, S. 1953. *The Interpretation of Dreams*. London: Hogarth Press.
Friedman, S. 1987. *Building Tomorrow Today: African Workers in Trade Unions, 1970–1984*. Johannesburg: Ravan.
Gay, J. S. 1980. Basotho Women's Options: A Study of Marital Careers in Rural Lesotho. Doctoral dissertation, Cambridge University.
Giliomee, H., and L. Schlemmer. 1985. *Up Against the Fences*. New York: St. Martins.
Gluckman, M. 1961. Anthropological Problems Arising from the African Industrial Revolution. In *Social Change in Modern Africa*, ed. A. Southall. London: Oxford University Press.
Goffman, E. 1959. *The Presentation of Self in Everyday Life*. Garden City: Doubleday.
——— 1961. *Asylums*. Garden City: Doubleday.
——— 1967. *Interaction Ritual*. Garden City: Doubleday.
Gordon, R. 1977. *Mines, Masters, and Migrants*. Johannesburg: Ravan.
——— 1978. The Celebration of Ethnicity: A Tribal Fight in a Namibian Mine Compound. In *Ethnicity in Modern Africa*, ed. B. M. du Toit. Boulder: Westview.
Gouldner, A. W. 1954. *Patterns of Industrial Bureaucracy*. Glencoe, Ill.: Free Press.
Gramsci, A. 1971. *Selections from the Prison Notebooks*. New York: International.
Greenberg, S. B. 1987. *Legitimating the Illegitimate: State, Markets, and Resistance in South Africa*. Berkeley and Los Angeles: University of California Press.
Guendelman, S., and A. Perez-Itriago. 1987. Double Lives: The Changing Role of Women in Seasonal Migration. *Women's Studies* 13.
Guy, J. 1990. Gender Oppression in Southern Africa's Pre-Capitalist Societies. In Walker 1990.
Guy, J., and M. Thabane. 1987. The Ma-Rashea: A Participant's Perspective. In *Class, Community, and Conflict*, ed. B. Bozzoli. Johannesburg: Ravan.
——— 1988. Technology, Ethnicity, and Ideology: Basotho Miners and Shaft-Sinking on the South African Gold Mines. *JSAS* 14, 2.
Habermas, J. 1989. *The Theory of Communicative Action*. Vol. 2, *Lifeworld and System*. Boston: Beacon Press.
Hansson, D., and D. van Z. Smit, eds. 1990. *Towards Justice?* Cape Town: Oxford University Press.

Harries, P. 1982. Kinship, Ideology, and the Nature of Pre-Colonial Labour Migration: Labour Migration from the Delagoa Bay Hinterland to South Africa, up to 1895. In Marks and Rathbone 1982.

——— 1983. Labour Migration from Mozambique to South Africa: With Special Reference to the Delagoa Bay Hinterland, c. 1862 to 1897. Doctoral dissertation, School of Oriental and African Studies, University of London.

——— 1990. Symbols and Sexuality: Culture and Identity on the Early Witwatersrand Gold Mines. *Gender and History* 2, 3.

Haysom, N. 1987. *Mabangalala: The Rise of Right-Wing Vigilantes in South Africa.* Johannesburg: Centre for Applied Legal Studies, University of the Witwatersrand (Occasional Paper No. 10).

Hildick-Smith, G. 1944. Remarks. *Association of Mine Managers of the Transvaal: Papers and Discussion, 1942–1945.* Johannesburg: Chamber of Mines.

Hoffman, L. 1981. *Foundations of Family Therapy: A Conceptual Framework for System Change.* New York: Basic Books.

Hunter, M. 1936. *Reaction to Conquest.* Oxford: Oxford University Press.

Ingram, D. 1987. *Habermas and the Dialectic of Reason.* New Haven: Yale University Press.

James, W. G. 1987. Grounds for a Strike: South African Gold Mining in the 1940s. *African Economic History* 17.

——— 1991. *Our Precious Metal: African Mine Labour in Modern South Africa.* Cape Town: David Philip.

Jeeves, A. H. 1985. *Migrant Labour in South Africa's Mining Economy.* Kingston and Montreal: McGill-Queen's University Press.

Jeeves, A. H., and D. Yudelman. 1986. New Labour Frontiers for Old: Black Migrants to the South African Gold Mines. *JSAS* 13, 1.

Jeppe, E. B. 1946. *Gold Mining on the Witwatersrand.* Johannesburg: Chamber of Mines.

Jingoes, S. J. 1975. *A Chief Is a Chief by the People.* London: Oxford University Press.

Jochelson, K., M. Mothibeli, and J. P. Leger. 1991. Human Immunodeficiency Virus and Migrant Labor in South Africa. *International Journal of Health Services* 21, 1.

Johnstone, F. A. 1976. *Class, Race, and Gold.* London: Routledge and Kegan Paul.

——— 1990. Quebec, Apartheid, Lithuania, and Tibet: The Politics of Group Rights. *Telos* 85.

Junod, H. A. 1962. *The Life of a South African Tribe.* Vol. 1. New Hyde Park, N.Y.: University Books, 1966 (first published 1912).

Kerr, C., and A. Seigel. 1954. The Industrial Propensity to Strike: An International Comparison. In *Industrial Conflict,* eds. A. Kornhauser, R. Dubin, and A. Ross. New York: McGraw Hill.

Kruger, H. J., and G. P. Rundle. 1978. *A Report on the Problems Associated with Excessive Drinking amongst Black Mineworkers.* Johannesburg: Chamber of Mines.

Kuckertz, H. 1990. *Creating Order.* Johannesburg: Witwatersrand University Press.

Lambert, R. 1987. Trade Unions, Nationalism, and the Socialist Project in South Africa. In *South African Review,* vol. 4, eds. G. Moss and I. Obery. Johannesburg: Ravan Press.

Lambert, R., and E. Webster. 1989. The Re-Emergence of Political Unionism in Contemporary South Africa? In *Popular Struggles in South Africa,* eds. W. Cobbett and R. Cohen. London: James Currey.

Lawrence, A. C. 1974. Human Error as a Cause of Accidents in Gold Mining. *Journal of Safety Research* 6.

Leatt, J., P. Zulu, M. Nchwe, M. Ntshangase, and R. Laughlin. 1986. *Reaping the Whirlwind? Report on a Joint Study by the National Union of Mineworkers and the Anglo American Gold Division on the Causes of Mine Violence.* Johannesburg: NUM and Anglo American Corporation.

Leger, J. P. 1985. *Towards Safer Underground Mining: An Investigation Commissioned by the South African Union of Mineworkers.* Johannesburg: Department of Sociology, University of the Witwatersrand.

——— 1990. Key Issues in Safety and Health in South African Mines. *South African Sociological Review* 2.

——— 1992. *"Talking Rocks"—An Investigation of the Pit Sense of Rockfall Accidents amongst Underground Gold Miners.* Doctoral dissertation, University of the Witwatersrand, Johannesburg.

Leger, J. P., and M. Nicol. [c. 1991]. *Gold Mining in South Africa: Priorities for Restructuring.* Cape Town: Economic Trends Research Group, Development Policy Research Unit, University of Cape Town (ET Working Paper No. 1).

Leger, J. P., and P. Van Niekerk. 1986. Organization on the Mines: The NUM Phenomenon. In *South African Review,* vol. 3, ed. Southern African Research Services. Johannesburg: Ravan.

McAllister, P. A. 1980. Work, Homestead, and the Shades: The Ritual Interpretation of Labour Migration among the Gcaleka. In Mayer 1980.

McNamara, J. K. 1980. Brothers and Workmates: Home Friend Networks in the Social Life of Black Migrant Workers in a Gold Mine Hostel. In Mayer 1980.

——— 1985. *Black Worker Conflicts on South African Gold Mines, 1973–1982*. Doctoral dissertation, University of the Witwatersrand, Johannesburg.

Malan, R. 1990. *My Traitor's Heart*. New York: Vintage.

Manganyi, N. C. 1990. Crowds and Their Vicissitudes: Psychology and Law in the South African Courtroom. In *Political Violence and the Struggle in South Africa*, eds. C. Manganyi and A. du Toit. London: Macmillan.

Marks, S., and R. Rathbone, eds. 1982. *Industrialisation and Social Change in South Africa*. London and New York: Longman.

Marsh, P. 1982. Rhetorics of Violence. In *Aggression and Violence*, eds. P. Marsh and A. Campbell. New York: St. Martins.

Marx, K. 1852. The Eighteenth Brumaire of Louis Bonaparte. In Marx 1974.

——— 1973. *Grundrisse*. New York: Vintage.

——— 1974. *Surveys from Exile: Political Writings*. Vol. 2. New York: Vintage.

——— 1975. *Early Writings*. New York: Vintage.

——— 1977. *Capital*. Vol. 1. New York: Vintage.

Mayer, P. 1961. *Townsmen or Tribesmen*. Cape Town: Oxford University Press.

——— 1978. *Wives of Migrant Miners*. Vol. 3 of *Migrant Labour: Some Perspectives from Anthropology*. Grahamstown: Institute for Social and Economic Research (unpublished).

——— ed. 1980. *Black Villagers in an Industrial Society*. Cape Town: Oxford University Press.

Mayer, P., and I. Mayer. 1970. Socialization by Peers: The Youth Organization of the Red Xhosa. In *Socialization: The Approach from Social Anthropology*, ed. P. Mayer. London: Tavistock.

——— 1972. Self-Organisation by Youth among the Xhosa-speaking Peoples of the Ciskei and Transkei. Typescript. Grahamstown: Institute for Social and Economic Research.

Mead, M. 1935. *Sex and Temperament in Three Primitive Societies*. New York: Morrow.

Moodie, T. D. 1980. The Formal and Informal Structure of a South African Gold Mine. *Human Relations* 33, 8.

——— 1983. Mine Culture and Miners' Identity on the South African Gold Mines. In *Town and Countryside in the Transvaal*, ed. B. Bozzoli. Johannesburg: Ravan.

——— 1988. The South African State and Industrial Conflict in the 1940s. *International Journal of African Historical Studies* 21, 1.

Moore, B., Jr. 1978. *Injustice: The Social Bases of Obedience and Revolt.* White Plains, N.Y.: M. E. Sharpe.

Moroney, S. 1982. Mine Married Quarters. In Marks and Rathbone 1982.

Moss, R. 1990. *Shouting at the Crocodile.* Boston: Beacon Press.

Murray, C. 1981. *Families Divided.* Johannesburg: Ravan.

——— 1987. Displaced Urbanization: South Africa's Rural Slums. *African Affairs* 86.

Nash, J. 1979. *We Eat the Mines and the Mines Eat Us.* New York: Columbia University Press.

O'Connell, M. C. 1980. Xesibe Reds, Rascals, and Gentlemen at Home and at Work. In Mayer 1980.

Offe, C. 1984. *Contradictions of the Welfare State.* Cambridge: MIT Press.

——— 1985. *Disorganized Capitalism.* Cambridge: MIT Press.

Palmer, R., and N. Parsons. 1977. *The Roots of Rural Poverty in Central and Southern Africa.* Berkeley and Los Angeles: University of California.

Penvenne, J. M. 1982. A History of African Labor in Lourenco Marques, Mozambique, 1877 to 1950. Doctoral dissertation, Boston University.

Piaget, J. 1971. *Structuralism.* London: Routledge and Kegan Paul.

Pycroft, C., and B. Munslow. 1988. Black Mine Workers in South Africa: Strategies of Co-optation and Resistance. *Journal of Asian and African Studies* 23.

Ramahapu, T. V. 1977. *Towards a Study of Basotho Labour on the Orange Free State Gold Mines: Mechanisms of Social Control.* B.A. thesis, National University of Lesotho.

Ramphele, M. 1986. The Male-Female Dynamic amongst Migrant Workers in the Western Cape. *Social Dynamics* 12, 1.

——— 1989. The Dynamics of Gender Politics in the Hostels of Cape Town: Another Legacy of the South African Migrant Labour System. *JSAS* 15, 3.

Ranger, T. 1978. Growing from the Roots: Reflections on Peasant Research in Central and Southern Africa. *JSAS* 5, 1.

Reck, A. 1964. *Selected Writings: George Herbert Mead.* Chicago: University of Chicago Press.

Rex, J. 1973. The Compound, Reserve, and Urban Location—Essential Institutions of Southern African Labour Exploitation. *South African Labour Bulletin* 1.

Richardson, P. 1982. *Chinese Mine Labour in the Transvaal.* London: Longman.

Riches, D. 1986. The Phenomenon of Violence. In *The Anthropology of Violence,* ed. D. Riches. Oxford: Basil Blackwell.

Rushton, M. W. 1945. Native Labour Control and Conservation. *Association of Mine Managers of the Transvaal: Papers and Discussion, 1942–1945*. Johannesburg: Chamber of Mines.

Saffery, A. L. 1940. The Liquor Problem in Urban Areas. *Race Relations Journal* 7.

Schapera, I. 1971. *Married Life in an African Tribe*. Harmondsworth: Penguin.

Schmidt, E. 1990. Negotiated Spaces and Contested Terrain: Men, Women, and the Law in Colonial Zimbabwe, 1890–1939. *JSAS* 16, 4.

Schutz, A. 1962. *Collected Papers*. Vol. 1. Amsterdam: Nijhof.

Scott, J. C. 1976. *The Moral Economy of the Peasant*. New Haven: Yale University Press.

Sebilo, P. 1976. *What Do the Miners Say?* B.A. thesis, National University of Lesotho.

Shaiken, H. 1986. *Work Transformed*. Lexington, Mass.: D. C. Heath.

Shanafelt, R. 1989. Worker Solidarity, Differentiation, and the Manipulation of Ethnicity: Conflict at Vaal Reefs, 1984–1986. Typescript. University of Florida, Gainesville.

Sharp, J., and A. Spiegel. 1985. Vulnerability to Impoverishment in South African Rural Areas: The Erosion of Kinship and Neighbourhood as Social Resources. *Africa* 55, 2.

——— 1991. Women and Wages: Gender and the Control of Income in Farm and Bantustan Households. *JSAS* 16, 3.

Simkins, C. 1981. Agricultural Production in the African Reserves of South Africa, 1918–1969. *JSAS* 7, 2.

Sitas, A. 1985. Moral Formations and Struggles amongst Migrant Workers on the East Rand. *Labour, Capital and Society* 18, 2.

Sloth-Nielsen, J. 1990. Corporal Punishment: Acceptable State Violence? In Hansson and Smit 1990.

Spiegel, A. 1980. Rural Differentiation and the Diffusion of Migrant Labour Remittances in Lesotho. In Mayer 1980.

Spiegel, A., and P. McAllister. 1991. *Tradition and Transition in Southern Africa*. Johannesburg: Witwatersrand University Press.

Steytler, N. 1990. Policing Political Opponents: Death Squads and Cop Culture. In Hansson and Smit 1990.

Stobart, W. T. 1960. Accident Prevention—Underground Native Labourers. *Association of Mine Managers of South Africa: Papers and Discussion, 1960–1961*. Johannesburg: Chamber of Mines.

Stone, L. 1979. *The Family, Sex, and Marriage in England, 1500–1800*. New York: Vintage.

Thompson, C. 1984. Black Trade Unions on the Mines. In *South African Review*, vol. 2., ed. Southern African Research Services. Johannesburg: Ravan.

Thompson, E. P. 1971. The Moral Economy of the English Crowd in the Eighteenth Century. *Past and Present* 50.

——— 1974. Patrician Society, Plebeian Culture. *Journal of Social History* 7, 4.

——— 1978. Eighteenth-Century English Society: Class Struggle without Class? *Social History* 3, 2.

Trist, E., et al. 1963. *Organizational Change*. London: Tavistock.

Van Onselen, C. 1980. *Chibaro*. Johannesburg: Ravan. Pluto Press: London, 1976.

——— 1982a. *Studies in the Social and Economic History of the Witwatersrand, 1886–1914*. Vol. 1, *New Babylon*. London and New York: Longman.

——— 1982b. *Studies in the Social and Economic History of the Witwatersrand, 1886–1914*. Vol. 2, *New Nineveh*. London and New York: Longman.

Wagner, H. 1970. *Alfred Schutz on Phenomenology and Social Relations*. Chicago: University of Chicago Press.

Wagner, H. 1986. The Challenge of Deep-Level Mining in South Africa. *Journal of the South African Institute of Mining and Metallurgy* 86, 9.

Walker, C., ed. 1990. *Women and Gender in Southern Africa to 1945*. Cape Town: David Philip, and London: James Curry.

Webster, D. 1991. *Afafazi Bathonga Bafihlakala*: Ethnicity and Gender in a KwaZulu Border Community. *African Studies* 50, 1 and 2.

Webster, E. 1988. The Rise of Social-Movement Unionism: The Two Faces of the Black Trade Union Movement in South Africa. In *State, Resistance, and Change in South Africa*, eds. P. Frankel, N. Pines, and M. Swilling. Johannesburg: Southern Book Publishers.

White, L. 1990. *The Comforts of Home: Prostitution in Colonial Nairobi*. Chicago: University of Chicago Press.

White, R. W. 1963. *Ego and Reality in Psychoanalytic Theory: A Proposal Regarding Independent Ego Energies*. Vol. 3, *Psychological Issues*, monograph 11. New York: International Universities Press.

Williams, R. 1981. *Marxism and Literature*. Oxford: Oxford University Press.

Willis, P. 1977. *Learning to Labor*. New York: Columbia University Press.

——— 1979. Shop-Floor Culture, Masculinity, and the Wage Form. In *Working-Class Culture: Studies in History and Theory*, eds. J. Clarke, C. Critcher, and R. Johnson. London: Hutchinson.

Wilson, F. 1969. *Labour on the South African Gold Mines.* Cambridge: Cambridge University Press.

Wolpe, H. 1972. Capitalism and Cheap Labour-Power in South Africa: From Segregation to Apartheid. *Economy and Society* 1, 4.

Young, M., and P. Wilmott. 1957. *Family and Kinship in East London.* London: Penguin.

Yudelman, D. 1983. *The Emergence of Modern South Africa.* Westport, Conn.: Greenwood Press.

Index

T. DUNBAR MOODIE is Professor of Sociology at Hobart and William Smith Colleges and the author of *The Rise of Afrikanerdom* (California, 1975).

VIVIENNE NDATSHE is a former teacher who now works as a domestic servant. She grew up in Pondoland, where her father was a migrant gold-miner. Her interviews with mine workers and their families added an essential dimension to this work.

Compositor: Impressions, A Division of
Edwards Brothers, Inc.
Text: 10/13 Aldus
Display: Aldus
Printer: Edwards Brothers, Inc.
Binder: Edwards Brothers, Inc.